P9-DXI-251

DATE DUE

MY 2 0 05			

DEMCO 38-296

EARL BATHURST
AND
THE BRITISH EMPIRE

Be famous then
By wisdom; as thy Empire must extend,
So let extend thy mind o'er all the world.

John Milton,
Paradise Regain'd
Book IV, lines 220–1

EARL BATHURST AND THE BRITISH EMPIRE 1762–1834

by

NEVILLE THOMPSON

LEO COOPER

Riverside Community College
Library
SEP '01 4800 Magnolia Avenue
Riverside, CA 92506

DA17.B38 T47 1999
Thompson, Neville, Ph. D.
Earl Bathurst and the
British Empire, 1762-1834

TO MY MOTHER
AND IN MEMORY OF MY FATHER

First published in Great Britain in 1999 by
LEO COOPER
an imprint of
Pen & Sword Books Ltd,
47 Church Street,
Barnsley, South Yorkshire, S70 2AS

ISBN 0 85052 650 0

Copyright © 1999 Neville Thompson

A CIP record for this book is
available from the British Library

Typeset in Bembo by Phoenix Typesetting, Ilkley, West Yorkshire.

Printed in England by Redwood Books Ltd, Trowbridge, Wilts.

CONTENTS

Acknowledgements   vi

Introduction   vii

Chapter 1   A Friend of the Monarch and Mr Pitt,   1
                                1762–1807

     2   Say Not the Struggle Naught Availeth,   27
                                1807–1812

     3   The Distant Triumph Song, 1812-1814   51

     4   The Awful Shadow of Some Unseen Power,   75
                                1814–1815

     5   The Idle Spear and Shield Uphung,   106
                                1815–1820

     6   War in Heaven, 1820–1825   135

     7   The Restraining and Liberating Hand   155

     8   Brave Men in Trouble   186

     9   A Friend of the Duke of Wellington,   211
                                1826–1828

   10   Reluctant Reformer, 1828–1830   230

   11   Crossing the Bar, 1830–1834   246

        Notes   261

        Bibliography   287

        Index   301

ACKNOWLEDGEMENTS

I am grateful above all to the Earl Bathurst, not only for permission to use literary and illustrative material but also for his friendly interest and encouragement from the beginning. I recall with pleasure our meetings on both sides of the Atlantic, particularly the one at which he pressed into my hands the recently-discovered Cirencester Papers which are an important addition to the main collection of Bathurst papers. I hope that the result is worthy of his confidence.

It is a pleasure to thank the many libraries and archives and their staffs for assistance and permission to reproduce copyright material. The British Library in particular has on loan the Bathurst Papers, as well holding many of the major related collections. The official papers in the Public Record Office are Crown Copyright, as are the Duke of Wellington Papers in the Hartley Library, University of Southampton, which are reproduced by permission of Dr C. M. Woolgar, the Archivist and Head of Special Collections, on behalf of Her Majesty's Stationery Office. I also acknowledge the gracious permission of Her Majesty the Queen to consult and reproduce material from the Royal Archives. The Wilmot-Horton (Catton) Papers in the Derbyshire County Council's Record Office are reproduced by permission of the County and Diocesan Archivist; the Goulburn Papers by kind permission of the Surrey History Centre and the depositor; the Sneyd Papers by permission of the Keele University Library; and the Newcastle Papers by permission of the University of Nottingham Library. The Mitchell Library, State Library of New South Wales, was good enough to provide copies of letters in the R. Wilmot-Horton manuscript collection; material from them is reproduced by permission of the Library. I am once again also much indebted to the D. B. Weldon Library at the University of Western Ontario Library.

The archival research was greatly assisted by a grant from the Social Science and Humanities Research Council of Canada. The University of Western Ontario and the Department of History provided smaller but no less appreciated research grants.

In this, as in everything else, my wife Gail has been an ever-present support and our daughter Elizabeth a distracting joy.

INTRODUCTION

The third Earl Bathurst is best remembered as Secretary of State for War and the Colonies from 1812 to 1827, and as such is still commemorated throughout what was then the British Empire, from Canada to Australia. He was practically the first Colonial Secretary and the founder of the modern Colonial Office, over which no one else ever held sway for so long. The nearest contender was Joseph Chamberlain (1895-1903), one of the few Colonial Secretaries whose position in cabinet ranked with Bathurst's.

The combination of responsibilities which Bathurst assumed in 1812 was of recent origin and uncertain future. A Secretaryship of State for War had been created in 1794, early in the conflict with revolutionary France; in 1801 the colonies were transferred from the Home Office, as a kind of make-weight at the Peace of Amiens. But until the end of the Napoleonic Wars the Secretary was primarily a War Minister and by no means the supreme authority in overseas possessions. In the zeal for economy after 1815 the staff was reduced by half, the Under-Secretary for War eliminated and the department even threatened with abolition or amalgamation with some other ministry. A decade later, when Bathurst left, what was by then principally a Colonial Office was securely established as a distinct branch of government. The post-Waterloo reductions had been reversed; a second Under-Secretary had been engaged; the administrative routine had been improved; consistent policies and a recognizable style had been established; an impressive staff had been recruited, which provided continuity of direction during the subsequent rapid change of ministers; and the Colonial Secretary was the dominant, if not the entire, British authority in the empire. This was essentially the Colonial Office which Joseph Chamberlain inherited seventy years later, shorn of its military responsibilities, which, after 1854, were the responsibility of a separate Secretary of State for War.

This office and these fifteen years were the most important in Bathurst's half-century in public life, extending from the aftermath of the American Revolution to the reformed parliament of 1832, from Pitt the Younger to the Duke of Wellington, from the age of turnpike roads and canals to the age of railways; from powdered wigs and knee breeches to natural hair and trousers. But some account of his earlier career and heritage is necessary in order to understand his high position in Lord Liverpool's government. Although he held only minor office before 1807, he was by then a well established member of the political inner circle with a reputation for moderation, good judgement, amiability and concern for what the most of the governing élite regarded as the best interests of the country. These qualities made him the friend and confidant of every Prime Minister from 1783 to 1830, with the brief exceptions of Addington (1801-4), Canning (1827) and Goderich (1827); and even with these he got along well when they were fellow cabinet ministers. Lord Grenville, his oldest and closest companion from school, was a special case as head of the largely Whig Ministry of All the Talents (1806-7); Bathurst would not join a government with Pitt's opponents, but their friendship endured and he never hesitated to advise and warn the Prime Minister. His family background as well as his outlook and personality also made him a favourite of every monarch from George III to William IV. And even some of his wife's Whig relations and other political opponents had a high personal regard for him and enjoyed his company.

By temperament sceptical of change, Bathurst realized the necessity of adapting to changing circumstances and the dangers of rigid resistance. He recognized the benefit of acknowledging the independence of the colonies of Britain's allies, Spain and Portugal, came to accept the wisdom of removing political restrictions on Catholics, and took a leading part in practical humanitarian efforts to improve the lot of the slaves and pave the way for freedom. He was far from being authoritarian in the administration of empire and constantly urged similar prudence on military officers who were governors of colonies.

From the time he entered the cabinet as President of the Board of Trade in 1807 Bathurst played a rôle in government far beyond the requirements of his offices. In particular, between 1812 and 1822 he, the Prime Minister and Foreign Secretary decided almost all foreign, military and colonial questions with scant reference to their colleagues. After Canning became Foreign Secretary Bathurst was consulted less frequently but remained deeply involved in foreign policy, partly because it was so closely related to the worldwide concerns of his own department but also from apprehension of the new Foreign Secretary, though he was far from being Canning's most determined critic.

Despite his prominence at the centre of the British state for a quarter of a century, and in the colonies for a decade and a half, Bathurst remains a shadowy presence in the history of the period, more easily appreciated in general than precisely understood: always present, always competent and reliable but never leaving the distinct impression of a Pitt or a Canning, Castlereagh or Wellington. This is to some extent due to his self-effacing, shy personality, masked and protected by gregariousness, wit and the kind of reserved decorum always described as old-fashioned, though never really in fashion or ever out of it. In 1818, when he was fifty-six, the Anglo-Irish novelist Maria Edgeworth described him as 'a chearful formalist with smiling usage of the world sufficient to be an *agreable* diplomatist — *flat* but not stiff backed — dry faced — of the old school. . . — the very first of that class.'[1] A poor speaker who never put himself forward or sought to shine in debate, he was ill at ease even in the customary informality of sparsely attended House of Lords. By contrast he was always a lucid and ready writer.

In all this he was very similar to Lord Castlereagh. But Bathurst's more indeterminate place in the history of the early nineteenth century can also be explained by his family's unusual failure to commission a tombstone Life and Times of the kind so famously disconsidered by Lytton Strachey[2] but so useful to historians (and to Strachey himself). This is all the more striking since his immediate heirs were well aware of the importance of their father's position and archive. In 1837 the fourth earl, an aide to Wellington at the Congress of Vienna and Waterloo, gave the letter books from 1813 to 1816 to the Duke for the publication of his despatches;[3] and his brother, the fifth earl, who had accompanied a couple of interesting missions while their father was in government, was Joint Clerk of the Privy Council for thirty-six years, as well as a fellow of All Souls College, Oxford. Whatever the reason for the neglect, it explains Bathurst's exiguous entry in the *Dictionary of National Biography*, which in turn perpetuated the impression that he was not of leading importance. Not until 1965, when many of the standard works on the political, imperial, military and diplomatic history of the period had been written, and even rewritten, did the Bathurst papers become generally available when they were deposited on loan to the British Library. Only one short study of the third earl has appeared from them.[4]

It is true that by 1923 there was the Historical Manuscripts Commission's *Report on the Manuscripts of Earl Bathurst*, edited by Francis Bickley, but even its 700 pages contain only a small selection from the extensive archive. Other Bathurst correspondence can also be found in such edited works as Arthur Aspinall's *The Letters of King George IV 1812-1830* (3 vols., 1938). As long ago as 1880 many letters on a wide variety of subjects were available, though sometimes extensively and silently edited, in the three series (36 volumes) of the Duke of Wellington's despatches, but this is still not the most obvious place to look for anything beyond narrowly military issues.

This biography is based on the 108 volumes of Bathurst Papers in the British Library, about three-quarters of which concern the third Lord, some seventy other letters (Cirencester Papers), a few unfortunately surviving only in typescript copies, which were discovered in the 1980s and remain in the possession of the present Earl, and the manuscripts of Bathurst's principal correspondents in public archives. Of these the most important are the Duke of Wellington's official papers at the University of Southampton, which contain many unpublished Bathurst letters as well as the parts deleted from those already in print. These various collections contain the private letters between Bathurst and his colleagues and administrators at home and abroad. Unlike official letters (easily distinguished by the formal salutation 'My Lord' or 'Sir' rather than the more familiar 'My Dear Lord' or 'Dear Mr Canning'), which had always to be written in the knowledge that they were public documents which members of either House of Parliament could try to have produced, any marked 'private' were considered personal and off the official record. The most confidential and sensitive were kept by Bathurst and other ministers not in their offices but at home.

These private papers clearly establish what his contemporaries well knew, that Bathurst was a very effective administrator of the Colonial Office and a figure of first rank in the war against Napoleon, in diplomacy and in domestic politics. The material which he retained also reveals his administrative and political priorities and sheds interesting light on many of his contemporaries: Wellington above all, in the Peninsular War, the Waterloo Campaign and as each other's closest associates after the death of Castlereagh in 1822; also Pitt, Grenville, Lord Wellesley, Liverpool, Castlereagh and Canning, the royal family, Colonial Office Under-Secretaries and a diversity of colonial governors.

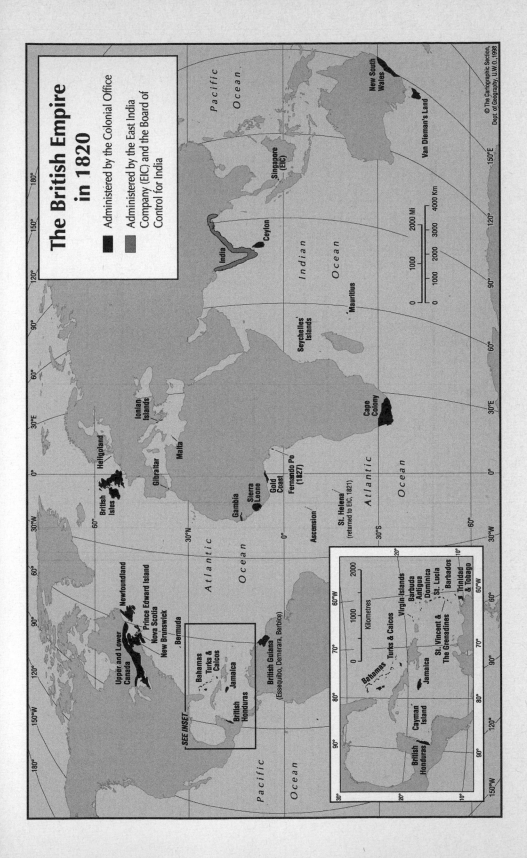

The British Empire in 1820

- Administered by the Colonial Office
- Administered by the East India Company (EIC) and the Board of Control for India

© The Cartographic Section, Dept. of Geography, U.W.O.,1998

New South Wales

Van Dieman's Land

Singapore (EIC)

India

Ceylon

Indian Ocean

Pacific Ocean

Mauritius

Seychelles Islands

Cape Colony

Ionian Islands

Helgoland

Gibraltar

Malta

British Isles

Gambia

Sierra Leone

Gold Coast

Fernando Po (1827)

Ascension

St. Helena (returned to EIC, 1821)

Atlantic Ocean

Newfoundland

Prince Edward Island

Upper and Lower Canada

Nova Scotia

New Brunswick

Bermuda

Bahamas

Turks & Caicos

Jamaica

British Honduras

British Guiana (Essequibo, Demerara, Berbice)

SEE INSET

Atlantic Ocean

Pacific Ocean

2000 Mi

4000 Km

1000

2000

3000

1000

2000

0

0

Kilometres

0

1000

2000

Bahamas

Turks & Caicos

Cayman Island

British Honduras

Jamaica

Virgin Islands

Barbuda

Antigua

Dominica

St. Lucia

Barbados

St. Vincent & The Grenadines

Trinidad & Tobago

180° 150°E 150°W 120° 90° 60° 30°E 30°W 0° 120°W 90° 60° 30°N 0° 30°S 60° 90° 120° 150° 180°

THE BATHURST FAMILY (SIMPLIFIED)

Sir Benjamin Bathurst = Frances Apsley
(1638–1704)   (1653–1727)

- Allen = Catherine Apsley
  (1684–1775) (1688–1768)
  1st Earl
- Peter Bathurst
  Clarendon Park
- Benjamin Bathurst
  Lydney Park
- Anne Bathurst = Henry Pye

1. Ann Phillipps = Henry = 2. Tryphena Scawen
   (1714–94)   (1730–1807)
   2nd Earl

Henry = Georgina Lennox
(1762–1834) (1765–1841)
3rd Earl

- Henry George
  (1790–1878)
  4th Earl
- William Lennox
  (1791–1878)
  5th Earl
- Louisa Georgina
  (1792–1874)
- Peter George Allen
  (1794–1796)
- Seymour Thomas = Julia Hankey
  (1795–1834)   (1798–1877)
- Emily Charlotte
  (1798–1877)
- Rev Charles
  (1802–1842)

1. Meriel Leicester Warren = Allen Alexander = 2. Evelyn Hankey
   (1832–1893)
   6th Earl

Seymour Henry = Lilas Borthwick
(1864–1943)
7th Earl

Allen Algernon Bathurst = Viola Meeking
(1895–1942)
Lord Apsley
(killed in action)

Henry Allen John
(1927–)
8th Earl

1

A FRIEND OF THE MONARCH AND MR PITT, 1762–1807

Henry Bathurst, the future third earl, was born on 22 May, 1762, into an old Tory family whose political fortunes were just beginning to revive after languishing for close on half a century under the first two Hanoverians. A modest revival had started in the last years of George II, but it was during the long reign of George III, from 1760 to 1820, that the Bathursts flourished again. In London he grew up at the centre of society and politics as the son of a judge, and later cabinet minister in Apsley House, more famous as the residence of the Duke of Wellington and now the Wellington Museum. At Cirencester, where the senior branch of the family had been established since the end of the seventeenth century, he lived in the house and umbrageous park created by his grandfather which remain over two centuries later as his monument.

The Bathursts traced their ancestry beyond the memory of man to Botehurst in the parish of Battle in Sussex, where the redundantly named Bathurst Wood ('hurst' being the old English term for forest) long survived. They rose in the world through trade and even more through association with the royal family after the restoration of Charles II in 1660. The same was true of the Apsleys, who took their name from lands in the Sussex parish of Thakenham near Pulborough. In 1682 Benjamin Bathurst, a director of various Tory dominated merchant companies, married Frances Apsley, daughter of the treasurer of the Duke of York, later James II, and friend of the Duke's two daughters, successively Queen Mary II and Queen Anne. The newly knighted Sir Benjamin became an MP and holder of various lucrative royal and public offices, as well as prospering in several trading enterprises. By his death in 1704 he had settled his two younger sons on substantial estates and purchased ones for himself and his heir at Cirencester and Paulspury in Northamptonshire. His oldest son Allen was only twenty when he inherited the estates. But even more was added by the marriage in the same year to his sixteen-year-old cousin Catherine, the Apsley heiress to whom he had been practically engaged for twelve years. The marriage joined the two families and estates, making their descendants also successors to the Apsleys.

If there was ever a man for whom every prospect pleased it must have been Allen Bathurst in 1704. Just down from Trinity College, Oxford, where his famous uncle Dr Ralph Bathurst had been president for forty years, he was handsome, gregarious, happily married to his beautiful cousin, amply provided for by his double inheritance and high in the favour of Queen Anne, which seemed to ensure a prominent and even lucrative place at court and at the centre of politics. Both he and Catherine were still very much alive when their grandson and eventual heir was born in 1762. The future third earl perhaps scarcely knew his grandmother, who died when he was six, but his grandfather, who lived on hale and hearty until his ninety first year in 1775, must have been a lively presence in his early years.

As one of the two MPs for Cirencester, Allen Bathurst naturally supported the Tory cause and at the end of 1711 was raised to the House of Lords as Baron Bathurst, one of twelve peers created to ensure the end of over twenty years of war with France which was finally settled in 1713 by the Treaty of Utrecht. But all his high standing and fine expectations came crashing down on 1 August, 1714, with the death of Queen Anne, predeceased by all her children. Whatever the achievement of the Treaty of Utrecht in securing British conquests overseas, it was seen as a betrayal by continental allies, and by none more than the Elector of the Protestant bastion of Hanover who now succeeded to the British throne as George I. Bathurst was one of those who hoped to bring to the throne the Catholic son of James II, whose birth in 1688 had precipitated the Glorious Revolution. But since the Pretender would not embrace Anglicanism, while the Lutheran Hanoverian readily would, there was no practical alternative to the prescribed succession.

With George I safely on the throne, his Whig ministers harried the Tories by claiming that they were Jacobites plotting with France to remove the Hanoverians and bring back the Catholic Stuarts. Bathurst was certainly involved in these schemes in some fashion and loyally defended his friends as they were persecuted, though he was never himself charged. Almost seventy years later, when the future third lord was travelling in Europe, the Duchess of Brunswick, George III's sister, told him that although his grandfather had been a good friend to her and her father (Frederick, Prince of Wales, who died in 1751), he was nevertheless 'a rank Jacobite'.[1] But the extent to which he was involved is impossible to determine since the second lord destroyed most of his father's papers on succeeding to the title in 1775. Horace Walpole was beside himself at this destruction of evidence that he was sure would justify his sainted father Sir Robert Walpole's persecution of the Tories in the 1720s and 1730s: '*cette tête à perruque*, that wig block the [Lord] Chancellor, what do you think he has done? Burnt all his father's correspondence with Pope, Swift, Arbuthnot etc. – why do you think? because several letters were indiscreet. To be sure he thought that they would go and publish themselves, if not burnt.'[2]

Lord Bathurst may not have been personally harassed by the Whigs but he was condemned to long decades of opposition after 1714. In 1727 he loyally and optimistically acclaimed the accession of George II, to no avail. In 1742, after twenty years' resistance, he was rewarded on the fall of Walpole by appointments to the Privy Council and as Captain of the Gentlemen Pensioners, a sonorous sinecure worth £1,000 a year.[3] But this was a short-lived triumph: when Walpole's successors returned in the Pelham ministry of 1744 he was ejected and returned to the familiar consolations of opposition. Even the anticipation based on association with the Prince of Wales, who in customary Hanoverian fashion hated his father, seemed doomed when 'Poor Fred' died in 1751; but the new heir showed himself a worthy son by detesting his grandfather and taking up most of his father's followers. Bathurst became Prince George's treasurer in 1757 and there were fears among ministerialists that the politically suspect septuagenarian would become the nineteen-year-old Prince George's tutor.

Nothing came of it, but the accession in 1760 of George III, the true born patriot monarch who gloried in the name of Briton, ended the proscription of Tories and completed the process of reconciling the die-hard remnants of 1714 to the Hanoverian dynasty.[4] Bathurst received a pension of £2000 a year and, even more pleasing, in 1772 his long-standing application for promotion to earl was finally granted.[5] As high in royal favour as he had been in his youth, Bathurst ended his days in 1775 at the age of ninety in the golden glow of a survivor from a legendary age, his astonishing vitality intact almost to the end. Until a month before his death he went riding for two hours a day and drank a bottle of wine after dinner.

In his enforced leisure after 1714 Bathurst poured his abundant energy into the improvement and ornamentation of his estate at Cirencester.[6] Lacking the great wealth of some peers and the lively prospect of supplementing his income from the public treasury, he could not afford a new house in the middle of a park in the highest fashion of the day. Instead he refurbished the existing E-shaped Jacobean structure at the edge of the town by knocking off the two wings and covering the remaining centre block in freestone. The result was a house with two fronts, facing both town and park, in the plain style of that good Tory architect Sir Christopher Wren, then considered out of date by the leaders of taste who favoured a Palladian design. A semi-circular, thirty-foot high stone wall covered on both sides by huge yew hedges and with a large classical gate in the centre opening on to the small courtyard screened the house from the town. A century later the third earl added a new entrance hall to the town front and a wing to the north, both designed by Sir Robert Smirke, the architect of the new Mint during Bathurst's Mastership. Otherwise the structure remains much as it was in the early years of George I.

In the changes to his estate Bathurst was truly innovative. Like all the countryside around, this originally consisted mainly of open sheep runs and a few woods. For sixty years he laboured to turn it into a beautiful and productive 3000 acre forest (in addition to 1000 acres of farmland) running five miles west from Cirencester to Sapperton. This involved buying adjacent land, selling other property, planting seedlings as well as cutting existing woods for rides and avenues, much earth-moving and the construction of ornamental structures. He may well have been inspired by John Evelyn's popular *Sylva, or a Discourse of Forest-Trees*, first published in 1664 as a call to reforest the country in order to prevent a dangerous shortage of domestic lumber for the navy, which in successive editions increasingly emphasized the aesthetic, social, philosophical and even the religious importance of woods.[7] And as a new man, and new to the county, he probably wanted to distinguish himself from the Duke of Beaufort, whose house at Badminton was then set in the middle of a symmetrical forest (which no longer survives). Whatever the reason, he decided on a more natural and picturesque forest than Beaufort's, though the park looks formal enough compared to those begun later in the century. In all his labours he was encouraged by Alexander Pope, who spent much time at Cirencester from his first visit in 1718 to his death in 1744. But Pope's influence is problematic since Bathurst knew his own mind and continued confidently and unaided for thirty years after the poet's death.

Even at his own death in 1775 there remained much for the second and even the third earl to do, though the outlines were all in place. The early seedlings were coming to maturity, just in time for the American war and the long wars against France, finally supplementing the farm rents which had hitherto subsidized the development of the forest. The staple tree was beech, though chestnuts, elms, oaks, yews, wild cherry and conifers were planted for variety and contrast. The woodlands were linked by a broad avenue running five miles west from the house through a variety of contours to the village of Sapperton, broken by intersections, glades and *rond points* which provided extensive and ever-changing views. This regular pattern was broken by more revolutionary serpentine walks, an asymmetric lake near the house and the first romantic follies in England, perhaps to endow a new family with the appearance of antiquity and continuity. In 1741 Bathurst erected a statue of Queen Anne on top of a seventy-foot Doric column in the centre of the Home Park as a tribute to the last of the dynasty under which the family had flourished and as a deliberate snub to the Hanoverians and their loathsome minister, Sir Robert Walpole.

The second Earl Bathurst was entirely different from his father. As the younger son he had no certainty of succeeding until late in life, though his elder brother had only one child who died in infancy. But when his brother also died in 1767, Henry at fifty-three became the heir.[8] With his own way to make in the world, he had chosen the law, a traditional career for younger sons. After three years at Balliol College, Oxford, then a centre of Jacobitism, he studied at Lincoln's Inn. He was called to the bar in 1736 and practised on the Oxford circuit and in the Court of King's Bench in lean years for a Tory lawyer. He also became MP for the family seat of Cirencester in 1735, as strong a Tory as his father and older brother, who was an MP for the county. Although he rarely spoke in the Commons, he could be depended upon to vote against Walpole. The family's opposition connections compensated somewhat for the lack of government favour and in 1745 he was appointed Solicitor General to the Prince of Wales, three years later being promoted to his Attorney General. When Prince Frederick died in 1751 he continued in the same office to the new Prince of Wales who, nine years later, became George III.

At the age of forty, when it must have seemed that it would be many a weary year, if ever, before he entered the long promised land of preferment, Bathurst made his peace with the ministry. His father applied to the government on his behalf for the vacancy in the Court of Common Pleas and, perhaps in the hope of winning over whole the Bathurst faction, the ministry granted the request. In May, 1754, he went to the bench, though the appointment did not diminish the Bathursts' opposition. His prosperity and security increased even further in the same year on his marriage to Ann Phillipps, a widow and heiress. They had no children in the four years before her death. In 1759 he married Tryphena Scawen who was twenty-nine to his forty-five. During the next ten years they had two sons and four daughters, all of whom survived to a good age save the younger son who died at forty-seven, but only the future third earl married.

In 1770 Judge Bathurst was surprisingly appointed one of three commissioners of the Great Seal following the sudden death of the Lord Chancellor. The astonishment increased further when he was chosen as Lord Chancellor in January 1771, appropriately taking the title of Baron Apsley. Writing in the nineteenth century, Lord Campbell, whose *Lives of the Lord Chancellors*, as Brougham said to Lyndhurst or Lyndhurst said to Brougham, added a new terror to death, sneeringly explained the elevation by saying that Bathurst was 'from his birth and family connections . . . very acceptable to the party in power; he was a man of inoffensive manners, and of undoubted honor and fidelity; and his insignificance was not disagreeable – being regarded as a guaranty that he would give no trouble in the Cabinet.' Certainly his family was an advantage since the Prime Minister, Lord North came from a Tory family and headed a kind of Tory government; and George III, even apart from his attachment to the Bathursts, also favoured such individuals. If Lord Apsley was not one of the ornaments of the wool-sack, even Campbell had to concede that his legal and ecclesiastical appointments were judicious. In 1774 he refused to nominate the celebrated preacher Dr William Dodd to St George's, Hanover Square after Dodd's wife offered a thumping bribe for the fattest living in the capital.[9] Dodd became the laughing stock of London and fled the country; three years later he forged the signature of the young Earl of Chesterfield, whose tutor he had been, on a bond for £8,400 and was hanged, despite a flood of petitions and enlisting the literary services of the great Samuel Johnson in his appeal to the Chancellor and Privy Council.[10]

In cabinet Bathurst was noted for caution and moderation, particularly in the conflict with the American colonies. In January, 1774, he opposed in vain closing the port of Boston and revocation of the self-government of Massachusetts which precipitated the revolution.[11] After the humiliating British surrender at Saratoga on 17 October, 1777, he was one of those who urged an end to the war since he thought that the imminent French recognition of American independence would make it impossible to retain the West Indies. 'With these apprehensions,' he told the Prime Minister, 'I own myself to be for peace on any terms.'[12] Early in 1778 he was threatening to resign over the insufficiency of North's peace proposals, as well as the deliberate failure to summon him to important cabinet meetings, and in June was allowed to go.[13] A more effective measure of sympathy for the colonists, which was accepted, was his recommendation of suspending Habeas Corpus in relation to Americans fighting against the crown. This would allow captives to be held without trial until the end of the war, thus avoiding the dilemma of acknowledging the authority and even sovereignty of the American Congress if they were considered prisoners of war, or executing them as traitors, which was contrary to the customs of civil war.

Despite the manner of his resignation, Bathurst was persuaded to return as Lord President of the Council in November 1779, when North was again trying to shore up his shaky ministry.[14] The most exciting moment in this undemanding post came in June 1780 when the anti-Catholic riots led by Lord George Gordon produced the most violent uproar in London in the whole eighteenth century. Members of the Lords and Commons were assaulted on their way to parliament and Bathurst was lucky to escape with having his wig pulled off and being taunted as 'the Pope'. The Lords engaged in emotional and unruly discussion while the crowd outside threatened to break down the door. When Bathurst was unable to bring it to order the House adjourned and the peers, protected by the Guards as they left, made their cautious ways home under cover of night. For the next five days houses in the capital were looted and burned, hundreds of people died or were wounded and more property was destroyed than in Paris during the whole decade of the French Revolution. Lady Bathurst described the fires that lit the night sky as 'the most dreadful scene you can conceive' and expected Apsley House to be burned to the ground.[15] But it was protected by the few troops who were in London until more were brought up from the country to restore control.

Apsley House, as the name suggests, was begun in 1771, before Bathurst succeeded to his father's title, and, although not completed until 1778, it continued to be known by its original name. In a backhanded compliment Lord Campbell claimed in a footnote that its building was 'the most memorable act in the life of Lord Chancellor Bathurst'. The architect was the fashionable Robert Adam and until 1828 it remained a medium sized, neo-classical brick structure with five bays. The interior was decorated with stylish plaster work and gilding, large windows made the rooms light and airy, and the furniture was specially designed for each room. In the centre was a large circular staircase, in the well of which is now displayed the huge nude statue of Napoleon by Canova given to the Duke of Wellington after Waterloo, with a window at the top to bring in the light. Some of the rooms remain much as they originally were, but the building was altered beyond recognition between 1828 and 1830 by Wellington's extensive remodelling, enlargement and covering of the exterior with Portland stone.[16]

Lord Bathurst was not best pleased at finding himself out of office when North's government finally fell in 1782. But he remained high in royal favour, and when, within a year, George III had imposed on him what he described to Bathurst as 'the most profligate and ungrateful coalition that was ever made in this country', the union of the former opponents North and Charles James Fox, he offered to return as Lord Chancellor. The King had to decline, but added the grateful comment: 'All I can say at present is that Lord Bathurst's handsome conduct shall never be forgotten whilst I live.'[17] Three years later, when Bathurst substituted for the ailing Chancellor, the King again wrote with feeling: 'No one can so properly act as Speaker during the absence of the Lord Chancellor than Lord Bathurst, whose zeal for my service at all times made me certain, if applied to, that he would willing[ly] come forth on the present occasion.'[18] He took advantage of this temporary opportunity to secure for his heir, then in very junior office, the succession to the Lord Chancellor's Tellership of the Exchequer, a rich sinecure worth £1200 a year whose duties could be assigned to a deputy for a fraction of the income.[19] But Lord Chancellor Thurlow quickly recovered and lived another twenty years. In the meantime the future third earl, by then a Lord of the Treasury, acquired an immediate Tellership in 1790 which he held until his death in 1834.

In his last decade the second Earl Bathurst spent most of his time at Cirencester, delighting in the park and continuing his father's planting. In July, 1788, he proudly entertained George III and Queen Charlotte on their way to Cheltenham, where the King hoped to recover from a recent illness. The royal party was impressed by the imposing stone arch at the eastern entrance to the two-and-a-half-mile Sapperton tunnel canal, which, when opened the following year, fulfilled the first earl's dream of uniting the Thames and Severn; but the holiday did nothing to restore the health of the King who by early November was mentally deranged for almost four months.

The second earl's letters to his agent at Cirencester, later Lady Bathurst's brother's agent at Carshalton in Surrey, show him to be a kindly and solicitous landlord, always worried about expenses but also concerned about his workers, particularly in hard times.[20] They do much to offset the impression conveyed elsewhere of a cautious, calculating and intellectually limited man. Indeed even Horace Walpole, who had a hereditary dislike of Bathursts, told friends when they went to live at Hyde Park Corner early in

1775 that they would find 'a very good neighbourhood there; Lord and Lady Apsley are mighty agreeable people.'[21]

Henry Bathurst, the second earl's elder son, was only five when his father became the first earl's heir, thirteen when his father succeeded to the earldom and he in turn became Lord Apsley. In temperament he was like his reserved father but his wide knowledge, easy learning and wit were more reminiscent of his ebullient grandfather. He was certainly put in the way of good opportunities to learn from the beginning by the books and acquaintances collected by the first earl at Cirencester. And he learned much from his relative and namesake, the Rev Henry Bathurst, eighteen years his senior. In the early 1770s Lord Bathurst summoned this young classics don at Oxford, one of his brother Benjamin's thirty-six children (with two wives), to be his intellectual companion. He read aloud to his uncle for four to six hours a day, and merely talking to one who had known most of the leading writers of the century must have been a liberal education for any scholar. Among the interesting visitors was the philosopher David Hume who, when unable politely to turn away the persistent questions of the Presbyterian clergyman at Cirencester about the atheism of the French writer Jean d'Alembert, finally exclaimed, no doubt to Lord Bathurst's delight, 'I don't know, Dr. Parry, much about my friend D'Alembert's religion. I only know he *ought* to have a great deal, for his mother was a *nun*, and his father was a *friar*.'[22]

After the first earl's death in 1775, the Rev Henry Bathurst was the thirteen year old Lord Apsley's tutor at Eton for a year, after which he was appointed a canon of Christ Church, Oxford through the patronage of his grateful cousin, the Lord Chancellor. His successor was the Rev Dr John Plumptre, who thirty years later was recommended to the King as Dean of Gloucester by the Prime Minister not only for 'the perfect orthodoxy of his character in all respects' but also for having had 'the care of the Earl Bathurst's education for several years to his perfect satisfaction and that of his family.'[23]

At Eton Apsley became a friend of two of the most accomplished scholars of the time, Richard, Lord Wellesley, and William Wyndham Grenville. By the time they reached Oxford they were the closest companions and stuck together after leaving the university. Apsley matriculated at Christ Church, Oxford, the college most favoured by the peerage, on 22 April, 1779, a month before his seventeenth birthday. Wellesley had preceded him by only four months, though Grenville was now in his fourth year. On one occasion this happy trio invaded the rooms of a don for a 'rouw'.[24] But in that highly stratified and status conscious society, tutors eager for rich benefices and other forms of patronage looked with indulgent if not blind eyes on the mischief of 'gold tufts'. At Christ Church the sprigs of aristocracy, conspicuous in gold-trimmed silk gowns and with gold tassels in their caps, had their own table in hall and could dine with the dons at high table as well as use the senior common room.

Little study was required; few troubled to take degrees; and many passed their university years in agreeable amusements, sports, violence and various forms of dissipation. But for those who wanted to learn there was plenty available at Christ Church, the leading college in raising standards in the late eighteenth century. The emphasis was more on training the mind than mere accumulation of information, but the curriculum was impressive: logic, mathematics, philosophy, the elements of religion and both the traditional Latin and recently revived Greek authors. The historians Thucydides and Xenophon were considered the best guides to civil government for a person who would be engaged in it: 'from none can he draw more instructive lessons, both of the danger of turbulent faction, and of corrupt oligarchy: from none can he better learn how to play skilfully upon, and how to keep in order, that finely-toned instrument, a free people.'[25] Modern history, including law and European languages, had also gained in importance through the century and was considered useful for aristocrats who might be involved in diplomacy or war, or at least interested in international relations.

As son of the Lord President of the Council, Apsley must have attracted much attention from ambitious dons. But his cousin, now Dr Bathurst, DCL, had a clear advantage. In 1780 he married Grace Coote, daughter of an Irish dean (whose first wife had been the canon's sister), over the objections of her father and his brother, Sir Eyre Coote, who had made a fortune as commander in chief in India. Both cut her off from any inheritance, but Apsley stood by the couple who were frequent visitors to Cirencester. In the following year he wrote from Hanover to say that he would be godfather to the child they were expecting.[26] And in 1790 Apsley's father added the living of Sapperton to the stall in Christ Church. By 1795 the new third earl had secured his cousin's advance to prebendary of Durham and in 1805 he persuaded Prime Minister Pitt to appoint him Bishop of Norwich. But this elevation marked the end of their thirty year friendship. When Pitt died at the beginning of the next year the Bishop threw in his lot with Lord Grenville rather than those of Pitt's followers, including Bathurst, who refused to join a coalition with the Whigs; he became a proponent of Catholic emancipation and over the next few years their formerly perfect harmony came to a conclusive end.

Like most aristocrats, Apsley did not trouble to take his degree at Oxford.

But in 1781, 1782 and 1783 he added to his education by visiting France and parts of Germany, including Hanover and Austria, though not Italy as most noblemen did in that neo-classical age. From Hanover Prince Frederick, later Duke of York told his brother, the Prince of Wales, 'We are agoing to lose Lord Apseley [sic] which I am exceedingly sorry for; he is excessively agreable and we have been great friends.'[27] This was the only time, save a brief excursion to Scotland late in life, that the man who directed the British Empire for longer than anyone else ever ventured outside England.

At the end of February, 1783, Apsley hurried home from Paris on hearing that North and Fox were about to bring down Lord Shelburne's government. A month later, when Fox and North were ensconced in office under the nominal leadership of the Duke of Portland, Apsley told his recent host, the Ambassador to Austria, that he had only narrowly escaped being pushed into office by his father who was anxious for him to become a Lord of the Admiralty even before he was an MP. He had gone to court to kiss hands on the appointment, but when some delay arose over the other members of the Board, managed to persuade his father to let him refuse. Apsley wrote that George III was hostile to the ministry, which was in any event unstable; there was not a shilling in the Treasury and everyone was obsessed with the scramble for favours before the administration collapsed. 'Such open prostitution & prevention of reduction [of government expenditure] by putting oneself up to sale was perhaps scarcely ever known in any Country,' pronounced the recent student of ancient political ideals. He predicted that there would be no secure ministry for some time and declared that he was anxious not to embrace any party, but particularly not one as discordant as the present administration.[28]

While keeping his own counsel during this fateful year, Apsley was returned to the House of Commons for Cirencester in July, two months after he came of age, the seat having been held in perfect silence since 1761 by James Whitshed, husband of Lord Bathurst's sister, Frances. The Bathursts were by custom entitled to one of the town's seats, but holding it was by no means cheap. There were about six hundred voters with a valuable franchise to offer and, even when, as in this case, there was no contest, there were substantial fees: ten guineas for the sheriff's precept, four guineas for the messenger who carried it to Cirencester, and £21 each for the steward and bailiff.[29]

By the end of the year Apsley had made his maiden speech, supporting the King by opposing the government's East India Company bill, the issue on which George III organized the defeat of the Fox-North coalition. The

King then commissioned the twenty-four year old William Pitt to form a new ministry. This extraordinary choice could only occur in a situation such as prevailed in the early 1780s: the confused aftermath of a great military and diplomatic defeat by the American colonists and their European allies; widespread demoralization among the governing classes; fears of national decline; the search for blame and reluctance to accept the responsibility and consequences of a humiliating peace. There had been three ministries within two years and no one knew when the process would end. In these kaleidoscopic changes Pitt, although one of the youngest MPs, had already been Chancellor of the Exchequer (in Shelburne's administration which concluded the treaty with the United States) and radiated the same confidence as his late father, Lord Chatham, that he alone could save the country. George III also shrewdly perceived that he was a fresh young reformer who presented no fundamental threat to the political system.

But with most of the experienced politicians standing aside, prudently as they thought, the new Prime Minister needed all the help he could get from his young friends. His cousin Grenville took office and Grenville's friend Apsley readily responded to the personal choice of the monarch to whom all the Bathursts were attached. Pitt in turn was glad to have the son of a political veteran and royal favourite, and on the last day of 1783 Apsley was appointed a Lord of the Admiralty.

Apart from the great advantage of royal support, the prospects of this precarious enterprise seemed no better, perhaps worse, than the others since the spring of 1782. No one expected the 'mince pie' administration to survive much beyond the twelve days of Christmas and the old political hands had no difficulty organizing defeats in the Commons in January and February. But by March Pitt was demonstrating an impressive authority and skill that won over many independent MPs whose inclination was always to support whatever ministry enjoyed the confidence of the monarch and preserved their interests. Seizing on this favourable opportunity, he and the King dissolved parliament and brought all the influence they could muster to bear in the hard fought contest. At Cirencester Apsley was returned without opposition for the third time within a year, the second having been required on his appointment to the Admiralty. Lord Bathurst also urged his former agent, now at Carshalton in Surrey, to do what he could to secure the return of William Norton and Sir Joseph Mawbey, 'who are friends to Mr. Pitt and the rest of His Majesty's Ministers'.[30] Whatever the effect of his intervention, both were elected for the county. The result of the general election was a House of Commons which customarily supported the government by large majorities, enabling Pitt to turn his formidable attention to improving public finance and the efficiency of public administration. Not least of the departments in which he took a keen interest was the Admiralty, where Apsley was beginning his undemanding apprenticeship.

The five civil lords, all MPs, were not expected to exhaust themselves in return for £1000 a year and a house adjacent to the Admiralty. Lord Palmerston, whose career also began there twenty years later, said in his hearty way that the duties, even in wartime, consisted merely of 'passing a couple of hours in the Board Room doing little or nothing'.[31] In practice the Admiralty was run by the First Lord and junior lords took turns attending meetings (usually every day except Sunday, and sometimes even then), primarily to ensure that there were three signatures for important letters. The Minutes record that Apsley attended the customary one third of the time. In 1784 the First Lord was Admiral Viscount Howe, a naval hero who shared the Prime Minister's dedication to reconstructing the navy, particularly since its shortcomings had undermined his own efforts as naval commander in the American War from 1775 to 1778. Howe's close attention was shared by the other professional member of the Board, Captain John Leveson Gower, and by the Secretary, Paul Stephens who supervised routine business and the two dozen clerks.[32]

But as with aristocratic university education, if there was little compulsion for junior lords to immerse themselves in the operations of the navy, there was plenty of opportunity to learn about the complexities of that department and of government in general. The interacting boards and departments which conducted state business may have exacted a price in lack of co-ordination, misunderstanding and confusion, but they did enable members of one to acquire considerable knowledge of many others. In the case of the Admiralty most of the correspondence was with the Secretaries of State, the Navy Board which constructed and maintained the ships as well as managing the civilian establishments, the Victualling Board which supplied the provisions, clothing and stores, and the Treasurer of the Navy who handled the funds. These were busy years for the Admiralty, which was exempt from the general programme of retrenchment. Five years of merely listening to discussions, glancing through the letters and witnessing the quarrels between the harsh and forbidding Howe and his rival Captain Charles Middleton, the hard-working Comptroller, head of the Navy Board and Pitt's confidant on naval matters, must have been useful training for Apsley. So too, in a different way, must have been his brief experience of the style of Howe's more courtly successor in 1788, Lord Chatham. Despite stiff competition, Pitt's brother has a strong claim to being the idlest minister in British history; when he left the Admiralty six years later hundreds of unopened letters were found in his house.

The five and a half years that Apsley spent at the Admiralty were also important in his personal life. About the time that he entered parliament he became engaged to a daughter of Sir Joseph Copley of Spotsborough, Yorkshire, but she fell ill and died in his arms. The only person whose company he could bear was Dr Bathurst, who slept in Apsley's room for fear of his mental state.[33] Five years later, on 1 April, 1789, Apsley made a wonderfully happy marriage to Georgina (Georgiana) Lennox, youngest of the three daughters of Lord George Lennox, a professional soldier and brother of the Duke of Richmond, the Master General of the Ordnance. It was a nice touch that the heir to Tory families closely connected with the Stuart monarchs should be united with a descendant of Charles II and his principal mistress, Louise de Kéroualle, Duchess of Portsmouth, sent abroad by Louis XIV to lie with his cousin for the good of France. Dr Bathurst, Lord Mornington (formerly Wellesley) and Grenville were naturally among the trustees of the marriage settlement.

Lady Apsley was twenty-three, four years younger than her husband, and remarkable for her beauty and good nature. She bore a striking resemblance to her famous aunt, Lady Sarah Lennox, who, when not yet fifteen, had captivated the young George III on the eve of his accession in 1760; but Duty, that stern daughter of the voice of God, prevailed on the conscientious monarch to marry a foreign princess rather than a subject, particularly one whose relatives were not above dangling her before him as a mistress if she could not be his wife. Lady Sarah considered her niece at fifteen to be the most vivacious of her brother's daughters, describing her as 'rather little & strong made; her countenance is reckon'd very like mine, for she has little eyes, no eyebrows, a long nose, even teeth, & the merriest of faces'. But she generously ascribed all Georgina's 'livelyness . . . all her witt, all her power of satyre, & all her goodnature too' to her mother and judged that she would be a delightful person so long as she was not tempted to overuse her wit.[34]

Two years before her marriage Georgina Lennox had at very least flirted with her handsome and clever cousin, Lord Edward Fitzgerald, son of the Duke of Leinster, whose wife was Lady Sarah's sister, but her father opposed their marriage. In despair the 'dear spirited boy', as Lady Sarah called him, went to North America, 'living in the wild woods to pass the time till my brother George & Ly Louisa may be brought to consent to his marrying Georgina who he adores'. But while he was away they 'cruelly married her to Lord Apsley, & the ungrateful girl has consented. We dread the effect this news will have on him.'[35] The disappointment may have encouraged

14

Fitzgerald, brought up by his mother as a disciple of Jean Jacques Rousseau, to support the French Revolution. He was a leader of the 1798 rebellion in Ireland and died of a bullet wound while awaiting trial.

Even before these radical adventures the heir to the broad Bathurst acres was in every way preferable to the unstable and impecunious younger brother of an Irish duke in the eyes of Lord George Lennox. But if the marriage was practically arranged, it provided them both with forty five years of perfect happiness. Five sons (one of whom died in infancy) and two daughters were born in the first thirteen years. As Apsley rose in power and influence he necessarily became involved in affairs of his wife's extensive family, many of whom were Whigs, led by her cousin Charles James Fox. And in 1819 he was instrumental in having the attainder against Lord Edward Fitzgerald posthumously reversed.

On 10 August, 1789, four months after his marriage, Apsley became a Junior Lord of the Treasury, when his colleague at the Admiralty, Richard Hopkins, declined the transfer on grounds of the difficulty of re-election.[36] The pay at the Treasury was somewhat higher, £1600 rather than £1000, though there was no house. The duties, however, were no heavier, being characterized later by George Canning as 'to make a House [of Commons], to keep a House, and to cheer the Minister'.[37] But the prestige of the Treasury was the highest of all boards, since its First Lord was the Prime Minister. In 1790 Pitt redeemed the promise to Lord Bathurst four years earlier by giving Apsley a Tellership of the Treasury. With the vast expansion of government in the long wars against France after 1793, its value also increased; by 1820, according to the *Extraordinary Black Book*, a radical compilation of sinecures, it was worth £2700 a year, minus whatever the deputy was paid to do the actual work.

The three other junior lords were all Apsley's contemporaries. One was his old friend Lord Mornington, the customary Irish representative since 1786. The Scottish representative, Edward James Eliot and Lord Bayham, heir to Earl Camden, Lord President of the Council, had both been at Trinity College, Cambridge, with Pitt. Apsley and Bayham became great friends, both succeeded to their fathers' titles in 1794 and were often together in office for the next two decades. The senior Joint Secretary of the Treasury Board was George Rose, a decade and a half older than these young lords, a man of industry and talent, Pitt's trusted confidential adviser and patronage manager, and a skilled pluralist on his own behalf. He and Apsley were also to have a long connection, particularly at the Board of Trade between 1807 and 1812.

Since the Treasury was not under the same pressure of time as the

15

Admiralty, the Board generally met about once a week but conducted more business at a time than the Admiralty. During Pitt's rare absences, Mornington customarily presided.[38] Even more than at the Admiralty, the attendant lords merely ratified the decisions of Pitt and Rose. But the Board did bring Apsley into frequent contact with the Prime Minister and laid the basis for their close connection a decade later, though Apsley was never one of those with whom Pitt relaxed from the strains of office in bouts of heavy drinking and masculine horseplay.

After only two years at the Treasury, in June, 1791,[39] Apsley asked to resign, probably to concentrate on family business, since his father was now seventy-seven. By 1793, with the family fortunes secured against his father's death (in the following year), he returned as a member of the Board of Control for India. This marked no great advance in his political position, but there is no reason to think that he wanted anything more at the time than an interesting place in government. On this board he again found pleasant company, being joined on the same day, 28 June, by Mornington and Robert Banks Jenkinson, the future Lord Liverpool, whose trusted colleague he would be from 1812 to 1827. The situation was also familiar, with Indian affairs being dominated by Henry Dundas, the rough, vigorous Scottish lawyer who was man of all work in Pitt's government and whose position on the Board since its inception in 1784 was now formally recognized by the title of President and a salary of £2,000 a year. Pitt, who was a member of the Board, rarely attended. Two of the commissioners were paid £1500 a year, but Apsley, who had his Treasury sinecure, and the other two were unpaid.

In the last nine years Dundas had worked out an easy relationship with the directors of the East India Company and the India Board met about every ten days to review the correspondence of the directors and discuss senior appointments. Apsley attended the usual proportion of a quarter of the meetings. When Dundas was absent Mornington generally presided. The vital issues of war, peace and negotiation with the Indian princes were handled by a secret joint committee of the Board and the directors of the company, usually chaired by Pitt or Dundas, of which Apsley was sometimes a member.[40]

A year after he joined the Board of Control Apsley succeeded as the third Earl Bathurst. Since the second earl was eighty and had been declining for some years, his death can have been no great shock. Far harder to bear was the death in October 1796 of the Bathursts' youngest child so far, the three year old Peter George Allen, from the effects of inoculation by Dr Edward Jenner, who had been at school at Cirencester and just begun experimenting with cowpox as a preventative against the scourge of smallpox. When he felt able to write to the new Earl Camden a few weeks later, Bathurst told him that 'there was something in the Age, beauty and manners of the poor Child we have lost, which will not let him be easily forgotten'. Camden in return hoped that having so many promising children would at least lessen the severity of the blow.[41]

Just before this great sadness Bathurst achieved some distinction by his maiden speech in the House of Lords when moving the Address in Reply to the Speech from the Throne on 6 October, 1796. In his decade in the Commons he had rarely spoken, and then only briefly, and he was to prove no less hesitant in the more conversational atmosphere of the Lords. But on this formal occasion he acquitted himself well in defending the government's actions against its opponents at home and abroad. 'It was also a matter of congratulation,' he said, referring to the domestic agitation and repressive legislation of the past few years, 'that the tranquillity of the country had been preserved and the views of those who wished to stir up anarchy and confusion, had been completely frustrated by the wisdom and energy of the laws.' Lord Grenville, now Foreign Secretary, told the King that it was the best speech he had ever heard on such an occasion. Of course no minister is on oath in making such a report about a friend, especially a royal favourite, but Grenville used the same terms to Mornington. The King in reply told Grenville that if Bathurst could 'conquer his natural diffidence, he cannot fail of making that figure which would be particularly agreeable to me for the memory of his grandfather'.[42] Although Bathurst never became an orator he did in other ways fulfil George III's hopes for him.

Unlike Bathurst, whose place at the Board of Control was primarily one of honour, Mornington, after chafing at the periphery of the great political world for a decade, finally saw in India a chance to improve his personal and family fortunes. In April, 1797, he was appointed Governor of Madras, with the promise of Calcutta in succession to Lord Cornwallis, who had held the post from 1786 to 1792 and had just accepted again; but when Cornwallis's military and political talents were more urgently needed in Ireland, Mornington was immediately given the senior governorship. He was so confident that Bathurst would accompany him as Governor of Madras that Dundas wrote to Cirencester offering the post. But Bathurst told Mornington that, although he would like it more than any other, particularly since it would mean acting with his friend, 'it would make Lady Bathurst so perfectly wretched that I have not hesitated a moment to give a positive refusal.'[43] If he had gone, he might have helped to moderate Mornington's imperious manner, though not necessarily the rapid expansion of British political involvement which so alarmed the traders of the East India Company. But for the first few years at least Mornington felt secure against this mercantile carping at his vigorous efforts to counter French influence, brilliantly executed by the military genius of his younger brother Arthur and supported by Pitt, Dundas and Bathurst at the Board of Control.

Mornington's wife, a French former actress at best who bore five children before they finally married in 1794, also refused to cross the ocean. This eight year separation destroyed the marriage, made it difficult for Mornington to adjust to British politics when he returned in 1805, and finally alienated most of his old companions. In his loneliness he wrote endless letters to his friends and Bathurst in turn kept the Marquess Wellesley (as he became in 1799) informed about politics and his family at intervals of at least four, and usually six, months that it took for letters to reach India. The loyal Bathursts were also one of the few families to receive Lady Wellesley and children, despite her dubious past and their illegitimacy.

Another absent friend with whom Bathurst had to keep in touch by letter in the later 1790s was Lord Camden, whom Pitt had done no favour in persuading to go to Ireland as Lord Lieutenant in 1795. His three years there had none of Wellesley's controversial success, but even apart from Camden's own shortcomings, the task was more difficult and he was too close to London to have the same freedom practically to make his own policy. The shield and defender of Ascendency privilege, he steadfastly opposed demands for removing Catholic disabilities and reforming the Irish parliament until, at the very end of the decade, he became a supporter of Catholic emancipation within a United Kingdom. But in February, 1798, while asking Bathurst to tell Pitt that he wanted to resign, he was still clinging to the preservation of the existing Irish system.[44] Camden was replaced by Cornwallis in June, in the middle of the uprising against British rule.

The dreaded French assistance to the Irish turned out to be a mere 900 troops at the end of August, too few and too late to have much effect. But the fear of a larger invasion in conjunction with rebellion meant that all the regular troops and even militia that could be spared in Britain were rushed to Ireland. More militiamen to replace them were recruited and finally a new provisional cavalry was formed which, in the words of William Windham, the Secretary at War (the House of Commons' watchdog over army expenses), 'passed over the country like a blight. It was a pleasant conceit to make every man ride another's horse, till at length when the men and horses were all brought together, no man knew how to mount, and so they all separated.'[45] Bathurst was given the command of this doubtful force in Gloucestershire, telling Wellesley in April 1798 that 'we are going to be embodied to my infinite surprise and regret'. A couple of weeks earlier he had written to Dundas, who had been directing the conflict since 1794 as the newly created Secretary of State for War, suggesting that if necessary the cavalry go no further than Bristol which was at least in the county; if it had to go outside he hoped it would be to Plymouth.[46] It was in fact soon disbanded, never to be revived, but in its brief existence provided the total military experience of the future Secretary of State for War and the Colonies.

A year after this martial interlude Bathurst became involved in a matter concerning his wife's sister Emily and her husband, Vice-Admiral George Berkeley. In 1796 the Admiral's brother, the Earl of Berkeley, had married Mary Cole, described by a former barrister on the Oxford circuit as 'a common prostitute at Worcester . . . [who] had often been with several of our fellow circuiteers, in the exercise of that profession, in houses of accommodation for such temporary amours'.[47] They had had four sons before they married and Lady Berkeley was not received at court. Suddenly they claimed that they had been secretly married in 1785, before the birth of their first child. This interposition of four supposedly legitimate heirs before himself and his children was a serious matter for the Admiral. From the squadron he was commanding in the Channel he asked his wife early in 1799 to urge Bathurst to have the parish register at Berkeley examined as soon as possible.[48]

Bathurst's agent was Joseph Pitt, a self-made lawyer, brewer, banker and land speculator; now a considerable figure in Cirencester, Cricklade and Cheltenham, he even claimed to be related to the Prime Minister and had his arms carved on his tomb.[49] To the Admiral's delight Pitt found no entry for the marriage or anything referring to it.[50] But when he returned a month later, this time closely watched by two people, he was astonished to discover a record of the marriage on 30 March, 1785, on a loose sheet, a certificate signed by three of Berkeley's retainers testifying that it belonged to the register and a record of the publication of banns in a section of blank pages. The certificate was in Lord Berkeley's handwriting; one witness was a relative of Lady Berkeley but Pitt could not learn the identity of the other. The clergyman, unfortunately deceased, had peculiarly signed the banns as curate and the marriage as vicar. Pitt was nevertheless able to recruit three good witnesses for the Committee of Privileges of the House of Lords.[51] Lord Berkeley was furious at his brother for preventing his claim of marriage from being accepted and the dispute rumbled on in the House of Lords for three decades. The eldest son following the 1796 marriage refused to assume the title and finally one of the Admiral's grandsons became earl in 1882.[52]

19

Joseph Pitt meanwhile, controlling or strongly influencing five seats in the House of Commons, in 1811 decided to become an MP for Cricklade himself, for which he solicited Bathurst's influential endorsement.[53] He was returned unopposed at the general election of 1812 and, although he spoke only once in twenty years, he could be relied on to vote for the ministry.

Just a few months after the Berkeley investigation Bathurst suddenly found himself out of office. The government managed to get the union of Ireland and Britain through the two parliaments, coming into effect on 1 January, 1801, but was hopelessly divided on the informal promise of full political rights for Catholics in the newly United Kingdom (in Ireland they had had the vote since 1793 and could hold most civil and military offices, though not sit in parliament). Pitt believed that this would secure the loyalty of Irish Catholics and was confident that he could manage George III as he had so often before. Bathurst was not enthusiastic about Catholic claims but accepted the argument of necessity. Some of their colleagues, however, saw true loyalty in telling the staunchly Protestant King what was afoot. With assurances from Henry Addington, Speaker of the House of Commons, that he could form a government to defend the Protestant constitution, the King finally set his face against Pitt.[54]

For other reasons the Prime Minister was not unhappy to have an honourable reason to resign. Bad harvests and high taxes had produced protests from all levels of society; he could not see how satisfactory terms to end the long, inconclusive and expensive war could be obtained from Napoleon Bonaparte; even if the cabinet accepted Catholic emancipation, there were probably not majorities for it in parliament. And after seventeen years his frail physique was exhausted by the strains of office and a decade of heavy drinking. The previous spring Bathurst had told Wellesley that Pitt was agitated by any vexation,[55] and his condition had not improved as the military situation deteriorated.

By the time the government broke up, Bathurst had been rewarded for his unpaid service at the Board of Control by appointment as Clerk of the Crown in Chancery, a sinecure worth about £1100 a year which he held jointly with his brother Apsley until the latter's death in 1816. Pitt's finances, which he had neglected while paying meticulous attention to those of the state, were, by contrast, calamitous. But he refused any lucrative sinecure and George III's magnanimous offer to pay his debts, though he did allow his friends to provide a loan of £11,700 so long as he did not know the names. Bathurst, who probably had no more expectation of seeing it again than anyone else, gratefully contributed £1000.[56]

The departure of the person he regarded as the indispensable leader in February 1801 finally prompted Bathurst, at the age of thirty-eight, to take an active role in politics. But he was soon shaken by Pitt's approval of the peace negotiated by Addington's ministry accepting French domination of the continent and restoring most of the overseas conquests to their European owners. When the terms were announced the former Prime Minister told Bathurst, 'I think on the whole the result highly satisfactory, and the stipulations in favour of our allies are particularly creditable.' He regretted the return of the Cape of Good Hope, 'but on that I know great authorities differ.'[57] To avoid disagreeing with his hero Bathurst withdrew to Cirencester, plausibly claiming love of rural family life.[58] Camden travelled thither to discuss their common dismay and Grenville wrote to the same effect.

Bathurst then wrote a long letter to Pitt in the hope of avoiding a division. He began on an encouraging note, glad to hear that Pitt was opposed to a rapid reduction of the armed forces and trusting that he was also aware of the danger of abandoning the Aliens Act of 1793 (which controlled the entry of foreigners and compelled them to carry passports and request permission to change residence) which would be impossible to reintroduce without war or at least apprehension of it. He hoped that Pitt would also recollect that the war had gone on so long from 'a just jealousy of the power, and the principles of the French. We may find it expedient to make Peace; but that has not lessened their Power (it unhappily increases it) nor does it alter their principles.' Bathurst saw no inconsistency in bending to events if peace was less dangerous than continuing the war but implored Pitt not to argue contrary to the apprehensions which everyone knew he felt, but rather to emphasize his reservations about the Cape and defence. Above all he warned him not 'in order to speak with zeal, to speak without discretion'.[59] Pitt in return agreed about the Aliens Act and the armed services, but insisted that, however he regretted the return of the Cape, it was not worth continuing the war to retain it. Downplaying their disagreement, he assured Bathurst that 'few things can give me more satisfaction and comfort than to find I concur with you on such an occasion; especially when I must have the mortification of differing from many with whom I have so long acted and whose opinions I so much value.'[60]

Bathurst unwillingly followed Pitt in accepting the peace treaty, but, like many others, became alarmed in 1802 when Addington abolished the income tax and began dismantling the army and navy while Bonaparte made preparations suggesting renewed hostilities. To the dismay of those who looked to Pitt as the only effective war leader, however, he practically

21

withdrew from the political scene; nor was he helping his delicate health by heavy drinking, which, Camden told Bathurst in October, his doctor was not firm enough to stop.[61] When Addington finally decided to increase the army and navy, Bathurst urged Pitt to attend parliament at the end of November to demonstrate to the country that he was not 'desirous of abandoning it altogether in a time of great difficulty'.[62] But Pitt would not budge from the fastness of Walmer Castle of which he was Lord Warden.

He did, however, spend a few days in December with the Bathursts and the veteran diplomat Lord Malmesbury and his family. 'Nothing could be more playful, and at times more instructive, than Pitt's conversation, on a variety of subjects, while sitting in the Library at Cirencester,' wrote Malmesbury's son. 'You would never have guessed that the man before you was Prime Minister of the country, and one of the greatest that ever filled that situation. His style and manner were quite those of an *accomplished idler*.' Malmesbury also admired Bathurst, 'who looks up to Pitt; rates Addington very low,' to be 'quite right and sensible on public affairs – moderate and candid in the true sense of word.'[63]

But even after war resumed in May, 1803, Pitt would not criticize the government for a year, at which point Addington's majority fell so low that he resigned. In the interval Bathurst tried to reconcile Pitt and Grenville, who agreed on the conduct of the war but not on Catholic emancipation. Pitt was willing to abandon it for what seemed the few years remaining to George III, but Grenville felt so strongly about the concession that he formed an alliance with their old opponent Charles James Fox. When Pitt was commissioned to form a new ministry in May 1804, Grenville would not join without Fox, which the King adamantly refused.

Patching together a ministry of those who did not stick to Grenville or Addington, the new Prime Minister optimistically assured Bathurst that 'The appearances of difficulty have diminished every day, and I think we shall on the whole start with a very fair prospect.' Bathurst, who could certainly have had one, must not have wanted a substantial ministry, but, all unbidden, Pitt offered him the Mint, 'with which for my personal satisfaction you must comply'. With his large family – the sixth and last surviving child had been born two years before – Bathurst was naturally delighted by this rich reward, though he assured Pitt that he was already well provided for with his two sinecures.[64]

If not quite a sinecure, the Mint did not require any onerous exertion of its Master in return for his salary of £3000 a year. The main activity during Bathurst's tenure was moving from its ancient home in the Tower of London to the new building on Tower Hill where modern machinery was also installed. The plans for the neo-classical Mint were completed by the young Robert Smirke, who later designed such buildings as the British Museum and Covent Garden Theatre, as well as the new entrance hall at Cirencester, drawn to Bathurst's attention in 1805 when the health of the present architect, James Johnson, was failing.[65]

Lady Bathurst's vitality was also declining, permanently as it turned out. Although not yet forty, she never again enjoyed robust health and her fitness became a staple topic in correspondence between Bathurst and his friends. But by taking good care of her ailments she managed to reach the age of seventy-five, outliving her vigorous husband by seven years.

The appointment to the Mint left Bathurst plenty of time to work on Pitt's behalf to attract their old friend Grenville and his followers while the Prime Minister concentrated on a third coalition against France under the newly-crowned Emperor Napoleon. But these efforts foundered on Grenville's insistence on the inclusion of Fox. At the end of 1804 Pitt instead came to terms with Addington, who became Lord President of the Council and went to the House of Lords as Viscount Sidmouth; this turned out to be a temporary help since he resigned six months later. The war, however, seemed to be going well. In September, 1805, Pitt cheerfully told Bathurst, 'Our prospects from abroad are improving every day.'[66] Russia and Austria were allies, an expeditionary force of 60,000 was on its way to Germany and there were high hopes that Prussia would also join. The great naval victory at Trafalgar on 21 October lifted the threat of a French invasion of Britain and even raised hopes of a triumphant advance against France itself. But from that moment the news rapidly deteriorated. On 2 December Napoleon defeated the Russian and Austrian armies at Austerlitz and the third coalition against France collapsed.

By the time the news of this calamity reached England, Pitt was once more at Bath trying to recover his health. Bathurst went to see him, but the Prime Minister was too ill to go to Cirencester. 'The progress of my recovery since the last fit [of gout] has been so slow that I believe it will be better the constitution should clear itself a little more,' he wrote to Bathurst on New Year's Day 1806. 'I have been taking the waters now for five days without much sensible effect unless as far as these sensations of gout can be charged to them.'[67] Bathurst was not deceived by this jocular tone and reported the Prime Minister's precarious condition to the King. But George III did not grasp the warning and his secretary replied with his gratification that 'Mr Pitt is mentally composed and that, notwithstanding his severe illness, his spirits are unshaken; which indeed the opinion which His Majesty has of the firmness of his character would have led him to expect, and His Majesty rejoices in the prospect of his speedy recovery.'[68]

On 9 January, the day of Nelson's state funeral, Pitt left Bath feebler than when he arrived. At that moment Wellesley arrived back from the East like Fortinbras in the last act of *Hamlet*. Writing to welcome him, Bathurst forbore comment on disputes among their old friends: 'Perhaps the only thing on which they agree is their regard and attachment to you.'[69] Wellesley hastened to the stricken leader and pronounced in his lapidary way: 'I saw that the hand of death was fixed upon him.'[70] After Bathurst had also been to Pitt Wellesley told him: 'I know not how we can ever meet again but with sorrow and pain. Lord Melville's affliction to-day is not to be described, and I never beheld any man more overwhelmed with grief than Grenville, who this morning desired to see me, but could scarcely speak to me; his heart is full of grief.'[71] Pitt, only forty-six, died in the early hours of the next day, 23 January, probably of stomach cancer. At a grim period in the war the political world was plunged into even greater confusion and Bathurst was not alone in finding himself for the first time since 1783 without a pilot to weather the storm.

Pitt's death destroyed the shaky ministry which he had directed in the last two years. Faced with powerful opponents in parliament and with Napoleon carrying all before him in Europe, the leading ministers told the King that they could not continue. Bathurst favoured Lord Chatham's idea of a broad coalition of Grenville, Fox and others under Lord Wellesley.[72] There was no doubt in Wellesley's mind that he was the obvious successor to Pitt, but he was still under a cloud for his expansionism and financial dealings in India. George III instead swallowed his animosity and commissioned Grenville to form a government without restrictions, which enabled him to include Fox. But any hopes of the devoted Pittites disappeared when Fox, in greater testimony to his consistency than good judgment, opposed, though he could not defeat, the motion in the Commons for a public funeral for Pitt.

One of those Grenville most expected to keep was of course Bathurst. But stung by the insult to Pitt's memory, Bathurst forestalled the offer by frostily telling Grenville that although he considered it unlikely that he would be included in the government, 'yet I am bound to tell you that I should feel myself obliged to decline any situation in an administration formed on such an occasion as the present'. He plausibly insisted that this was not due to hostility but because 'after such a loss, I cannot wish, or bring my feelings to think of immediately entering into any new political engagements'. Grenville understood what was being said but hoped that, even in the unlikely event of political disagreement, 'I should still look with entire confidence to the continuation of your friendship to which you will know how much value I attach.'[73]

The much blunter refusal of others dealt a fatal blow to Grenville's hope of a comprehensive ministry. He put together what was soon ironically styled the Ministry of All the Talents with Fox as Foreign Secretary; and, his bellicosity having given way to defeatism, Grenville even supported Fox's vain efforts to come to terms with his hero Napoleon. To balance these supporters of Catholic emancipation, Sidmouth, the King's Protestant champion, became Lord Privy Seal.

The Peelites finally settled on the decrepit Duke of Portland, who had served in both the Addington and second Pitt administrations as Lord President of the Council, as their leader. But they also regarded Grenville as a great man led astray by Fox and looked to the day when they would replace Fox and Sidmouth in their rightful places in a restored version of Pitt's government before 1801. Bathurst in particular, given his personal friendship, adopted an attitude of benevolent and optimistic neutrality. In July, 1806, he told Camden that the best hope at present was for Grenville to assert himself on his administration; and when Fox died in September he took no joy in the prospect of turning out the ministry, but again told Camden that his inclination was to support the monarch's wishes 'as far as is consistent with one's duty to the Country,' now that Grenville might show himself a real leader.[74]

The fall of the Talents came six months later, when Grenville and other pro-Catholics decided to open the higher ranks of the army and navy to Catholics. This involved the clever deception of the King, but Sidmouth was not deceived, and Bathurst implored Grenville to consider the King's views and the fact that no one wanted another clash on the issue. 'The country is not in a situation to bear it,' he warned, 'and it would lose much more by such a battle than you could possibly gain by a victory. I do hope therefore that you will be able to listen to some modification.' Grenville disingenuously replied that the King had understood what was intended, insisted that the proposal had had a good effect on Ireland and that this concession alone would have prevented consideration of full Catholic relief. Hoping to win over Bathurst, perhaps bring him into the cabinet to replace Sidmouth, Grenville invited him to dinner to advise on what he should do.[75]

Perhaps on Bathurst's recommendation, Grenville did drop the bill, but when the King insisted on a written undertaking 'never under any circumstances to propose to him *any* concessions to the Catholics', it was too much. What would be said of him, Grenville asked Bathurst, if after championing full Catholic relief he should publicly bind himself 'never to give any, even the smallest, part?' But by this time, perhaps, he was also weary of office and glad to depart in peace rather than face ignominious defeat.[76] Its initial expectations in ruins, the Ministry of All the Talents sloped out of office in March 1807, leaving as its monument the abolition of the slave trade, a testament to the strength of religious and humanitarian feelings in what was seen as a righteous war against the revolutionary forces of atheism.

2

SAY NOT THE STRUGGLE NAUGHT AVAILETH, 1807–1812

When the King called on the Duke of Portland to form a ministry after the fall of the Talents, it was inevitable that Bathurst would be invited to join the cabinet and that he would be obliged to accept. His political involvement since 1801 required him to take a prominent part if requested and his moderate temperament certainly appealed to the new Prime Minister. He was appointed President of the Board of Trade, which was not necessarily a cabinet post though Portland reminded the King that it had recently become customary for it to be included, 'considering how intimately it is connected by its duties with the first & most confidential offices of State'.[1] But since it was unpaid he again became Master of the Mint. On the eve of his forty-fifth birthday, after twenty years of undemanding minor offices and advice to powerful friends, Bathurst himself was now one of the country's ten decision makers.

The Board of Trade, formally 'The Right Honourable the Lords of the Committee appointed for the Consideration of all Matters relating to Trade and Foreign Plantations', had in its present manifestation been reconstituted by Pitt in 1786 after the abolition of its predecessor in the mood of despair and retrenchment following American independence. As an advisory body to other departments it had a long list of statutory members and some specifically named individuals (most notably in 1807 Sir Joseph Banks, the

27

famous botanist and President of the Royal Society), none of whom was paid and few of whom attended unless matters in which they had a particular interest were being discussed. It recommended means of promoting trade, safeguarded the rights and interests of British merchants, fixed duties and other charges on imports and exports, and considered the validity of acts of colonial legislatures.[2]

In practice, like other offices in commission, the Board consisted of the President and Vice-President. It was rare for more than four members to be present at meetings, which were held about twice a week. Banks was a frequent attender, but often there was only Bathurst and George Rose, the Vice-President, sometimes only one of them, and on occasion, such as when colonial acts were being routinely referred to the legal officers, no members were present as the secretary read the orders into the minutes. The Board shared the two Clerks of the Privy Council, who, along with one of its own, acted as Secretaries. It also had a chief clerk and half a dozen juniors, by no means too many to handle the complaints of merchants and traders as the economic warfare between Britain and Napoleon intensified at the end of 1807.

Bathurst was particularly fortunate to have as Vice-President the experienced George Rose, who for seventeen years had conducted the business of the Treasury as Secretary under Pitt, whose loyal friend and adviser he remained to the end. In 1807 he was sixty-three, Treasurer of the Navy and holder of numerous other sinecures accumulated over a long career. Bathurst naturally depended heavily on his professional expertise in trade and finance.

Another person with a wealth of technical knowledge was the law clerk, John Reeves, formerly the first Chief Justice of Newfoundland, a considerable legal scholar and, like Banks, a Fellow of the Royal Society. In 1795 he had aroused the anger of the House of Commons by his *Thoughts on the English Government*, which concluded that all authority rested in the monarch and that parliament and juries were merely subsidiary and occasional bodies. The House had ordered him prosecuted for libel by the Attorney General but he was acquitted by a jury which fairmindedly overlooked his reflections on that institution to find the publication no worse than improper. His views, however, were not necessarily unwelcome to the executive and Reeves like Rose flourished as a wealthy pluralist, becoming King's Printer and Superintendent of Aliens, as well as law clerk to the Board of Trade from 1787 to 1823. For thirty-six years he pronounced on colonial acts and the Board was not disposed to alter his judgements. Only after his retirement was this duty transferred to the Colonial Office where Bathurst was then minister.

One of Bathurst's main occupations was to attend meetings of the Privy Council, generally about twice a week, when it deliberated on Orders in Council regulating trade with Napoleonic Europe. In practice this also often consisted only of Bathurst, Rose and Banks; even Lord President Camden rarely troubled to put in an appearance. The real decisions about trade regulations and charges were made by the Chancellor of the Exchequer, but the Privy Council ruled on such particular matters as licences for ships to sail through the British blockade of Napoleonic ports, requests for variations in such matters as ship size, petitions from ship owners claiming compensation for losses resulting from official directives, as well as keeping a watchful eye on merchants trying to disguise the nature or true provenance of their cargoes.[3] The other duties of the Privy Council, such as hearing appeals from the colonies, the Channel Islands and the Isle of Man, were necessarily of minor concern in the half decade after 1807.

The Board of Trade provided Bathurst with plenty of routine work and established his reputation for efficiency and dependability. It also gave him intimacy with his cabinet colleagues, much knowledge of the work of other departments and ample opportunity to consider general policy. Of his nine fellow cabinet ministers, Bathurst was closest to Lord Camden. But among the others were several with whom he was to work closely for the next twenty years, notably the Home Secretary, Lord Hawkesbury (who succeeded his father as Earl of Liverpool in 1808), Lord Castlereagh, Secretary of State for War and the Colonies, and Lord Eldon, the Lord Chancellor. He also had a trusted relationship with the Leader of the House of Commons and Chancellor of the Exchequer, Spencer Perceval, and a good association with the mercurial and prickly Foreign Secretary, George Canning, the rival in the Commons of both Castlereagh and Perceval.

Lord Harrowby, who was not included, congratulated Bathurst, and even more the cabinet, on his appointment: 'Your advice has always been so good out of it that I am truly glad it will have the advantage of having it upon all subjects to be discussed'.[4]

Another friend who remained out of office was Lord Wellesley who was offered the Foreign Office but told Bathurst that he had decided to decline.[5] He did not feel that he could abandon Grenville, who had stood by him during the attacks on his Indian administration, and undoubtedly thought it only a matter of time before he was summoned to replace the ailing and unimpressive Portland. In the meantime his interests were well protected by three of his brothers, who had hitherto also supported Grenville: William Wellesley-Pole, Secretary to the Admiralty, Henry Wellesley, Secretary of the Treasury, and General Sir Arthur Wellesley who became Chief Secretary for Ireland under the new Lord Lieutenant, the Duke of Richmond, Lady Bathurst's brother.

Later in the year, following his mother's death, Bathurst sold Apsley House to Lord Wellesley for £17,000. He was relieved that the purchaser was a fellow aristocrat since he would have been unwilling to sell to a financier or merchant 'East of Temple Bar'.[6] Ten years later Wellesley sold the house to his brother Arthur, by then the great Duke of Wellington. Bathurst himself spent the rest of his life in London in a succession of rented houses and until about 1820 also had a villa, Lime Grove, at Putney, in which the historian Edward Gibbon had been born and from which he attended the local school.[7]

In joining Portland's government Bathurst felt that he had to justify his decision to Lord Grenville, whose ministry he had refused to join. He explained that he had not been able to remain even neutral on Grenville's Catholic bill and that to oppose Portland would be contrary to all his feelings, habits and opinions. Each assured the other that political differences would not destroy their old friendship,[8] probably expecting that another turn of the political kaleidoscope would unite them in office or opposition before long. But in fact the new governmental arrangement endured and the two were estranged for over a decade.

Bathurst's place in the cabinet naturally made him concerned about matters affecting his brothers in law, the Duke of Richmond, the Irish Viceroy, and more immediately Vice-Admiral Berkeley, who was a pressing problem for the entire ministry. He had been appointed commander of the North American waters at Halifax in 1806 at the express desire of Grenville, his relative whom he supported as MP for Gloucestershire. In the continuing dispute with the United States over the right to inspect ships for British deserters, Berkeley sent his flagship, the *Leopard*, to search the USS *Chesapeake*. On 27 June, 1807, after unsatisfactory negotiations, the *Leopard* opened fire and several sailors were killed before the *Chesapeake* surrendered. One British subject who had been particularly vituperative against his own country was hanged at Halifax, but the other sailors who were seized embarrassingly turned out to be Americans.

The outraged President Jefferson demanded an apology, reparations and a commitment from the British government to keep its warships out of American waters. But Berkeley was unmoved, telling Bathurst that the American government did nothing to check the violence of the newspapers which were the only guide for public opinion. He was not exactly opposed to negotiations but thought that any olive branch should be accompanied by force, preferably a strike against the rich port of New York.

He asked Bathurst to have his colleagues send him more ships and munitions and a flying army of 5,000 troops in fast transports to spread alarm and despondency on the American coast. Six months of this, he confidently predicted, would force the Americans to accept British terms.[9] War in America in the midst of its troubles in Europe was the last thing the government needed and no one paid any attention to Berkeley's helpful suggestion. But neither would the ministry accept the American demand to end its searches.

It could, however, remove the provocative Admiral, despite his connection with Bathurst and Richmond, to say nothing of his own important family. At Bathurst's request the First Lord of the Admiralty, in November, 1808, posted Berkeley to the warm water command at Lisbon,[10] where he soon became a great trial to the military commander. At the beginning of 1810 Sir Arthur Wellesley protested that Berkeley interfered in everything in Portugal, 'civil Military political Commercial, even ecclesiastical I believe'. He had never known a man

> who had so good an education, & had been employed in publick stations, & had some communication with the world, whose understanding is so defective & who has such a passion for new invented modes of doing ordinary things & such contempt for every thing that is practicable.

But despite Wellesley's protests about being 'teazed to death by this Man,'[11] Berkeley remained on the Lisbon station until his retirement full of honour in 1812.

In the summer of 1807, just as Bathurst was settling into office, Napoleon began enforcing his Continental System in order to ruin his most persistent opponent and force her to accept his domination of Europe. He declared that Britain was in a state of blockade, prohibited imports of British manufactures and colonial goods, excluded any ship which stopped at a British port or one of its colonies, pronounced all British property lawful prize and all British subjects prisoners of war, and even forbade correspondence. Until substitutes for British imports could be found, essential commodities could be purchased only from neutrals.

The British government might simply have ignored this overweening scheme as it had others since the beginning of the wars with revolutionary France, confident in its naval superiority and the connivance of continental ports. But the Portland ministry was determined to act more vigorously than the spineless Talents, which had merely prohibited neutral trade between ports controlled by France. Perceval, Hawkesbury and Castlereagh were the most ardent in insisting that all trade with Napoleonic Europe must be channelled through Britain and controlled on British terms. Bathurst, by nature more cautious, feared that this would cause more harm to Britain than to Napoleon. He warned that Britain's ability to continue the war depended on commerce and that raising other taxes would increase the government's difficulties. He also pointed out that 'The enemy forms one great military empire. The extent of country he covers does not render him so dependent on an export and import trade. The whole of that trade might perish and he could still continue the war. If one-third of our's were to fail, we should soon be reduced to a peace'.[12] But the more belligerent ministers carried the day.

By Orders in Council of 11 and 25 November, 1807, all ports closed to Britain were declared to be under blockade. Ships bound for them must land their cargoes at British ports, pay the duty and buy a licence for inspection and protection by the Royal Navy. Any ship sailing for a blockaded port without a licence, any not bound for a British port from a blockaded one, or about which there was suspicion, was to be seized for adjudication by the Admiralty Court; but properly licensed direct trade between Britain and continental ports was to be protected in order to promote British prosperity and Napoleon's distress.[13] These regulations gave British shipping interests a great advantage over their rivals by not having to pay duties or interrupt the voyages. But manufacturers insisted that the country would be better off exporting as much as possible to neutral countries, particularly the United States, which should then be allowed to sell directly to Napoleonic Europe.

The Orders in Council controlling and taxing trade were subject to constant adjustment as countries slipped in and out of Napoleon's control. The various changes were the daily round and common task of the Privy Council and the Board of Trade, in effect Bathurst, Rose and their officials. But their wide-ranging effect meant that almost all departments were involved to some extent in the officially sanctioned provision of forged papers and false flags, smuggling and the encouragement of regular trade through every scrap of mainland Europe over which it had any influence, the most important at the end of 1807 being neutral Sweden. Although the precise means were altered from time to time, the essential aim was always the same: to frustrate Napoleon, to encourage resistance to his Continental System, to maintain as much British trade as possible and to increase revenue to pay for the war. As Bathurst said in one of the many debates on the subject in the House of Lords: 'In the exercise of belligerent rights for the purpose of embarrassing the commerce of the enemy, and making him feel the effects of his own acts of violence, every possible attention had, at the same time, been paid to the commercial interests of [this] country'.[14]

The American government was outraged by the arrogance of the Orders, which it regarded, like the right of search, as a refusal to accept its sovereignty and the forced subordination of its interests to British naval hegemony. The New England shipowners, to whom British licences were liberally granted, pragmatically accepted the Orders and prospered from the war, but pressure from other parts of the United States produced various retaliatory embargo acts and ultimately war against Britain.

Unfortunately for Portland's eager ministers, apart from economic warfare, 1807 was as unfavourable a year for decisive action as any since 1793. In early July, by the Treaty of Tilsit, Napoleon and Tsar Alexander I became allies against Britain and Russia joined the Continental System; by secret clauses Austria, Sweden, Denmark and Portugal were also to be compelled to enter. Even before this fairly obvious news arrived the British were negotiating with the Danes to surrender their fleet for the duration of the war in return for an alliance and an annual financial subsidy. When this was refused Copenhagen was bombarded into capitulation and the Danish navy confiscated, which turned Denmark into Napoleon's loyal ally. The Danish island of Heligoland off the German coast was also seized and became a major base for exports, mostly smuggled, to the continent. When the merchants complained to Bathurst that the pilots were increasing the opportunities of their fellow islanders for salvage by refusing to go out in bad weather, the Board of Trade ordered the governor to have the magistrates and the harbour master determine the danger, set the pilots' rates and compel them to perform their services.[15] A morally and strategically clearer triumph was achieved at the end of the year at the other end of Europe when the Royal Navy escorted the Regent, Prince John, from Lisbon to re-establish his capital at Rio de Janiero just as Napoleon's army arrived to force Portugal into the Continental System.

By the summer of 1808 the Portuguese were in revolt against the French, as were the Spanish after Napoleon forced the royal family to abdicate in favour of his brother Joseph. A fatal breach seemed to have been made in Napoleon's empire and British government hopes soared for his early defeat if Austria also rose. But when it offered troops to the Spanish representatives, they confidently replied that they could deal with the French alone if they were properly supplied and suggested that Britain send its soldiers to liberate Portugal and prevent the French army there from attacking the Spanish insurgents. A force was promptly despatched under the command of the Irish Secretary, Sir Arthur Wellesley. But he was prevented from following up his triumph over the French General Junot at the battle of Vimiero by the senior generals, Sir Harry Burrard and Sir Hew Dalrymple, who seized the opportunity to remove the French from Portugal by agreeing to transport the 25,000 troops, their arms and property (including booty) back to France, with no restrictions on future service in Portugal. Wellesley was obliged to sign this Convention of Cintra as the officer equal in rank to the French negotiator, but the next day wrote to the War Minister, Lord Castlereagh, listing his objections.

News of the convention fell like a bombshell on London after the victory of Vimiero, itself following the heady Spanish triumph of Baylen, at which 18,000 French troops surrendered, and King Joseph's hasty retreat from Madrid. Canning was so furious at Wellesley's conduct and Castlereagh's bad judgment in appointing him that Bathurst wrote a letter of nine sides pointing out that, however bad the treaty turned out to be when the official despatch arrived, the government could not refuse to comply. Violating the terms would lead to 'a state of warfare of the worst kind; and they who set the example of it are answerable for whatever afterwards happens'. It could only be repudiated if it could be shown that the terms were fraudulently obtained or that they had not been fulfilled by the French.[16] When the official account did arrive, Canning was somewhat mollified that the naval commander had repudiated the return of the Russian fleet, which fell under his jurisdiction, but still insisted to Bathurst that the troop repatriation amounted 'literally to have conquered Portugal not Junot, and to have saved Junot with advantages which no other possible combination of circumstances could have given him'. He claimed that the expedition to Portugal was 'the most disastrous that I can remember; and if we are forced by circumstances to approve that convention, the sooner our army is recalled, the better.'[17]

The embarrassed ministers put the best possible face on the humiliation by having bells rung and guns fired for the independence of Portugal. Fortunately for his government colleagues Wellesley also defended himself well at the court of inquiry, which on 22 December, 1808, gratifyingly recommended no further proceedings against any of the officers. Wellesley returned to his Irish duties and was thanked by both Houses of Parliament for Vimiero.

But more bad news arrived from the Peninsula early in 1809 when Sir John Moore was driven across the snow-covered mountains of northern Spain by the French. Although his operation saved Portugal from a new French onslaught, Canning criticized him for fleeing before an army whose size was exaggerated and which was supposed, incorrectly, to be led by

Napoleon. 'The truth is that we have retreated before a rumour – an uncertain speculation – and Moore knows it,' Canning complained to Bathurst before the final outcome was known: 'O that we had an enterprizing general with a reputation to make instead of one to save!'[18] Moore made his immortal reputation, at the cost of his life, in the battle covering the embarkation of the exhausted army at Corunna on 16 January. But although this was also hailed as a victory, like Dunkirk in the Second World War, it could not disguise the fact that the British were leaving Spain. All the high hopes of the summer of 1808 were fast fading at the beginning of 1809.

An incidental consequence of the Iberian revolt was to widen the breach between Bathurst and Grenville. In the summer of 1808 Grenville encouraged his nephew and half-pay diplomat, Henry Williams-Wynne, to put his enforced leisure to good use by travelling to Portugal and the friendly areas of Spain. But Canning not only refused consent but threatened to cut off Williams-Wynne's pay on the grounds that it would be supposed that he was travelling on some secret government mission. Grenville took great umbrage, complaining to Bathurst that an honest diplomat was being prevented from going where any other subject might and insisting that his whole family had suffered serious injury and insult. He was not mollified by Bathurst's assurance that the ministry was trying to discourage anyone from going to the Peninsula, but was at least glad to learn that his friend had not known of the decision or been a party to it. Canning for his part told Bathurst that Williams-Wynne and his relations were using excessively impertinent language about him and that he would meet insolence with contempt.[19] In the divide between these two proud individuals Bathurst's relations with Grenville suffered when he would not champion his friend against his colleague.

Even as the ministry was recovering from Cintra and putting the best construction on Corunna, it suffered further mortification from charges that Mrs Mary Ann Clarke, the aggrieved former mistress of the royal Duke of York, Commander in Chief of the Army, had taken bribes for promotions gazetted as being without purchase. An inquiry occupied the Commons for most of February and March and outside parliament became the focus of a storm of criticism against the whole established order. At the beginning of the investigation Bathurst told Richmond that York's friends were sure that he would be cleared, but when Mrs Clarke's letters were read the sentiment of the Commons turned against him. 'The disposition now is most unfavourable, the disposition of the country still worse,' Bathurst gloomily wrote. 'I am afraid there is not much hope of being able to resist a Motion for his removal if no resignation is to take place.'[20] The Duke did resign on

18 March, but, although the Commons finally concluded that he had been no worse than imprudent and had not himself accepted payments, his departure and the nature of it were yet more blows to the government.

In this accumulation of difficulties a ray of hope appeared when an Austrian envoy arrived at the end of March seeking aid for an impending revolt against France, while other intelligence suggested an uprising in northern Germany. Once again the possibility rose of Napoleon's early defeat. The government offered financial support, but, having been disappointed by Austria so often, would not accept an alliance or regular subsidies. The point was made clear enough by sending as envoy the twenty-five year old Benjamin Bathurst, who had served briefly at Vienna at the beginning of his career in 1804 before going to Stockholm as secretary to the legation in 1805. Even though he had returned suffering from a nervous illness, from which it was by no means clear that he had recovered, he was nevertheless Canning's choice. This was in large part to gratify Bathurst, who had helped the son of the Bishop of Norwich to a place in the Foreign Office, and consolidate his support for Canning's scheme to replace fumbling and incompetent Castlereagh as War Minister by their friend, the man of push and go, Lord Wellesley.

Trusting that Napoleon would be preoccupied in Germany, the ministry also sent Sir Arthur Wellesley, this time resigning his seat in the Commons and Irish Secretaryship, with a force of 20,000 to secure Portugal and encourage the resistance in Spain. Driving the French troops out of northern Portugal, he fought a major battle in conjunction with the Spanish army just over the border at Talavera on 27 and 28 July. Although this was at best an ambiguous, even pyrrhic victory, marked by misunderstandings and recriminations between him and the Spanish commander, the government thankfully cried it up as a glorious triumph and created its hero Viscount Wellington.

Just after Sir Arthur had sailed for Portugal, his brother Lord Wellesley was appointed ambassador to the Supreme Junta at Seville. He was certainly an impressive figure, though his temperament was not necessarily suited to dealing with the Spanish in the sour aftermath of Talavera. Bathurst was one of the few who knew that Canning's main purpose was to increase Wellesley's reputation before bringing him into cabinet. Since Wellesley did not actually leave for three months, he was able to take with him Bathurst's second son, William Lennox, then eighteen and a student at Christ Church, Oxford. Bathurst urged Wellesley to work him hard but not to keep him so long in Spain that he would be late for the beginning of term, 'as I am very anxious that he should have no interruption in his studies there; and I have receiv'd repeated lectures from the Dean [the formidable Cyril Jackson] on the risk I run in turning his mind from those studies by letting him go with you'.[21] William Bathurst spent about a month at Seville and went on an expedition to Grenada before being consigned through Wellington's army in the middle of September to his uncle, Admiral Berkeley at Lisbon for passage back to England.

A month after their arrival Wellesley told Bathurst: 'The heat here is insufferable, but I am in good health, and I keep up my spirits by scalding the Secretary of State twice a day'.[22] But he tried as best as he knew how to soothe Wellington's anger, to goad the inexperienced Junta into mobilizing that poor country's resources more effectively and to assure the wary Spaniards, in words if not in manner, that Britain would neither abandon nor try to dominate their country.

In contrast to Wellington's achievement in the Peninsula, the other major expedition to help and take advantage of the Austrian revolt was an unmitigated disaster. By the time the British strike across the channel against the fleet in the Scheldt was launched on 28 July, Napoleon had crushed the Austrians three weeks earlier at the Battle of Wagram. The military command was given to Lord Chatham, Master General of the Ordnance, to raise his military reputation; but 'the late Lord Chatham', as he was soon called on account of his listlessness, was no Wellington and the admiral commanding the fleet, with whom Chatham was soon at loggerheads, no Nelson. The island of Flushing nevertheless fell on 15 August and Bathurst, seeing it as a more convenient Heligoland, wrote enthusiastically to his Vice-President: 'There is no calculating the advantages to be derived from Walcheren, if we can keep it'. Since duties and regulations would have to be established, he urged Rose to 'make it fall in with your Holiday amusements to go over to Walcheren – for you would in three or four days get us some information, and form a System which we shall not be able to do for many months'.[23] Rose did hurry over, but his trip was to no avail when the British were forced to withdraw by a combination of Napoleon's military power and 'Walcheren fever', primarily malaria, against which no precautions had been taken.[24] By that time the Walcheren expedition had also destroyed the government. The only transitory compensation was a trade boom with the continent while Napoleon's troops were otherwise engaged.

Throughout the summer Bathurst was much occupied by Canning's conspiracy, which ended much like Walcheren.[25] In April the Foreign Secretary told the Prime Minister that unless Castlereagh left the War Department, he would go himself. Since neither Bathurst, who was the confidant of both, nor Portland seems to have questioned that Castlereagh should be removed, and Bathurst of all people could not object to bringing in Wellesley, discussion focused on a way to manage it that would spare Castlereagh's feelings. Portland, even more ill than usual, offered to retire to allow Castlereagh to be moved in a general reorganization, but the King would not hear of it. Bathurst also offered to resign or change offices several times, but Portland refused, telling him that he intended to recommend him as Prime Minister when he left.[26]

The Walcheren expedition provided an excuse to postpone a decision, despite Canning's protests, and if it had prospered it would have been difficult, if not impossible, to dislodge Castlereagh. But at the beginning of September, when it was obviously failing, Canning demanded that Castlereagh be dismissed and Wellesley recalled as his replacement. This time Portland, who had suffered a slight stroke, insisted on resigning, and Bathurst helped to persuade the King that he must allow him to go. Canning then pointedly told his other rival, Perceval, that the new leader should be in the Commons but made it clear that he would not serve under Perceval.

Confident that the Prime Ministership was his, Canning did not attend the cabinet to discuss its future. Castlereagh, probably the only minister who did not know that he was to be pushed out, was only told of it after the meeting by Camden, his uncle, in what the latter described to Bathurst as 'a very long and painful conversation . . . in which I made him acquainted with the whole transaction softened in most respects. The promise with respect to Wellesley I did not mention.' Castlereagh took the news 'firmly and reasonably',[27] but immediately resigned and ten days later fought a duel with Canning. The remaining ministers tried to come to terms with the opposition Lords Grey and Grenville, but when this foundered on the Catholic question unanimously recommended at the end of September that Perceval become Prime Minister. Canning then had no choice but to live up to his threat by resigning.

Perceval's ministry was essentially a reshuffling of the old, but without the energy and optimism with which Portland's government had succeeded the Talents on that glad confident morning in 1807. Bathurst carried on at the Board of Trade and Lord Wellesley was invited to become Foreign Secretary. But since it would take about six weeks to ensure that he would accept, Bathurst took on the additional appointment of the Foreign Office in the meantime. This meant leaving the Board of Trade largely to Rose, who was closely attached to Canning and had intended to resign with him. But when Canning revealed his insistence on being Prime Minister, Rose, after a sleepless night reflecting on what Pitt would have wanted, concluded that it was his duty to stay. He was much pleased by Bathurst expressing his pleasure 'in terms and in a manner that astonished me, and said he knew that his colleagues would not feel less delight at it'.[28]

The Foreign Secretaryship, which Bathurst assumed on 11 October, was not a post that he sought or hoped to keep if Wellesley refused. He told the departing Under-Secretary, the experienced old diplomat Lord Malmesbury, in soliciting his guidance, that 'the terms on which I hold it, which to many would be an objection, is that which makes it acceptable to me'.[29] And he was certainly right in expecting that Wellesley would accept. As soon as he received Perceval's letter Wellesley told Bathurst that he would leave within a week: 'I am as eager to return, as you can be to receive me: as for abuse, I am so accustomed to that Diet, that it is now become necessary to my constitution'.[30]

Bathurst received this letter on 24 November, just two days before Wellesley himself landed at Portsmouth. In the interval Perceval decided to put this seemingly impressive recruit in the right humour by giving him the Garter vacated by the death of the Duke of Portland at the end of October. Wellesley had for years claimed that it had been promised him by Pitt, Grenville and Portland, and Bathurst himself had thought him entitled to it ten years before. Unfortunately, before deciding on Wellesley, Perceval had promised it to the Duke of Richmond, and Bathurst had the unenviable task of assuaging his brother-in-law. 'I think there is a difference between Lord Wellesley accepting office & having the Ribbon at the same time; and Lord Wellesley asking it as a reward for past services when he supported the Government,' he told Richmond in embarrassed terms, 'but he is so great a card at the moment, and *so aware of it*, that I know not what to say'. Richmond, however, knew perfectly well what to say: 'The world will never be persuaded that the Garter was not the price Govt. offered and he accepted for his taking office; it will make him extremely unpopular, and consequently it will hurt Governt'. All too accurately, he predicted: 'People in general will think he can carry what he pleases and indeed it will be difficult to prevail on him not to join in this opinion'. Richmond also said that he would never ask for the Garter again,[31] though he was pleased enough finally to receive it in March 1812. In the meantime Perceval took the edge off the Viceroy's discontent a year and a half later by adding £5000 a year to his salary.[32]

The other delicate manner of honour and prestige raised by Portland's death was the Chancellorship of Oxford, for which Grenville had long yearned. Since one of the other candidates was that staunch defender of the Protestant constitution, Lord Chancellor Eldon, the election became a fierce political election, government versus opposition, pro-Catholic versus anti-Catholic, confused by the third candidate, the Duke of Beaufort, a Protestant supporter of the administration though not a leading political figure. Despite partisan feelings, Bathurst, who had no vote since he had not taken his degree, supported Grenville and tried to get Eldon to withdraw.[33] Wellesley went further, immediately antagonizing his new colleagues on his return by openly championing Grenville, who won by the split in ministerial vote between Eldon and Beaufort. Cabinet ministers could understand Bathurst's discreet personal loyalty, but were less forgiving of Wellesley who further signalled his political intentions in congratulating Grenville by saying that his sojourn in Seville, particularly 'holding the tapers for two hours at the high mass performed in the cathedral for the repose of Sir John Moore's soul,' had altered his sentiments on the 'No Popery' system.[34]

In the month and a half that Bathurst served as Foreign Secretary the main concern was the end of the Austrian revolt. The last flicker of hope was the peasant revolt in the Tyrol, which four years earlier Napoleon had forced Austria to cede to Bavaria. Protesting the loss of local autonomy, conscription and the curbs on clerics and nobles, the peasants, led by Andreas Hofer, won a great victory over the Bavarians at Mount Isel on 13 August. Two delegates then went to England, promising that they could bring a large force to the shores of the Adriatic. This raised giddy prospects of an attack on Venice, even a revolt of the whole Adriatic, but by the time the emissaries arrived at the beginning of November Bathurst knew that Napoleon was in a strong position to crush this minor uprising, following Austria's submission. He was willing to risk £10,000 through a banker in Vienna, with the promise of an additional £10,000 a month later. But any further aid, as he told the King, 'must depend on the safe receipt of the first, and on the continuance and state of the insurrections'. He assured the delegates that it was not the British government's intention 'either to create any obligation or to afford any inducement to continue the resistance one hour longer than they would otherwise be inclined to do, if no such supplies were afforded. . . . [I]t is not for those who are not to participate in the danger to counsel others to incur it.'[35] Even as he wrote, the Tyrolese had been defeated and their territory divided until it was finally returned to Austria at the end of the war.

At the same time as he was dealing with the Tyrolese, Bathurst was also bidding farewell to the Austrian Ambassador, since Napoleon's peace terms required breaking relations between the two countries. He told the emissary that he could 'only lament the most unfortunate conclusion of a war in which the Austrian Army had given such signal proofs of their valour, and the whole country such undeniable evidence of their attachment to their Sovereign'.[36] Austria nevertheless remained vital to any future prospect of destroying Napoleon's empire and Canning urged Bathurst to keep on the Foreign Office payroll Friedrich Gentz, who provided valuable information from inside the Austrian chancellery. Although he conceded that Gentz was an enthusiast and a spendthrift, the former Foreign Secretary was convinced that his principles were sound and he had 'this certain recommendation and guarantee for his sincerity, that he would infallibly be shot, if Bonaparte should catch him'. Canning enclosed a sixteen page letter dated 29 September, warning Bathurst to keep such communications to himself: 'not the *substance* of them of course — but the letters themselves, and the name of the writer, and not [leave] them in the office'. After sending the letter to the King (without concealing the identity of the author) Bathurst carefully took it home.[37]

The British envoy to Austria, Benjamin Bathurst, also had to leave. After a horrendous outward voyage through Trieste, he decided to return over-land to Hamburg where a British warship would take him to England. But the Austrians had forgotten to request a safe conduct from Napoleon, and Metternich, the Chancellor, dared not issue one on his own authority. Fearing for his life in French-occupied territory, Bathurst decided to travel in the guise of a German merchant, though his slim, six-foot figure, luxurious clothes and four-horse carriage immediately suggested a rich foreign nobleman. His companions, however, the Swiss servant he had brought from England and the embassy messenger, were native German-speakers.

Departing the Austrian court at Buda on 9 November, the party stopped to rest in the afternoon of 25 November at the small Prussian town of Perleberg, half-way between Berlin and Hamburg and close to the border with Napoleon's Confederation of the Rhine. Bathurst was in a highly agitated state and asked the military governor for protection. Two soldiers were provided, whom he dismissed a few hours later. He spent most of his time in the inn writing and burning papers. But when the others looked for him to resume the journey at 9 pm he could not be located. Despite an extensive search, no trace was discovered, though three weeks later a pair of overalls, evidently left where they would be certain to be found, came to light. In the pocket was an incomplete letter to his wife saying that he was surrounded by enemies and entreating her not to remarry if he did not return. Forty years later, when an old house was being demolished, a skeleton with a hatchet mark on the skull was discovered under the floor. But Bathurst's sister, who by chance arrived at Perleberg shortly afterwards, confidently, if not necessarily conclusively, pronounced that it could not be his.

It was generally supposed that he had been killed by the French or their agents for his despatches, but these, which would have been carried by the messenger, were apparently untouched. Indeed all his effects were carefully packed up by the Prussians and sent to England. And in the spring of 1810 Napoleon made an extraordinary exception to his prohibition on Britons under the Continental System by granting Bathurst's wife passports to search for him.[38] She travelled for four months, investigating in Berlin and Perleberg and returning through Paris, where she saw two of Napoleon's ministers, though the Emperor himself would not receive her. She concluded that her high-strung husband had been driven by mental strain to commit suicide in some remote place where his body would not be found, but in later years came to believe that he had been murdered for some French political reason.

The most convincing explanation of Bathurst's fate was proposed by Sir John Hall in *Four Famous Mysteries* (1922): that he was murdered by the *Tugenbund*, a secret Prussian military association against Napoleon, provided with funds by Britain, which feared that his mental condition would lead him to betray them to the French. Bathurst certainly knew of the organization's activities and probably met some of its members when he stopped at Berlin for a couple of days. If they did decide to kill him before he left Prussian territory, it must have helped that the military governor of Perleberg was a member. Hall's solution accounts for the British government's failure to protest at his disappearance, its neglect of a major propaganda opportunity against Napoleon and the half-hearted inquiries of the British and the Prussian governments. It may also explain the shortage of material on the subject in the Foreign Office files, though Lord Wellesley was notoriously careless about papers.

Whether Bathurst or other ministers knew the true fate of Benjamin Bathurst is impossible to tell, but there are bits of tantalizing evidence that he at least knew more than is documented. In 1815 his son Lord Apsley wrote from the Congress of Vienna that the British Foreign Under-Secretary had showed him a letter from Hanover about Bathurst's murder - not suicide - 'which he seemed to think not worth following up now, as there is no doubt of his being no more'. Apsley told his father that he would put down what he remembered of the letter on a separate sheet, but if he did, it has not survived. He also told his father that 'Govt ought to look to the murder of one in his situation abroad as much as they do to those at home. If however you think the thing had better be given up, the less said the better.'[39] There is no record of a reply from Lord Bathurst.

The British secret agent at Berlin and paymaster to the secret society was

George Mills, a bankrupt former MP posing as an American merchant, who was engaged by Bathurst while he was Foreign Secretary. Mills was sent by the Prussian government to make inquiries at Perleberg on behalf of their King.[40] And in 1824, despite his dubious financial reputation and strong opposition to the government as MP again from 1818 to 1820, Bathurst appointed him registrar of the supreme court of New South Wales at £800 a year. This curious selection, when many loyal friends of the ministry would have welcomed such a lucrative and undemanding post, was obviously a reward for Mills's services in Prussia, whether or not they included collusion and silence about Benjamin Bathurst's fate. After three and a half years in Australia Mills again failed in business and committed suicide. Reporting his death to Bathurst, the Governor described him as 'a Man of profligate Character and dissolute habits . . . deeply involved in debt'.[41]

Just as Benjamin Bathurst was approaching Perleberg Lord Wellesley arrived to take over the Foreign Office. The King thanked Bathurst for the 'able and regular manner' in which he had conducted business and did not 'expect that the office in question can be filled more to his advantage than at present'. Nor was he alone in this feeling. A month earlier Lord Malmesbury had told Bathurst: 'If *you* wish Lord Wellesley back so must *I*, although I should be well pleased to see you fill permanently the office you have in so honourable a way consented to hold *pro tempore*.'[42]

From the moment he entered the cabinet Wellesley was arrogant and overbearing, quarrelsome and contemptuous of the Prime Minister and other colleagues. He expected everyone to defer to him until it pleased the King formally to place him at the head of a stronger administration. He was soon on bad terms with everyone save Bathurst, and even that old friend's patience was eventually exhausted. The seemingly mild Perceval never feared to stand up to him, though others were more wary. And for someone who constantly urged decision and firm action, Wellesley turned out to be as idle as Lord Chatham, reducing the Foreign Office to inefficiency and confusion. Less than a year after his appointment there were seventy unopened boxes of official papers at Apsley House. The person who sorted them out concluded that only six were still worth attention.[43] Among those weeded out may well have been some relating to Benjamin Bathurst.

After the military humiliations of 1809, the other ministers rejected what they regarded as Wellesley's reckless demands for greater commitment to the risky Peninsular War. They doggedly supported Wellington's efforts to tie down large numbers of French troops and encourage more decisive resistance elsewhere on the continent but warned him to be careful of the troops they supplied. Their difficulties were increased by the bad harvest of 1809 which added to social tension during the winter; and, although the harvest of 1810 was much better, Napoleon now could use his army to police the ports and restrict British imports. Smuggling from Heligoland practically ceased and the goods returned to Britain simply increased the glut and industrial distress.

Wellington railed against the government's restrictions but succeeded brilliantly within them. In great secrecy – perhaps the greatest secret in military history – he constructed the fortified lines of Torres Vedras outside Lisbon as he was forced to retreat before the French throughout the summer of 1810. He also had Admiral Berkeley assemble transports in case the lines did not hold. The day before the army withdrew into the lines, Berkeley told Bathurst that the wealthy Portuguese were fleeing aboard his ships with whatever they could carry. 'You can have no conception of the consternation which pervades this great country,' he wrote. 'My ship is crammed with the valuables of the richest people, plate money and jewels,' which he hoped the government would allow the refugees to bring into Britain duty-free to support themselves. But just four days later he added that the fortifications were holding and courage returning.[44]

After camping outside the lines all winter the French commander was forced in March to withdraw across the Spanish border pursued by the British and Portuguese armies. If not exactly a splendid victory, this was at very least a vindication of the ministry's policy and its choice of commander. There was now a safe base at Lisbon which could be supplied from the sea and the likelihood of yet another mortifying evacuation was much reduced. It was perhaps also fortunate that the transports were not needed since Berkeley told Bathurst that their condition was 'too dreadful to be known publicly, and might almost occasion a mutiny in the army, if they knew to what rotten and dangerous ships they were consigned'.[45]

While Wellington was holding the French at bay that autumn, ministers at home faced the prospect of being overcome by their political opponents when George III again lost his mind. Everything was kept quiet in the hope that the symptoms would abate, but on 3 November the cabinet decided that he must again be attended by a specialist in insanity. As Bathurst put it to Richmond, the ministers did not 'think themselves justified in letting an experiment to be tryed whether in the last illness the King could be cured without the usual aid'. When the Duke of York and the Queen, remembering the brutality with which he had been treated twenty years earlier, threatened the Prime Minister with the King's eternal wrath when he recovered, the cabinet recorded all the royal family's objections and took the whole blame on themselves as a body.[46] A month later Bathurst sent the King a backgammon board which one of the doctors assured him was 'excellently adapted to the purpose for which your Lordship intended it. It shall be made use of whenever it can be of benefit to his Majesty'.[47]

Although the Prince of Wales protested at the restrictions that were imposed on the first year of his regency, justified on the grounds that the King might recover as he had in 1789, to the disappointment of his opposition friends he decided to keep the present ministers, at least for the time being, when he assumed the powers of monarchy in February, 1811. The cabinet expressed its relief by accepting the reappointment of the Duke of York as Commander-in-Chief of the Army, for which he was obviously the fittest person. And Bathurst also issued licences for the pleasure-loving Regent to import wine and other articles from France.[48]

For the country generally 1811 was the hardest year of the Napoleonic wars. The United States and the Baltic markets were practically closed, the over-supplied South American market collapsed and only Russia offered a small outlet for commerce under the guise of neutral trade after breaking away from the Continental System at the end of 1810. The vast accumulation of goods for export persuaded the ministry to offer merchants £6,000,000 in 5% Exchequer bills, repayable in instalments from January 1812, to save them having to sell their goods at a loss. Bathurst defended these loans in the House of Lords on 28 March by observing that the plight of the traders was not the result of excessive speculation but rather of Napoleon's prohibition over which they had no control. The government also set its face firmly against the opposition's arguments for withdrawing paper money and resuming cash payments, which in the desperate shortage of specie could only have made the economic situation far worse and might have forced abandonment of the Peninsular War.

While the opposition attacked the government for obstinately persisting in the hopeless cause of the Peninsula, it continued to be assailed from within by Lord Wellesley who claimed that more resources would produce decisive victory. In September a member of Lord Grenville's faction claimed that the Foreign Secretary and the Prime Minister were quarrelling 'like Cat and Dog' until finally the piously Evangelical Perceval exclaimed that

tho' he had succeeded in begetting ten [actually 12] Children, that supply fell very short of the Army which Wellesley wanted and that he saw no other mode, except the efforts of the united vigour of the Cabinet, of creating it, and that as for the money, it was out of the question.

When Wellesley stormed that he would never act with Perceval again, the Prime Minister told the Foreign Secretary that he 'might kiss his – – – !!!'[49]

By this time Wellesley was manoeuvring to become Prime Minister himself. On 17 January, 1812, he asked Bathurst to tell the Prime Minister that he intended to resign, claiming that he had already informed the Prince, though he did not want the decision to become public immediately; indeed he was willing to stay at the Foreign Office until a successor was appointed. He added that he had wanted to leave as early as October, 1810, and had been prevented only by various political difficulties; but once the Regent's restrictions were removed 'and the administration had taken on a new character' then would be the appropriate moment to go. Wellesley's justification was that 'he had long found he had not that lead in the Cabinet which at the time he accepted office he had expected, and that he was frequently executing the suggestions and opinions of others, not his own'. When Bathurst protested that even Canning had accepted changes to his draft despatches, Wellesley loftily replied that 'it might be so, but that his habits in India had not accustomed him to this'. The only difference of policy he mentioned was that 'more might have been done for Spain'. But he signified clearly enough those with whom he intended to act by adding that he did not think that 'the door ought to be for ever closed against the Catholics,' though relief should not be granted until real security was found for the established Church.[50]

This announcement, as Wellesley intended, threw the government into turmoil, though the result was not as he expected. On 15 February, with full regency powers, the Prince, to the dismay of his opposition friends and of Wellesley, confirmed Perceval as Prime Minister. Two days later Wellesley tried again, telling the Regent that he could not continue under Perceval, that both Castlereagh and Canning must be in government, and that he was the only person who could persuade both to accept. As actual Prime Minister he disingenuously suggested the Prince's friend, Lord Moira, a soldier whose only ministerial experience had been as Master General of the Ordnance in Grenville's administration. That evening the cabinet unanimously agreed that Wellesley must resign immediately. As Bathurst recorded: 'It should be further represented to the Prince that not one of the present Cabinet would continue, if Lord Wellesley remained in office'.[51] Even he, who had endured his friend's eristic manner better than most, was finally estranged by his treachery, and the break was complete.

To Wellesley's astonishment the government survived his departure very well. Castlereagh accepted the Foreign Office, for which he had hitherto demonstrated no particular aptitude, and Sidmouth also joined. But even for those who were well disposed to the ministry, its chances of survival did not seem very bright. Perceval may have exercised firm control and ministers may have been competent, experienced and more harmonious than any since 1801, but all the glittering figures stood outside and were in varying degrees hostile, while the Regent's endorsement was at best grudging and provisional. The country also faced enormous difficulties at home and abroad. Manufacturing had been depressed for two years; provincial banks had failed and industrial areas were racked by discontent, rioting and Luddism. Nor was there any end in sight to the Peninsular War, despite the fall in January, 1812, of the great Spanish fortress of Ciudad Rodrigo, the key to the security of northern Portugal. The ministers were so relieved that Wellington was immediately promoted to earl, but even this triumph raised the fear of massive retaliation by Napoleon.

In parliament the government was attacked above all for the Orders in Council which seemed to many to be the root cause of the country's distress. Perceval remained convinced that they were helping British trade and harming Napoleon, but even he may have given some verbal promise of alteration to win over the free-trade Sidmouth. Responding to a flood of petitions, Bathurst defended the administration in the Lords on 21 April by insisting that repealing the Orders would 'open the ports of France to importations from the Baltic, from the United States of America, and various other places,' transferring 'the entire advantages of a traffic to the enemy, which might otherwise direct itself to this country'. But despite counter-petitions from the West Indian interests, from shipowners who thought licences were too readily granted to foreigners and from pillars of Church and state, the cabinet was clearly faltering in its resolve. It announced that the Orders would be repealed in relation to the United States if Napoleon's clever revocation of his decrees in 1811 could be authenticated, if the US admitted British warships to its ports to refit on the same terms as other belligerents and if all American restrictions against British commerce were annulled.

Committees of inquiry were established by both Houses of Parliament. On Monday, 11 May at about 5 pm, as Perceval was hurrying through the lobby to the Commons committee, he was shot dead by John Bellingham, a deranged bankrupt trader who blamed his losses and imprisonment in Russia on the Orders in Council. Bathurst arrived at the House of Lords a few minutes later and found Lord Eldon standing by the table with several other peers while the Sergeant at Arms, looking pale and terrified, spoke with great vehemence. Fearing that the assassination might be part of a larger conspiracy, the Lords ordered the doors locked to any passages through which Bellingham's accomplices might escape until they were assured that he had acted alone.[52]

Radicals may have rejoiced at the removal of the chief obstacle to repeal of the Orders in Council, but the cabinet had to postpone the matter to deal with yet another political crisis. The Regent assured the ministers of his confidence, but they were not themselves convinced that they could survive in the Commons without additional strength. When nothing had been resolved ten days after Perceval's death, a mortifying motion by a government MP and relative of Lord Liverpool, calling on the Regent to form a strong and efficient administration, was carried by 174 votes to 170, virtually compelling the cabinet to resign.

Wellesley finally got his chance from the Regent to see if a government could be created from the present ministers with the addition of Grey and Grenville. The now-antagonistic Bathurst protested to Rose that Wellesley's proposals to consider Catholic claims 'in order to come to a final and satisfactory arrangement of them; and to prosecute the war in the Peninsula with the *best means* of the country' were 'conveniently lax in the expression'. Even apart from the fact that he and most of his colleagues believed that the Catholic question should not be disturbed and that they were doing as much for the war as parliament and the country would stand, he told Rose emphatically that '*all* of us thought we were bound to decline, especially after recent events, to accept the proposals of belonging to an Administration formed by *Lord Wellesley*'.[53] When the Regent responded to their cabinet minute of refusal by canvassing each minister, Bathurst reiterated that they could not honourably form a juncture with Wellesley and Canning after what had passed in recent months or on the basis of Catholic relief. He warned the Prince that 'an administration formed under such circumstances, if under such circumstances any could be formed, would be ill-calculated to obtain the confidence of Parliament, and by its early overthrow would expose your Royal Highness to aggravated embarrassments'.[54]

The Regent nevertheless supported Wellesley until he came to grief over Grenville and Grey, who were united on Catholic emancipation but hopelessly divided on the war. He then tried Lord Moira, who had no better luck. Finally tiring of this ineffective exercise, he confirmed Lord Liverpool as Prime Minister on 8 June. The Duke of Richmond, who had sent Bathurst his resignation to be submitted if a pro-Catholic government were formed, gloomily judged that the administration might last out the parliamentary session.[55]

In this atmosphere of low expectation there was only a slight rearrange-

48

ment of the ministry. The most important appointment was that of Liverpool's own successor as War Minister. The new Prime Minister offered this to William Wellesley-Pole, the Irish Secretary, to blunt the attacks of Lord Wellesley and send a strong signal to Wellington that the government intended to support the war in the Peninsula as strongly as when Wellesley had been in office. But Pole, unimpressed by the ministry's prospects, decided to join Wellesley in opposition, even to the extent of repudiating his hitherto extreme Protestantism. Liverpool then turned to his reliable colleague since 1807 and Bathurst did not refuse him. But since the arrangement, if not the entire ministry, might only be provisional, he continued at the Board of Trade and as Master of the Mint as well as Secretary of State for War and the Colonies until the end of September.

In June, 1812, the outlook was as bleak as any time since the beginning of the conflict with France almost twenty years earlier. Wellington had followed up his victory of Ciudad Rodrigo with the capture in April of Badajoz, the Spanish fortress controlling the southern entry to Portugal, but had not advanced far into Spain. In parliament ministers were again tackled on the Orders in Council and on 16 June Castlereagh announced in the Commons, in terms that were confused even by his standards, that the government had decided to suspend the Orders. The cabinet then delayed for a further week, for no better reason than, as Castlereagh said, 'One does not like to own that we are forced to give way to our manufacturers'.[56] The Orders were withdrawn on 23 June in respect to the United States, provided that its ports were open to British commerce and warships, though with the threat that they might be reimposed in May, 1813, if the British government was not satisfied with the conduct of the United States and France. This grudging and conditional repeal, fatally delayed for a month by Perceval's assassination, came too late. Five days earlier the United States had declared war on Britain and begun preparations for the invasion of Canada. But at least the ministry had better luck on the Catholic issue, which had divided politicians more than the war for over a decade, by Liverpool's expedient of making it an open question on which ministers might support either side, while carefully balancing the cabinet between the two views.

Then suddenly the whole prospect before them was transformed. On 22 July Wellington won a great victory at Salamanca and three weeks later entered Madrid, though he was not strong enough to hold it. In northern Europe Napoleon launched a massive invasion of Russia to force it back into the Continental System, which within a few months was turning to catastrophe. At home a good harvest promised cheaper food and less discontent during the coming winter. In fact, though no one could be sure of it even in 1813, the tide of war had finally turned. There was still a long struggle and many difficulties ahead, but at last an end was in sight. And in this final phase, and long after, Bathurst played a leading part in the office to which he had been so casually called.

3

THE DISTANT TRIUMPH
SONG, 1812–1814

However accidentally Bathurst, at the age of fifty, found himself at the War and Colonies Office in June, 1812, he was at least as qualified for it as Castlereagh for the Foreign Office and, like his close colleague in foreign policy, soon demonstrated that he was a skilled administrator of military and imperial matters. Unlike Pitt and Grenville, he had never wavered in his support for the war against France and the conviction that the United Kingdom and its possessions and interests overseas would not be safe until France was defeated and forced back into something like its previous boundaries. Unlike Grenville he never doubted that the Peninsular War, however risky, offered the best opportunity after 1808. And, unlike Wellesley, he recognized that, although the political nation had a general will to win, there were limits at all levels of society to the sacrifices that they would make for efforts in the Peninsula and elsewhere. The challenge for government in this situation was to mobilize as many resources as practically possible and use them to best advantage.

Bathurst was well suited for his difficult and stressful duties by his diligence, equable temperament and long political experience. Two of the departments in which he had served in a minor capacity, the Admiralty and the Board of Control, were important for Britain's widespread commitments and interests; the Treasury had given him some sense of financial limits; at the Board of Trade he had been closely involved with economic warfare; and even his brief tenure at the Foreign Office had given him some training in diplomacy. Apart from the importance of his department, his judgement was so trusted by the Prime Minister and the Foreign Secretary that he quickly became a member of the triumvirate that for all practical purposes decided the country's foreign, military and imperial policy for the next decade.

The War and Colonies Office was located in a house at the end of Downing Street, where the steps now lead down to St James's Park. A new, third, Secretaryship of State for War had been created in July, 1794, to accommodate Henry Dundas when he surrendered the Home Office to the Duke of Portland, who brought his followers over to the government from the opposition. The colonies were transferred from the Home Office in 1801 when the Peace of Amiens threatened the seemingly redundant War Department with underemployment or abolition. In the rapid changes of government in the decade from Addington to Liverpool there had been five Secretaries of State for War and the Colonies, four of whom now sat in the cabinet: Liverpool who had held the office since 1809; Castlereagh (1805–6 and 1807–9); Camden (1804–5); and the Earl of Buckinghamshire (1801–4, as Lord Hobart). Given the preoccupation with the war, the colonies were of necessity handled at best by an Under-Secretary, and were often neglected for years on end unless some major problem arose.[1]

Once military policy was decided by the inner cabinet of Liverpool, Castlereagh and Bathurst, the Secretary of State conveyed the orders in the name of the monarch (the Prince Regent until 1820) to military commanders and the various government departments and boards which supported and co-ordinated the efforts in the field. The celebrated division of responsibility among the Secretary of State, the Commander in Chief, the Master General of the Ordnance, the Secretary at War and a host of lesser officials which had developed since the Glorious Revolution to guard against the army becoming an instrument of autocratic monarchy on the one hand and what was considered a democratic House of Commons on the other had notoriously been achieved at the cost of elaborate, hampered and inefficient administration.[2] But the many instances of division and confusion during the Napoleonic Wars that were cited then and ever since should not obscure the fact that the real power to make decisions and see that they were carried out by the other appropriate departments lay in the hands of the Secretary of State, supported by the authority of the cabinet and the monarch, and that they were usually effectively executed.

How many troops were to be employed, where they were to be sent, who was to command them and what arms, money and other supplies were to be provided, were obviously matters of primary concern to almost all ministers. But the fact that Liverpool, Castlereagh and Bathurst made most of these decisions among themselves meant that the Treasury, Foreign Office and War Department acted harmoniously. To clarify their thoughts or ensure that what they decided could be properly carried out, they occasionally consulted Lord Mulgrave, the Master General of the Ordnance (who commanded the artillery and engineers and was the army's professional representative in the cabinet), Lord Harrowby, the Lord President of the Council, and Lord Melville, First Lord of the Admiralty. But it is a measure of the confidence and smooth functioning of Liverpool's cabinet, in refreshing contrast to the tensions and quarrels of the Portland and Perceval administrations, that other ministers never questioned the right of the three to run the main effort of government. Although important issues were submitted to the whole cabinet, this was largely a matter of form and to ensure greater authority. Even the Regent only occasionally asked for some refinement in the decisions of the inner cabinet.

In his office Bathurst had two Under-Secretaries, one each for war and the colonies, a private secretary and about twenty clerks. The Military Under-Secretary was Colonel Henry Bunbury, then thirty-four, a man of tact and polish, good military judgement and literary skill. He was obliquely related to Bathurst as nephew and heir of Sir Charles Bunbury, the first husband of Lady Sarah Napier (Lennox), Lady Bathurst's aunt. He had served in Holland in 1799 and from 1805 to 1809 in Malta and Sicily under General Henry Fox, brother of the Whig politician and nephew of Lady Sarah; he had been on expeditions to southern Italy, and at the Battle of Maida in 1806 so distinguished himself as chief of staff that he was awarded a gold medal. In 1807 he married a daughter of General Fox; but despite his connections with the opposition, Liverpool appointed him as his Under-Secretary in 1809. This was a professional post which did not require him to be an MP or departmental spokesman in the Commons. In domestic matters Bunbury was, like his relatives, a reformer, even a Radical, and after the war became increasingly critical of government. But until its end he was a strong opponent of Napoleon, a good assistant to Bathurst and an intimate friend of the whole family.[3]

The Colonial Under-Secretary, who represented the entire department in the Commons, was Robert Peel, the future Prime Minister, appointed by Liverpool in 1810. But in August he became Irish Secretary in succession to Wellesley-Pole. He was replaced by his close friend, Henry Goulburn, then twenty-eight years old and Under-Secretary at the Home Office since 1810. In his unpublished memoirs Goulburn wrote:

It was my good fortune to secure the good opinion of Lord B. He treated me with every kindness, & I can truly say that the 10 years during which I remained with him were those to which I look back with the greatest satisfaction both as regards the nature of the business committed to me & my constant intercourse with one who was a really good man & united to a kind disposition very considerable ability.[4]

A rather different recollection, also long after the event, was that of Bathurst's private secretary, Charles Greville. Grandson of the late Duke of Portland, the famous diarist was only eighteen when Bathurst appointed him as secretary on assuming his new office. Greville's uncle, Lord William Bentinck, the envoy to Sicily, commander of the British forces and practically ruler of that island, commented ironically on Greville's suitability for the job in thanking Bathurst for it: 'It is most fortunate for my nephew that out of your extreme kindness he should have obtained such an advantageous situation for himself. No doubt he recommended himself by his character of *extreme diligence*'.[5] Twenty-two years later, on Bathurst's death, Greville bitterly criticized his patron for indulging this indolence: 'So far from feeling any obligation to him, I always consider his mistaken kindness in giving me that post as the source of all my misfortunes and the cause of my present condition'. By not working him harder Greville claimed that Bathurst 'abandoned me at the age of eighteen to that life of idleness and dissipation from which I might have been saved had he felt that my future prospects in life, my character and talents, depended in great measure upon the direction which was at that moment given to my mind'. He thought that he would have resisted Bathurst's efforts to make him a Tory, 'but I should have become a man of business'.[6]

Greville was always reproaching himself for his supposed failure, and perhaps Bathurst might have pushed him to some political or administrative distinction, instead of which he left the Colonial Office in 1821 for the easy berth of Clerk of the Privy Council, arranged by Portland when his grandson was only ten, combined with the sinecure of Clerk of the Stables. But Greville might then not have had the time and inclination to gather the news of the day for his incomparable diary. It is also clear from that journal, which was at first only sketchy and discontinuous, that, whatever he said later, he did a fair amount of work at the War and Colonies Office and was certainly a welcome visitor to the whole Bathurst family in London, at Lime Grove and Cirencester. It did not apparently occur to Greville to criticize his grandfather for condemning him to such a pleasant and undemanding life.

★　　★　　★

The most pressing issue for the War Department in 1812 was of course the campaign in the Peninsula, still nowhere near fulfilling the high hopes raised by the Spanish revolt four long, difficult, expensive and discouraging years ago.[7] This was of such consuming importance that Goulburn had to act for Bunbury whenever the Military Under-Secretary was away, while the reverse was only nominally the case. Almost the only colonial matter allowed to intrude on the conflict with Napoleon was the war against the United States. There was no question of not continuing the Peninsular War, despite the criticisms of expense and the disappointing results, but the lively sense of disaster still made the government hesitate to send everything it could possibly raise, giving Wellington ample scope to continue complaining that he was being prevented from success by lack of troops, money and supplies. Bathurst's most important task by far during the next two years was dealing with Wellington, on whose achievements the government so heavily depended. He had to explain why the ministry could not always do more, smooth out embarrassments and misunderstandings, placate his anger, send him news of home and military operations and developments elsewhere, and generally try to keep him as well-disposed as possible. This was a particularly delicate matter in the summer of 1812 with Lord Wellesley and Wellesley-Pole in opposition.

On 10 June, two days after becoming Prime Minister, Liverpool wrote to tell Wellington of the new political arrangements. He excused his failure to do so sooner on the 'confusion and uncertainty' of the last three weeks, including 'the untoward turn which events have taken with respect to some of those with whom you are most nearly connected [which] must have made it painful for me to write, or for you to receive a letter upon some part of the transactions in which we have been here engaged'. He told Wellington that the 'unaccountable conduct of the Opposition' resulted in the government continuing to be 'the remains of Mr. Perceval's party . . . with a reasonable chance of their being able at least to get through the present session'. In this uncertain situation he tactfully remarked that Wellington would not be surprised to learn that Pole had refused the War Department, which had been given instead to Bathurst: 'I believe you are sufficiently acquainted with him to know that there are few men so assiduous at business, and that you could not have a more agreeable correspondent.' He also assured Wellington that his government was as determined as ever to make every effort in the Peninsula 'compatible with our resources, and which is consistent with the security of the British empire'.[8]

After this nervous overture, the cabinet must have been much relieved by the letter which arrived about a month and a half later from Colonel

Alexander Gordon, a military aide and brother of Lord Aberdeen, saying that Wellington was by no means displeased by the changes in the ministry and expressing the highest regard for Bathurst. Gordon told the new Secretary of State that Wellington was 'sure he should do business with you very well. He is not in the least hurt at his brothers not being in the Government, except in the way of regret at Poole [sic] having been in so great a hurry to refuse office, which opinion he has written to him person-ally'.[9] Wellington had himself written directly, and more laconically, three days earlier to assure Bathurst that 'the arrangement by which you have been placed at the head of the War Department is perfectly satisfactory to me; and you will find that I shall correspond with you with the same freedom and confidence as I have with you predecessors'. As formidable with the pen as the sword, Wellington was true to his word. During the remaining two years of the Peninsular War he and Bathurst exchanged over five hundred letters. Despite the inevitable misunderstandings, embarrassments and tensions between a high-strung field commander and even the most sympathetic and conciliatory minister, they developed a mutual trust and confidence that lasted until Bathurst's death.

In the first letter, short as it was, Wellington repeated what he had so often told Liverpool, that his most pressing need was for gold and silver coin to pay the troops some of their arrears in order to preserve discipline and morale and prevent looting, to pay local contractors and muleteers and gain the goodwill of locals who were suspicious of the foreigners' promises of future payments, and even to purchase grain and flour from abroad since scarcity in the United Kingdom prevented supplies being sent from there. As he never failed to point out at every opportunity, cash was a cheaper means of waging war than credit or bills of exchange on the British Treasury which were discounted at varying high rates by individual dealers. A month later, for example, he told Bathurst that the timely arrival of specie had enabled him to save two-thirds of the cost of grain for the troops and horses. In this first letter he pleaded: 'Our principal and great want is money, with which I am afraid you cannot supply us sufficiently. But we are really in terrible distress; I am afraid, in greater distress than any British army has ever felt.'[10]

This, however, was no simple matter for the government. There was a shortage of specie all over the western world as the gold and silver mines of Central and South America declined in production, while paper money and the uncertainties of war drove cash out of circulation. By 1812 gold imported into England was worth 42% over the Mint price, and the value of silver, as Bathurst told Wellington in September, was also rising to a level that threatened silver coinage. Even so, speculators could still make a 30% profit by buying specie and sending it to Russia.[11]

British commanders had the authority to purchase specie with bills of exchange, but even though Wellington was willing to pay more than the rates set by the Treasury, he could not pry much out of the millions that the well-informed British Commissary in Chief believed were hoarded at Lisbon and Cadiz. His efforts were not made easier by a currency consortium at Malta with agents in Spain and Sicily aiming at a monopoly by driving out other dealers.[12] Nor was he consoled by Bathurst's rehearsal of the familiar difficulties of acquiring specie in England and his reminder that the problem was compounded by the bills drawn in Portugal. 'All this,' Bathurst wrote in tones designed to assuage, 'I am aware does not in the smallest degree lessen the difficulties you experience, but it accounts for our not being as able, as we are willing, to remedy them.'[13] But although Bathurst did not then know it, just the day before he wrote this letter, on 22 July, a major obstacle to sending more gold had been removed by Wellington's great victory at Salamanca. 'I hope that you will be pleased with our battle,' he wrote to Bathurst two days later when he was able to pause in pursuit of the French. 'There was no mistake; every thing went on as it ought; and there never was an army so beaten in so short a time.'[14]

When the first news reached London on 5 August, Bathurst told Wellington, the ministers were in a 'tumult of joy', after contradictory rumours and were now convinced that the official news would confirm their most sanguinary hopes.[15] When Lord Clinton arrived with the despatch ten days later it was greeted by 'the acclamations of all London'. Even the equable Bathurst had to apologize for his unintelligible hand as he scribbled immediate congratulations on 'the most eventful victory this country has been for some time blessed with'. In this brief, hurried message he assured Wellington that all his needs were being met: £100,000 chiefly in gold had already been sent; almost 1000 cavalry remounts and artillery horses were on the way; the Medical Board was assembling and the next day he would go to the Ordnance to order arms.[16]

After four years of equivocal effort the long-awaited triumph seemed finally to have arrived. The expectation of decisive victory in the Peninsula had come again and vindicated the government's course. Wellington had succeeded despite his complaints and the ministry was also safe, at least for the time being. Even Lord Wellesley, who was at once informed by Bathurst, hurried to the Regent with mixed feelings of pride, chagrin and eagerness to demonstrate his transcendence of mere party politics. The Prince, Wellesley told Bathurst, 'was so gracious as to communicate to me the

57

general outline of the despatches.' Perhaps expecting an offer from his former colleagues, he thoughtfully advised of his movements.[17] But in its triumph the cabinet did not need to suffer the return of this imperious cuckoo.

In a moment, in the twinkling of an eye, the relationship between Wellington and the government was also transformed. Their fortunes were now even more closely linked than before. If he succeeded the administration would share the glory; if he failed the danger would be greater than before the victory. But he could now demand greater support, and the ministry was more willing to take risks in supplying it.

On a personal level the cabinet could hardly do enough to show its gratitude. Wellington was immediately promoted marquess; a grant of £100,000 was recommended to parliament, 'for,' Liverpool told Bathurst, 'I know that at this time he is rather poor'; and his case for an increase in pay was anticipated by granting £5,000 a year table money. There was unfortunately no vacant Garter but the Prime Minister asked Bathurst to turn his mind to 'what it may be fitting to do with respect to *new honours* to Lord Wellington'.[18] Lord Mulgrave suggested that the parliamentary grant should be at least £50,000 more and that the ministry should not quibble about an 'excrescent Ribband' disfiguring the Order of the Garter until death restored the pristine number: 'I do not think much mischief could have followed, unless *Garter* in horror and despair should have hanged himself in his own Garters.'[19] An extra Blue Ribbon was not granted, even on this triumphant occasion, but Wellington received one at the next vacancy, on the death early in 1813 of the Marquess of Buckingham, whose aide-de-camp in Dublin he had been in 1787. In the meantime the Prince Regent allowed Wellington to add the Cross of St George to his coat of arms, as had been granted to the Duke of Marlborough.[20]

Even as these marks of distinction were being considered, yet more good news was on the way from Spain. When the allied armies entered the capital and King Joseph and his army fled, Wellington told Bathurst: 'It is impossible to describe the joy manifested by the inhabitants of Madrid upon our arrival.' He hoped that the Spaniards' detestation of the French would finally 'induce them again to make exertions in the cause of their country, which being more wisely directed, will be more efficacious than those formerly made'.[21] When the despatches reached London four weeks after the event, Bathurst, in congratulating Wellington, wrote: 'It is not in the Peninsula alone that your Lordship's triumphant entry into the capital of Spain will be heard with delight: there is not a country labouring under the yoke of France, or dreading her progressive power and dominion, which will not hear of this event with exultation.' He trusted that Wellington's rapid victories would lead to 'the liberation of Spain at no distant period; by the blessing of Providence it may ultimately effect the salvation of Europe'.[22] It was certainly a good omen for this happy issue and closer co-operation between the three armies that Wellington was appointed commander of the Spanish forces for the duration of the war.

But he was still short of supplies, particularly cash. After entering Madrid he told Bathurst that lack of pay for the army was producing 'acts of plunder and indiscipline by which we are disgraced every day,' while the sick and wounded officers at Salamanca were even obliged to sell their clothes to raise money.[23] By the end of the month the War Minister had prised all the foreign gold (a mere £76,424) out of the Bank of England and even commandeered silver dollars from captured American ships, perhaps returning from selling grain at Lisbon, in exchange for treasury bills before they were judged by the Admiralty court.[24] But these and the earlier shipments were still grossly inadequate for Wellington's needs. After the military successes of the summer, however, Bathurst and his colleagues were willing to chance more extraordinary and hazardous expedients. When the Bank was reduced to British guineas, which it was illegal to export, and foreign coins were hard to acquire, the ministers invoked a provision of the 1797 Act suspending the Bank's requirement to exchange gold for paper money which permitted them by Order in Council to require the Bank to issue gold for the payment of troops. This had never been construed as extending to the army abroad, but after difficult negotiations Bathurst was able to tell Wellington in late September that the directors would release £400,000 in guineas at the rate of £100,000 a month, with the commander being left to determine their local value in Spain and Portugal.

Bathurst then went even further – beyond any letter of the law – in authorizing Wellington to use this money not just for payment of the troops but in whatever way he considered would help the army. 'If things turn out well,' he wrote, 'I shall probably never hear much about it, but if there is a great alarm again on the subject of specie, and there should not have been any brilliant success *at the time*, this transaction, if it comes out, will I am aware expose me to some trouble.'[25] Lord Harrowby put it more bluntly, hoping that Bathurst would not lose his head over this arrangement, but encouragingly adding: 'You and all of us should deserve to lose it, if we refrained from using a vigour beyond the law to enable Lord W to pursue his successes, and it is fortunate that you have a decent legal cloak for so good a deed.'[26] Luckily the opposition did not get wind of this and the directors, who had parted with the £400,000 in return for a promise that the demand would not be repeated, were induced to release a further £300,000 in guineas in the spring of 1813.[27] Thereafter the government kept up as great a supply of specie as it could by importing and reminting gold from India.[28]

Lord Mulgrave at the Ordnance applied himself to providing arms, relatively easy compared to specie, and seasoned horses, which was more difficult. As he told Bathurst, old or untrained horses would be 'a prodigal waste of money and an inevitable disappointment to him in all his measures'. He was willing to withdraw good horses from the army in Ireland and England, despite complaints from the Irish commander and the Duke of York, since the Peninsula was the most important object: 'Artillery horses for *home service* may be fully dressed and groomed long before we shall have to resist an invasion.'[29] Even so Wellington was still complaining to Bathurst in the spring of 1813 that he was so short of horses that 'I shall, as usual, take the field with an equipment of artillery far inferior to that of the enemy, and to what I intended to take with me; and we shall have no spare horses whatever'.[30] The Ordnance was loath to increase the price of horses, which would drive up the cost for all those needed by government, but Bathurst assured Wellington in May that an adequate supply would be obtained by paying the dealers a premium to drive horses to military depots.[31]

Food for Wellington's army was also a problem closely connected to specie. Even the good harvest in 1812 did not permit the risk of exports from the British Isles and not until the 1813 crops were safely gathered in was there a clear surplus for the Peninsula. In the meantime the troops continued to depend on grain and flour from the United States, despite the war with that country. Under the circumstances the Americans naturally insisted on cash, which increased the scarcity in Spain and Portugal. These licensed imports continued as a matter of necessity, but war with the United States raised the whole issue of trade with that country.

After five years at the Board of Trade Bathurst was in a better position to discuss this than his replacement, Lord Clancarty. At the beginning of October, 1812, he took the matter up with the Prime Minister at length, recommending that US ships be granted licences and encouraged to bring flour and grain to Britain, but cotton, rice and tobacco, the products of the 'Anti-Anglican' south, should be banned. There were good stocks of all of these on hand and more could be obtained from British, Spanish and Portuguese colonies. Rice was necessary only in a real scarcity and, if US cotton was required, it could be imported in neutral ships at a price ensuring that the quantity would be kept to a bare necessity. Refusing these imports and vigorously blockading the rivers of the south, Bathurst thought, would make that part of the United States feel the pressure of the war of which it was the main author. In principle he thought that Britain should refuse import licences to American ships on the same basis as it did the French, since the US was 'evidently becoming a formidable maritime power, both as to the construction of their Ships, & the Skill of their Seamen – and we should be unwilling to encourage their Shipping as we are that of France'. But in practice allowing trade to continue was the most effective way of discouraging its fighting navy. Banning American merchant ships would simply lead to the arming of privateers and men of war, while 'all the Vessels which may thus trade under licences, together [with] the Men on Board will not venture to return to the United States, the laws against such Ships & Men being very severe'.[32]

Despite this pragmatic compromise, the government wanted to reduce the dependence on American food. In the spring of 1813 Wellington told Bathurst that he had authorized the purchase of grain in Egypt and Brazil to decrease imports from the US.[33] And at the same time Bathurst despatched the diplomat William A'Court (later Lord Heytesbury) to the Barbary States of Morocco, Algiers, Tunis and Tripoli, which for some reason came under the War and Colonies rather than the Foreign Office, to induce them by threats, bribes and financial advantages to supply the Peninsula with cattle, horses, mules and grain. In the case of Algiers, the most piratical state, A'Court was to point to the strength of the Royal Navy and threaten that Britain would not tolerate harassment of its shipping at Malta and the Ionian islands or of its allies, Spain and Portugal. He was empowered to offer a British ransom by instalments for Sicilian slaves, since the government of Sicily could not afford it, but if this did not produce an Algerian truce with Sicily as long as the British remained in that island, it was to be regarded as an act of hostility against Britain itself.[34] The mission no doubt improved the situation in the Peninsula as well calming the Mediterranean somewhat for the time being, but it was better agricultural, social and economic conditions in Britain as well as the improved fortunes of war that were more significant in increasing support for Wellington's campaigns.

In the autumn of 1812, when jubilation at the Spanish victories was at its height, Bathurst also had welcome news from North America. The declaration of war in June had bitterly divided the United States, with the shipping interests of New England being overwhelmingly opposed, as they had previously been to measures restricting trade with Britain, while the War Hawks of the south and west were eager to strike a decisive blow to end British harassment at sea, break through the Indian barrier to westward expansion and seize the British North American colonies which threatened to replace the American export trade.[35] Although the US was not prepared for war, an attack was quickly mounted on Upper Canada (Ontario), considered the most vulnerable British possession, with only 1600 regular troops and many American settlers who had gone there for cheap land and who were thought to be eager to rejoin the United States. At the end of May Major General Isaac Brock, the military commander and acting civilian administrator, reported in a despatch that would have arrived in London at about the same time as the declaration of war that he had found in travelling through the colony 'a good disposition and a high degree of industry. A general determination has been manifested to defend the province in the event of hostilities with the United States, and I am reliably assured that the people, taken in a wide sense, are as sincere as they are ardent in their profession.'[36]

This was soon put to the test. On 12 July the Governor of Michigan Territory, Brigadier General William Hull, pressed against his inclinations by President Madison, crossed the river from Detroit and issued a proclamation promising the Upper Canadians freedom from tyranny. Unfortunately, on his way back from Washington, his baggage, including instructions and the muster roll, had been inexplicably shipped across Lake Erie after the declaration of war and was captured by the British. Brock put this heaven-sent intelligence to good use by exaggerating the strength of his own force, which was about equal to Hull's, deceiving American spies and allowing a fraudulent despatch stating that 5000 Indians had joined him to fall into the hands of the Americans. Believing himself greatly outnumbered and with Fort Michilimackinac in the north having fallen to the British on 17 July, Hull retreated to Detroit on the eve of Brock's arrival on the frontier in the middle of August. When the Upper Canadian force, numbering about 1300 regulars, militiamen and Indians to the Americans' 2000, carried the war into Michigan on 16 August Hull surrendered the fort, troops, arms and supplies after the first barrage and Michigan became an appendage of Upper Canada for a year. Hull himself was sentenced to death for cowardice and neglect of duty but pardoned by President Madison who perhaps recognized his own responsibility for the disaster.[37]

Colonel Bunbury, who had no inkling of Brock's luck and deception, told Bathurst when news of the fall of Detroit arrived in terms reflecting the conventional British view of American military capacity: 'Accept my congratulations upon the brilliant achievements of General Hull and his invading army. This occurrence forms an amusing episode in the great epic of the war.'[38] Bathurst in turn told Wellington that Brock 'seems to be a man of energy and resource', but took the occasion to reiterate the risks the government was taking in order to support the Peninsula:

This news is a great relief to me. After the strong representations which I had received of the inadequacy of the force in those American settlements, I know not how I should have withstood the attack against me for having sent reinforcements to Spain instead of sending them for the defence of British possessions.[39]

Brock was immediately made a Knight of the Bath, but the honour came too late. On 13 October he died leading a charge against the Americans at Queenston on the Niagara frontier. This incursion was also repelled by the beginning of December, and a mismanaged march on Montreal collapsed when the American militia refused to cross the border. These initial successes against the Americans provided valuable time to organize the militia and volunteers of both colonies, but the home government could spare very few regular troops. Any strong defence, or effort to recover them if they fell to the Americans, depended on the war in Europe. In the overall scheme of things this was a marginal war, handled by the Colonial rather than the Military Under-Secretary, with Bathurst himself devoting little time to it.

In the North American maritime colonies, despite much better relations with the neighbouring US states and the continuation of trade, the war did not begin so well. The British had only three ships on the Halifax station and the American navy proved better than the British expected. But some ships at least could be spared from Europe and by 1813 the British had regained the initiative and were blockading the major points of the American coast.

Far more important than the news from across the Atlantic was that from northern Europe. The fate of the Peninsular War, and indeed of all Europe, depended on the success or failure of Napoleon's invasion of Russia with an army of over 500,000 in June 1812. Reports were slow to arrive and not always reliable, but they were eagerly digested by Bathurst and other ministers and immediately conveyed to Wellington, now becoming a kind of proconsul whose opinions and advice were solicited and carefully considered by his colleagues at home.

When he first heard of the invasion from Bathurst on the morrow of Salamanca, Wellington thought: 'If the Emperor of Russia has any resources, and is prudent, and his Russians will really fight, Bonaparte will not succeed.'[40] Napoleon did fail, but not in the way Wellington expected. As the Russians retreated before Napoleon's huge force, scorching the earth behind them, British ministers put an optimistic interpretation on

63

events. But by the time the two armies reached the former Russian capital, Bathurst in trying to make sense of contradictory French and Russian accounts, told Wellington that Moscow had probably fallen to Napoleon, and 'the fear which the Russian government has to let the truth be known will induce them to make a sudden peace'.[41] In fact the Russians did not capitulate. Moscow began to burn as soon as the French entered; there was not enough food for the winter for even the third of Napoleon's army that survived; no warm clothing had been brought for what had been intended as a mere summer campaign; there was a desperate shortage of medicine and Napoleon was 1500 miles from Paris, where there were plots to overthrow him.

On 19 October Napoleon ordered a withdrawal to Poland. His ragged army struggled over roads that were passable when frozen but quagmires when thawing, across rivers that were death traps when they melted, all the while being harassed by Russian soldiers, various irregulars and murderous serfs. The retreat became a rout and only about 60,000 soldiers staggered back across the River Niemen in December. Even before the extent of this disaster was known in England, Bathurst could confidently assure Wellington on 12 November: 'In whatever way the Campaign in the North may terminate, the French Armies must suffer so much that they cannot hope to begin another, or make preparations for it, without such reinforcements from France, as will prevent her sending any considerable forces to Spain.'[42]

The news from Russia did something to offset the disappointment that Wellington could not drive the French armies out of Spain and continue into southern France. Unable to take the fortress of Burgos, a hundred miles north of Madrid, and with the French consolidating their stronger forces under Marshal Soult to begin a powerful offensive, he had to order a familiar retreat to safe winter quarters in late October. This was not to be compared with Napoleon's withdrawal from Russia, but it was bad enough. 'The people of England,' Wellington bitterly told the Prime Minister when he reached his final destination of the Portuguese border in late November,

> so happy as they are in every respect, so rich in resources of every description, having the use of such excellent roads &c., will not readily believe that important results here frequently depend upon 50 or 60 mules more or less, or a few bundles of straw to feed them; but the fact is so, notwithstanding their incredulity. I could not find means of moving even one gun from Madrid.[43]

Even worse was the disorderly condition of the army, which Wellington told Bathurst at length had deteriorated further than ever before. Most of those lost along the way were 'Men who broke into wine cellars, and made themselves so drunk, that they could neither march nor be removed at the time the Army was ordered to march; or men who straggled from the column in search of plunder and were taken by the enemy.' Five hundred drunken men had to be abandoned in one cellar when the officers could not get them to move. And in addition to drink, Walcheren fever and other illnesses had made the British army 'almost a moving hospital'. About a third were either sick or attending those who were, and having to take along hospitals added to the difficulties. Wellington considered most of the supposed infirmities to be of 'a very trifling description', sufficient to make soldiers incapable of service but not of 'committing Outrages of all descriptions on their passage through the Country'. The last time the hospitals had been evacuated, the soldiers had not only plundered the local inhabitants but even 'the Hospitals Stores which moved with the Hospitals; and have sold the plunder'.[44]

This mortifying retreat after the high expectations only a few months before produced an angry philippic in the House of Lords on 12 March, 1813, from Lord Wellesley, standing forth as his brother's true champion. He demanded to know 'what secret cause amidst the splendid scene that has been exhibited on the peninsula – what malign influence, amidst the rejoicings and acclamations of triumph, has counteracted the brilliant successes of our arms, and has converted the glad feelings of a just exaltation into the bitterness of regret and disappointment?' Not knowing Wellington's description of the rabble that reached Portugal, he declared the army to be the best that had ever been assembled and its leader 'a general pronounced by the whole world to be unsurpassed in ancient or modern times, the pride of his country, the refuge and hope of Europe'. The gravamen of this orotund charge was that his brother had not been properly supplied since he had left the government. Wellesley focused particularly on the shortage of money, which he insisted could have been provided by economies elsewhere, by obtaining greater quantities from Spanish America and by prohibiting cash purchases of silk and other luxuries from France under special import licences. Rising immediately after Wellesley, Bathurst did not attempt to compete with this powerful rhetoric, but he did firmly insist that Wellington was not dissatisfied with the efforts of the ministers and that as much specie and everything else as possible was being sent to him. The same case was also made by the Prime Minister. But neither even hinted at the questionable device for supplying specie.

Wellesley was at least a month late in moving for an inquiry into the Peninsular War, which was easily defeated by 115 votes to 38. By the time of the debate there was sufficient evidence that 1813 would at last see a decisive, perhaps even conclusive, advance against Napoleon from every direction which would increase parliamentary confidence in the ministry and the ministers' confidence in themselves. The Prussians joined the Russians as they relentlessly pursued the French beyond their border. And on 3 March Britain concluded a treaty with Sweden to provide 30,000 troops in return for a British subsidy and an agreement not to oppose the conquest of Norway as compensation for the loss of Finland to Russia. As Napoleon raised a huge new army Bathurst told Wellington in March, on the basis of information from the Swedish Crown Prince John Charles (the former French Marshal Bernadotte), who kept in touch with his compatriots at Paris, that Napoleon would remove at least 40,000 troops from Spain.[45] In fact he once more confounded the British by removing only half that number, leaving 200,000 soldiers in the Peninsula.

Whatever the uncertainty about Napoleon's intentions in Spain, the omens were certainly excellent as Wellington set out in the spring with his 100,000 British, Portuguese and Spanish troops. He told Bathurst that, although he did not know if he was more powerful than the enemy, he was certain that he would never be stronger or the French weaker and that he would never have a better opportunity of driving them out of Spain. Even the health of the army seems to have improved with the weather and the lively prospect of success: 'Some few men have fallen sick since the troops marched; but in general, the troops are more healthy than I have ever known them to be.'[46] Napoleon ordered Joseph to leave Madrid and concentrate his forces closer to France. Burgos was destroyed by the French rather than being held. And on 21 June Wellington achieved a smashing triumph at Vitoria, just eighty-five miles from the French border. Joseph and his army abandoned arms, equipment, horses, cash and booty in their flight. Wellington's exhausted troops fell on the treasure trove and only a small part of the military chest was rescued by the authorities to help pay the troops. Among the less practical items that fell into the hands of the commander were magnificent paintings from the Spanish royal collection which Joseph had been taking with him. At the end of the war these were formally given to Wellington by Ferdinand VII and may still be seen in Apsley House. The baton of Marshal Jourdan was also captured and sent home with the despatches. When they arrived Bathurst asked Wellington to send the cabinet some of the most interesting of Joseph's papers, promising that he should have them back as trophies. Wellington was happy to comply, but he warned that 'as the Secretary of State's Office is a sink of papers, and these are really curious, and will hereafter tend to illustrate many things that have occurred here, particularly in the last year, I shall be glad to have them again, and that they should remain among my papers'.[47]

Vitoria, which effectively drove the French out of Spain, caused an even greater sensation than Salamanca when the news arrived in London on 3 July. 'It is impossible to express the exultation felt by everyone on this occasion,' wrote Bathurst,[48] while the Prince Regent immediately ordered Wellington promoted to field marshal. Four days later Bathurst told the House of Lords with considerable ministerial and even family pride that the battle, 'as decisive in itself, and as gigantic in its results, as any which had graced the military annals of England,' had been won by a man who only four years ago had been merely Chief Secretary to the still-serving Lord Lieutenant of Ireland. Lord Wellesley naturally added his congratulations and was even obliged to concede that, on this occasion at least, Wellington had received proper support from the government.[49]

The battle had an even greater effect on the continent. Britain had at last redeemed itself for the peripheral bungling of the past twenty years, shown itself capable of great military effort and produced in Wellington a leader of genius. The war in Germany was at a standstill since Napoleon, after brilliant victories in the spring, had proposed a much-needed armistice, and his opponents had agreed on 2 June in order to gather their own reinforcements. Both sides wrestled for the support of Austria, but Vitoria decisively tipped the balance to the allies. On 12 August war began again and Napoleon was driven out of Germany by the Battle of the Nations at Leipzig on 16–19 October. And in the middle of November Holland also rose in revolt.

Apart from continued incompetence on the east coast of Spain, an operation directed from Sicily and effectively separate from Wellington's, the only place where war was not going well for Britain by the end of 1813 was Upper Canada. The Americans, reversing their losses of the previous year in Upper Canada, looted the capital, York (Toronto), and either deliberately or accidentally burned the legislature. They failed to cut the supply line of the St Lawrence River, but the US naval build-up on Lakes Erie and Ontario certainly threatened it. In July an aide-de-camp to Sir George Prevost, the Governor General at Quebec, arrived with despatches and told Bathurst that reinforcements were needed to hold Upper Canada. At least 600 sailors were required for the lakes, which must leave by the end of August to reach the St Lawrence before it froze. Bathurst impressed on the messenger the difficulties, but he also wrote to the First Lord of the Admiralty to see what could be spared, and 300 prime seamen were added to the 400 who had already gone.[50] This was little enough, but with the prospect of victory in Europe at hand the British government was confident that it would soon be able to recover Upper Canada if it fell to the Americans.

The decision over North America is an indication that the dramatically improving situation in Europe did not make Bathurst's task any easier. New allies required assistance even beyond financial subsidies and in the Peninsula Wellington was more imperiously demanding than before, suspicious of any diversion of effort and apprehensive that he would not be strong enough to carry his latest victory through to final success, particularly if Napoleon sent reinforcements against him. No further French troops could in fact be spared for Spain after Austria's declaration, but it took all of Bathurst's tact and store of goodwill to explain, a few weeks after Vitoria, that confusion between the Ordnance and the Transport Board had for weeks held up a battering train needed for the attack on San Sebastian on the French border. He sent a clerk to Portsmouth to investigate, but a month later Wellington was bitterly complaining that he was still waiting for it and had lost sixteen valuable days. 'A British Minister cannot have too often under his view the elements by which he is surrounded,' he sharply reminded Bathurst, 'and cannot make his preparations for their operations of the campaign at too early a period'.[51]

This delay was all the more infuriating since Wellington had shortened his line of communication with Britain by moving his naval base from Lisbon to the north-eastern Spanish port of Santander. This made possible the establishment of a depot for supplies and the reception of sick and wounded soldiers at Plymouth,[52] but it did little to reduce the hazards of shipping. Wellington protested that Spain was being neglected by the Royal Navy while the French were able to reinforce their two posts in the north from the sea. No British army, he insisted, had ever been left in such a vulnerable situation since the country became a naval power, but if no more than 'one frigate and a few brigs and cutters, fit and used only to carry dispatches' could be supplied for the seige of San Sebastian, he grumbled, 'I must be satisfied, and do the best I can without such assistance'.[53] Bathurst passed these complaints to the First Lord of the Admiralty, who told Wellington that in the last twenty years it had been impossible to protect even the coast of England from privateers, and the situation had become worse with war against the United States.[54]

The powerful fortress and port of San Sebastian finally fell at the end of August but was put to such a brutal sack that scarcely a building was left standing by the end of the third day. Wellington, however tired and angry he must have been by this time, was greatly criticized for permitting such plunder and atrocities, not least by the Spanish who were furious at the destruction of a major port by their allies. When parliament met in November, Bathurst told Wellington that the government was rescued from censure only by news of Leipzig.[55]

More good tidings were also arriving from the Peninsula to overshadow San Sebastian. Pamplona, twenty miles inland, the other key to the roads through the Pyrenees, was starved into submission at the end of September, securing Wellington's advance into France. Bathurst told him that he had 'brought us back after the lapse of a century to the time when, under the auspices of the Duke of Marlborough, the military glory of this country was raised to a height at which, until lately, it was imagined it would never arrive again'.[56] But since he could not adequately supply the Spanish troops under his command, Wellington was obliged to send them back to their own country. 'If I could now bring forward 20,000 good Spaniards, paid and fed, I should have Bayonne,' he complained to Bathurst: 'If I could bring forward 40,000, I do not know where I should stop. . . . Without pay and food, they must plunder; and if they plunder, they will ruin us all.'[57] Not until the following spring, when he was well provided with cash, could he summon the Spanish soldiers back for the conclusion of the campaign in France.

The revolt of the Dutch in the middle of November also added to the difficulty of supplying the Peninsula and other war efforts. The only leading minister in London when that news arrived was Lord Liverpool, who immediately summoned the Colonial Under-Secretary and the Commander-in-Chief to decide what troops could be spared.[58] A few days later Bathurst called home the hereditary Prince of Orange, who was serving as Wellington's aide-de-camp, and told the latter that 5500 soldiers, some of them Guards from London replaced by militia units, had been scraped together for Holland.[59] This was bad enough as far as Wellington was concerned, but he was beside himself with anger when Bathurst followed this with an inquiry about further British advances into France during the winter. In scorching terms he reiterated his straitened circumstances, the government's misjudgment in spreading its resources too thinly and the primacy of his own campaign. Properly supported, he insisted that he could do 'ten times more to procure peace than ten armies on the side of Flanders'. Instead he was short of everything – troops, supplies and shipping, but above all cash: 'We are overwhelmed with debts, and I can scarcely stir out of my house on account of the public creditors waiting to demand payment of what is due to them.' He bluntly told Bathurst that he must give up either the Peninsula or Holland.[60]

Bathurst and his colleagues could not give up the military efforts in Germany and the Low Countries since valuable trading opportunities helped pay for the war and they wanted to ensure that Antwerp did not remain in French hands. But on New Year's Eve Bathurst tried to reassure Wellington that he was not giving preference to Holland over the south of France.[61] Since Wellington was now so close to England, at St Jean de Luz, he also despatched Colonel Bunbury to discuss personally what would be provided for the 1814 campaign, even though Bunbury was sceptical about an advance into France from the south, which, he feared, might provoke massive national resistance.[62] Along with him Bathurst sent his eighteen-year-old third son Seymour, who, he told Wellington in mollifying tones, had been intended for the Church, 'but I am desirous that he should see a British army, before he finally decides, whether he is to wear a black coat or a red one. It will at any rate be something for him to boast that he had the honour of seeing your's in France.'[63] Perhaps to give him some standing in the mission, Seymour was appointed ensign in the Foot Guards the day before this letter was sent, and in the Guards, rather than the Church, he remained.

There is no record of the conference in France, though Bunbury brought back a familiar list of what Wellington expected: to keep his veteran troops; more supplies; better sea transport; and more effective assistance from the Royal Navy.[64] But as a professional soldier as well as the representative of the Secretary of State Bunbury undoubtedly guaranteed that everything necessary would be provided, and certainly the list was carefully attended to by Bathurst. Bunbury must also have told Wellington confidentially that the government had sent the banker Nathan Rothschild to the continent to organize a network of agents to buy French coins for him; indeed a large shipment was on its way before Bunbury returned.[65] Finally Wellington admitted that he had ample specie,[66] as well as the unusual advantage for an invader of being able to pay for his requirements in the currency of the country.

The Dutch operation, towards which Wellington was so hostile, was also going well with Prussian assistance, The sovereign Prince of Orange returned from exile in England to organize his country's own military effort and his son, the hereditary Prince, told Bathurst when he arrived at The Hague on 19 December, 'The reception I met with by the people cannot be described'.[67] Everything augured well for a strong advance to seize Antwerp. But Bathurst and his colleagues also hoped to secure a loyal Holland by a dynastic marriage between the two heirs, the twenty-two-year-old Prince William and the seventeen-year-old Princess Charlotte, the only child of the Prince Regent and the estranged Princess Caroline. This had already been agreed to in principle by the ministers, the Regent and the sovereign Prince before he left England, with all acknowledging that the succession in the two countries would be separate.

In the few days that the hereditary Prince spent in London between the Peninsula and his own country a determined effort was made to promote, even conclude, the arrangement. On 12 December the Regent held a dinner at Carlton House for the Prince and Princess, the Dutch emissary, the Prime Minister and the Foreign Secretary and their wives, Bathurst and a few others. Lady Bathurst, who with her daughter Georgina was a confidante of the Princess, was out of town, but her husband sent her a long account the next day. Bathurst himself was assigned to escort the Prince to Carlton House. On the way he revealed that the Princess had overcome her earlier aversion to the Prince and would be at the dinner to meet him. At the Regent's request he added that the Prince's father wanted him to marry her; depending how things went, the Regent might even announce that evening that the Princess was willing to accept. Prince William was understandably taken aback by this sudden news but seems to have recovered his equanimity and adjusted to his heady prospect by the time the carriage reached Carlton House.

Once there, the romance progressed with gratifying speed. Bathurst observed that the Prince and Princess begin talking together as soon as dinner began; and just three-quarters of an hour after the men joined the ladies the Regent came up to Bathurst and Liverpool and said, 'It is all settled. I never was so anxious. Feel my hand.' After dinner the Princess had told her father that she had made up her mind to accept. The Regent let them have a little conversation together, then 'join'd their hands together, upon which . . . the young Prince gave her a hearty kiss, with which she was much pleas'd'. At the end of the evening Bathurst returned the Prince, who told him that he and the Princess had agreed on everything. 'All this sounds well,' Bathurst wrote to his wife, adding that the engagement was to be kept secret for the present. He also told her that he thought the Prince 'an amiable ingenuous Boy', which was not the customary opinion of this remarkably unhandsome, frequently drunk and generally loutish youth. His comment on the more comely, golden-haired Princess was more conventional and a compliment to his spouse: 'I should like to have her for my wife for an hour, but afterwards I think I could put up with my own.'[68]

Having apparently settled this important item of foreign policy and sent the hereditary Prince on his way rejoicing, the cabinet decided on 20 December that the Foreign Secretary should go to allied headquarters with full negotiating powers to keep the partners together and prevent them from making separate agreements with Napoleon. He was to insist that France be reduced to an approximation of its frontiers in 1792, to create strong barriers against its expansion and ensure that Britain kept its principal conquests of Heligoland, Malta, the Cape of Good Hope and Mauritius. Although originally given leave of absence until 1 March, Castlereagh was away for five months as the floating summit conference followed the army to Paris and settled the preliminary peace; he was then away for another four months in the autumn at Vienna. During these long absences, which amounted to most of 1814, the natural person to act as Foreign Secretary in London was Bathurst, who had been closely involved in policy since 1812. This also had the advantage of not requiring a formal appointment, as it had in 1809, since each of the three Secretaries of State had the power to convey the orders of the others. And adding the department to the already busy War and Colonies Office was not quite as onerous as it seemed, since Castlereagh continued to make the most important decisions and issue directives with the help of the small staff he took with him. Those matters that had to be settled at home were resolved by Bathurst and Liverpool together, so that Bathurst's main individual responsibility was to write and supervise the despatches and other routine business. But for one of the busiest members of the government it was a significant additional burden, though one which he bore with his customary lack of complaint.

By the time Castlereagh reached the headquarters at Basle the allied armies had invaded France, but Russia, Austria and Prussia were quarrelling over peace terms and the division of central Europe. They had more respect for British military capacity following Wellington's victories, but were still suspicious of the insistence on maritime rights and the reluctance to give up most of the colonial acquisitions. And as usual they clamoured for larger British subsidies.

In February Napoleon defeated the armies of his divided opponents and contemptuously rejected their offer of the 1792 boundaries. The British cabinet was also split by this unforeseen reverse, with some ministers being tempted to concede better terms to Napoleon. Only Bathurst, Eldon, Harrowby and Melville were adamantly opposed.[69] The situation was resolved by Napoleon overplaying his hand and demanding more than the allies would grant. But even then it was only with great difficulty and by conceding a subsidy of £5,000,000 a year to the other three powers by the Treaty of Chaumont that Castlereagh got them to concentrate on defeating Napoleon and agree not to make any separate peace. Despite the pessimism this revealed about the length of fighting which was still required, Napoleon had finally exhausted his resources. On 9 March, the day the treaty was concluded, he was defeated at the Battle of Laon and on 31 March the allies entered Paris. Two days later Sir Charles Stewart, Castlereagh's half-brother, told Bathurst from the French capital:

> I believe I may safely congratulate you on the fate and exit of Bonaparte. I was at the opera here last night. The Emperor [of Russia] and the King [of Prussia] were there, the [Napoleonic] Eagles were torn down, '*Vive le roi*' resounded from every part of the house and the whole was a scene of the greatest enthusiasm.[70]

In the south of France Wellington also had great success. On 23 March his armies captured the rich port of Bordeaux, the second city of France and a centre of royalism. As he continued to pursue Soult's army up the Garonne River, Bathurst, fearing another trick from Napoleon, warned him not to give up any territory until he received official instructions from London.[71]

But even Napoleon's options were severely limited once Paris had fallen and Talleyrand had organized a provisional government and persuaded the Senate to depose the Emperor. Napoleon's proposal of renouncing the throne in favour of his four-year-old son was rejected by the allies and on 11 April he was compelled to abdicate unconditionally. When the news arrived in London, Colonel Bunbury wrote to tell Bathurst that Napoleon had had the effrontery to propose '*an Asylum in England*' but had settled for the island of Elba, retaining the title of Emperor and a pension of two million francs a year from the French government, and the allies had undertaken to deter the Barbary pirates from molesting his miniature dominion. His wife would also retain her title of Empress as ruler of Parma, which would descend to her son; other members of the Bonaparte family were similarly pensioned off. Castlereagh had sent for Wellington and also requested that the restored Louis XVIII be sent to Paris to sign the preliminary treaty.[72]

The return of the eldest surviving brother of Louis XVI was particularly gratifying to Bathurst, who just two weeks earlier had told Wellington that he would prefer to fight on alone for the Bourbon cause if Spain and Holland were safe rather than accept Napoleon in concert with the other allies.[73] The newly recognized Louis XVIII, who had been living for the past seven years as a pensioner of the British government at Hartwell in Buckinghamshire and treated coolly as a possible impediment to ending the war, was now bidden to London to be received in proper state. On 20 April the Regent met his Christian Majesty on the road and accompanied him to London in a state carriage, attended by Guards, trumpeters and a hundred gentlemen on horseback. The procession made its way to Grillon's Hotel in Albemarle Street, where, in a room magnificently decorated with fleurs-de-lys, the King was formally welcomed by Liverpool, Bathurst, the Earl of Buckinghamshire, the foreign ambassadors and about a hundred and fifty French emigré aristocrats. The Regent and King read each other addresses of congratulations and thanks. There were further greetings in London and on the way to the coast until finally the regular rightdown royal King was seen off at Dover by the Regent after an absence from France of over twenty years.[74]

In the south of France the news of Napoleon's abdication arrived too late for such an unambiguously happy ending. On 10 April, Easter Sunday, Wellington launched a mighty assault against Soult's army in the fortified city of Toulouse, expelling him at the cost of about 3000 French casualties and 4500 for the British and their allies. On the night of the twelfth, when a great dinner in Wellington's honour was held in that royalist city, couriers finally arrived from Paris with the official despatches of Napoleon's fall. But even Toulouse was not quite the end of the fighting, since the governor of Bayonne launched a forlorn but bloody sortie against the besieging British troops two days later.

Writing to congratulate Wellington on what he expected would be the last such occasion, Bathurst blamed the 'unwarrantable delay' in communicating the restoration of the monarchy from Paris for the loss of so many of Wellington's brave soldiers. He pronounced the Battle of Toulouse 'the last effort in an expiring cause, consistent in evil, to protract the miseries which its supporters had occasioned, and to postpone as long as possible the return of that harmony and peace which they had for upward of twenty years too successfully laboured to disturb'. Even before this victory, at what seemed at last the return of peace on earth, Bathurst had told the great hero that he was to be promoted to duke and five of his leading generals were to be peers.[75]

Neither Bathurst nor Wellington could have predicted that they would be working together on yet another major military operation within a year. But despite the tensions and vicissitudes between them in the past two years, they had created the basis of firm relationship that would continue not just in the renewed fighting but in peacetime for twenty more years.

4

THE AWFUL SHADOW OF
SOME UNSEEN POWER,
1814–1815

As soon as the war ended in April, 1814, Paris was flooded with British visitors eager to enjoy pleasures denied them for twenty years apart from the short interval of the Peace of Amiens. Not all of these made Castlereagh's diplomatic work easier, but among the most welcome was Lord Apsley, Bathurst's twenty-four-year-old heir, a Guards officer, MP for Cirencester and member of the Board of Control for the past two years, who supplemented the Foreign Secretary's despatches by describing for his father the atmosphere in the defeated capital. Apsley was warmly welcomed by Castlereagh and his wife, and, as the son of the British War Minister, was soon introduced to the Emperors of Russia and Austria, the King of Prussia, Talleyrand and Marshal Blücher. The King of France was still on his way back to Paris but Apsley went to a levée held by his brother, the Comte d'Artois (later Charles X) which Castlereagh was unable to attend. Apsley told his mother that the royal host, spotting his British army red coat, came through the crowd to greet him, shook his hand (a rare condescension) and said in a voice loud enough for all to hear 'that he should never forget the treatment he had received from you & my father & that he begged I would tell you how sensible he was of it'. As for Castlereagh, the rulers and diplomats considered him 'the cleverest man of the Alliance'.

Apsley reported that the Austrian Emperor would probably not go to England for the celebrations of peace and talks on the future of Europe since he disliked being cast in the shade by the grandstanding, ostentatiously liberal Tsar Alexander, who would probably take some of his magnificent guards: 'He is very fond of show, & has them stuffed out about the chest & girt so wasp-tight about the loins, that they walk as if they had the stomach ache.' But the news that most pleased Bathurst must have been the reported judgement of Napoleon that Wellington was 'the greatest man in the world, & his Marshalls say they cannot ever hope to stand against the English Troops, but that they should like to have a day with the Allies upon any thing like equal terms'.[1]

The Duke, who had just been appointed ambassador to France, visited Paris to see Castlereagh briefly at the beginning of May. But before he could take up his diplomatic post he had to go to Madrid to help the ambassador, his brother Sir Henry Wellesley, try to reconcile the restored Ferdinand VII to the liberal leaders who had helped drive out the French. Apsley went to Toulouse with despatches in time to accompany him on the mission, but, although Ferdinand had promised to uphold the constitution of 1812, once safely returned he adamantly refused. Even Wellington could not shake him and soon the whole apparatus of absolutism, even the inquisition and persecution of liberals, was re-established.

While Apsley was on this dispiriting journey, his brother Seymour wrote from Bordeaux, the main embarkation point for Wellington's army, to say that he had thought of joining the contingent going to North America, but since his father was already negotiating with the US and that detachment was being reduced he decided instead to ride across France with another part of the army and return to England. He also told his parents that even royalist Bordeaux was getting so tired of the British that 'it is no longer reckoned prudent to play "God Save the King" in the theatre for fear the audience should not receive it quite well'. Otherwise the territory was perfectly quiet.[2]

At the end of May Bathurst's protracted stewardship of the Foreign Office drew to a close, at least for the time being, when the allies concluded the Treaty of Paris with Louis XVIII. The country was returned to its 1792 borders, but to counter French resentment and help safeguard the restored monarchy, claims for indemnity were abandoned; Britain also returned all the captured French colonies save Mauritius, St Lucia and Tobago, and reopened the Newfoundland fisheries. France agreed to abolish the slave trade within five years, though Castlereagh had to defend himself against the anger of the Evangelicals at this delay by insisting that he had done the best he could. Three weeks later the allies agreed to the annexation of Belgium by Holland as a barrier to French expansion. The general settlement, particularly of central Europe, and the means of preserving the new arrangements, were then postponed to the Congress of Vienna in the autumn.

Shortly after Castlereagh's return, in June there arrived for three weeks of festivities and discussions the King of Prussia, Metternich, representing the Emperor of Austria, and the Russian Emperor. The last did indeed bring his guards and also aroused great curiosity and popular enthusiasm by playing to the crowd and courting opposition politicians, and was barely restrained from insulting the Prince Regent by visiting the despised Princess Caroline. Just as these luminaries prepared to depart, the Duke of Wellington arrived for a further round of adulation and celebrations which concluded on 1 August with a collective commemoration in London's royal parks of the peace, the Battle of Trafalgar and the centenary of the Hanoverian succession. Bathurst attended the various ceremonies and finally received a degree from Oxford, an honorary Doctorate of Civil Law (DCL), on 16 June, along with Wellington (who had never attended university), the Russian Emperor, the King of Prussia, Blücher and many others. And he must certainly have been present in the House of Lords on 28 June when the Wellington was introduced in all five ranks of the peerage by the Dukes of Richmond and Beaufort.

While attention was fixed on these grand figures, Bathurst was involved in a lesser but nevertheless important royal and diplomatic matter. On 24 April, five months after the engagement had been settled, the hereditary Prince of Orange sent Bathurst a letter for Princess Charlotte and asked when communication of the marriage would be made to parliament: 'and is it true as she says that the voice of the country is decidedly against her coming over to Holland, or is it a story somebody had told her to give her solid reasons to combat my wishes on that subject?'[3] Bathurst confirmed that 'some ill-disposed persons' (including Princess Caroline) had indeed encouraged the idea that the heiress presumptive might be forced to live outside her country and that she was not satisfied with her intended husband's replies on the subject. His advice to the Prince was to make a sudden, unannounced visit to the Princess. If he took this advice and travelled incognito, he should announce himself at Bathurst's house as Colonel St George, an emissary from Sir Thomas Graham. Bathurst would then tell him all he knew before he went to see the Princess.[4]

The Prince followed this advice and confronted his fiancée on 30 April, when they came to an apparently amicable agreement that they would spend part of the year in each country.[5] But on 16 June the Princess broke off the engagement saying that she could not live abroad and that it would be

77

prejudicial to her mother, who, the Regent was hoping, would go abroad with their daughter to help his divorce. Among those in whom Princess Charlotte confided was Lady Bathurst.[6] But reluctance to live outside England was only part of the reason for this change of heart. During the war there had been a dearth of suitable Protestant princes in the Princess's life, but the royal visits produced several candidates more pleasing than the drunken and disorderly Prince of Orange. Her leading favourites were Prince Frederick of Prussia and the penniless Prince Leopold of Saxe-Coburg-Saarfield, who arrived in the suite of the Tsar, though the Russian Emperor and his sister tried to promote a Russian candidate. The Regent was furious at his daughter's change of heart, but when she would not be dissuaded the cabinet agreed that she could not be compelled. Prince Frederick lost interest after returning home, but Prince Leopold remained constant and they married in May, 1816. But this decision was a blow to the dream of the Netherlands becoming a dependable British outpost by dynastic marriage.

Even before the fighting ended in Europe Bathurst was turning his attention to settling matters in North America. At the end of January, 1814, with allied troops still on French soil, he raised with Wellington the possibility of sending 20,000 of his men to strike a decisive blow against the Americans. Otherwise, Bathurst feared, if Napoleon continued as ruler of France he might recommence hostilities by aiding the United States, to which none of Britain's allies would object.[7] Wellington evaded the issue of releasing troops, but he told Bathurst that, although he had not given much thought to North America, the success of any operations based in Canada must depend on naval superiority on the Great Lakes and he did not see where coastal landings could be made that would be injurious enough to force the Americans to sue for peace.[8]

Nothing was in fact done to reinforce North America until Napoleon abdicated in April, when Bathurst instructed Wellington to assemble troops at Bordeaux so that there would be 'no delay in embarking them & that they may arrive in America before the Season of Action shall be passed'.[9] About 16,000 hardened veterans were sent to carry out swift punitive attacks that it was confidently expected would force the United States to accept humiliating peace terms.

The only hope for the Americans, who dreaded the troops being commanded by great Wellington himself, was to strike a telling blow against the British colonies while time remained. This began well enough with victories on the Niagara frontier of Upper Canada in July, but the aim of a well co-ordinated attack all around Lake Ontario was a miserable failure, and by November the American troops had entirely withdrawn across the border. In the meantime the British soldiers were harrying the seacoast, from which US troops had been withdrawn for the interior. The most spectacular raid was against Washington on 25 August. Since this had not been considered a likely target, the Americans had made no preparations. When the British approached the city, the President, the government and troops simply fled, allowing the British to enter unopposed. British officers ate the dinner prepared for President Madison while the troops treated the city almost as if it had been taken by storm, looting and burning the public buildings, including the President's mansion. After two days, since there was no one with whom to negotiate, they withdrew to attack Baltimore, where they failed, as they also did at Plattsburg in the middle of September.

But the brutal treatment of the American capital, in what had hitherto been a relatively restrained conflict, provoked condemnation in Europe and called into question the British sincerity that they were simply trying to bring the Americans to a moderate peace. From his embassy at Paris Wellington wrote that the French newspapers presented the British operations in a manner which 'increased the ill temper and rudeness with which in too many instances His Majesty's subjects are treated in this town'.[10] In a letter to his Colonial Under-Secretary, who was negotiating with the Americans in Belgium, Bathurst did not mention retaliation for the American burning of the parliament buildings at York the previous year; but he did defend the restraint of the British army, pointing out that no capital had ever been so abandoned to the mercy of the enemy, and, even though there was no one to propose terms for the inhabitants, their lives and private property had been respected and they had even thanked the troops. When an attempt was made to assassinate the military commander, which by the laws of war meant that the lives and property of the city were forfeited, the only action was against the house from which the attempt was made.[11]

But, embarrassing as the triumph at Washington was for the British government, it was infinitely better than the humiliation at Plattsburg. Early in September the Governor-General of Canada, Lieutenant General Sir George Prevost, reinforced with Peninsular troops, marched south at the head of the largest army of the war to attack the stronghold on Lake Champlain by land and water. When the naval force was defeated, however, he abruptly withdrew to Lower Canada to preserve his army. This was not what those who had served under Wellington expected, nor the government at home, and several officers wrote to protest Prevost's conduct.[12]

Bathurst had already considered recalling Prevost for his unforthcoming communications with the Colonial Office and unsatisfactory military conduct,[13] but when he lost the confidence of the army at Plattsburg his fate was sealed. Asking Wellington's advice on a successor, Bathurst conceded that the criticisms of Prevost were 'in many respects I make no doubt, unfair & grounded on very exaggerated representation: but he has not the means of re-establishing himself in the good opinion of those he has to command'. If it had not been for the public comment that it would provoke, Bathurst said that he would have liked to appoint his brother-in-law, the Duke of Richmond. He had returned from Ireland in 1813 but his rank of general without field experience had prevented him from realizing his ambition of serving under his former Chief Secretary in the Peninsula. With a good military second-in-command in Canada, however, Bathurst was confident that he could 'get the better of my difficulties'.[14]

Wellington did not question Prevost's removal – 'I see he is gone to war about trifles with the general officers I sent him which are certainly the best of their rank in the army; and his subsequent failure and distresses will be aggravated by that circumstance'[15] – but a suitable replacement was no easy matter. The obvious candidate was the Duke himself, who did not fail to remind Bathurst of his unique qualifications: 'I see that the public are very impatient about the want of success in America and I suspect they will never be quiet till I shall go there.' But he considered Europe too unsettled for him to leave and, in any event, he could not arrive before the spring: 'If, however, in March next you should think it expedient that I should go there, I beg you will understand that I have no objection whatever.'[16]

The government seized on this hint and formally offered him the command, partly to remove him from the hostile atmosphere of Paris, but Wellington in effect refused, pointing out that if war began again in Europe, 'there is nobody in whom either yourselves or the country, or your Allies, would feel confidence'. Leaving the door open to accept later, however, he pronounced:

> There are enough troops there for the defence of Canada for ever. . . . I am
> quite sure that all the American armies of which I have ever read would not
> beat out of a field of battle the troops that went from Bordeaux last summer,
> if common precautions and care were taken of them.[17]

Finally Sir George Murray, Wellington's Quartermaster General in the Peninsula, was sent to Lower Canada as military commander, with the civil power being given temporarily to Lieutenant General Sir George Drummond, the administrator of Upper Canada and senior officer in North

America. Bathurst had already offered the Governor Generalship to Murray who replied that he would prefer to be chief of staff in a multi-national European army under Wellington. Although the pay would be better in Canada, Europe was more desirable 'in respect of Society and all the comforts and pleasures of life'. 'On the other hand,' Murray mused, 'although Canada is remote from the most conspicuous theatre of our interests as connected with European Nations, it is likely, nevertheless, to attract occasionally a large share of the immediate attention of our own Country'.[18] When nothing better turned up in Europe, Murray agreed to a military appointment on the second time of asking. He reached Quebec by sleigh from Halifax on 2 March, 1815, to tell Prevost of his dismissal and recall to explain his conduct at Plattsburg, just one day after Prevost learned that the peace treaty between Britain and the United States had been ratified in Washington. On his return to London Prevost was censured by a naval court martial but died before the military one he requested could be convened.

Even more humiliating than Plattsburg was the expedition launched directly from Britain late in the season against New Orleans. Colonel Bunbury protested to Bathurst against this, arguing that it would rob the country of troops that might be needed for disturbances in Ireland or Britain or even required in the Low Countries against France before the general peace settlement was concluded. He thought it better to wait until the spring of 1815, when the fate of Europe and the progress of negotiations with the United States would be clearer; then, if necessary, a strong assault might be launched at the vital centre of the Chesapeake rather than the periphery where the risk of failure was greater. He thought there was a good chance that the fleet might be dispersed and the troops lack supplies in the Gulf of Mexico; and even if Britain won, was it worth the trouble of fortifying New Orleans and keeping an army there?[19]

But this prudent advice was as dust in the balance in the general eagerness for an advantageous peace settlement, to say nothing of control of the Mississippi, prize money and booty from a rich port. A contingent of 8000 troops, mostly Peninsular veterans, set off in September and arrived in Louisiana in the middle of December. At the battle for New Orleans on 8 January, 1815, the British were massively defeated by General Andrew Jackson's artillery which killed the commander and about 2000 others. But this American triumph turned out to be of no diplomatic advantage since peace had already been concluded.

During these varied fortunes of war in North America Bathurst was once more in charge of the Foreign Office after Castlereagh left for Vienna in the middle of August. The deliberations there were expected to be short, but quarrels over the division of Europe continued in heated fashion for over half a year until hastened to a conclusion by a new threat from Napoleon. Castlereagh again decided most policy without reference to his colleagues in London, and the main issue for Bathurst in both of his offices, as well as for Liverpool, whom he regularly consulted, was the negotiations to end the war with the United States.

The Americans made overtures even before Napoleon's abdication, and the Russian Emperor had offered his services as mediator from the beginning of the war, but Castlereagh and the other British ministers insisted on direct negotiations, distrusting the Tsar's showy liberalism. The site was eventually fixed at Ghent, less neutral than it seemed since it was garrisoned by British troops to secure the union of Belgium with Holland. It was also close to London, so Bathurst and Liverpool were able to direct the British side of the talks in considerable detail, though this did not prevent much misunderstanding of tone and tactics by their negotiators. The five American commissioners arrived in late June, 1814, but the three British representatives did not join them until early August, when the British troops had embarked on what were expected to be devastating assaults on the United States.

The leader of the British delegation was Vice-Admiral Lord Gambier, reflecting the importance of the rights of search and impressment. He was supported in this and other maritime matters by the Admiralty lawyer Dr William Adams. But the most important of the three plenipotentiaries was in fact Bathurst's Colonial Under-Secretary, Henry Goulburn. He was familiar with British North American territorial issues as well as the wider diplomatic context of the war and carried on the correspondence with his chief, with the Prime Minister and occasionally with Castlereagh at Vienna. Goulburn not only took his family to Ghent but even much of his colonial business, which was carried back and forth by messengers. Yet for all his political and administrative experience and close relationship with the leading ministers, Goulburn was inclined to be more intransigent than his principals and from the very beginning, when Britain seemed in a strong position to demand concessions, had to be told to be more conciliatory. The atmosphere might have been better if Bathurst had sent Bunbury, though his departmental title and army rank might have created the wrong initial impression.

The other difficulty in negotiations was lack of precision in the British instructions. Preoccupied with the end of the war in Europe and the victory celebrations, the Foreign Secretary and his colleagues did not make clear their final demands and what they were prepared to concede. This was to some extent deliberate, since both political and public opinion expected a more vindictive settlement than Bathurst, Liverpool or Castlereagh, who would have been satisfied with an honourable return to the situation before the fighting began. But the imminent success of their army in North America also seemed to guarantee the British a strong hand in whatever they demanded.

The list of topics for discussion was narrowly interpreted by Goulburn and his colleagues, who failed to understand that they could be modified or traded for other concessions. They frequently went beyond their instructions, notably in raising search and impressment at the beginning of the discussions when the ministers had hoped that the Americans would not even mention an issue that in practice had disappeared with the end of the war in Europe. They also took a hard line on American fishing rights off Newfoundland, which the British regarded as being abrogated by the declaration of war, revised boundaries for greater Canadian security, good terms for Britain's Indian allies by means of neutral territory that would prevent US expansion, the instructions added a few weeks later requiring US disarmament on the Great Lakes and the prohibition of new fortifications, British navigation rights on the Mississippi, Florida, the Louisiana purchase and much else.

The US commissioners could not accept any of these demands, but lengthy deliberations seemed to work to British advantage, since, apart from the military raids, the naval blockade was driving up the cost of US imports and reducing the volume of its exports. Liverpool confidently told Bathurst in September: 'I confess I cannot believe that with the prospect of bankruptcy before them, the American government would not wish to make peace, if they can make it upon terms which would not give a triumph to their enemies.'[20] But the British government also had its reasons for wanting a speedy treaty. The very next day Bathurst told Goulburn that the clamour for economy would not make the war popular for long and continental allies would not acquiesce in the naval blockade much beyond the end of the year. Above all he urged Goulburn not to let negotiations be broken off, which would give the opposition an opportunity to raise the issue in the Commons before Castlereagh returned from Vienna.[21]

But almost immediately the British position weakened precipitously. The attack on Washington attracted reproach and Plattsburg was an even greater blow. The disputes at Vienna, which seemed to be leading towards a renewal of war, increased the need for the British government to concentrate its financial and military capacity to influence a secure peace settlement or, if necessary, take an effective part in the fighting. All the demands against the US were quickly abandoned and, on Christmas Eve, a treaty was signed practically restoring the situation of 1812. Occupied territory was returned and the unresolved issues of warships on the Great Lakes, the Canadian boundary and the east coast fisheries were postponed for future negotiations. From Vienna, where he had gone with the Foreign Secretary, Apsley told his father: 'The news of the American peace came like a shot here, nobody expecting it.' Talleyrand, the French foreign minister who had skilfully insinuated himself as mediator among the allies as well as defender of his own country's interests, epigrammatically pronounced it *'la paix sterling'*.[22] Britain's prestige soared with this assurance of financial and military security and Castlereagh's authority increased further in taking the lead to settle differences among the victors.

A less happy item that fell to Bathurst during Castlereagh's absence was the forced transfer of Norway from Denmark to Sweden. This had been reluctantly agreed to by Britain in March, 1813, to gain Sweden's army against Napoleon, and, by the Treaty of Kiel in January, 1814, compelling Denmark to join the allies, it was required to surrender Norway in exchange for Swedish Pomerania and the return of all Danish possessions seized by Britain save Heligoland. The Norwegians, who rallied round Prince Christian Frederik, their governor since May, 1813, and heir presumptive to the Danish throne, sent an envoy to plead with the British government. But the most that he could get from Liverpool, who pointed to Norway's hostility towards Britain since 1807 and Christian Frederik's suspect motives in light of his father's renunciation of Norway, was an assurance that the Norwegian constitution and institutions would be respected by Sweden.

The British government was nevertheless uneasy about the transfer, and not merely because the opposition in parliament supported Norway's claim to independence. The Swedish Crown Prince Charles John (Bernadotte) seemed more concerned with his own interests and ambitions than defeating his former commander Napoleon. From Paris in April, 1814, Castlereagh told Bathurst that although Charles John had 'certainly forfeited all claim to personal favour,' there were not sufficient grounds to break an agreement on which Russia in particular insisted. He thought that the best solution was 'to finish the business, without suffering the people of Norway to embark in a contest in which we must, at least navally, fight against them, under the stipulations of our treaty'.[23]

The stubborn resistance of the Norwegians did force the Royal Navy to blockade the country and prevent it from importing food, but the British

1. Cirencester town, House and Park from the Church tower, looking west to Queen Anne's Column *(photograph by F. Westley, Country Life Picture Library)*.

2. Cirencester Park looking east to the House and Church tower *(photograph by F. Westley, Country Life Picture Library)*.

3. Apsley House c. 1819, substantially as it was built by the second Earl Bathurst in the early 1770s.

a. View from Piccadilly

b. View from Hyde Park

(Meissen plates from the Saxon Service: The Wellington Museum, photograph Victoria & Albert Picture Library).

4. Henry, Lord Apsley, and his brother by Nathaniel Dance, c. 1775 *(The Earl Bathurst: photograph Courtauld Institute of Art)*.

5. Georgina, Countess Bathurst by Sir Thomas Lawrence *(The Earl Bathurst: photography Courtauld Institute of Art)*.

6. The Earl Bathurst, 1818,
   by Sir Thomas Lawrence.
   Painted to the order of the
   Duke of Wellington *(The
   Duke of Wellington:
   photograph Courtauld
   Institute of Art)*.

7. The Earl Bathurst by Thomas
   Phillips *(The Earl Bathurst:
   photograph Courtauld Institute
   of Art)*.

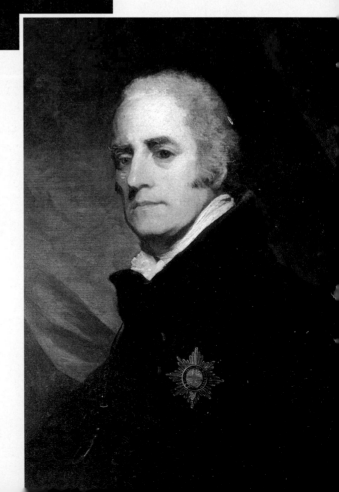

also tried to reconcile the Norwegians to the union and get the Swedish Crown Prince to guarantee Norwegian institutions. In the middle of July the British minister to Copenhagen assured Bathurst that he would make 'every exertion in my power to bring about an arrangement that will leave Norway almost an independent state,' adding that the Norwegians 'seem so English in their sentiments that I really believe, if it were to be proposed to them, they would to-morrow consent to Norway becoming a part of his Majesty's dominions.'[24]

Despite these efforts, Charles John shortly afterwards invaded Norway. But when he encountered strong resistance and the prospect of a long campaign, he conceded that the union would be only a personal one under the crown, preserving significant Norwegian autonomy and distinctiveness. This was a considerable thing gained, though not enough for strong Norwegian nationalists. In November their envoy tried to present a memorial against the union to Bathurst. But the acting Foreign Secretary decided that he could have no communication with an unofficial representative which would not only anger the Swedish government but, 'by giving encouragement to those in Norway who may still continue indisposed to the union of the two countries, expose them to the consequence of a fruitless resistance'. He did, however, return the memorial to the agent personally, 'lest the sending it back to him should appear to proceed from indifference to its contents or to the happiness of the people of Norway, for which the British Government must always be sincerely interested'.[25] With this tactful rebuff, dictated by the necessities of war against Napoleon, Norway's fate was sealed until 1905 when the union was peacefully dissolved.

Troubling as Norway was, almost as much attention was paid by Bathurst, Castlereagh and others connected with the Foreign Office to the comic opera marriage of Lord Herbert, heir to the Earl of Pembroke. While travelling in Spain and Sicily in the last year of the war, the handsome twenty-two-year-old milord became infatuated at Palermo with the Prince of Butera's wife, who was about his own age. When the Prince died in June, 1814, and Herbert proposed to marry the widow, Pembroke rushed to Sicily to prevent it. He arrived on 17 August, just as the couple were about to sail to Naples for the ceremony. That night, while Pembroke was still on board ship in quarantine, the couple went through a form of marriage, throwing a piece of paper inscribed with their two names and those of two footmen as witnesses at the foot of a priest, taking each other by the hand and saying, 'This is my wife: this is my husband'. This, though clandestine, was a valid marriage in Sicilian law, but still punishable by five years' imprisonment – in a convent for the woman, a castle for the man.

The local authorities tried to help Pembroke remove his son from the island, but when Herbert adamantly refused, his father had him confined, while his wife was sent to a convent. Pembroke then hurried to Paris to seek the aid of the Papal representative at the peace talks in having the marriage annulled. But by the time he reached there in September, the envoy had left for the Congress of Vienna. However, Wellington promised to ask Louis XVIII to use his influence with the Pope. Lady Pembroke wrote Bathurst hoping that he would also see her husband when he arrived in London.[26]

The Foreign Office machinery was duly enlisted in the cause, but Castlereagh discouragingly reported to Bathurst from Vienna that the Pope could not dissolve the marriage 'either upon the ground of incongruity of religion or the culpable manner in which it was contracted,' even though in civil law Lord Herbert was under age in Sicily and the widow prohibited from marrying so soon after her husband's death. But the Foreign Secretary took comfort from the fact that the two parties were at least sequestered, 'and no further mischief can happen, whilst we are using every exertion to avert this painful case of domestic scandal'.[27]

A month later Apsley told his father that Castlereagh's Under-Secretary had suggested that the marriage be invalidated on the grounds of scandal, at which the Vicar General, also at Vienna, merely shrugged his shoulders. Castlereagh, in turn, asked Bathurst if Pembroke would be willing to pay £1000, which he undertook to put quietly into the best hands in Rome since the more he asked the annulment as a favour 'the more they hold back, to keep it if possible as a set off against us for something'.[28] Pembroke readily agreed, provided that the final sum was not be paid until the marriage was annulled, having been assured by a relative of his wife (daughter of Count Woronzow, the former Russian Ambassador to Britain) that money was 'as necessary an ingredient to procure anything that was legal and right as to procure anything illegal and wrong'.[29]

A short time later Lord Herbert managed to exchange clothes with a British naval officer, slip by the guards and escape from Sicily. At Pembroke's request Bathurst wrote to Wellington urging him to hasten Herbert home in case he was disposed to linger in Paris: 'You may tell him that you have reason to believe he will be well received, if he does not delay his return.'[30] But the return of the prodigal did not solve the problem of the marriage, which remained valid in canon, Sicilian and English law. An annulment proved impossible but Herbert and his wife never saw each other again, the Countess of Pembroke, as she eventually became, being supported by a pension until her death in 1857.

From the Congress Apsley also told his father of the strange conduct of

Lord Stewart, the Ambassador to Vienna and one of the British pleni-potentiaries at the peace talks, these appointments being entirely due to the affection of his half-brother Castlereagh. Alternately charming and abusive, Stewart quarrelled with Metternich and most others, carried on numerous affairs and generally conducted himself in a fashion compelling attention, not all of it favourable. On one occasion in the palace square his carriage prevented the Emperor of Austria and his court from setting out in state, despite two requests from the Emperor himself, until finally the officers took the heads of his horses; on the other hand he gave a grand ball on Queen Charlotte's birthday which delighted everyone. Apsley reported that such behaviour made Britain unpopular in the city and at the Congress, 'as they think that the character of the English'. Even the more restrained Castlereagh sometimes did peculiar things, such as ostentatiously wearing a diamond Order of the Garter around his neck 'and thinking that people know nothing about it, while there is nothing they are so curious about as orders and particularly ours, of which they have hitherto seen so few'. The only explan-ation that Apsley could offer for such vulgarity was that the brothers were Irish rather than English.[31]

Despite such peculiarities, Castlereagh was eventually able to impose his mediation on the other allies for a territorial settlement and agreement to preserve it. When Prussia and Russia threatened to go to war over Saxony he negotiated a secret alliance with France and Austria on 3 January to face them down. This astonishing diplomatic reversal had been anticipated by Bathurst three weeks earlier in a circular to the cabinet in which he observed that 'Our foreign relations have essentially changed since Lord Castlereagh's departure'. He argued that it was necessary to bind France to Britain in order to prevent it from siding with Russia and Prussia in return for being allowed to reconquer Belgium, in which 'All Europe from Sicily to Sweden would acquiesce, some secretly, others openly wishing France success'.[32] It was nevertheless with astonishment that ministers learned that Castlereagh had actually signed an alliance with the recent enemy, if only as a bluff, raising the possibility of a new war in association with France against former allies.

Most of the cabinet was dispersed in the country when the news arrived. Bathurst, who remained in London, stood by the Foreign Secretary as he canvassed his colleagues' opinions by letter. From Bath the Prime Minister only reluctantly endorsed this daring action: 'I am sure we had no alterna-tive but to ratify the treaty, which under the circumstances I am persuaded is an advantageous one. It will secure the Low Countries for a time and give more *éclat* to Castlereagh's presence at Vienna, which was certainly wanting.' Three days later he even more grudgingly added that, since the cabinet had decided on ratification, it could not repudiate the treaty without recalling Castlereagh and breaking up the government in a manner disgraceful to all who had agreed. 'I am not sure that in Castlereagh's situation I should have proposed it,' he told Bathurst finally, 'but if it had been proposed by Austria and France I would not have refused to be a party to it.'[33]

Lord Harrowby put his finger on the problem for those outside the inner triumvirate who were accustomed to their colleagues unquestioningly ratifying their decision when he irritably told the acting Foreign Secretary:

> Your information is so astonishing that it seems to have turned your own head while you were relating it, for after telling me that *no* opinion can be formed without seeing the treaty, you *ask* for mine. Now, as not only the treaty, but all that has brought matters to this strange state, would be necessary to enable me to judge, I can only stare and be silent, the matter being decided.[34]

In the end only three of the thirteen cabinet members (Harrowby, Mulgrave and Westmorland) withheld their support and the treaty was approved by the Prince Regent. As the principle, though not the details, became known at Vienna, Castlereagh's gamble succeeded without the government having to try to explain to parliament why it was again preparing for war.

After solving this major impasse, the Foreign Secretary was eager to press on with the remaining reconstruction of Europe. 'I do not think Lord Castlereagh means to go home if he can possibly help it,' Apsley correctly told his father. 'I do not think he at all likes the idea of giving up the business to another to sign, after he has worked through so much of it.'[35] But Liverpool was far more concerned about the clamour for economy in the Commons when parliament met on 9 February, 1815, and insisted that the Leader return for the main financial debates in March. To replace him Wellington was sent from Paris, the only person outside the cabinet who could be trusted with the power and discretion to settle the affairs of Europe and the only one apart from Castlereagh with the prestige and authority to deal with heads of state and such astute diplomats as Metternich and Talleyrand.[36]

When the messenger reached Vienna at the end of January with the Foreign Secretary's recall and announcement of the Duke's approach Apsley told his father that Castlereagh took the news very quietly, but Apsley commented that it was 'a bad example to shew an opposition that they can so bully you as to force home the man whom they allow to be the fittest negotiator'.[37]

*   *   *

88

Castlereagh had scarcely settled in London before the astounding news arrived of Napoleon's escape from Elba and landing in the south of France on 1 March. Fortunately Wellington was at Vienna, immersed in negotiations that showed no sign of an early end, rather than across the Atlantic or even at Paris. The various rulers and representatives quickly sunk their differences, proclaimed Napoleon an outlaw, announced their resolve to oppose him and asked the Duke to command one of the three armies, that on the lower Rhine, along with the combined force of occupation in Belgium. Blinded by his adamant royalism, Wellington confidently pronounced that Napoleon had acted 'upon false or no information' about the opposition to Louis XVIII and confidently expected that the King would 'destroy him without difficulty, and in a short time'. Even if Napoleon managed to establish a significant base in France, 'such a force will be assembled by the Powers of Europe, directed by such a spirit in their councils, as must get the better of him'.[38]

But Napoleon's desperate gamble soon became a triumphant progress as he gathered troops and support on his march to Paris. From Brussels, the joint capital of the United Netherlands, the hereditary Prince of Orange told Bathurst in panic the day after Wellington wrote his letter that Napoleon had reached Lyons. Pleading for British supplies and heavy artillery to put the frontier fortresses in a state of defence, he also urged a rapid advance by British, Prussian and Dutch troops to stop Napoleon and save Louis XVIII. Bathurst, like Wellington, was not yet convinced that the situation was desperate, but, more justifiably sceptical of the Prince's military skill, he instructed him to co-ordinate defensive measures with the Prussian commander on the Rhine but not to invade France or take the offensive without further orders.[39] The British government, even before it knew that the command had already been offered at Vienna, also appointed Wellington to supersede the Prince as commander of the combined force in Flanders.[40] This saved the Prince's vanity and his standing in his own country, since, as he told Bathurst, he was happy to serve under the Duke again but would have found it mortifying to submit to anyone else. This graceful acceptance prevented future embarrassment after Bathurst privately told Wellington that whatever instructions the Prince had, 'they are not to regulate your Conduct, as you are left with full power to act in whatever way it shall appear to you most fit'.[41]

Despite the prompt step of entrusting everything to the Duke a couple of weeks after Napoleon's return Bathurst was still not convinced that war was inevitable. He told Sir George Murray in Canada that, although fighting could not be avoided if the great opportunist managed to get back into power, 'If this enterprise of Bonaparte's fails, we shall have a better Prospect of a general Peace than we have hitherto had.'[42] Unfortunately for these high hopes, on that very day, 20 March, Napoleon entered Paris. Louis XVIII had ignominiously fled the night before. He was persuaded to halt his retreat and establish his court at Ghent, but within a few weeks was demanding that a vessel be held at Falmouth to take him to England if Belgium were attacked.[43]

Before Wellington left Vienna to take up his command he agreed to the renewal of the Treaty of Chaumont, extending it beyond the original Britain, Russia, Austria and Prussia to include France, the Netherlands, Spain, Portugal, Denmark and several smaller German states, and again committed the British government to providing £5,000,000 for the three major allies and £2,500,000 on behalf of his own country to hire 100,000 soldier from the smaller states. Fortunately the subsidies were in the form of credits and paper transactions since the turmoil had once more driven specie out of circulation. But again the efficient Commissary in Chief, J.C. Herries, had immediately sent orders to buy coin at Paris until the market closed. He also had a die made for French louis and, after the French King had given his approval on 1 June, the British Mint struck close to £700,000 worth of them.[44]

When the Duke finally arrived in Brussels on 5 April, two weeks after Napoleon had taken control of Paris, he instantly saw that providing subsidies was the least of the British problems. The Prince of Orange's shortcomings were painfully obvious; the fortifications on the French frontier had not been strengthened; there were only about 24,000 troops, including a mere 4000 British, mostly recruits, and 7000 Belgians, who were of dubious loyalty since most of them had served under Napoleon. Despite his exhortations from Vienna and Bathurst's assurances that everything was being done for the Low Countries, there was no evidence of military reinforcements. In blistering tones he told the War Secretary the next day: 'It appears to me that you have not taken in England a clear view of the situation, that you do not think war certain, and that a greater effort must be made, if it is hoped that it shall be short.' He berated the cabinet for not calling out the local militia to release regular troops for service abroad and charged: 'How we are to make out 150,000 men, or even the 60,000 of the defensive part of the treaty of Chaumont, appears not to have been considered.' But finding himself in the familiar situation of having to make the best of limited resources, evidently only grudgingly provided by an uncomprehending government, he grimly professed that he would be satisfied with a mere 40,000 British and German Legion infantry, 18,000 cavalry of the same, 150 pieces of field artillery fully horsed and a long list of ammunition, pontoons and supplies, and would then 'take my chances for the rest, and engage that we would play our part in the game. But as it is, we are in a bad way.'[45]

The tone of this outburst was familiar enough to Bathurst and Wellington offset some of his asperity the next day by saying that he would be delighted to have Apsley on his staff. He also appointed Seymour Bathurst, already stationed with the Guards in Belgium, as an aide-de-camp while continuing to serve with his regiment.[46] From Vienna, Apsley told his father that he had been afraid to ask for an appointment 'as he had abused the Head Quarter Idlers; but I have written to the Duke to thank him extremely & to tell him I shall set off in a day or two'.[47] Another relation whose hopes of employment soared was the Duke of Richmond who had lately moved his family to Brussels, a traditional refuge of the impoverished. Wellington assured Richmond that he would be glad to have him, and Richmond optimistically wrote to Bathurst about 'the only military employment I see a chance of in my life'. But recognizing the practical difficulties of his rank, he added: 'Being refused it I need not tell [you] would make no difference in my political opinions.' Once again he was denied the chance to serve, since, if Wellington were killed, he would become commander by seniority, which even he had to admit was beyond him.[48]

Perhaps anticipating the Duke's reaction to the situation when he arrived in Belgium, the cabinet had already despatched a delegation to discuss the requirements with him. This consisted of Lord Harrowby, Lord President of the Council; William Wellesley-Pole, detached from Lord Wellesley the previous September and given the unusual distinction of a seat in the cabinet as Master of the Mint; and Sir Henry Torrens, the Commander-in-Chief's military secretary. They arrived at Brussels two days after the Duke and reported that he was in a remarkably receptive and optimistic mood, having perhaps sufficiently relieved his feelings and apprehensions in his letter to Bathurst. He was perfectly easy in discussing the long list of diplomatic and military questions the Prime Minister had sent and confident that he could raise the necessary troops with the subsidy and lead a successful invasion of France.[49]

Wellington continued to radiate calm assurance which was a vital part of the great trust he inspired whenever he was in the company of his officers or the aristocratic admirers and lovers who transformed Brussels into the most fashionable of cities as they flocked to be with their relatives in the army and bask in the glory of the great Duke. But in his letters to Bathurst and others he did not conceal the anxiety he had plenty of reason to feel. A month after the cabinet delegation's visit he bitterly told the Foreign Secretary's brother:

> I have got an infamous army, very weak and ill equipped, and a very inexperienced Staff. In my opinion they are doing nothing in England. They have not raised a man; they have not called out the militia either in England or Ireland; are unable to send me any thing; and they have not sent a message to Parliament about the money. The war spirit is therefore evaporating as I am informed.[50]

He was not, in fact, well informed, but he certainly had his work cut out for him in welding together the ill-assorted troops, some inexperienced, others unwilling, into an effective fighting force. He achieved it by mixing dubious units with reliable ones, and perhaps only he could have done it so well. But the main problem was still the absolute shortage of troops which it was not easy to supply.

In retrospect Colonel Bunbury had been perfectly right to warn Bathurst at the time of the ill-fated New Orleans expedition that a large effective army should be kept in Europe until peace on the continent was definitely assured, but the demand for economy in parliament and the country at the end of the war was overwhelming. Apart from that part of the Peninsular infantry which had been dispersed to North America and various other colonies around the world, many soldiers had been discharged by the beginning of 1815 and Bathurst had to tell Wellington that renewed recruiting had not produced any great response.[51] Troops fit for service returning from New Orleans and Halifax were shipped directly to Belgium, while the unfit went to Ireland to replace more efficient regiments already sent to the continent.[52] But it took time for the overseas troops to arrive and not all reached Europe before the decisive confrontation.

Wellington's seemingly sensible demand that regular home troops be replaced by militia also presented real difficulties. As Bathurst explained, the crown had no legal right to call out the militia except in cases of war or insurrection. Since the declaration of the allies was against Napoleon personally rather than France, whose King was a party to the agreement which provided an international force for his defence against usurpation, there existed no formal state of war.[53] The difficulty was eventually overcome, only very late in the day as it turned out, by acts of parliament embodying the militia on the grounds of prospective war with France.

There were similar difficulties with the Ordnance, despite Lord Mulgrave's assurances to Bathurst that he would do his utmost to supply artillery and would suspend all home fortifications to provide sappers and miners for the Belgian fortresses.[54] Seasoned horses and drivers were particularly difficult to find. And at the end of April the Duke was sharply complaining to Bathurst that apparently only 42 of the 150 pieces of field artillery he required would be forthcoming while the Prussian army had hundreds, which they did not take into the field, 'for show or amusement'.[55] So long as hostilities did not begin until July or August there was a good chance that most of these deficiencies could be overcome from the rapidly depleted British resources, but no one could be sure how much time there was.

It was a great disappointment for Wellington not to have the Portuguese fighting cocks under Marshal Beresford with the latter as his second-in-command. After lengthy negotiations the regency at Lisbon finally informed the British government, on the very eve of Waterloo, that it could not send troops on foreign service without express orders from the capital at Rio de Janeiro.[56] They might, in any event, not have lived up to the Duke's expectations. In the middle of May Bathurst had forwarded to him an account from a British general at Lisbon saying that the Portuguese soldiers had been so badly paid and underfed since the peace that it would take two months' good feeding to restore their strength. The best troops – volunteers who had been discharged at the end of the war – would probably not return, and, while junior officers would serve under Wellington in Belgium, the senior ones would not, 'partly as having got into the habits of indolence and ease', and partly from a conviction that the Low Country must by its very name be conducive to ague, 'and that they will all suffer by going there. From this impression they have taken of Flanders, nothing will divert them.'[57]

Wellington also complained to Bathurst about the officers that were sent by the Commander-in-Chief: 'I might have expected that the Generals and Staff formed by me in the last war would have been allowed to come to me again: but instead of that, I am overloaded with people I have never seen before; and it appears to be purposely intended to keep those out of my way whom I wished to have.' In fact most of the officers had served in the Peninsula, but the Duke did have some particular grievances. Sir George Murray was still in Canada and, although summoned back by Bathurst at the end of March, did not even receive the letter until the end of May.[58] Wellington also wanted Lord Combermere (formerly Sir Stapleton Cotton) to command the cavalry as he had in the Peninsula, but the Regent insisted on Lord Uxbridge who became second in command by seniority. This was a matter of some personal awkwardness since Uxbridge had eloped with Henry Wellesley's wife five years before, and he was at pains to assure the

Duke that he had not sought the appointment. But, despite regretting that he was deprived of his 'old friends and assistants', Wellington ended his litany of grievances with the grim assurance to Bathurst: 'I'll do the best I can with the instruments which have been sent to me.'[59]

In the midst of these military preparations the government also faced considerable condemnation for waging an unjust and immoral war against a manifestly popular ruler of France in order to reimpose a monarch who had not even had the courage to stay and face the challenge. On 7 April the Radical Sir Francis Burdett told the Commons that no one could foresee the end of this new war, while his colleague Samuel Whitbread went even further by saying that Wellington and the other British diplomats who had signed the treaty against Napoleon at Vienna should be impeached. Earl Grey, Whitbread's brother-in-law, offered similar criticism in more measured terms in the Lords on 23 May. But by insisting that it was not seeking to impose any particular government on France but simply opposing an adventurer who was aiming again at the domination of Europe, the ministry was able to defeat the motions brought forward before the fighting began.

A far greater threat came from Lord Wellesley, who saw an opportunity to destroy the government and become the peacemaker of Europe. On 12 April he criticized the ministers in the Lords for not making better arrangements to confine Napoleon and their negligence in allowing him to escape. But as he observed the contrast between British and Napoleon's preparations he became increasingly pro-Napoleon, perceiving a chance to unite the opponents of war and some of the ministry's lukewarm supporters in coming to terms with Napoleon, whether he remained within the borders of France or tried again to divide his opponents and embark on expansion. Wellington's great military reputation may have hung in the balance in the coming confrontation, but so too did the existence of the government, as well as the fate of the country for the foreseeable future.

Weeks before Wellington or anyone else expected, Napoleon left Paris with his army and crossed into Belgium during the night of 14/15 June. The Duke learned of this at about 3 pm and, after directing his army towards Quatre Bras, went to a grand ball given by the Duchess of Richmond in the workshop of the carriage maker's house which the family was renting. Apart from the Richmonds, the other Bathurst relations at this famous event were the retired Admiral Sir George Berkeley and his wife, Lord Apsley and Seymour Bathurst. Always calmest in a storm, Wellington's assurance never wavered as despatches kept arriving and he directed various officers to join their troops. At some point he asked Richmond for a map of the country and, putting his finger on Waterloo, said that the battle would be fought there.[60] After supper, about 3 am, he went home to sleep for a couple of hours and then rode out to join the army at Quatre Bras, the crucial crossroads just beyond Waterloo.

Later that day (16 June), the seventeen-year-old Lady Georgina Lennox wrote to her cousin Lady Georgina Bathurst: 'The Army is alas! ordered to march . . .. We had a great ball last night, and fancy the horror of hearing this news in the middle of it, and seeing all one's friends fly to the right and the left.' The garrison at Brussels had been under arms all night 'and I hear so many drums and such a noise that I think they must be marching. I am afraid we are just near enough to hear the cannonading which I think will just kill us with anxiety'.[61]

That day Napoleon defeated the Prussians at Ligny, forcing them to retreat, while Marshal Ney engaged the Anglo-Dutch army (including Hanoverians and other Germans) under Wellington in the inconclusive battle of Quatre Bras. The following day Lady Georgina, perhaps forgetting that Lennox was a Scottish name, assured her cousin: 'The Scotch were chiefly engaged, so there are no officers wounded one knows.' Believing that Wellington had won a great victory and was pursuing the French, she optimistically wrote: 'The Prussians are come up, so if Bony is not soon annihilated I shall be surprised.' She also took heart from the fact that 'The Duke's baggage is still here, so I suppose he will not go far today. I hope you will not be in a fuss, we will let you know by every opportunity'.[62]

Wellington did not fight on the 17th, as Richmond told Bathurst on the 18th, since the Duke had been too busy to write a despatch during the last few days, because Blücher could not collect his forces after the encounter on the 16th. Instead Wellington withdrew to Waterloo, which Richmond described to Bathurst as

a strong position about eight miles hence. When the Prussians have joined him and if they will stand he is perfectly safe. Buonaparte did not venture to prevent his retreat and has not yet attacked. I doubt his doing so. His loss has been severe, as well as that of the Allies.

Richmond added that he was just going to look at the position and would write on his return if there was any news. Many of the English colony had already fled to Holland or England, but, although his own family was ready to start, Richmond did not think it would be necessary.[63] Napoleon's many sympathizers in Brussels thought otherwise and one of them was even preparing a victory dinner for the hero to celebrate the beginning of a new liberation of Europe.

Accompanied by his fifteen year old son William, who had been prevented by a riding accident from joining his brother Lord March in the army, Richmond reached Waterloo in mid-afternoon on that famous Sunday, the 18th, to discover the battle well under way. He had after all contrived to be at the great confrontation, if only as a civilian spectator. After watching the action for some time and having a chat with Wellington, Richmond and his son rode back to Brussels with their news.

The battle, which began about 11 am when the ground had dried some-what after heavy rain in the night, raged back and forth until mid-afternoon when the Prussians, who had already fought the French earlier in the day at Wavre twenty-five miles to the east, arrived to turn the balance. By 8 pm, while still light, it being practically the longest day of the year, the French were retreating. An hour later Wellington waved his hat to order a general advance while Napoleon was in full flight to Paris.

The exhausted Duke, who had managed only a few snatches of sleep in four days, had dinner and lay down for a few hours. But by 3 am he was up again receiving reports of the dead and wounded while one of his aides, Colonel Alexander Gordon, lay dying in the adjoining room of the inn. Tears streaming down his face, Wellington was finally able to begin his report to Bathurst of events since the 15th. In his fatigue and haste to get the good news to London, many individuals and units were omitted from special mention in the despatch, which long remained a source of grievance. Later in the morning he rode back into Brussels to complete the despatch, still dated from Waterloo where he began it, write some other letters and arrange matters before joining his army and the Prussians in pursuit of the French. He told the Whig MP Thomas Creevey, who was among those who had stayed despite the danger, that the battle had been 'a damned nice thing – the nearest run thing you ever saw in your life. . . . By God! I don't think it would have done if I had not been there'. He also saw the Richmonds and assured them that there would be no more fighting.[64] When the Waterloo despatch had been copied in a fair hand, he gave it and three stan-dards with gold Napoleonic eagles for the Prince Regent to one of his aides, Major Henry Percy, grandson of the Duke of Northumberland, who had been hit in the foot by a ball at Waterloo, to take to London.

The government in London meanwhile was in a state of anxiety and gloom. The tremendous cannonade of Ligny on the 16th could be heard at Dover, but when no news arrived from Wellington it was generally assumed that he had been defeated. Those who fled Brussels on the morning of the

18th encouraged this assumption when they reached England. But Bathurst told his Colonial Under-Secretary: 'The Duke has long since fixed upon the position at Waterloo as that on which he meant to fight & I will not believe that in a position taken by himself he can be otherwise than victorious.'[65] A confused Dutch report of a British victory was received by the government on the morning of the 21st through Nathan Rothschild, but there was still no news from Wellington when the cabinet met for dinner that night at Lord Harrowby's house in Grosvenor Square. Even if some of the letters from the Richmond family had arrived by this time, they would not have provided Bathurst with evidence of Wellington's ultimate success.

About 10 pm Major Percy arrived in Downing Street with the French standards sticking out of his carriage seeking directions to Bathurst from his office. Charles Arbuthnot, who lived in one of the government houses in the street, thought the uproar was another demonstration against the corn laws, but when he learned the happy cause he jumped into the carriage and accompanied Percy to Grosvenor Square.

Bathurst and the other ministers eagerly scanned the long narrative of the battles and plied Percy with questions before allowing him to take the despatch and the eagles to the Prince Regent who, along with Castlereagh, was at a ball in St James's Square. The Prince immediately promoted Percy to colonel, after which, still wearing the clothes he had at the Duchess of Richmond's ball six days and half a lifetime ago, he was able to go to his father's house where a surgeon removed the bullet from his foot.[66] Two days later he was on the road again, bearing the official thanks of the Prince Regent and a personal letter from Bathurst congratulating Wellington 'most heartily on a victory which is not only splendid beyond comparison, but is most fortunately timed, and will, I trust, hasten the conclusion of our contest'.[67]

As the tone of Bathurst's letter indicates, no one in Britain could be sure that Waterloo marked the end for Napoleon. But it was certainly a stunning blow. On 23 June votes of thanks for the battle were easily carried in both Houses of Parliament. Lord Wellesley, his latest hope of becoming Prime Minister shattered by his brother's 'transcendent increase in glory', plausibly told Bathurst that, having been out of town, he was not aware that the matter was to be discussed in the Lords, though Bathurst had given notice the day before. 'I should otherwise have attended, and probably expressed my sentiments,' he wrote, tepidly adding, 'I sincerely hope that this victory will accelerate the conclusion of the war, and I shall be most anxious to observe its consequences in that view.'[68]

As gratifying to Bathurst and his wife as the outcome of this momentous battle was the news that their two sons were safe. They were particularly relieved to hear about Seymour, who had been in the final charge against Napoleon's Imperial Guard. The next day Apsley wrote to his father from Brussels, enclosing a brief but reassuring note from his brother to their mother. Apsley told his father: 'The victory was entirely won by the Duke's own personal courage and conduct. He stood in the squares as the French cavalry charged them, and led them on when the cavalry retreated.' But he also added, noting in pencil 'do not mention this', 'Some of our German and *also English* cavalry gave way.' Wellington had forgotten to mention in his despatch that 'the French not only left all their cannon, baggage, etc, but that they threw away their arms and knapsacks. Such a sight as the field of battle was never seen'. But on the other side: 'You will all be horrified at our loss, which I fear it will be some time before we can exactly ascertain.' He did mention some of the more prominent dead and wounded, including his future brother-in-law, Colonel Frederick Ponsonby, who was 'very badly wounded', and Lord Uxbridge, whose leg had been amputated after being crushed by a cannon ball which flew over the neck of Wellington's horse. Despite his suffering, Uxbridge was in 'ecstasies about the Duke, says there never was such a man, indeed the whole army give him the whole credit'.[69]

Three days later Lady Georgina Lennox sent her cousin more news of the invalids at Brussels, saying: 'I long to nurse even the poor privates. We have several people we know well wounded here, all slightly, it is such a pleasure to be useful to them now, poor creatures.' The Duke's military secretary, Lord Fitzroy Somerset, whose arm had been amputated after being struck by a bullet, was very low and 'says all his prospects in life are blighted'. His wife of less than a year, the daughter of Wellesley-Pole, had been 'nearly distracted with anxiety during the action – she went to Antwerp but she is now with him here'. To console Lady Georgina in her own grieving, Wellington had given her a miniature of himself, 'extremely like, I am so pleased with it'.[70]

On the same day, 22 June, Seymour Bathurst, now with the army on French territory, told his father: 'We do not as you may suppose think *small beer* of ourselves since we licked the Imperial Guard. I beg you will mention in the house [of Lords] that it was the *1st Regiment*.' (Bathurst did not mention any particular units except the Prussians in a general way.) He also assured his father that the wounded were doing well. Uxbridge was particularly cheerful, saying, 'It is but fair that he should no longer cut the young men out as a handsome well-made fellow which he has done for many years.'[71]

As the allies advanced across France, Napoleon tried to save something of his gamble by abdicating in favour of his son, with a regency of five people named by himself, but this was rejected by the Chamber of Deputies and the Senate. As Wellington told Bathurst three days later, this was not the security that the allies had in mind when they combined against Napoleon. The Duke announced that he intended to go on fighting and thought it impossible for Napoleon to collect an effective force.[72] The next day, before receiving this letter, Bathurst instructed him to do the same, adding that the cabinet had that morning decided to send Castlereagh to allied headquarters to discuss the expected peace proposals from the provisional French government under Joseph Fouché.[73]

At the same time as this letter Wellington wrote an angrier one to Bathurst complaining that he had not one quarter of the ammunition he needed, owing to a shortage of drivers and carts. Despite what he had said on the morrow of Waterloo, he now insisted that, apart from the Spanish soldiers, he had the worst troops, the worst equipped army and the worst staff ever brought together and his only hope was a speedy end to the campaign.[74] The exhilaration of victory had given way to exhaustion which found outlet in a familiar tirade to a familiar recipient. Lord Apsley, less accustomed than his father to the Duke's temper, wrote to take the edge off it when he discovered that it had not been exhausted in expostulation against himself. He explained that, having lost both his Adjutant and Quartermaster General as well as his secretary, Wellington had been forced to take on himself the whole business of the army for the past week. And it did not help that he was having to fend off Blücher's demand to be allowed to execute Napoleon.[75] But even as Wellington was listing his shortages reinforcements were on the way, including further Peninsular veterans from North America sent directly to Ostend, and Bathurst assured him that Combermere was being sent to replace Uxbridge as commander of the cavalry.[76]

In the event the troops being rushed to the continent turned out not to be needed for fighting. Although Seymour Bathurst told his mother from just outside Paris on 2 July that no one knew for certain if Napoleon even commanded the army and everyone was waiting to hear the outcome of Wellington's negotiations that day with the French peace commissioners,[77] Napoleon had left for the west of France three days before in the expectation that the provisional government would secure him a passport through the Royal Navy to the United States. But the French commissioners informed the Duke, who immediately relayed the information to Bathurst. Wellington also reported that he had informed the commissioners that any ruler other than Louis XVIII was a usurper and that he would not cease his

99

military operations until the rightful King was restored, ideally without conditions.[78]

With the Duke and his advance guard dictating terms for the whole alliance, the gates of Paris were thrown open to British and Prussian troops on 7 July. The next day the King sloped in behind them. Seymour Bathurst told his mother that 'the enthusiasm of the people for the King within these few days is beyond description. One could almost suppose them to be sincere if we had not seen them petting white cockades a week ago. Brutes how I do hate them!!' He added that Blücher wanted to destroy all the monuments to French victories and had attempted to blow up the Jena Bridge, commemorating the defeat of Prussia in 1806, from which he was prevented only by Wellington.[79]

Encouraging Napoleon to go to Rochefort and then betraying him to Wellington was probably a humane trap by Fouché to save him from Louis XVIII or more vindictive allies than the British. Captain Frederick Maitland was sent to blockade the harbour and on 16 July Napoleon voluntarily surrendered, appealing to the Regent for asylum in Britain. On the 24th Maitland's ship arrived at Torbay. 'I cannot conceive the state you must all be in with Bonaparte in England,' Seymour Bathurst wrote to his mother on the 22nd: 'What are you going to do with him &c. Pray go & see him & be civil to him. I am all for his being treated well.' He said that the French believed that if 'Cochon' (Pig) or 'le Préfet du Prince D'Angleterre', as Louis XVIII was variously called, did not behave well towards the British, they would turn Napoleon loose again.[80]

The British ministers had no intention of using Napoleon for diplomatic advantage, but neither would they let him live in their country, the United States or anywhere else where he might threaten the peace of the world. The day before he surrendered Liverpool told Castlereagh at Paris that if the King of France did not feel strong enough to bring Napoleon to justice as a rebel, Britain would undertake his custody on behalf of the allies, but, in that case, 'it is but just that we should have the choice of the place of confinement, and a complete discretion as to the means necessary to render that confinement effectual'.[81] By 21 July, when Napoleon was sailing to Torbay, the cabinet had practically decided on the East India Company's tiny way station of St Helena in the South Atlantic (no longer vital with the Cape of Good Hope in British hands), the island furthest from any mainland in the whole world.[82]

Three days later Bathurst relayed the decision to Wellington, telling him (perhaps not knowing that the Duke had spent some weeks there on the way back from India in 1805) that the climate of St Helena was unobjectionable, 'and its situation will enable us to keep him from all intercourse with the world without requiring that severity of restraint which it would be otherwise necessary to inflict upon him'. With neutral ships banned from the island and little communication with the rest of the world, Bathurst hoped that Napoleon's very existence would soon be forgotten. He added that it was intended to appoint as the new governor and effectively Napoleon's jailer Major General Sir Hudson Lowe, then still fighting Bonapartist diehards in the south of France. Lowe, who had brought the news of Napoleon's first abdication to London, probably owed this honour to his friendship with Colonel Bunbury, with whom he had served in the Mediterranean between 1805 and 1809. Bathurst confidently pronounced in words he was soon to regret: 'I do not believe we could have found a fitter person of his rank in the army willing to accept a situation of so much confinement, responsibility, and exclusion from society.'[83] But even Wellington, under whom Lowe had served briefly as Quartermaster General in Brussels before being sent into the field by the authorities in England, saw no reason to object.

After a couple of days at Torbay Napoleon was ordered to Plymouth to be told his fate and transferred to a faster warship, the *Northumberland*, for the 5000-mile voyage to St Helena. Maitland was instructed to break the news informally on 30 July, and the next day Napoleon was officially told of the decision in the form of a letter from the First Lord of the Admiralty to Admiral Lord Keith, commander of the Channel fleet, personally conveyed by Colonel Bunbury. Goulburn was greatly disappointed at not being chosen by Bathurst,[84] but, apart from the fact that this was a matter which properly fell under the War, not the Colonial Department, Goulburn's rigid nature, recently exhibited at Ghent, would have done nothing to help reconcile Napoleon to his fate. On this memorable assignment Bunbury took along the minister's son, William Lennox Bathurst, the twenty-four-year-old MP for the snug burgage borough of Weobley.

Just before noon on Monday the 31st, Bunbury and Keith went aboard Maitland's ship, the *Bellerophon*. William Bathurst was not allowed on board and saw only the back of Napoleon's head as they talked inside his cabin. Keith handed Napoleon a copy of Lord Melville's short letter stating that 'General Buonaparte' was to be taken to St Helena by Admiral Sir George Cockburn, along with three officers he might select from those with him and twelve servants. At Napoleon's request Bunbury orally translated the letter into French. For about half an hour Napoleon railed against the decision and insisted that he had been trapped, that he was not a prisoner of war but merely a passenger aboard a warship after negotiations with the

101

captain. He appealed to the British people and laws, demanding the right to become a British citizen, if necessary after a period of supervised residence, insisted that he should be styled Emperor or at very least First Consul, and claimed that he would not last three months on St Helena: 'If your Government wishes to put me to death, they may kill me here. It is not worth while to send me to St Helena. I prefer death to St Helena.'

When Napoleon paused in this outpouring for a reply, Bunbury pointed out that he was 'little more than bearer of the despatches to Lord Keith; that I was not authorized to enter into discussions; and that I could only undertake to hear General Buonaparte's representations and to communicate them to the king's ministers'. But he added that he was convinced that the cabinet had decided on St Helena because 'its local situation admitted of his enjoying a greater degree of liberty and personal indulgence than could be allowed in any part of Great Britain'. A few minutes after Bunbury and Keith left, Napoleon recalled the Admiral in a brief but futile attempt to soften the decision.

In the notes that Bunbury made on Napoleon's appearance, he recorded that there was 'something particularly agreeable in [his expression]. Yet, in the course of his long talking I observed changes both in his tone and look, which made me suspect that there was a good deal of the fox as well as of the lion in the composition of the great conqueror.' In a brief informal letter to Bathurst, after putting a rough draft of his memorandum on the conference in the post to London, Bunbury confessed himself at a loss to determine Napoleon's true intentions: 'Whether he only means to render it necessary to send him to his island-prison *by force* or if he means to put himself to death. At least he intends, I think, that we should draw the latter deduction.' He added that he would stay at Plymouth until the middle of the next day in case Napoleon wanted to see him again,[85] but Napoleon did not.

William Bathurst complained to his father about not being allowed to approach Napoleon:

There are no people of any *consequence* here who seem anxious to see him, and not many boats near the ship, so that I think if I had been on board nobody would [have] taken any notice of the matter but the orders are so infernally strict that there is no room for disagreement.

Since Napoleon usually walked on deck about 5 pm, however, he hoped to see him then: 'The boats gave Buonaparte three cheers yesterday, as he was very obliging in showing himself and pulled off his hat when he retired. Perhaps that circumstance may induce him to do the same thing to-day, though of course he was not well pleased with the conference.'[86]

On the authority of a convention quickly concluded at Paris on 2 August by the five powers, Britain was formally entrusted with the custody of Napoleon, including the right to choose the place and manner of his confinement, to say nothing of the responsibility and considerable cost. But this clear, simple arrangement caused the Lord Chancellor great anxiety when asked to affix the Great Seal to what he regarded as irregular third-party treaties, on which parliament could not be consulted since it was not sitting. In the end Eldon told Bathurst:

> it may be a simple way of considering the case to say, you made war against *Buonaparte only*: you have conquered *him*, and made him a *prisoner of war*: as he is such, and was the only person against whom you made war, you have no occasion to make *with him* any treaty of peace. You have your only enemy in your power, and you may, without more, keep him in it all his life long. But this is better for Parliament too.

As far as the last was concerned, Eldon took great comfort that bills of in-demnity securing ministers against legal action 'may save our necks: but when a question of justice arises, which the Law of Nations must determine, bills of indemnity must be considered as very good things, but not settling all points.'[87]

That these were not simply pettifogging objections was revealed when the House of Lords discussed the bill for detaining Bonaparte on 8 and 9 April, 1816. Lord Holland raised many of the same legal points that Eldon had expressed and recorded a formal protest in the journal of the House that it was unworthy of the magnanimity of Britain to confine Napoleon to distant exile, both he and Lord Lauderdale insisting that he should have been allowed to live in England under custody. But the Chancellor, observed smiling at Holland's arguments, did not allow his earlier hesitations to prevent him from supporting Bathurst and Harrowby's case for St Helena. Bathurst told the Lords, what was practically impossible to deny, that handing Napoleon to Britain ensured that he would be treated far more leniently than by any other party to the arrangement.

It was no surprise that the modern Prometheus did not adjust to life on the tiny, remote, humid and windy St Helena, denuded by generations of passing Europeans and more recent settlers. He was full of resentment, complaints and self-pity and did his best to remain before public attention in Britain and on the continent. The arrival of Lowe in April, 1816, simply played into his hands. Despite his extensive military service in the

Mediterranean, with the Russian and Prussian armies, and his command of French, Italian and Portuguese, the new governor lacked the tact, confidence and detachment needed for this particularly provoking post and prisoner. He was conscientious to a fault, insecure, abrupt and overly fearful his prisoner would escape, even though the island was stiff with 3000 soldiers and its waters patrolled by a squadron of frigates. It would have been difficult to contrive a better foil for Napoleon. But their stormy relationship from the beginning was made even worse by Bathurst's first letters reducing Napoleon's annual expenses from £12,000 to £8,000 and ordering away four of his attendants to help the reduction.[88] Even at a time of obsession with government austerity, this mean-spirited saving caused far more trouble than it was worth. Lowe and Napoleon met for the last time on 18 August, 1816; for the last five years of his life Napoleon refused to see the governor.

Napoleon's version of events soon reached Europe and on 18 March, 1817, Lord Holland again attacked Bathurst in the Lords for confining the fallen hero too closely, not permitting him the reading material he requested, interfering with his correspondence and not allowing him sufficient to live on in that expensive island where almost everything had to be imported. Bathurst made light of all this and his tone was considered far too jocular by Napoleon's admirers. He insisted that the restrictions on Napoleon's movements and correspondence were no more than prudent, that Napoleon was allowed all the reading material he requested and could be obtained, except for newspapers which might be the means of communication with his accomplices in Europe, and said that he had already, on Lowe's recommendation, restored Napoleon's allowance to £12,000 (the same as Lowe's own).[89]

This was by no means the end of the matter and until Napoleon's death in 1821 Bathurst was besieged by long letters on small points from Lowe, who also had to endure double-dealing by his own staff, the tedium of the Russian, Austrian and French commissioners (Prussia declined to send one) and the kind of intrigues only to be expected in such a tight little island. Bathurst shared Lowe's fears that Napoleon might be rescued and generally supported him. But reading Lowe's interminable letters was a great weariness of the flesh and each time one arrived Bathurst must fervently have wished that he had sent someone else.

Many years later, with the benefit of hindsight, Wellington pronounced Lowe, 'a stupid man . . .. He was not an ill-natured man. But he knew nothing at all of the world, and like all men who know nothing of the world, he was suspicious and jealous.' The Duke claimed that he would have guarded the few landing places on the coast and allowed Napoleon to wander about the island as he pleased, so long as he showed himself to a British officer each morning and night, and would have allowed him to correspond as he wished without requiring his letters to be read by the governor.[90] But not every officer had Wellington's supreme confidence and no one made the absurd suggestion that Napoleon's conqueror go to St Helena as his jailer. Failing that, it might at least have been better for all parties if Colonel Bunbury had continued, as Under-Secretary, to deal with Lowe. But with the return of peace Bunbury went, as the War and Colonies Office was itself under seige .

5

THE IDLE SPEAR AND SHIELD UPHUNG, 1815–1820

The detention of the retired General Buonaparte, as the British insisted on styling and treating him, was far from being Bathurst's most important concern with the second coming of peace in 1815. Apart from the business of his own threatened department, he was also again in charge of the Foreign Office until November, while Castlereagh was in Paris negotiating the latest peace treaty with France. Bathurst's two sons, who were there, continued to provide him with interesting, supplementary informal news.

Two weeks after the allied entry to Paris Seymour Bathurst complained to his mother about the dullness of the city, hoping that social life would improve with the imminent arrival of Lady Castlereagh. In the meantime the troops passed the mornings in reviews. That very day the Emperors of Austria and Prussia at the head of their own armies had watched 3000 smartly attired Prussian guards march past to the tune 'the Downfall of Paris': 'Can you conceive any thing so humiliating to the French[?].' In a couple of days the Emperors were going to review the British army, which he feared would suffer by comparison with the Prussians; if only the Prince Regent were there, he lamented, to improve the British uniform.[1] Two months later Lord Apsley attended a more elaborate review near Châlons at which the Prussians manoeuvred 152,000 troops and 540 cannon in perfect order. Even Wellington, who had a keen understanding of the difference between parade ground smartness and performance on the battlefield, was impressed, 'saying that there never was anything so magnificent, but adding that in two hours his little fellows would be in [the] middle of them all'.[2]

Amid these military entertainments, the heads of state, their representatives and advisers at Paris negotiated a permanent peace settlement that would ensure that France could not again easily challenge the arrangements agreed on at Vienna. French acclaim for Napoleon's latest adventure made the continental powers harden their hearts further than in 1814 and in Britain Bathurst and Liverpool also wanted severe terms. Even when they were persuaded by Castlereagh and Wellington that lenient treatment offered the best hope for the Bourbon cause and a successful peace, they remained under pressure from parliamentarians and the press for a more exacting settlement. But this time, until the issue was resolved, the British government wisely decided to maintain a strong military presence in France. In the middle of July Bathurst told the Duke that he was sending him seven of the strongest regiments ordered back from Canada and offered three additional companies of artillery, though making it clear that in the clamour for retrenchment at home this army must be maintained at the expense of the French.[3]

After months of arduous bargaining a treaty was finally concluded on 20 November by which France generally lost all the territory acquired since 1790 (rather than 1792), including several strong fortresses. Seventeen other fortresses in the north-east of the country were to be garrisoned by an allied army under Wellington for up to five years at French expense to safeguard the monarchy and the new borders. This army of occupation was to consist of 30,000 troops each from Britain and the other three powers and the same collectively from five smaller states. The victorious Quadruple Alliance also agreed to Castlereagh's proposal for periodic congresses to discuss the maintenance of peace and most rulers, though not Britain's, undertook to be guided by the Christian principles of the Russian Emperor's Holy Alliance. With considerable relief the Prime Minister told Bathurst as the negotiations finally drew to a close: 'I am quite satisfied from all I hear that the treaty will satisfy the public in general, and that you will find it to be the opinion of most persons that the terms are as *severe upon France* as would in any way be consistent with maintaining Louis XVIII upon the throne.' He also assured Bathurst that he need not trouble to summon those members of the cabinet who were far from London in order to approve the treaty.[4] A week later Bathurst duly reported to the Prime Minister, who remained at Walmer Castle, that he and the other ministers in town - Sidmouth, Vansittart and Wellesley-Pole - had agreed to the terms, though remaining concerned about the possible costs of occupation to Britain.[5]

While the discussions were going on at Paris, Bathurst was involved in an only slightly less difficult diplomatic effort to persuade the Duke of Cumberland to leave England and spare the royal family further dissension over his wife. When in 1814 Cumberland had announced his intention of marrying his twice-married and once-divorced cousin Princess Frederica, both the Prince Regent and Queen Charlotte had sent their congratulations. But by the time of the wedding at the end of May, 1815, the Queen had learned from her German relations that her niece's second husband had died on the eve of their divorce and was also reminded that Frederica in her first widowhood had been engaged to Cumberland's brother, the Duke of Cambridge, until pregnancy caused her hastily to marry the father, the minor Rhineland Prince of Solms-Braunfels. The primly moralistic Queen then announced that she could not receive her new daughter-in-law, while the House of Commons at the beginning of July artfully combined righteousness with economy to deny Cumberland the allowance customary on marriage by one vote.

Although the Regent was friendly enough when the couple arrived in London at the end of August to be remarried in his residence according to the rites of the Church of England, he was clearly in an awkward position and his ministers made strenuous efforts to persuade the couple to leave as soon as possible. Since the Bathursts were particular friends, Cumberland asked Lady Bathurst to call on his ostracized wife. Bathurst carefully explained the circumstances to the Regent, and also sent along a letter urging Cumberland to spare his failing mother further distress by returning to the continent. If the Queen died, he warned, people would conclude that 'the calamity is to be attributed to your continuing in England, and mischievous persons will be able so to work on the public feelings as to expose her R.H. [the Duchess] most unmeritedly to personal insult & reproach'. Bathurst provided the convenient justification of joining the royal assembly in Paris as a reason for leaving. When the Queen died the couple could return with great public respect and those who now felt compelled to avoid their company would make them welcome. The Regent approved of this initiative and the Prime Minister offered money for the journey.[6] But the proud and choleric Cumberland was not so easily moved, even by Bathurst. When the Regent feared to give him an appointment in Hanover, he decided to remain in England, either to win over or defy his family and society. And there he stayed with no diminution of awkwardness for the next three years. His wife meanwhile was transformed from an object of scandal to a virtuous and wronged victim of a selfish royal family and voted a parliamentary grant in the event of her widowhood. Finally, in 1818, on the eve of Queen Charlotte's death as it turned out, Cumberland admitted defeat, leaving in great bitterness for Berlin where his wife's sister was Queen of Prussia. There he lived for ten years until the news that those who had betrayed him socially were undermining the Protestant constitution brought him storming back again.

This royal embarrassment was not, of course, in the league of Bathurst's concern about the army in the rage for economy. He, and Liverpool and Castlereagh in particular, remembered all too well the consequences of rapid demobilization in 1814 and were by no means convinced that peace in Europe was really secure. But in the face of parliamentary insistence on cutting the armed services to the lowest possible level they had no choice but to make reductions.[7] In the course of long discussions between his department and the Commander-in-Chief, Bathurst told Wellington in October that, once Ireland and the colonies were provided for, it might not be possible to supply more than 20–22,000 of the 30,000 troops of occupation specified in the treaty and he hoped that the balance could be hired cheaply from Hanover. The difficulty was the House of Commons, 'where our establishments are always canvassed, and where there is a foolish doctrine too prevalent, that we are not to consider ourselves a military country in time of peace'. For his own part, Bathurst assured the Duke that he would be happy to press for more if Wellington could get assurances from Castlereagh, the Leader of the House, 'who has to do with these gentlemen'.[8] The Duke replied in blistering terms: 'Now that we have toiled like slaves [in Paris] to make the arrangement which has been made, Government do not like it because some newspaper writer or some friend in Parliament dislikes it, and they will not carry it into execution'. Nor, he added, did he appreciate the Duke of York's plan to foist on him the more expensive cavalry rather than 'the best troops we have, probably the best in the world . . . the British infantry, particularly the old infantry that has served in Spain. This is what we ought to keep up; and what I wish above all others to retain.'[9]

After further painful exchanges with Wellington, the treaty obligations were finally met with British troops acceptable to him, and about 33,000 soldiers and officers were stationed in northern France and the adjacent United Netherlands. But by the spring of 1816 the opposition in parliament was charging that the army of occupation would still in some degree be a cost to the British Treasury and Bathurst warned the Duke to make sure that its expenses stayed within the sum provided by France. Wellington irritably replied that he had already cut the number of horses from 13,500 to 10,000 and would send home every person not absolutely necessary for the efficiency of his contingent, but could not resist pointing out that it was parliament that was to blame for the rapid growth of the civilian departments of the army: 'I think the evil can be traced to the desire of government to provide a more efficient control over the expenditure, and to force the holders of public money to account for it, as well as the necessity of raising the salaries of the clerks &c.' He nevertheless enclosed his proxy vote in the House of Lords in the ministers' favour.[10]

The army of occupation was, of course, only a small part of the general target attacked by foe and friend of the government. When the ministry in 1816 proposed a total army of 170,000 (from 300,000 in 1814) for the British Isles, the colonies and France, MPs fell on it like the wolf on a lamb in the fold. Although the administration managed to carry its proposed total, the hostility was such that on 5 April it announced further cuts. The naval estimates were also attacked, though less violently. And on 18 March the ministry's move to lower the rate of income tax was defeated and the tax abolished entirely by a majority of 37.

When Wellington pronounced in the summer that the state of France was such that the army of occupation might safely be decreased, the cabinet grasped at his statement and would not let him retract. In February, 1817, at the beginning of the parliamentary session, the Duke publicly announced that his army would be decreased by twenty percent, starting on 1 April,[11] two days after Castlereagh had assured the Commons that there would be great reductions in the army establishment (amounting in all to about 40,000), as well as in the navy. But even this did not entirely satisfy the criticism of the size of the armed services.

In this atmosphere of economy Bathurst's department was particularly vulnerable. There seemed on the face of it a strong case for abolishing the third Secretaryship of State now that the war was over and returning the colonies to the Home Office with an additional four clerks, as had been done at the end of the American revolution. This was the argument of George Tierney in the Commons on 3 April, 1816, when he was countered by Henry Goulburn pointing out that the colonies were too important to be entrusted to the part-time attention of a busy minister. Nothing abashed, a year later, on 29 April, 1817, Tierney tried again, this time merely moving for a committee to inquire into the abolition of the office, though there was no secret as to what he hoped its recommendation would be. Forearmed on this occasion, Goulburn cited the increase in colonial correspondence to prove the growth in business since the beginning of the war. He was power-

110

fully supported by William Wilberforce, generally a government adherent but an MP of great moral authority and independent views who wanted the Colonial Office to remain strong in order to force better conditions for slaves on their owners.

Goulburn's later claim that part of the problem was that most politicians simply did not understand the business of the Colonial Office was true enough,[12] but the government had to respond to the demand for reductions from MPs of all stripes. In the year between the two debates Bathurst's department, like most others, was substantially diminished as the government scrambled to demonstrate its commitment to economy by paring administration to the bone. When the post of Military Under-Secretary was abolished, Bathurst wanted to keep Bunbury and let Goulburn go, but Bunbury, who had wanted to leave in 1815 and had stayed only for the crisis of Napoleon's return, did not feel that he had sufficient knowledge of the colonies. He would also have had to become an MP and defend a government with whose domestic policies he now disagreed, believing that it should be conciliating the population in the difficult aftermath of war rather than using the army as a police force.[13]

In addition to Bunbury, three of the thirteen regular clerks, four of the six extra clerks, the précis writer and the Arabic interpreter (an otiose Russian emigré who could neither speak nor write Arabic) were also pruned,[14] reducing the total establishment from twenty-five to fifteen. Among those who survived was the well-connected Charles Greville, who continued in his professed light duties as Bathurst's private secretary.

Nor did the Bathurst family have any personal reason for complaint during this period of retrenchment. After his only brother, Apsley, died at the age of 47 in January, 1816, Bathurst drew the entire salary of the Clerk of the Crown. In the same month he appointed his second son, William, as his sufficient deputy as Teller of the Exchequer, the other sinecure that he had held for quarter of a century at a generous half of the total income. Goulburn told his wife that William Bathurst was unwise enough to complain that this required him to give up his seat in the Commons, observing enviously that the appointment gave him £1200 a year 'and leaves him at liberty to attend to the study of the Law to which he otherwise would never have attended at all for Parliament and the society in which it places a young man is quite incompatible with legal pursuits'.[15] William Bathurst was called to the bar in 1821 and four years later found a comfortable berth as a commissioner for victualling the navy until an even better appointment appeared at the end of the decade.

In June, 1817, Lord Bathurst was surprised and delighted to be told by

111

the Prince Regent that he would receive the Garter in succession to the dying Duke of Northumberland.[16] Lord Eldon rejoiced that 'the Knights of the Garter have got some True Blue among them'. And the Duke of Wellington, on the second anniversary of Waterloo, welcomed his political chief to the Order by saying: 'As no person has had more official communication with you than I have, so there is no person so convinced as I am, how well you deserve it'.[17] As usual the honour involved passing over the claims of others who were not slow to express their disappointment. Chief among them was the new Duke of Northumberland, who evidently felt that he had as good a claim to the Blue Ribbon as to the title and the estates. But the Regent told him that Bathurst deserved the Garter for 'his long and arduous political services, in his laborious Department, during the most severe and gloriously terminated contest,' while promising Northumberland the next vacancy but one.[18]

In July Bathurst formally became a Knight of the Garter. He received detailed instructions for the ceremony and a list of charges: £100 for the knighthood; £30 10s. for the badge, ribbon and clasp, to be returned on his death; £8 10s. for an engraved gilt plate over his stall in St George's Chapel, Windsor; and £12 for recording his pedigree, arms and military services in the books of the Order.[19] After returning from the induction he told his wife, 'All that has passed on this occasion is most gratifying to those who wish me well.' There had been knights aplenty in attendance, including the royal Dukes of York and Cumberland, his cabinet colleagues Liverpool, Castlereagh and Westmorland, and his old friend Lord Camden. And the Prince Regent directed the Chancellor of the Order, the Bishop of Salisbury, to allow Bathurst to wear the star as a civilian, though he did not intend to dispense with the rule in future.[20]

The edge was taken off his joy when Bathurst shortly afterwards received a further bill for £533.14.1 from the College of Heralds. When he asked for an itemized list, it was clear that the College was not included in the drive for economy. The Dean of Windsor, as registrar of the Order, was entitled to £37.13.4; the Chapel of St George, Windsor got £90.3.8; the Garter King of Arms £45 and a further £25 in lieu of installation; the herald painter's bill was £124; the Town Ringers of Windsor got £2.2.0; the Housekeeper of the Castle £10; the Chelsea Drums £1.1.0; the St George's Waits £1.1.0; the Women who strew flowers £1.1.0; the Marrowbones Cleaners £2.2.0; and £25 was allowed for contingencies, presumably in case anyone with a claim had been missed.[21]

Another, completely free but no less welcome, mark of esteem soon arrived when Wellington presented Bathurst with a lifesize portrait of himself at the Battle of Waterloo riding Copenhagen, his celebrated horse, wearing his blue cloak and pointing with his hat to signal the advance of the army at the end of the day. The painting by Sir Thomas Lawrence, the most fashionable and highly paid artist of the day, cost the Duke 200 guineas, expensive even by Lawrence's standards,[22] but the sheer size of the painting (152" by 103") was an indication of Wellington's high regard and gratitude to the civilian minister, however many hard letters he had written. It hangs still in the new entrance hall constructed at the time at Cirencester, and since Copenhagen (borrowed by Bathurst for a time after Lawrence had finished his work) was painted from life, the picture was used in the 1880s as the model for the equestrian statue of Wellington by Sir Edgar Boehm which now stands opposite Apsley House. A few months later Bathurst also received a gift of porcelain from the King of Prussia in appreciation of his services to the allies during the wars.[23]

In the midst of this happy life, Bathurst was present at the sad and momentous death of the heir to the throne in the autumn of 1817. As one of the official witnesses to the birth of the first child (in her third pregnancy) of Princess Charlotte, he was summoned to Claremont, the Princess's house at Esher, on 4 November, optimistically sending a note to his wife at 4.30 pm asking her not to delay dinner, though he expected to be back at Lime Grove, Putney, within three hours.[24] In fact the Princess's terrible labour extended for about forty-six hours, with Bathurst, the Archbishop of Canterbury, the Bishop of London, the Lord Chancellor, the Home Secretary and the Chancellor of the Exchequer in attendance for well over the last day. After sending periodical medical reports to the Prince Regent, Bathurst wrote at 9.30 pm on the 5th to say that the Princess had safely delivered a stillborn but well-formed male child and was herself doing well.[25] Five hours later, however, Dr Matthew Baillie, the royal physician, sent Bathurst a hasty note saying that at about half past midnight the Princess had been seized with 'great difficulty of breathing, restlessness and exhaustion. She is not yet better, and we cannot avoid being in very great alarm about her state.' Twenty minutes later Baillie sent a one-sentence message: 'It is with the deepest concern that we inform your Lordship that Princess Charlotte has this moment expired.'[26]

Just before 7 am Bathurst went with the Duke of York to break the news to the Regent at Carlton House. The Prince, who had travelled to London through the night, had only learned of the stillborn child on his arrival at 4 am. When he now asked about his daughter, Bathurst had to tell him that she had also died. He told the Prime Minister that the Prince 'struck his two hands on his forehead & bowed down without saying a word for a minute.

He then held out his hand to me, & calling his brother threw himself into his arms.' Eventually he asked Bathurst and York to return to Claremont with offers of assistance to the bereaved Prince Leopold.[27] Two days later Sir Benjamin Bloomfield wrote to express the Prince's appreciation of Bathurst's attendance and solicitude.[28]

Princess Charlotte's death was not only a family tragedy but also a serious matter of state. As soon as he received Bathurst's letter the Prime Minister set out from Walmer Castle to meet Bathurst, Sidmouth and Eldon in London the next morning[29] to discuss what to do if the Regent pressed for a divorce in order to remarry and try to produce an heir. If the Prince, who had himself recently been very ill, died without a child, the throne would pass in turn to his numerous brothers. But since they had not one legitimate child among them, the succession thereafter would be more complicated than at any time since 1714.

The Regent stayed his hand for the time being, but the prospect of a large parliamentary allowance for marrying and the honour of fathering a prospective monarch spurred three royal dukes to shed their mistresses and scour the minor German Protestant courts for eligible wives. This produced the usual row over marriage allowances in 1818, provoking the mild-mannered Charles Arbuthnot, Patronage Secretary to the Treasury, to tell Bathurst: 'I may be influenced by feelings of irritability, but the inclination of my own mind would be to abandon the marriages altogether, and then let the House of Commons feel what it is to leave the succession in its present alarming state.'[30] The matter was finally patched up, to no one's real satisfaction, and the three promptly married. The winner in the royal sweepstakes was the Duke of Kent, George III's fourth son, whose only child was born in Kensington Palace on 24 May, 1819, with Bathurst and Wellington among the witnesses.[31] Almost exactly a year before, on 27 May, 1818, Bathurst had attended the birth in St James's Palace of the son of Kent's next younger brother, the Duke of Cumberland,[32] who, by the later birth, derived no benefit from having beaten the royal rush. In 1837 Kent's daughter came to the throne as Queen Victoria.

The War and Colonies Office was by this time not only smaller but far less hectic than during the tense years of war. Bathurst, like other ministers, continued to do most of his reading and writing of despatches at home or wherever else he happened to be, while Goulburn supervised the staff, did his own work and spent long nights in the Commons during the parliamentary session. The conventional hours for clerks were more leisurely but more constrained - from eleven to six, Monday to Saturday - though they had occasionally to work longer when parliament was sitting and when correspondence had to be completed in time for the colonial packets.[33]

The postwar tenor of the Office was caught by Goulburn in a letter to his wife at the end of January, 1816. 'Today has been dull enough,' he wrote, 'for though I have had incessant visitors they have not been of an amusing kind - complaining Chief Justices & discontented officers.' Among the latter was Colonel Sir Neil Campbell, 'who with due deference be it spoken is a great bore'. Campbell, who was now commanding the 3000 troops of the Hanseatic Legion in the army of occupation in France, had been absent from Elba, to which he had accompanied Napoleon, when the Emperor escaped in 1815. When he was announced Goulburn excused himself from walking with Bathurst to Drummond's Bank. The very reason he should go, Bathurst replied, since Campbell was accustomed to escapes. 'This,' Goulburn dolefully told his wife, 'is the only joke with which I can enliven my dullness.'[34]

Although Bathurst continued to be involved in military and foreign policy and other issues, he now had more time to devote to the vast worldwide empire. So too had his much reduced staff, most of whom had also hitherto been occupied with the war. For the first time since the War and Colonial departments had been combined in 1801 the office was now primarily a colonial one and Bathurst himself the first true Colonial Secretary, though he always considered himself far more than that.

The diverse and widely scattered territories over which he had charge ranged from the tiny, now largely abandoned island of Heligoland in the North Sea to the sugar islands of the West Indies; from the settlement, fishing and lumber colonies of North America to the prison territories of Australia; from the ancient polities of the Knights of Malta and the Ionian Island to the former Dutch colonies of South Africa and Ceylon. Bathurst's approach to this official patrimony was like that of a well-disposed landlord with estates over all three of the United Kingdoms, the Channel Islands and even the Isle of Man. The main consideration was for the enterprise to be as profitable as possible, even if some parts were temporarily in financial difficulties or had to be subsidized for a time. Local forms and customs were respected and only slowly and carefully altered to what was axiomatically assumed to be a superior as well as more familiar British system. Experienced stewards had to be selected who could be trusted to exercise sound judgment in territories up to six months' sailing time away from the Colonial Office, and these had to be supported against the complaints of the local populations and critics at home unless their conduct was so imprudent as to jeopardize the good order of the area under their charge or the security of the ministry at home. In any such conflict Bathurst almost automatically insisted that the authority of the Crown must be sustained, but, ever alert to potential criticism, particularly in the Commons, he constantly advised the mainly military governors whose instincts were authoritarian to protect their control by tact and discretion rather than heavy-handed insistence that would make confrontation far worse both in the colony and at home.

The Crown was in effect the British government, and among the many and often competing ministries and agencies with jurisdiction in the colonies – the Army, the Ordnance, the Admiralty, the Treasury, the Board of Customs and the Post Office – Bathurst by his high standing in the cabinet increasingly managed to establish the ascendency of the Colonial Office. Since there was no well worked-out departmental routine directed by senior permanent officials until his last few years, he was also, like his counterparts in other ministries, the person who made all major appointments and policy. He necessarily had to leave most of the detail to Goulburn, James Stephen (still at this time in private practice, acting as legal adviser on a fee basis) and other able assistants; but he did a great deal of the work himself, keeping himself well informed beyond the private despatches he received and wrote by also reading most of the other incoming and outgoing correspondence. He remembered much of what he read and by long experience in this department and government generally was well prepared to make decisions or judgements in any crisis. The control he exercised over his office was exactly the same as that of his fellow Secretaries of State, Castlereagh and Sidmouth, and only rarely did he trouble the cabinet for formal endorsement on important issues. For far away governors and colonists the awesome Earl Bathurst was for all practical purposes the Crown in whose name he acted.

At home, in the aftermath of Waterloo, the colonies attracted attention mainly for their cost. The opposition in the Commons concentrated on colonial garrisons which, it insisted, were too large, too expensive and too great a threat to civil liberties. They thought that Malta, the Cape and Ceylon at very least could well afford to pay for their own defence. Bathurst, Goulburn and other ministers countered by insisting that the colonies were a bargain at the price for their trade and security of communications. They claimed that 48,000 soldiers were the absolute minimum required for protection, particularly of the Mediterranean, the West Indies, North America, the Cape, Ceylon and Australia. But the force of the attack on this subject, even from the friends of government, was so great that Bathurst was forced to make concessions.[35]

In February, 1816, he sent a circular to the governors of the prosperous

8. Bust of the Earl Bathurst after the manner of Sir Francis Chantry by an unknown sculptor *(The Earl Bathurst: photograph Courtauld Institute of Art)*.

9. The Earl Bathurst by Sir Thomas Lawrence, 1822. Commissioned by George IV for the Waterloo Gallery, Windsor Castle *(reproduced by gracious permission of Her Majesty the Queen; Royal Collection Enterprises Ltd)*.

10. The House of Lords, 1820. The Trial of Queen Caroline, painted by Sir George Hayter. Lord Chancellor Eldon presides. The Queen is seated with the lawyers at the bar of the House. Earl Grey, arm outstretched on the right, is questioning the Marchese di Spineto, who leans forward on the left with Theodore Majocchi beside him. Beyond and between the two witnesses stands the Duke of Wellington, arms folded. Seated on the front bench to the right of Majocchi are Lord Sidmouth, Bathurst, Lord Harrowby, Lord Liverpool (standing) and the Duke of York. The Duke of Clarence stands in the middle of the gallery on the left. Charles Arbuthnot observes the proceedings from the aperture below the gallery on the right. (*Reproduced by courtesy of the National Portrait Gallery, London.*)

11. The Waterloo Banquet at Apsley House, 1836, painted by William Slater. The Duke of Wellington is speaking. To the right of the Duke is the Hereditary Prince of Orange, who twenty years before had been betrothed to Princess Charlotte; to his left are King William IV and Bathurst, partly obscured by the trophy, as usual the only civilian. Although Bathurst had died in 1834 he was included, presumably on instructions from Wellington, since he had been War Minister at the time of the battle and was customarily invited to the annual commemoration. (*The Duke of Wellington; the Victoria and Albert Picture Library*.)

12. Watercolour by J.C. Buckler of the western end of Downing Street, 1827. The Colonial Office, number 14, is in the centre. In 1827 it also took over the adjoining house, number 12, in the right corner, previously occupied by the Judge Advocate General. The combined building, already jeopardized by seepage, was fatally weakened by the excavations for the new Foreign Office on the south side of Downing Street (left side of the picture) in the early 1860s and part of the building had to be taken down. The rest was razed in 1876 and replaced by steps down to St James's Park. *(©The British Museum).*

West Indies, where troops guarded the planters against slave insurrections (there was one that year in Barbados), explaining the government's financial difficulties and appealing for contributions (in the case of Jamaica, an increased contribution) for their maintenance. With the single exception of Demerara, which offered to support 300 soldiers if an additional 500 were provided by Britain, the replies were predictably negative, with the colonists citing their own real economic troubles as trade declined with the return of peace. In face of this adamant resistance, the slow whittling down of colonial forces to 30,000 and increasing the colonies' financial contribution from about 10% to 13% of the total was a process that took thirteen years.

Bathurst also tried to reduce other costs, impressing on Governor Macquarie of the expensive penal settlement of New South Wales for example, 'the necessity of accurately investigating upon the Spot every branch of the Civil and Military Expenditure of the Colony, with a View to its immediate Reduction'. He ordered the governor to decrease the rations provided to free settlers from six months' supply to three and assured him that new emigrants had been warned not to expect anything beyond a land grant and some convict labour. He also urged Macquarie to advise on the Treasury's recommendation of opening commerce to free competition rather than government regulation of prices of the main articles of consumption. And as a spur to these exertions he pointed out that the governor could not give himself 'a stronger Claim to the Approbation of His Majesty's Government, than by proving, from the Retrenchments made by you on the present occasion, the sincerity of your desire to adopt, as the Rule of your Government, a System of regular and rigid Economy'.[36]

But reducing civil costs turned out to be every bit as difficult as reducing the garrisons. Even governors eager to comply with Bathurst's directives ran into strong resistance from those whose status, to say nothing of their standard of living, was derived from official largesse. From Ceylon Sir Robert Brownrigg told Bathurst, in tones suggesting that the conquest of the Kingdom of Kandy in the interior two years earlier had been the easier task, that he had been trying to cut the travelling expenses of the two judges of the Supreme Court. He had expected that 'the invidious work of retrenchment would not be unattended with some heart-burning. I could not however have predicted to your Lordship nor myself believed the degree of irritation which the attempt had in fact produced.' When he decided to delete 'as necessary Expenses of the Circuit, those of mere food and entertainment, which gentlemen in all situations must require for themselves independent of their publick avocations,' the judges raised a storm of protest. Brownrigg allowed them to carry their grievances against him to the Crown, but hoped that Bathurst would at least tell the Prince Regent the real nature of the dispute.[37]

A more reliable way of saving a modest but significant amount, as well as meeting some of the flood of supplications for employment from officers made redundant by the reduction of the army, was to appoint them as colonial governors. Since their military pay could be set off against their colonial salaries, this produced a saving to the Colonial Office as well as decreasing slightly the list of senior officers waiting for purely military commands. There was no shortage of high-ranking half-pay or under-employed heroes who considered themselves entitled to consideration from government, particularly by the very cabinet minister who had had so much influence over their military careers. Bathurst would have tended to appoint such individuals anyway, even if the War and Colonies departments had been totally separate, since they were used to obeying orders and exercising independent authority under general instructions, and the main concern of colonial government from the British perspective was military rather than political and civilian. But the parliamentary opposition, far from welcoming the financial advantage, asserted that the ministry was creating an authoritarian system and inflicting military despotism on the hapless colonists perhaps in preparation for the same at home.

As was the case with such coveted honours as knighthoods, peerages and sinecures, there were never anywhere near enough colonial governments for the number of deserving applicants. Disappointment was the lot of many, relieved only by bitter reproach and the hope of future consideration. Those who had some connection with Bathurst or some other minister or powerful figure, above all those who were supported by that transcendent hero the Duke of Wellington, naturally stood the best chance.

One such doubly fortunate individual was Major General Sir Peregrine Maitland, commander of the first brigade of Guards in the Peninsula, at Quatre Bras and at Waterloo, to whom at the end of the day Wellington gave the famous command 'Stand up Guards' to charge Napoleon's Imperial Guard. Seymour Bathurst had served with Maitland on the great day and was then appointed Maitland's aide-de-camp until his cousin, Lord William Lennox, was well enough to take up his duties.

Maitland's first wife had died ten years before and at Brussels before Waterloo he had enchanted the Duke of Richmond's twenty-three-year-old daughter, Lady Sarah Lennox. Her father probably had less objection to the fifteen-year difference in age than to Maitland's lack of fortune or prospects. Richmond may have been living in reduced circumstances but the least his daughters, for whom he could not afford large settlements, could do was to marry advantageously. His disapproval was overcome to some extent by the Duke of Wellington who had a high regard for Maitland and had liked Lady Sarah since the days when he had been Chief Secretary in Ireland, and they were married at his headquarters at Paris on 9 October, 1815. Two months, before Lady Sarah had written excitedly to Lady Georgina Bathurst from Brussels: 'I am delighted at what you tell me about my friend Genl Maitland, I am sure he deserves all the praise, he is a most delightful person and I am sure you and Aunt B. will be quite captivated by him. He has sent me a Legion of Honor taken by his Brigade of Guards at Waterloo which I am very proud of.'[38]

While this impecunious nephew by marriage was serving in the army of occupation in France, Bathurst sounded out Wellington about appointing him Lieutenant Governor of Upper Canada. The new Lady Sarah Maitland was told of it by the Duke and consulted her father, who agreed rather ungraciously, telling Bathurst: 'I have no doubt it would be the best thing for them. When people make inconsiderate marriages they must expect long absences from their friends, and I know of no other objection to Canada'.[39] The appointment was duly made and Maitland embarked on a second career as a colonial administrator, later serving in Nova Scotia, Madras and the Cape before retiring to London in 1847 at the age of seventy. But even before the Maitlands had made their arrangements for sailing to North America, Richmond was also turning his mind to a similar appointment that would help relieve his own financial troubles.

Another favoured individual was Lord Combermere, who had served with Wellington in Dublin in the early 1790s, in India, in the Peninsula and in France, and had also supported the government as MP from 1807 to 1814. Almost as soon as Bathurst became Secretary of State in 1812 the Duke of Newcastle (brother of Combermere's first wife, who died in 1807) began pestering him for honours until Combermere received a peerage at the end of the Peninsular War in 1814. After commanding the cavalry in France until the reductions of 1817, he became Governor of Barbados and Commander-in-Chief of the Leeward Islands. But neither Newcastle nor Wellington considered this good enough. 'You are too young [at 44] to withdraw yourself from the troops in order to take a civil government,' Wellington told him, 'and I don't think it will materially improve your fortune'. He undertook to push him forward, even promising to raise the possibility of the Governor Generalship of Canada with Bathurst.[40]

When Canada did not materialize, Newcastle in 1819 pressed Bathurst at least for something better than Combermere's present post. The Colonial Secretary apparently held out the prospect of Ceylon in succession to

Brownrigg when he returned in 1820, but Newcastle wanted the Cape Colony. Bathurst patiently explained that there was no expectation of a vacancy there and told Newcastle: 'I have found it absolutely necessary to lay down a rule not to make any engagement with respect to the succession to any Government, unless it be actually vacant, or that I have good reason for judging that it will immediately become so.'[41] Newcastle then had the effrontery to suggest that Bathurst simply dismiss Lord Charles Somerset, brother both of the Gloucestershire magnate the Duke of Beaufort and Wellington's military secretary Lord Fitzroy Somerset, to which Bathurst sharply replied: 'Lord Charles has conducted himself at the Cape in a manner which entitles him to every Protection; & his family is one, for which I have always entertain'd the greatest respect & regard. Your Grace therefore will readily imagine I could not be a party to such a measure.'[42] When Combermere returned to England in 1820, however, he was well provided for by appointments as Commander-in-Chief in Ireland from 1822 to 1825 and then in India from 1825 to 1830.

The request for a mere consulship from the wife of his cabinet colleague the Earl of Westmorland must have come as a welcome relief from the barrage of desperate and minatory petitions, giving Bathurst an opportunity to indulge his wit without fear of unpleasant consequences. 'All the Consuls in Europe, & indeed in every part of the world, except the Barbary States, are appointed by the Foreign Office,' he told Lord Lonsdale, the other northern grandee, whose wife, Westmorland's sister, had conveyed the application: 'From the moment I belonged to the Colonial Department I thought this very wrong, and am now completely convinced by Lady Westmorland's letter that the whole Patronage should all have good Salaries, & Deputies into the bargain'. But he feared that this would not happen until Lady Westmorland was herself an MP and helpfully suggested that Lonsdale have one of his sons vacate a seat for her: 'She is as eloquent as [the Whig] Mr. Brougham, & her pretty face is as good as his pretty plan for a qualification to be the representative of the County of Westmorland.'[43]

The Duke of Richmond was a different case since he was not really a military veteran, despite his rank of general. The refusal to employ him in the field was part of what he considered to be shabby treatment after he left Dublin in 1813. He grumbled to Bathurst from Brussels early in 1818 that the former Viceroys Camden and Westmorland had been given cabinet office (the latter apparently in perpetuity), while he had not even been allowed to fight for his country. Much as he yearned for it, he accepted that he could not return to England until most of his debts were paid off, except in the unlikely event that he could rent out the dilapidated Richmond House in London and keep his family away from that ruinously expensive city. But he welcomed his brother-in-law's offer to find him an appropriate appointment and expressed himself willing to accept anything – though hinting at the Cape – on which his eldest son, Lord March, and Bathurst could agree.[44]

The Cape was not available, even to Richmond, but Bathurst had recently heard from Sir John Sherbrooke that his health required him to give up the Governor-Generalship of Canada, and in fact, since writing, Sherbrooke had had a stroke. Richmond accepted with alacrity this succession to his friend: 'a good fellow but he has a violent temper,' he pronounced, confidently casting a stone from his own glass house. If he remained at Quebec for over two years he calculated that he would be able to save enough to return in comfort to his beloved Goodwood, and since his wife's aversion to the sea would make her a difficult companion on the voyage, 'and I very much fear she would dislike Canada so much as to make it most unpleasant to the whole family,' she would remain in a small leased house in London. Richmond also told Bathurst that he could furnish the requirements of his new post by buying perfectly good, once washed linen cheaply at Brussels.[45] A couple of weeks later he added that he had already sent wine and other economical purchases to Quebec and asked Bathurst's advice on taking the plate for fourteen from Richmond House. He also reported a storm, 'short but necessary to manage,' over his decision to take only a few of his fourteen children: 'It would not have done for the *whole* family to have gone to Canada.'[46]

The person most stunned by this appointment was the Peninsula veteran and Lieutenant Governor of Nova Scotia, Lord Dalhousie, who had been assured by Bathurst that he would be promoted to the senior government when the Colonial Secretary first heard of Sherbrooke's intention to resign. 'What can have led to this appointment, not more extraordinary as to the person than the manner in which it has been done, I cannot imagine,' he raged in his journal: 'I have been deceived to the last minute by Lord Bathurst. I have had not a line upon the subject.' But after a week's reflection he decided not to resign but 'to bear up with as much moderation and firmness as I can'.[47]

Richmond travelled to Quebec in the same ship as Sir Peregrine and Lady Sarah Maitland, arriving on 29 July, 1818, after which they proceeded to Upper Canada. Within a couple of weeks he was assuring Bathurst that the situation in Canada perfectly answered his private needs: something could be saved in three years and 'There is a good deal to do, but not too much'. Having been instructed to improve the defences of the colonies against American attack, he pointed out that it was essential to strengthen the fortifications of Quebec itself: 'Nothing but a citadel can save it if attacked, and indeed that would only save the garrison. The town would be knocked down by guns from Point Levy [Levis] across the river.' Although it was in fact never needed, a mighty citadel was built between 1823 and 1832 atop the cliff rising out of the St Lawrence at the enormous cost of £7,000,000 and further construction continued inside the walls until the middle of the century. Richmond also urged his brother-in-law to stop the flow of emigrants if possible, apart from those who could bring some money, since 'I cannot see the unfortunate people starve,'[48] perhaps strengthening Bathurst's own scepticism about encouraging the poor to leave for the colonies.

The population of Lower Canada, Richmond's principal charge (he had only military authority over the other colonies), was largely French but devoutly Catholic and practically unaffected by the secularism of the French Revolution. The Catholic bishop had been alarmed at the prospect of a 'red hot Protestant', but Sherbrooke had assured him that the new governor had been 'strenuous against the riotous Irish Catholics not on account of their religion but on account of their revolutionary principles. This quite satisfied him,' Richmond reported to Bathurst with satisfaction, 'and we are great friends'.[49] Before long, however, Richmond was predictably favouring the vociferous Protestant British minority, looking towards a union of Upper and Lower Canada which would reduce the French to a minority and perhaps prejudicing the Colonial Office against the French Catholics, if indeed Goulburn and other Evangelicals needed any prejudicing. Bathurst himself continued to be tolerant of Catholics in Lower Canada as elsewhere in the empire.

In the summer of 1819 Richmond went on a lengthy tour of both Canadas, visiting the Maitlands as well as Niagara Falls in the interior colony. On the return journey he began to show signs of hydrophobia, probably from a fox bite a few weeks before. On 28 August he died in agony in a barn (as he had been born in one when his mother suddenly went into labour) close to the hamlet named in his honour north of Kingston. As he lay dying he asked to be remembered to his wife, his mother, who could rejoice that her son had died in honour although denied the risk of battle, and all his children, particularly Sarah and Sir Peregrine Maitland, whom he forgave for their marriage, '& they and their family have my blessing'. He also desired that his wife remember him to the Duke of York, with whom he had fought a duel so long ago, to the Prince Regent, and gave his love to 'Bathurst, to my sister Bathurst, to Apsley & Georgiana Bathurst'. Then, rallying himself for his last testament, he pronounced: 'Let Bathurst know that I am firmly persuaded that if the Catholics succeed Ireland is lost'. He instructed his attendants to give his defence plans to his successor and requested Bathurst to do the same with Wellington's masterly scheme for defending Upper Canada through a system of waterways by which troops could safely move from Montreal to Kingston away from the American frontier of the St Lawrence.[50] At his express wish he was buried a week later in the Anglican Cathedral at Quebec.

Maitland was shocked to learn the news when he returned to his own capital at about the time of the funeral. 'Nothing,' he told Bathurst, 'could be kinder [than] the poor Duke was to us when he was here, and he went from hence in a state of health and spirits, on which we were congratulating ourselves. So sudden is this tremendous blow'.[51] Hurrying to Quebec, he told Bathurst a week later that the Richmond children there were as tranquil as possible, though his own wife had suffered severely and was far from well. A transport ship was fitted out to take the family to England while he remained at Quebec in expectation of being relieved by Dalhousie.[52]

An officer reached Halifax, Nova Scotia, with the news ten days later. 'The unlooked for event has confounded & stupefied us all,' wrote Dalhousie. Lord Frederick Lennox, who was with him, wanted to go immediately to Quebec, but Dalhousie convinced him that his family would have left and sent him instead by packet with despatches to England. This time Bathurst at once appointed Dalhousie Governor-General and Dalhousie was now full of gratitude. But, having achieved his ambition, he reflected, as many another governor must: 'Success in it will carry distinguished honour, but if the reverse, I have a dreadful example before my eyes in the unpitied fate of Sir Geo. Prevost.'[53]

When the account of Richmond's death reached London on 1 October Bathurst forbore giving the details to his grieving wife since she had a particular abhorrence of hydrophobia; indeed he himself doubted the diagnosis since Richmond was apparently so lucid between paroxysms.[54] He enlisted Wellington's aid in helping the family and the Duke undertook not only the education of the youngest son but to do whatever else he could.[55] There was a flurry of activity by Bathurst, the Prime Minister, the Regent and others to make decent public provision for Richmond's large family and spare the new Duke, who inherited the debts that had beset his father and estates so strictly entailed that, as Bathurst told Liverpool, he could not even solve his financial problems through 'the common recourse of cutting down timber'.[56] The Bathursts for their part took one of the daughters, Lady Georgina Lennox, to live with them until her marriage to William Fitzgerald de Ros in 1824.

But Richmond's death provided hope as well as grief. As soon as he heard of it Sir James Kempt, a Peninsula and Waterloo veteran and Lieutenant Governor of Portsmouth, was quick off the mark. Anticipating Dalhousie's promotion, he urged Wellington to make an early application to Bathurst in his favour. The Duke mentioned it in his first letter to Bathurst and Kempt was immediately appointed to Nova Scotia.[57]

While Richmond was settling into his new post in the autumn of 1818 Bathurst once more acted as Foreign Secretary for over a month when Castlereagh attended the Congress of Aix-la-Chapelle along with Wellington for the formal ratification of the revised French reparations agreement and the end of occupation. Far more contentious was the issue of admitting France to the alliance system in order to increase the defence of the post-war settlement. Most British ministers were more wary of this than Castlereagh and the Duke, though they did recognize the danger of allowing the ancient enemy to mobilize continental discontent. The solution proposed by the cabinet and accepted by the allies was to maintain the existing alliance, to be invoked if necessary against France, while creating a new quintuple alliance to include that country.

The other matter that exercised British ministers was the proposal for regular meetings of the great powers. Bathurst told Castlereagh, following a cabinet attended by himself, Liverpool, Sidmouth, Melville, Canning and Vansittart, that they were all sceptical of a regular schedule, but Canning had gone further, claiming that this was a new and questionable policy that 'will necessarily involve us deeply in all the politics of the Continent, whereas our true policy has always been not to interfere except in great emergencies, and then with a commanding force'. He had also pointed out that 'the people of this country may be taught to look with great jealousy for their liberties, if our Court is engaged in meetings with great despotic monarchs, deliberating upon what degree of revolutionary spirit may endanger the public security, and therefore require the interference of the Alliance.' None of the other ministers had agreed with Canning, but, as Bathurst added: 'If this is felt by him, it is not unreasonable to apprehend that it may be felt by many other persons as well as by our decided opponents. And what I wish to ask you is, why take the bull by the horns?' He suggested simply agreeing on a date for the next conference (to which even Canning had no objection) rather than a permanent calendar.[58] This prudent advice had in fact already been anticipated by Castlereagh, and when Austria and Russia tried to use the alliances to stifle change in Europe Castlereagh neither went himself nor sent a formal representative to the conferences of Troppau (1820) and Laibach (1821).

Just when Europe seemed to be settled to general satisfaction by the Treaty of Aix-la-Chapelle an embarrassing issue at the imperial fringe threatened the close relations between Britain and the Netherlands. In the summer of 1819 Bathurst suddenly learned from Lord Hastings, the Governor-General of India, that Sir Stamford Raffles had taken possession of Singapore in January through a treaty with the local sultan. A physically frail but energetic and scientific servant of the East India Company, Raffles had been instrumental in the conquest of Java when Holland was part of Napoleon's empire and had then been its administrator. He was not alone in his anger at the unconditional return of the East Indies to the Netherlands in 1814. British merchants, rivals of the Dutch in the east for over a century, were also astounded at this supine return of a valuable trading area to their competitors.[59] But the British ministry had a pressing interest which transcended commercial considerations to ensure that the Kingdom of the United Netherlands was economically and militarily strong and well-disposed to Britain, though the Dutch merchants did not help the situation by ruthlessly excluding British traders from the posts that they had occupied during the war.

Hastings shared Raffles' feelings and, in the spirit of Lord Wellesley, encouraged his lieutenant to find a base in the vital Straits of Malacca on territory not claimed by the Dutch in order to protect the East India Company's trade with China and the coast of Bengal. Singapore, which in time became a greater Malta of the east, was a superb choice, but the Dutch naturally protested the infringement in an area they regarded as their monopoly by the very country that was professing such great friendship.[60]

This precipitate seizure caused great discomfort to the government, particularly to those like Bathurst who considered a strong and amicable Netherlands far more important than another small overseas possession. But with economic desire competing with diplomatic necessity, the government tried to find a solution through negotiation. Because of its wide ramifications, this involved, in addition to the Colonial Office, the Foreign Office, the Board of Control (of which Canning was President) and the East India Company. The last two were determined to retain Singapore, while Bathurst and Castlereagh were more concerned about the European consequences. Discussions began at the end of 1819, but were then abandoned for three years while the British government was preoccupied with more pressing matters. The Dutch for their part were in no hurry since they did not regard Singapore in itself as important and were in any event in no position to demand that Britain withdraw. But by the time talks resumed in 1824, and the abrasive Canning was Foreign Secretary, Singapore was a British boom

125

town. A treaty was finally concluded allowing the East India Company to keep it and even to add Malacca and the Dutch bases in India in return for Britain promising not to establish any settlements on the islands south of Singapore, both governments covering their awkwardness by blaming their distant agents. Singapore turned out to be a great triumph for Britain, but at the time Bathurst was not alone in thinking that it had been won at the risk of alienating the Netherlands and jeopardizing British security in Europe.[61]

One of the great benefits of withdrawing the army of occupation from France at the end of 1818 was that the British government could strengthen its hand and undermine its critics before meeting the new parliament, elected in the summer of 1818, by further reducing the army. Both the Duke of York and the Prince Regent were strenuously opposed, but, as Liverpool told Bathurst at the end of September, 1818, the Regent simply had to be informed that the fate of the ministry depended on the first parliamentary challenges in 1819: 'Economy and reduction are the passions of the day, and . . . if he wishes to preserve his Government, he must allow them to manage the questions of establishments of all descriptions in such a way as to give no pretext to our friends to vote against us.'[62] Bathurst had his work cut out for him in getting the Commander-in-Chief to accept the point,[63] but by the time parliament assembled cutbacks in the army were well under way.

The other advantage of the end of occupation was acquiring the Duke of Wellington as a cabinet colleague. Liverpool lost no time in offering him the post of Master General of the Ordnance in succession to Lord Mulgrave, who was allowed to keep his seat in the cabinet, and the Duke as swiftly accepted. He was still only forty-nine, had no intention of slipping into an honoured retirement and the cabinet assured him of a place in national affairs commensurate with his great standing until he was needed once more in the field. At first he treated the post as a strictly professional one, taking little part in discussion outside his own department and foreign policy, but by 1822 he was drawn into a position of partisan leadership from which he could not easily withdraw. Among the old friends and acquaintances in the cabinet, some of whom had served with him in the Portland ministry a decade ago, only Castlereagh was closer than Bathurst.

Liverpool's ministry certainly needed all the help it could get in 1819, the most difficult of all the troubled years since the war as economic distress and popular agitation focused on the demand for parliamentary reform. This culminated in the great meeting and 'massacre' of Peterloo outside Manchester on 16 August, when eleven people were killed and hundreds injured in a cavalry charge to arrest the speaker,'Orator' Henry Hunt. Greater injury was added when the ministers sent a message in the name of the Regent congratulating the magistrates on their handling of the situation. Sympathy meetings for the victims were held all over the north of England and elsewhere condemning the authorities and calling on the Prince to dismiss the cabinet, while Home Secretary Sidmouth persuaded his colleagues to summon parliament in November to enact measures against disturbances which might well escalate to something far more dangerous.

Among those who were thoroughly alarmed was Lord Grenville, who saw the spectre of the French Revolution once more stalking England's green and pleasant land. After close to a decade and a half of opposition, he and his faction now supported the ministers against the Whigs and Radicals and endorsed the six acts introduced at the autumn session. Hoping that this would lead the small remaining band of independent Pittites to join the government, Bathurst proposed visiting Grenville before parliament met, but Grenville put him off, saying that 'he should be in town long enough before the meeting, to enable him to communicate and consult with him on the points brought forward'.[64] For the time being the Grenvillites were not willing to go beyond buttressing the ministry from outside.

The last of the six acts against treason and sedition was passed at the end of December and parliament recessed until the middle of February, 1820. But at the end of January George III, the friend and patron of three generations of Bathursts, died after sixty years on the throne. In many ways this made little practical difference. His son, already effectively monarch for a decade, simply changed from being Regent to George IV; the ministers formally surrendered their seals of office and received them back again and the meeting of parliament was put off for two days to accommodate the royal funeral. The only other inconvenience seemed to be that the new parliament had to be elected within six months. But the transition proved to be more eventful than anyone expected as George IV's reign fundamentally transformed the constitutional order that Bathurst and most of his friends had spent their whole careers defending.

During the difficulties of 1819 and the distressing news of Richmond's death Bathurst was primarily engaged, as he had been for much of the period since 1815, with the Ionian islands, the most delicate and potentially dangerous of the overseas responsibilities which called for his personal handling. At the beginning of September he had bidden a heartfelt farewell at Cirencester to Count Capodistria, a native of Corfu and one of the two Russian foreign ministers, who had come to England to complain about the British administration of the protectorate assigned to it in 1815.

The importance of the seven islands off the western coast of Greece

127

(Corfu, Paxo, Santa Maura, Ithaca, Cephalonia, Zante and Cerigo) had been obvious since ancient times.[65] Corfu in particular, with its magnificent harbour, was the gateway to the Adriatic and one of the keys to the Mediterranean, while Zanthe had prospered since the seventeenth century by exporting vast quantities of its unrivalled currants to Britain for plum puddings. For four centuries the islands had been the possession of Venice, but in 1797 Bonaparte had insisted that they be surrendered to France. As elsewhere, the French were at first welcomed as liberators and then resented as oppressors for imposing new taxes and their contempt for local Orthodox Christian practices. In 1798–99 the islands were captured in a combined operation of Russia, Turkey and Britain and formed into a Septinsular Republic, effectively under Russia, until the Tsar returned them to Napoleon in 1807. Capodistria, who had been a member of the governing council, left in despair and shortly afterwards entered the service of the Russian Emperor.

In 1809, in response to appeals from the islanders, the Royal Navy once more took all but Corfu and Paxo. The latter fell in February, 1814, but Corfu held out against a naval blockade until ordered to surrender a few months later by Louis XVIII. British occupation of these islands, which had been an important centre of smuggling during the Continental System, however, did not mean sovereignty, which had to be settled by the Congress of Vienna. Castlereagh at first favoured giving the islands to Sicily as compensation for the loss of Naples, still ruled by Joachim Murat, who had adeptly abandoned his brother-in-law Napoleon, or neutralizing them and opening their commerce to all. But Bathurst, encouraged by Bunbury, who had served in the Mediterranean, was anxious to maintain the British interest and at first thought the least dangerous solution would be to assign them to Austria.[66] The return of Napoleon, this time supported by Murat, guaranteed the reunion of Naples and Sicily under Ferdinand I after the two adventurers were defeated, which changed the Ionian situation. Capodistria, given a free hand on the matter by the Russian Emperor, objected to handing over his beloved islands to Austria, Russia's rival in eastern Europe, preferring Britain if independence was impossible. British protection would provide the islands with security and great commercial advantages. As Castlereagh told Bathurst: 'The great motive the Ionians have to become *our subjects* is our flag now being the *only one* respected.' In order to keep up the pressure for this happy issue, the Foreign Secretary asked Bathurst to hold his hand in sending an expedition against the Barbary pirates; otherwise the islanders would press for a real republic with the protection of a British garrison.[67] By the treaty of 5 November, 1815, 'the single, free and independent state, under the denomination of the United States of the Ionian Islands' became a British protectorate; but Bathurst got far more than he had bargained for, not least in trying to reconcile freedom and independence with the authority of the British Lord High Commissioner.

While this was being worked out, in 1816 Bathurst orchestrated a move against the piracy of the Barbary states (Tripoli, Tunis, Algeria and Morocco). Britain had tolerated petty outrages during the war while trying to protect her allies since she needed food for Gibraltar and the Peninsula; but in peacetime it was determined to stop the danger to trade, to end the enslaving of captured Christians who could be redeemed only by purchase, and to ensure the recognition of British jurisdiction over the Ionian islands. The mission was entrusted to Admiral Lord Exmouth, Commander-in-Chief of the Mediterranean since 1811. He reported good progress as he sailed around the states, from Tunis for example telling Bathurst that he really believed that slavery would now be abandoned. He reported that over 2500 slaves had been released by his visit, 'among which are cases which harrow up every feeling in the human heart, and would melt a flint. . . . The blessed name of King George and England resounded through these caverns of wretchedness from the moment the fleet arrived until the doors were thrown open to the British officer who received them.'[68] But when the Dey of Algiers refused to reply to his ultimatum to accept the same terms as the other states, Exmouth opened a barrage that destroyed the entire Algerian navy, much of the city of Algiers and many inhabitants, including those who ignored his warnings and gathered on the piers to witness the spectacle, while his fleet, joined by the Dutch, lost not a single ship. The next morning the Dey capitulated; 3000 slaves were freed and repatriated to Spain and Italy and the commander, with becoming modesty, wrote to congratulate Bathurst on a lasting success.[69] It was a famous victory and Exmouth was hailed as a hero by all of Christian Europe; but, as so often before, within a few years the danger arose again while the British were occupied by the Greek revolt against the Turks.

With the Mediterranean apparently at peace, Bathurst could concentrate on the new British possession. Before the final Ionian treaty was signed, he decided that the ideal Lord High Commissioner would be the seemingly indefatigable governor of Malta since 1813, Sir Thomas Maitland. Bunbury doubted whether Maitland would accept, but readily concurred with Bathurst's efficient and economical proposal of combining all the British governments in the Mediterranean (save Gibraltar) – Malta, the Ionian islands and even the consuls on the North African coast, who would thereby enjoy military support – under the formidable Maitland.[70] And in December, 1815, he was appointed to his new post.

At forty-seven Maitland had already had a remarkable career. After varied military service he had served from 1806 to 1811 as Lieutenant Governor of Ceylon, captured from the Dutch in 1796 to prevent it becoming a French base for attacking India; returning home he had firmly but humanely suppressed the Luddites in the north of England; and in July, 1813, he was appointed Governor of Malta, finally annexed as a crown colony after fourteen years of occupation. A commission of inquiry, established by Liverpool just before Bathurst replaced him at the War and Colonies, recommended, as practically instructed, that the military authority be supreme, since the island, ruled from 1428 to Napoleon's conquest in 1798 by the Knights of St John of Jerusalem, was unsuited to self-government and was happy and prosperous without it. The commissioners also advised that local institutions and practices be respected and modified only as necessary but that the corrupt judicial system be reformed, the English language be elevated to equal official status with the Italian of the élite (the ordinary Maltese spoke an Arabic patois) and that English education be encouraged. All this was well and good in Bathurst's eyes and Maitland was commanded to proclaim the inhabitants of Malta British subjects entitled to its protection and the arms and emblems of the Knights of Malta on public buildings were replaced by British ones.[71] Maitland threw himself into his duties with energy and enthusiasm, ridding the island of the plague within a year, abolishing torture and carrying out a host of reforms which transformed Malta into a model of paternalistic autocracy. Even his critics half-admiring called him 'King Tom' and it was natural that Bathurst wanted to use his skills in the Ionian islands.

After sailing to Corfu and casting a cold eye over these new charges in January, 1816, Maitland told Bunbury:

> To a British mind the feelings of the people of these countries are equally repugnant and revolting - and it does not require a positive experience and knowledge of their character to be able to make up one's mind to the belief that people exist with principles so degrading, and feelings so debased as mark the character of those living in Italy and Greece - and in all those countries that in former days constituted the glory and form still the admiration of the civilized world.

He considered the Ionians interested in power only for corrupt ends and understanding nothing other than a strong hand. They preferred Russian rule to British liberty, and 'any Government however corrupt, and however tyrannical, to the only Government Great Britain can ever wish to give them – one that would tend to their general happiness, prosperity and security'. The character they most detested was 'that of an honest and upright man'.[72] But that was what Maitland was, according to his own strong lights.

The Lord High Commissioner enforced rigorous quarantine regulations on shipping to reduce the plague, appointed good (British) subordinate residents in the islands other than Corfu which he governed himself, increased the efficiency and fairness of government and the courts, favoured pro-British nobles and excluded those, particularly the Capodistria family, who looked to Russia. He also supervised the election and work of the Primary Council in devising the new constitutional chart, as it was called, which was presented to the Prince Regent for ratification in 1817. (The 1815 treaty made no mention of the British parliament, which was not consulted.) Despite its Byzantine complexity and elaborate division of powers, the constitution was simply a façade to mask the absolute power of the High Commissioner acting under the Colonial Secretary. Even Lord Chancellor Eldon, no advocate of democracy or stranger to legal obfuscation, asked Bathurst to provide him with a copy in plain English so that he could understand 'how much or how little my Sovereign should promise or pledge himself for under the Great Seal'.[73] Eldon's legal scruples were eventually assuaged and the Regent in all his glory ratified the constitution before a delegation from the islands. Maitland's practical understanding of how the arrangements really worked was reflected in his request in 1819 for warrants signed by the Colonial Secretary for the dismissal of officials, 'leaving a Blank for the name to be filled in here, to use as occasions may require'.[74]

To help reconcile the Ionian élite to the new dispensation, the chivalric order of St Michael and St George was devised (and continued as a general order for overseas service with the Ionian symbols after the islands were ceded to Greece in 1864). This gratified loyal servants and defenders of British rule and helped counter the honours that the Russians had distributed during their occupation. The High Commissioner represented the sovereign as local head of the order, but, as Bathurst bluntly told the First Lord of the Admiralty in proposing that the admiral on the Mediterranean station always be the Principal Knight Grand Cross: 'We must have a few Englishmen who are in the service either of the Ionian or the Maltese Government, belonging to it, in order to give it some consequence in the eye of the States.'[75]

Apart from those nobles who preferred the good old corruption and who were now deprived of their fees, bribes and attendant status, the Ionian islanders were apparently grateful for even-handed British rule and the security of its flag. Russia raised no objections to the way in which the treaty

131

obligation to design a 'single, free and independent state' under British protection had been fulfilled. But the discontented in the islands had a powerful advocate in Capodistria. In 1819 he travelled to Corfu with the permission of the Tsar and was appalled by what he saw. But although Maitland expressed a wish to see him, Capodistria did not accept.

On the way back to Russia Capodistria stopped in England to take up the matter with the British ministers. He first sought out Wellington, who admitted that he had not thought about the matter since the treaty four years earlier. The Duke reported to Bathurst, who had just left London for Cirencester to recover from a minor operation, that Capodistria claimed that Britain had breached the treaty in devising the constitution, in the proportion of British to native troops, in its involvement in the details of administration, and was guilty of 'misgovernment in a variety of instances'. Since Bathurst was not in town Wellington advised Capodistria to see Castlereagh. Wellington also saw the Foreign Secretary and gloomily reported to Bathurst that, since Capodistria was charging treaty violation, 'at all event it will be necessary to enter upon the subject with a view to satisfy him'.[76]

Bathurst in reply conceded the Russian Emperor's right to intervene if Britain broke the treaty, but was confident that no such breach could be demonstrated, and at the time of the treaty the Russians had been given solemn assurances that they would not interfere in the internal administration of the islands. 'We cannot satisfy Capo d'Istria,' he told Wellington,

> except by abandoning the British interest and placing his family and friends at the head of the government in which case we had better give up the Ionian Islands altogether and the very appearance of entering into a communication with him on this subject will create a sensation in the islands which will have the worst effect.[77]

Castlereagh also wrote to Bathurst after his interview with Capodistria and the Russian Ambassador, Count Lieven. Although not familiar with the details of government in the islands, he had insisted that Maitland was 'a distinguished officer placed in a very arduous and responsible trust'. When he read over the written complaints after his visitors left, the Foreign Secretary was struck by the bitterness of tone and expected that Capodistria had left copies with his family at Corfu: 'We must regard them, therefore, if not intended for publication, as liable to come out at any moment it may suit the opposition party in the islands to bring forward a public appeal.' He was particularly concerned that the grievances might reach the House of

Commons, where suspicions of the islands' government, 'already inconveniently strong, would be augmented by an avowed difference with Russia'. Since Bathurst had invited Capodistria and Lieven to Cirencester, Castlereagh hoped that he would manage to keep the matter unofficial. A couple of days later he jocularly added: 'I don't envy you your party, but you are a great master in managing difficulties, and I should not be surprised to hear that you pressed the Count to stay another day with you.'[78] Bathurst tried to get Wellington to join the party but he begged off, though he did entertain the travellers overnight at Stratfield Saye. By this time, perhaps under the influence of Lieven, Capodistria was much less vehement and maintained that he was merely a concerned individual. Wellington seized on this to hint that breach of treaty was the only grounds for Russian interference.[79]

Thus armed with reports from his colleagues, Bathurst was in a strong position to receive his visitors at Cirencester, where the library and other parts had recently been refurbished under the supervision of his daughter Georgina.[80] Although Capodistria later complained to Wellington that Bathurst seemed not to know most of the essential details, the Colonial Secretary told the Russians that he could find no abuses of the treaty in Capodistria's written complaints and pointed out that liberty and independence were necessarily limited in a country occupied by a foreign power which had to approve its constitution.[81] After the Russians left, Bathurst asked the Duke to use his standing to remind the Tsar that 'the bad effect of foreign interference was . . . foreseen at the time the treaty was made, and that all appearance of it is to be avoided as much as possible'. Capodistria, realizing that the British ministers were defying him to recommend a formal complaint to the Tsar, with all the unpredictable risks of international disagreement, not least to himself and his position, confined himself to expressing his gratitude for Bathurst's friendly reception and his confidence that justice would be done and oppression ended in the Ionian islands.[82]

Sir Thomas Maitland lost no time in supplying Bathurst with material for defence against Capodistria's charges. Far from being a despot, he claimed that he never did anything decisive until he felt forced to act, though that did not mean that he would 'permit the essential interests of the Crown of England to be assailed by any quarter, or by any set of men whatever, without putting down all such attempts in the most effectual manner'. Half a year later he more emphatically added that he could not publicly state the true justification for his system of government, that the Ionians were 'the most profligate and vile of mankind' and that the only means of ensuring the happiness of the ordinary people was 'to maintain all power in the hands of

H. Majesty's Lord High Commissioner'. But he did point out that if the government allowed Capodistria to bring about his dismissal British rule would be impossible and the sooner the country abandoned the islands to Russia the better.[83]

Goulburn was undoubtedly right in telling his chief that the real grievance was Maitland's replacement of fees by fixed salaries which deprived the great families (including the Capodistrias) of huge profits,[84] and Lieven privately agreed that Capodistria had been misled by his family. After pondering the material sent by Maitland, Bathurst enlisted Wellington in the autumn of 1820 to tell Capodistria that Britain was governing in the interests of the local inhabitants and was not going to change the new constitution. Far from increasing taxes, eleven had been abolished and only the export duty on oil had been increased, which had no effect on the Ionians; the abandonment of tax farming had produced a less burdensome system and greater revenue; the courts were open to the poor (previously unable to afford the fees); and steps had been taken to repair the Catholic church's buildings and to reclaim the land it had lost during the French occupation, without suddenly disrupting those who had enjoyed uncontested possession.[85] With this firm and detailed defence, Britain's position in the Ionian islands seemed secure. But almost immediately the protectorate was demanding even more of Bathurst's attention when war for Greek independence from Turkey erupted in 1821.

6

WAR IN HEAVEN, 1820–1825

George IV's reign got off to an ominous start three weeks after his accession with an attempt to assassinate the cabinet while dining with Lord Harrowby on 23 February. This Cato Street conspiracy was fortunately averted when two of the plotters betrayed their colleagues. But there was no such merciful deflection from the King's insistence on ridding himself of his wife. The ministers accepted his demand that Caroline be omitted from the state prayers of the Church, agreed that she should not be crowned and recommended that she be given a large allowance to remain on the continent where she had been living a raffish life since the end of the war; but they refused a divorce, since a trial would bring out the King's own well-known conduct, perhaps even his illicit marriage to the Catholic Maria Fitzherbert.

The return of the Queen at the beginning of June, to the delight of the radicals, finally forced the issue of divorce. Since there could be no question of going to the courts, the government agreed on a parliamentary act of pains and penalties to deprive her of her titles and dissolve the marriage. Canning, who claimed to have been one of Caroline's earliest lovers, refused to be a party to the accusations and offered to resign, but neither the government nor even the King could afford such evidence of dissent within the cabinet, much less risk losing this powerful debater to the opposition. At the end of June Bathurst told the Prime Minister that there must be no delay in telling Canning that his resignation was not accepted.[1] Canning instead took himself to Paris.

The bill was introduced on 5 July in the House of Lords, which was not only more likely to be more sympathetic than the Commons, but also, as the highest court, had established procedures for judicial hearings. The 'trial',

135

with lawyers and witnesses at the bar, began on 17 August. To counter the radical activities in favour of Caroline, which had continued unabated since her return, troops were brought up from the country to safeguard the Palace of Westminster by land and water. From Cirencester, before he was summoned along with all the peers save those who were ill or had special excuses, Bathurst warned Liverpool against trying to ban reports on the evidence until the matter was concluded. Apart from the fact that there was probably no precedent for such a prohibition, which might in turn create a dangerous one for the future, he considered that the testimony against the Queen would allay popular agitation, while 'If this be not allow'd, the grossest misrepresentations will go forth'.[2] The government did not interfere with publication and a month of this low entertainment may have prevented greater violence, though it did nothing to diminish Caroline's popularity as she travelled back and forth each day to take her place in the chair at the bar of the Lords.

Despite what they heard, the Lords were by no means convinced of the expediency of the bill when it was debated after the hearing ended. When it passed the third reading by only nine votes on 10 November the Prime Minister moved that it be abandoned, since sending it to the Commons would provoke even sharper debate and almost certain defeat. The King threatened to dismiss the ministry and was particularly furious against Liverpool. At his wits' end, the Prime Minister told Arbuthnot: 'I wish only to be thoroughly & honourably released. I will not abandon others, but I am by no means sure that they will not abandon me & leave me to be the *sole* victim of the present clamour.'[3] Canning now insisted on resigning and when the King sent for Lord Grenville, ostensibly to consult him about a precedent for excluding the Queen from the Church liturgy, Arbuthnot told Bathurst that it put Liverpool into a fever. Grenville, however, not only refused to give an opinion but took the opportunity to warn that the Whigs were 'so mixed up with Radicalism that they did nothing which was not abominable'.[4] But he still would not join the government.

If the Prime Minister could not recruit support, he could at least relieve his feelings against apostates. When Sir Henry Bunbury followed disapproval of Peterloo with promoting an address in favour of Caroline, Liverpool angrily advised Bathurst in January, 1821, to strike him out of the army and remove him from any other position he could. Even though he had himself appointed Bunbury to the War and Colonies Office in 1809, 'I do not see why a man is allowed to add the sin of ingratitude to that of treason.'[5] The more equable Bathurst permitted Bunbury to continue as a major general, though he did deprive him of the pension of £650 a year granted

136

in 1816 and the post of colonial agent (to the Colonial Office, almost a sinecure) for Malta, worth £600 a year; even in the latter case he was allowed the decency of resignation and was replaced by the more reliable Seymour Bathurst.[6] But the deprivation simply increased Bunbury's opposition to his former associates.

The support for Queen Caroline dwindled after she accepted an allowance and a house from the government; and when she was refused admission as Queen to George IV's grandiose coronation in July, 1821, she drove away to more jeers than acclaim from her former supporters. But her death a month later and the request that her body be returned to Brunswick for burial provided one last opportunity for opponents of the King and the ministers to use her for their purpose. Despite George IV's orders that the coffin be taken from Hammersmith by water to a warship at the Nore, strong westerly winds caused the Admiralty to advise overland transportation to Harwich. A route was chosen well north of the radical City of London and all the troops were ordered out or put on alert.

Since Sidmouth and Castlereagh were with the King on a state visit to Ireland, Bathurst was the only Secretary of State in England, and he was in the country. The day before the procession Goulburn reported that he had just seen a public notice calling on all London to follow the Queen's coffin the next day. If this had been known sooner Bathurst would have been summoned in case there was a riot, but since Liverpool was in town and arrangements were well in hand, neither thought that he should come before he intended at the end of the week, unless he wished to repair his own windows, which Goulburn thought would be too tempting to be overlooked.[7] Bathurst nevertheless sent instructions in case matters did get out of control. There was to be no interference with the procession unless the civil authorities were attacked; if that happened, the riot act was to be read and placards, prepared in advance, were to be held up to inform the crowd. Only if the magistrates certified that they could not quell the riot by means of the police were written orders to be sent for troops.[8] But the radicals had also made preparations and when the cortège reached the western edge of London the streets were barricaded in order to force it through the City. When the soldiers tried to clear the streets there were clashes with the crowd and disorderly firing by angry troops in which a couple of people were killed. The procession reached Temple Bar and was escorted in state and triumph through the City by the Lord Mayor, aldermen and members of the Common Council. It then continued with little incident to the ship at Harwich.

The disregard of his explicit instructions made it likely that the King would seize on the incident to dismiss the ministers. Bathurst told Eldon: 'As we have been for some time at single anchor, I think the storm may most probably carry us out to sea,'[9] while from Walmer Castle the Prime Minister told Bathurst, now in charge in London, that it was essential to seize the initiative and attack those responsible for the disturbances. Even if it did not succeed, it would at least demonstrate the ministry's resolve and make monarchical retribution more difficult.[10]

The chief individual selected for attention was Major General Sir Robert Wilson. A thorn in government flesh as reform MP for Southwark since 1818, Wilson, at the end of a chequered military career, had been officially reprimanded and jailed in Paris for three months for helping one of Napoleon's supporters escape the sentence of death. He had played a typically ambiguous part in the Queen's funeral, even attempting to stop the troops from firing on the crowd, but in the view of the cabinet it was enough that he was on the side of the demonstrators and was a friend of Caroline to whom his son was equerry. Once Wellington had ascertained that the non-commissioned officers and troops who would make depositions against Wilson were 'all old soldiers of most unexceptional characters; and in every way deserving of credit,' Bathurst, Liverpool, Wellington and the Duke of York swiftly agreed to strike him off the army list without calling for an explanation which, as Wellington warned, would 'infallibly lead to a trial by a general court martial and the acquittal of Sir Robert or some very lenient censure'.[11] Eight years later, when William IV came to the throne, Wellington, as Prime Minister, was persuaded to restore Wilson to the rank of lieutenant general, retroactive to 1825 when he would have achieved the promotion by seniority.

Despite their prompt action following the funeral demonstration, the ministers awaited the King's eight-day sojourn in London between the visits to Ireland and Hanover with trepidation. Liverpool told Bathurst that the First Lord of the Admiralty, at whose insistence the funeral order had been altered, should be brought back to London. Melville breezily agreed, confidently assuring Bathurst that the matter of the 'water party' would be 'speedily blown out of the water, at least at headquarters'.[12] On Sunday, 16 September, the King pointedly kept Liverpool waiting while he interviewed other ministers, including Bathurst and the Lord Chancellor.[13] But when they all stood solidly behind the Prime Minister, and with no real alternative group available, he had to abandon the idea of dismissal once more.

The other significant death in 1821 was that of Napoleon on 5 May. As soon as the news arrived in July Bathurst informed Lady Holland, one of Napoleon's greatest admirers in Britain, that he had received a snuffbox bequeathed to her by her hero. Lady Holland replied from Paris that, although she and Bathurst would never agree on Napoleon, she appreciated his allowing her to send three trifles to St Helena during the past three years, 'which were an indication of my respect & admiration of the greatest man of our times, which I have now the satisfaction of learning afforded him some little comfort & which I am sure he had more than rewarded by so affected an acknowledgment of them'.[14]

The death of Napoleon permitted Bathurst to order the removal of troops and ships from the island, which reverted to the administration of the East India Company. This was a financial bonus to the government but a blow to the economy of the island and to the Cape of Good Hope which had been the main supplier to the garrison and the navy.

Among those returning from St Helena was Sir Hudson Lowe. At the next vacancy he was appointed colonel of the 93rd Highland Regiment, but he never ceased pestering Bathurst to protect him against criticism of his treatment of the icon of liberal Europe, while refusing Bathurst's advice to publish the documents that would vindicate his conduct.[15] His patience finally worn down, Bathurst sharply reminded the almost paranoid Lowe that the colonelcy was 'an unequivocal proof of his Majesty's approbation of your services' and that his promise of a government in the West Indies as soon as possible was because Lowe's services entitled him to one, not to silence any clamour against him. If Lowe allowed this last impression to circulate, Bathurst warned, 'Believe me it will only give to your opponents the occasion of renewing their attack.'[16] Lowe was soon appointed Governor of Antigua but resigned before sailing for personal reasons. He did serve as second-in-command in Ceylon from 1825 to 1830, but then spent the remaining fourteen years of his life bombarding successive Colonial Secretaries with his grievances and claims for recognition.

Once the storm over Queen Caroline's funeral had died down, George IV became better disposed to his ministers than he had been in the two years since his accession. He was buoyed up by his reception in Ireland, where he was far more popular than in London, and was in even better form after his triumphant tour to Hanover, which included an inspection of the field of Waterloo with the Duke of Wellington. He had never been hostile to Bathurst, and after his return had his private secretary tell the Colonial Secretary how much he looked forward to his audiences: 'Your Lordship never failed to mix up so much good-humour & fun with your business, that it was rather a recreation than a fatigue.' The King also hoped that the portrait of Bathurst that Sir Thomas Lawrence was painting for the Waterloo

Gallery in Windsor Castle would be as successful as those already completed.[17]

By the end of 1821, too, the government had finally managed to acquire more badly needed support in parliament. Although the King adamantly refused to take back Canning, despite the Prime Minister's pleas about the need for his debating skills in the Commons, it did gain a considerable figure in Robert Peel who, after dithering for a year, agreed to become Home Secretary in place of Sidmouth, who was allowed to keep his cabinet seat. Lord Grenville and his followers were also won over on extravagant terms, including a dukedom for his nephew, the Marquess of Buckingham, and the Board of Control and the embassy to Switzerland for two other nephews, Charles Watkin Williams Wynn and Henry Watkin Williams Wynn, popularly known as Bubble and Squeak for their high voices. This reunion with the last of the independent Pittites also meant a resumption of happy personal relations between Bathurst and Grenville.

No such reconciliation occurred with Lord Wellesley, a loose adjunct of the Grenvillites, who was secured by appointing him Lord Lieutenant of Ireland. Having frittered away the fortune he had brought back from India in high living and low company, Wellesley was overjoyed at the prospect of enjoying again something like the style of Calcutta. But the memory of his idleness as Foreign Secretary a decade earlier, as well as his support of Catholic emancipation, made it essential to appoint a strong and efficient Protestant minder as Chief Secretary.

Lord Harrowby told Bathurst at Cirencester that the cabinet 'with one accord cried out Goulburn,' and indeed Liverpool had sounded out Goulburn even before Wellesley was approached.[18] Bathurst added his own encouragement and Goulburn, given a pension of £1000 a year for his services at the Colonial Office, felt financially able to accept the office he had refused three years before.[19]

After his initial interview Goulburn told Bathurst that Wellesley had leaped at the offer 'with quite eastern ecstasy, which appears to be equally excited by his view of the situation itself and of his secretary'.[20] Bathurst's reaction to the resurrection of his former friend who had tried to undermine the government in 1812 was more restrained. According to the new cabinet minister Charles Wynn, who dined with Bathurst early in 1822, he was 'very hostile and bitter against Lord Wellesley, quizzing his speeches, &c., &c.'[21] But Bathurst managed a correct if formal letter of congratulation to Wellesley, commending Goulburn in the highest terms: 'He has been now nearly ten years in my Office & in addition to excellent abilities & great diligence I have uniformly found him the most upright honourable man

140

imaginable.' And in a none too subtle reference to Wellesley's own short-comings, he added: 'You will find in him all the qualities which you could desire in his situation, & will well know how to call forth all the advantages to be derived from them.'[22]

Bathurst was obviously sorry to lose his trustworthy and energetic assistant, but he had no alternative in face of the needs of the government, and it was a consolation that they continued as colleagues. To replace Goulburn, someone in the cabinet suggested the thirty-seven-year-old Robert Wilmot, a reliable and useful MP since his election in 1818. In 1819 he had defended the provision for George III at Windsor Castle against opposition charges of extravagance; in 1820 he had opposed a radical motion for parliamentary reform and in 1821 he had seconded the Address in Reply to the Speech from the Throne. Bathurst and Goulburn agreed that he was a good choice.[23] But far from being a dependable supporter of the old order, Wilmot soon became an enthusiast for change.

The Colonial Office on Wilmot's arrival was not the happiest place. In common with all departments, salaries had been decreased, to take effect at the beginning of 1822. The stipend of the Secretary of State remained at £6000 a year, but most others were reduced, including the Under-Secretary's from £2500 to £2000. 'The office is in a dreadful state of dissatisfaction in consequence of the new Establishment & the complaints made to me are not very agreeable,' Goulburn told Bathurst just before leaving for Ireland, 'but I think the storm will blow over before Wilmot's installation.'[24]

The House of Commons was also in a surly mood in 1822 as landowners suffered from low grain prices. George Canning, a loose cannon while awaiting the promised golden exile to India as Governor General as consolation for the King's refusal to take him back into the cabinet, managed to get a bill through the House allowing Catholic peers to take their places in parliament, though it was rejected by the Lords. And the strain of leading the fractious Commons as well as conducting foreign policy for a difficult decade was now telling on the fifty-three-year-old Marquess of Londonderry (as Castlereagh became in succession to his father in 1821, though as an Irish peer preferring to continue as an MP). By the end of the session the Foreign Secretary was so worn out by late night sittings that he had to stay in bed until it was time to go back to parliament in mid-afternoon. Having been enticed into a brothel by what turned out to be a young man in woman's clothes, he was also being taunted outside his house with what were then illegal homosexual practices.[25] On 7 August he attended a cabinet to approve the instructions he had drafted for his attendance at the Congress of Verona, and those of his friends and colleagues who remained in London were alarmed at his deteriorating condition. A week later he committed suicide at his house in Kent by cutting his throat with a penknife.

Bathurst, who was at Cirencester when he received the news, was immediately summoned to London, as was Wellington from the Netherlands, and as many cabinet ministers as could be collected from around the country. The easy matter was the replacement for Castlereagh at Verona, which it was quickly agreed should be the Duke. Even before this was known on the continent, the new Lord Londonderry (Lord, formerly Sir Charles, Stewart) wrote to tell Bathurst from his embassy at Vienna that Metternich specifically hoped for that kindred spirit, 'not only from his genius and transcendent reputation in Europe, but from his intimate knowledge of everything connected in that [Iberian] peninsula, in which so large a proportion of his career has been seen'.[26]

Far more difficult was replacing Castlereagh at the Foreign Office and as Leader of the Commons. This could not finally be settled until the King returned from Scotland where he had gone with Peel and Melville two days before Castlereagh's death. In the interval Bathurst stayed with the Prime Minister at Coombe Wood, his house near Kingston-upon-Thames, and Wellington frequently joined them for dinner. Apparently much influenced by a letter from the new Duke of Buckingham threatening to withdraw the support of the Grenvillites if Canning was not appointed, Bathurst and the Duke reluctantly agreed to recommend this difficult former colleague, and Peel even waived his considerable claim to the Leadership. Bathurst and Wellington were confident that their experience of foreign policy and their influence would keep Canning from straying from Castlereagh's path, however trying he might be. The Duke provided a gracious way for the King to overcome his personal objection by observing that royal honour would be perfectly safe in extending forgiveness to an erring subject, but George IV's objections were at least as much overcome by Bathurst. The King told his current mistress, Lady Conyngham that 'he was more satisfied by what Lord B. had said to him on that subject than by any of the Ministers'.[27]

Canning was not best pleased that his colleagues welcomed him back as Foreign Secretary and Leader of Commons by agreeing with the King that there was some transgression to forgive, though he was not willing to risk the office he had yearned for ever since leaving it in 1809 by standing on his dignity. He did take the opportunity to request that his friend William Huskisson also be brought into the cabinet. But having endured enough in getting the King to agree to Canning, Liverpool refused another immediate engagement. After a series of retirements and reshufflings in the next few months, however, Huskisson did join the cabinet in 1823 as President of the Board of Trade, replacing Frederick Robinson who became Chancellor of the Exchequer. A minor consequence was that the colonial agency for Ceylon which Huskisson had to resign could, after being reduced from £1200 to £800 a year to meet the demand for economy, be used by Bathurst to permit the retirement of Richard Penn, a senior clerk who had served in the Colonial Office since 1801, by exchanging his £500 a year agency for Mauritius.[28]

Whatever the new ministerial arrangements did for government efficiency, debating strength in the Commons and the satisfaction of various claims, they took a high toll in personal emotions. The Prime Minister in particular was reduced to a nervous wreck by the end of the process. It was reasonable to expect that the partisan bitterness would subside once Canning and the other ministers settled into office, but in fact the government was immediately divided by the new Foreign Secretary's policies and even more by his eristic personality and manner. The unity of purpose and personal harmony of Liverpool's government during a decade of war, peacemaking, domestic tensions and threats to its very existence was gone forever and Bathurst was not alone in soon regretting that he had supported Canning's return. Even though he continued as a member of the inner cabinet for foreign, imperial and military matters, along with the Prime Minister, Wellington and Canning, this was not the happy group it had been in Castlereagh's day.

Canning strode back into the Eden he had left thirteen years before with a light heart and heavy tread. The change of tone was immediately obvious as Wellington set off for the Congress of Verona bearing Castlereagh's instructions. He had no objection to telling the meeting that Britain would not support an invasion of Spain to restore Ferdinand VII, forced by the army to accept the liberal constitution of 1812 and still a captive, nor to Canning's supplementary order to raise the scandalous continuation of the slave trade in defiance of promises in 1815, but he did protest at being pursued by messages from the new Foreign Secretary, instead of being trusted to use his own judgment as he had at the Congress of Vienna. On his return he told his confidante, Mrs Arbuthnot, that he would never again go on a mission so fettered.[29]

Canning was blissfully unaware that he was antagonizing the Duke, who regarded himself as Castlereagh's true heir. He was so pleased with Wellington's conduct at Verona that, early in 1823, he tried to enlist his prestige further by sending him to Spain to negotiate the freedom of the

King without a French incursion and risk of occupation. But Bathurst, who was also offended by Canning's manner and the fact that he was not consulted as he would have been by Castlereagh, strongly reinforced Wellington's reluctance to become involved in a confused situation where his presence might do no good and his failure much harm. 'To whom are you to be sent?' Bathurst asked. 'With whom are you to negotiate? What rational hope is there of success? You are too great a card to be employed on such an adventurous mission.' More importantly he believed that the Duke should remain in England as the only person who could control Canning.[30] Lord Fitzroy Somerset went instead, but to no avail. In the summer the army of Louis XVIII freed the Spanish King, who in the remaining ten years of his reign imposed more severe repression on the country. And the presence of the French army raised once more the familiar issues of Portugal and the colonies of both Iberian states.

Canning was no revolutionary, supporter of revolutions or, at home, sympathizer with the demands for moderate parliamentary reform. But his public criticism of autocratic régimes, his greater distaste for acting with them and his determination to separate Britain further from the continent than Castlereagh, made him seem far more friendly to constitutionalism, national liberty and the destruction of the postwar order than his predecessor, or than he really was. He was also supremely confident of his ability to handle foreign affairs without advice from Bathurst or Wellington, and after only perfunctory consultation with the Prime Minister and the rest of the cabinet. Bathurst and the Duke found that their views were resisted and were further antagonized by Canning's showy self-promotion, delight in his own verbal cleverness and unconcealed low opinion of such veterans as Eldon and Westmorland.

It was bad enough that the new Foreign Secretary proved more obstreperous than those who had practically guaranteed his conduct had expected, but far worse when other ministers sided with him. It was only to be expected that Huskisson would support him. It was more surprising of Frederick Robinson, hitherto considered a Tory of pleasing orthodoxy. But it was truly astonishing that the Prime Minister seemed to change his whole outlook and surrender his judgement to Canning. The hostility and suspicion within the government became so strong that Bathurst did not feel that he could even trust his own Under-Secretary, Robert Wilmot. Asking Charles Arbuthnot to come to his office, he explained that he did so only because Wilmot was gone. In future he would go to Arbuthnot's house (only a few doors away in Downing Street), since Wilmot 'repeated everything to the Canning party & that, if he saw them talking together, he wd suspect something & tell Canning! Such is the state of confidence in which we are with our new ally!' commented Mrs Arbuthnot. Bathurst thought that the only thing that could save the country from Canning's mismanagement was Wellington's 'authority & his excessive good temper, which he said was beyond any thing he ever knew'.[31]

The split in the cabinet owed something to Canning's personality, but much also to his efforts, along with Huskisson, Robinson and the Prime Minister, to increase the prosperity of the country by the same means as Pitt in the 1780s: reducing tariffs and rationalizing taxes (which in the prosperity of the early 1820s seemed to have the effect of eliminating the chronic budget deficit). Sympathy with nationalism was a natural corollary in promoting trade and was not incompatible with what Castlereagh had done. But to the Ultra Tories the advent of Canning and the new tone marked a dangerous reversal and subversion of the ministry's previous course, and their suspicions were not allayed when the Whigs stopped criticizing foreign policy in the hope of separating Canning from his colleagues, perhaps even forming a coalition with him. The Ultras looked to Wellington as their champion, had a powerful ally in the King, who now found new grounds for detesting Canning and Liverpool, and in the Commons put their hopes in Peel, a reformer at the Home Office but at least a sound defender of Church and State and no follower of Canning.

Bathurst's loyalty was particularly torn by this conflict. He was Wellington's closest associate and temperamentally agreed with the Ultras; indeed within a year and a half of Canning's appointment he was threatening to resign if the Foreign Secretary did not stop sending despatches before consulting his colleagues and the King.[32] But he had a better grasp than the Duke of the subtleties and flexibility of Castlereagh's policy, which had been based more on British diplomatic and trade interests than a rigid defence of the existing order, and a greater appreciation of the importance of trade. As a veteran of office for the best part of forty years, rather than a Great Man who considered himself well above the ruck of ordinary politicians, Bathurst was also more accustomed to compromise and living with less than an ideal policy. And as an intimate of Liverpool for over a decade, he could not lightly break this connection, however much he grumbled and complained about Canning and his policies.

This loyalty to the Prime Minister must have severely tested Bathurst's attachment to the person if not the institution of monarchy when the King put on a disgraceful display of hostility to the ministry at the Royal Pavilion at Brighton in March, 1823. Apart from Bathurst, the only other guests at dinner were the royal mistress, Lady Conyngham, her husband and Countess

Lieven, wife of the Russian Ambassador, who egged on the King. Bathurst was forced to endure the monarch's abuse of Canning's attitude towards the Spanish insurrection, of the Prime Minister, of the country's 'abominable Constitution' and his declaration that he would 'rather be a shoe-black than a member of that odious Parliament'. The King afterwards told Madame Lieven that he merely wanted to show her how he treated his ministers, and even she had the decency to confess to her lover by correspondence, Prince Metternich, that she had found the episode unseemly and hoped that Bathurst, whose agitation had been physically obvious, had understood that she did not take the outburst seriously.[33] But this mortifying episode must have confirmed in Bathurst's mind the need to tread a careful line between Canning and the Ultras, and the need, above all, to keep the only obvious person who could preserve the combination.

The strain of the conflict on him and others was nevertheless very high. At the beginning of 1824 Arbuthnot urged Bathurst not to remain silent but to speak out in cabinet when he agreed with the Duke, lest he resign over his apparent isolation. Various ministers assured Wellington after cabinet meetings that they supported what he said, 'but as the leaders in the two Houses [Liverpool and Canning] had taken a different view they thought it better to acquiesce'. The Duke's blunt nature prevented him from understanding this and he imagined himself the object of suspicion by his colleagues. 'It would be very painful to *you*, I am sure,' Arbuthnot warned, 'and very injurious to all were he to retire'.[34] But, however true this might be, Bathurst would not take a stand against Liverpool by openly confronting the Foreign Secretary.

The main dispute was over recognition of the independence of the Spanish and Portuguese colonies in Central and South America. This had been an issue during the French Revolutionary and Napoleonic wars, but became more pressing after the 1820 revolt against Ferdinand VII in Spain and the similar civil war between absolutists and constitutionalists in Portugal. The colonies of both countries, which had resisted the efforts to reimpose the systems of metropolitan control after 1815, took advantage of the conflicts to assert their claims to independence.

Britain did not want to lose the major stake in trade that she had gained during the wars to other countries, and independence was supported by British merchants and bankers as well as opponents of absolutism and those who believed that free governments would abolish the slave trade. At the time of his death Castlereagh was on the point of recognizing the flags of the most effectively autonomous colonies, but Wellington was not only more of a legitimist but had also been sharply critical throughout the

Peninsular War of British merchants trying to steal the colonial trade and poison relations with the country's allies. He did not relent in his opposition to recognition after Canning took over the Foreign Office, and neither did the King. Bathurst, who had strongly promoted this colonial trade while at the Board of Trade, did not go as far as the Duke and the King in his objections, but he did not consider that commerce required formal diplomatic recognition which would jeopardize British friendship with the Iberian countries and further separate her from the continental powers. He tried to bridge both sides by urging caution on Canning, writing from that centre of resistance, Windsor Castle, early in 1824 of Mexico: 'I have long thought that the insurgent States must be sooner or later recognized, but in doing it we must be govern'd by circumstances.' Although neither the present nor any prospective government of Spain could recover its colonies, it seemed to him 'desirable on many accounts to put as much of the appearance of deliberation & even of reluctance in the act as possible'. As an argument for delay he suggested that since 'Men are not apt to set a high value on what appears to be too readily given,' speedy recognition would simply encourage the colonists to demand more, even an alliance with Britain.[35]

But Canning and Liverpool were no more willing to accept the case for cautious gradualism than adamant opposition and by the end of 1824 got their way by threatening to resign. Early in 1825 commercial treaties, carefully drafted to assume rather than assert independence, were concluded with Mexico, Buenos Aires and Columbia; a treaty with Brazil was signed later in the year, and others followed. But this did not end the acrimony in the cabinet. Nor were the benefits of recognition as great as had been imagined. By the end of 1825 the speculative fever since 1822 for investment in Latin America finally broke. Enthusiasm for South and Central America cooled as many investors were ruined and others (including Wellington) lost considerable sums. Small local banks in Britain failed as depositors rushed to withdraw their deposits and the whole country was plunged into a financial crisis.[36]

The other great dividing issue in the cabinet was Catholic emancipation, and here Bathurst was more successful in harmonizing the antagonistic colleagues. The compromise of leaving it an open question within government, which had served well enough for a decade after 1812, came under severe pressure with the new appointments between 1821 and 1823. Canning was more determined than Castlereagh to achieve full political rights in order to reconcile Irish Catholics to the Union of 1801 and he was encouraged by the fact that by the end of 1823 all the ministers in the Commons save Peel were of the same opinion. Matters came to a head in

1825, hard on the heels of the dispute over Latin America, when an opposition motion for relief, supported by Canning, passed the Commons. A bill was then introduced accompanied by two 'wings' to allay Protestant fears: one raising the property qualification for the franchise in Ireland, the other providing for some degree of influence over the Catholic church through state payment of the clergy. Peel then decided that he must resign as a matter of honour, throwing the neurasthenic Prime Minister into a panic. Summoning his fellow Protestants, Peel, Bathurst and Wellington, Liverpool told them that if Peel went he must too.

Bathurst and Wellington were desperate to avoid this since Canning would be the leading candidate to become Prime Minister. The Duke suggested a scheme of carefully controlled emancipation through a concordat with the Pope, while Bathurst assured Liverpool that the bill would be defeated in the House of Lords and urged him to stay for the sake of his reputation and out of a sense of duty. He pointed out that Peel might well 'plead that his resignation is a relief to himself and the consequences affecting the Government of a very limited nature; your resignation is the dissolution of the Government'. He also reminded the Prime Minister that he would be exposed to bitter reproaches from those who had relied on his assurance that Catholic relief would not be a ministry question: 'Your Government was formed upon it: your friends have trusted their political fortunes upon it, and now you without notice turn round and consider it as a vital question.' Far better, Bathurst advised, to dissolve parliament, whether Peel resigned or not; and, if there was a strong mandate for Catholic claims after the election, Liverpool would at least have better grounds for resignation than the wounded feelings of one of his colleagues.

Liverpool replied in great agitation the same day saying that he could not continue with dignity without 'some organ' of his own Protestant feelings in the Commons. 'Who could replace Peel?' he asked Bathurst. 'It must not be an *ordinary man*. A moment's reflection will convince you that the man cannot be found.' No practical compromise could be devised and he would soon be forced out by a confrontation that could not be long averted: 'Whenever the *crisis does come*, the *Protestants* must go to the *wall*.'[37] Liverpool and Peel increased their determination to leave when the Relief Bill passed the Commons by twenty-three votes on 10 May, but on the eve of the debate in the Lords Liverpool relented to the extent of saying that he would remain if Peel did.

Bathurst then applied himself to persuading Peel to stay, reinforcing Wellington's efforts with a long and frank letter motivated by 'a sincere interest in [Peel's] character as well as a conscientious solicitude for the well-

148

being of the country'. If he went so would the Prime Minister, which would mean the end of the government. 'He must justify his resignation by the necessity which your's imposes upon him, & upon you alone therefore rests the responsibility,' he warned and asked whether it was fair for Peel, as MP for Oxford University, suddenly to abandon the cause with which the Church of England '(whether wisely or not is another question)' was so strongly identified. Did resignation demonstrate responsibility to the King and the public which admired his opinions? Bathurst also pointed out that, although it was easy to achieve popularity through indifference to office, 'you will find that public men, who have by their resignations exposed the country to great trouble & sudden convulsions are not easily forgiven. The public confidence in them is shaken in a way which is not soon recover'd'.[38] This appeal from age and experience to youth and promise succeeded. Peel relented and the bill was defeated in the Lords by 178 to 130.

But the end of debates in parliament for 1825 was not an end of the matter for the government. Canning was furious at the Protestant triumph in the Lords in defiance of the Commons and demanded that Catholic emancipation be adopted as government policy under threat of his resignation. This was a prospect that Bathurst and Wellington could bear with equanimity, but not the Prime Minister, who was plunged back into agitation. The day after the debate in the Lords he once again summoned Bathurst, Wellington and Peel to discuss this latest development.[39] After several conversations Liverpool told Bathurst that he could not agree to let Canning resign, even if a majority of the cabinet decided that the Catholic question should continue to be an open one. Once formally raised in cabinet, Catholic emancipation must be resolved like any other, and in this case either way meant the end of the government. Liverpool believed that he would have to advise the King that 'the formation of a Government upon the principle of resisting the Catholics' claims is *absolutely impracticable*, whereas the formation of a Government upon the opposite principle, even from amongst his present servants with some few additions, is within his power.'[40]

Once again Bathurst patiently recalled his colleague from his febrile defeatism by repeating many of the statements that he had made earlier. He reminded Liverpool that the crucial matter was his principle of cabinet neutrality and abandoning it would open him to the criticism of all the friends who had trusted it.[41] In the end the Prime Minister was saved by Canning who shrank from destroying the ministry, which might endanger his chances of becoming Prime Minister, agreeing instead to discourage further consideration until the new parliament met after the general election of 1826.

* * *

Meanwhile, in his own diminished and sombre office following the 1821 salary decreases Bathurst was occupied above all with the Ionian islands. Early in 1821 Greek revolts organized by a secret society of merchants at Odessa broke out in Moldavia and Wallachia (Romania) and the Greek Peloponnesus.[42] The Turks, aided by the hostility of the local population to Greek administrators, quickly suppressed the former, but in Greece proper, where the Turks had been a small minority living in amity with their neighbours for centuries, 20,000 were slaughtered in the uprising. The Sultan's government retaliated by hanging the patriarch of Constantinople, who, as a government official, was responsible for the conduct of his co-religionists, three bishops and a dozen other Greek administrators on Easter Sunday, then allowing a reign of terror for three weeks against Greeks in the capital and other cities of the empire. In October there was a massacre on the other side when Tripolitsa, the principal fortress in the Peloponnesus, fell to the Greeks and another 10,000 Turks were slain. An assembly at Epidaurus in January, 1822, proclaimed Greek independence, but endemic localism and factionalism were not cured at the ancient shrine of medicine and soon there were two major warring groups, and many smaller ones, which helped to prevent a decisive victory over the Turks.

The British government's great fear was that the revolt of Orthodox Christians would lead to war between Russia, their self-proclaimed protector, and the Ottoman empire, with Russia expanding into the Mediterranean and upsetting the balance between the powers established at the end of the Napoleonic wars. Russia broke off diplomatic relations with the Sublime Porte after the Constantinople massacre, but the Tsar was restrained from war by Castlereagh and Metternich warning of the danger of supporting revolt that elsewhere he was opposing.

The barbarities in Greece continued on both sides. But, with little accurate information, classically educated Britons, particularly those of a liberal disposition, saw only the slaughter, rape, forced circumcision and sale into slavery of noble and innocent descendants of classical and early Christian Greeks rightfully struggling for their freedom. The government, however, had better intelligence on both the Greeks and the Turks from the Ionian islands. This included not only reports from the islands themselves but also copies of intercepted correspondence from the mainland, easily obtained under the requirement that letters be fumigated.[43]

Bathurst put some of this early news to good advantage in December, 1821, when he learned that Lord Aberdeen, the 'Athenian Thane' as his distant relation Lord Byron called him, had made a financial contribution to

150

the Greek cause. Bathurst warned that the name of a prominent government peer on the subscription list would be used by the opposition to embarrass the government. 'You must be aware,' he told Aberdeen, 'that the Greek cause is supported by every Jacobin in France & England; and that it is impossible for Government to do anything but remain neuter.' He enclosed a graphic report of the Greek atrocities following the surrender of Tripolitsa from one of Aberdeen's neighbours in Scotland who had joined the Greek cause but fled to Corfu after witnessing that sickening triumph: 3000 people, mainly women and children, had been led to a gorge, stripped and butchered; pregnant women had had their bellies ripped open and their severed heads exchanged with those of dogs, and the large Jewish population had been tortured to reveal its wealth, after which many of them had been buried alive.[44]Abderdeen quickly saw the wisdom of neutrality on moral as well as diplomatic grounds, but the opposition never did.

If the ministry would not support the Greeks, as the opposition and other philhellenes demanded, neither would it aid the Ottoman Empire which it was concerned to preserve. At the beginning of the conflict Bathurst ordered Sir Thomas Maitland to proclaim neutrality in the Ionian islands, from which many had rushed to join the revolt, with the threat that those who went to fight would lose their property. With his equally low opinion of Greeks, Turks and other Mediterranean people, to say nothing of the bulk of humanity, Maitland was the ideal person to enforce this even-handed policy. But neither Bathurst, the two successive Foreign Secretaries, Maitland, nor anyone else would go so far as to deny asylum and even government maintenance in the islands to Greek refugees fleeing the Turks when the fortunes of war turned against them. Bathurst did, however, warn against allowing the Greeks to send their women to the islands so that the men could fight unencumbered. To prevent British leniency becoming an occasion for Turkish protest, the ambassador at Constantinople was provided with copies of the proclamation and instructions to assure the Sultan that Britain was still neutral.[45] Despite charges from the friends of Greece that government policy was merely a façade for injuring the Greeks and helping the Turks, it was in fact one of tempering strict legal neutrality with compassion for the Greeks.

In the summer of 1822 Maitland told the Colonial Under-Secretary from Geneva, where he was on medical leave, that it was quite impossible to tell who was winning the sporadic war in Greece: 'The imbecility and nullity of both sides, considered in a military point of view, is beyond all credibility.' He was also unable to understand why the opposition kept on harping about the lack of true neutrality in the islands. He conceded that he had done his best to keep out a flood of Greek refugees, but insisted that he had carefully considered each case on its merits and pointed out that it was ironic for his critics that those seeking refuge in the islands were ones who had opposed the revolt.[46]

Even as the High Commissioner wrote, a Turkish army of 30,000 was arriving in Greece and soon regained control of the area north of the Peloponnesus. This brought a significant change in Maitland's attitude. Back in harness at the end of September, he told Bathurst that neutrality should be further modified in favour of the Greeks flying before the Turks, 'in order to support those principles of humanity, for which our country is so justly celebrated'. Considering the Greek cause lost, he urged that they no longer be considered 'Insurgents by whose acts the quiet of Europe might be destroyed, but as mere fellow creatures who, whatever their former conduct may have been, now demand commiseration; and any relief we can afford them, without inflicting intolerable burdens on ourselves'. Indeed he told Bathurst that he intended to protest to the Turkish government against the slaughter he thought inevitable from the Porte's lack of control over its officers, not from any presumed right of interference but from a concern for Turkish honour.[47]

By the time this letter arrived in England Canning was Foreign Secretary. As with so much else, the change in approach to the Greek question was largely a matter of style, rhetoric and degree from that of Castlereagh. Canning did have a warmer solicitude than his predecessor for those struggling to be free and was more interested in securing autonomy for Greece within the Ottoman Empire, but he was also concerned to maintain that empire and had, as he said, no intention of going to war 'for Aristides and St Paul'. But the alteration in attitude and manner was sufficient to make him seem a friend of real Greek independence. When some other Greek islands applied to come under British protection in 1823 Maitland gave them an encouraging response and forwarded the request to Bathurst. The Foreign Secretary wanted to pursue the matter, but Bathurst and Wellington managed to dissuade him and even considered reprimanding Maitland, wanting nothing to do with what Mrs Arbuthnot called 'such a horde of savages'.[48]

No Greek islands were allowed to transfer their allegiance, but neither was any step taken against the generally excellent if angular High Commissioner in whom Bathurst had great confidence. He was even permitted to compromise the neutrality of the Ionian islands still further in favour of the Greeks by allowing British philhellenes, the most famous being Lord Byron, to stop there on their way to and from the fighting in Greece.

Bathurst, without relenting in his commitment to the Ottoman Empire, also demonstrated his own practical, humanitarian and prudent partiality towards the Greek victims by taking a strong stand against the attempt of Algiers and Tunis to evade the terms extracted by Lord Exmouth in 1816 in order to revive the slave trade while the British government and navy and were absorbed in Greece.

As soon as he heard that the ruler of Tunis was allowing the sale into slavery of captured Greeks sent from Constantinople in the summer of 1823 he sent an ultimatum by way of Maitland and asked the First Lord of the Admiralty to spare a couple of warships to compel the Bey's signature. If he refused, the vice-consul was to 'strike his flag & come on board & the port to be declared in a state of blockade, and the commencement of hostilities to take place.... The details of the sale of these Greek prisoners would make a great sensation, if we appear'd to have done nothing to prevent the recurrence of a similar transaction.' Melville happily provided the ships and when Tunis was blockaded the Bey reaffirmed the 1816 agreement, agreeing to treat Greeks sent there as prisoners of war rather than as slaves.[49] In the case of Algiers a more formidable expedition, which as in 1816 again involved bombarding the city to overcome the Dey's resistance, achieved the same result in the following year.

When Bathurst requested a report of the Greek war at the end of 1823, Maitland sent a long account based on intercepted correspondence from Byron, Capodistria (suspended as joint foreign minister by the Tsar in 1821) and others. He thought the odds still fearfully against the Greeks, but the astonishing incapacity of the Ottoman government prevented the slight exertion that would effectively crush the insurrection. This incompetence and the very length of the rebellion, now entering its fourth year, suggested to Maitland that it might eventually succeed, though he also thought that any victory would be destroyed, as every Greek one had so far, by jealousy and love of plunder.[50] Five days later Maitland was struck down by a fatal stroke. Autocratic, arrogant, loutish and frequently drunk, he had been an outstanding governor of the Ionian islands at a tense time with far more humanitarian sympathy for the Greeks than his many detractors then and later appreciated.

Maitland's lieutenant and military commander at Malta, Major General Sir Frederick Adam, immediately wrote to Wellington, under whom he had served in the Peninsula and at Waterloo, asking for his influence with Bathurst for the succession. Lord Beresford, the commander of the Portuguese army, also asked the Duke for the post.[51] But Bathurst quickly decided on Adam, who was on the spot and had the qualifications for governing at that critical moment. The new High Commissioner was at least as irascible as Maitland, but at least as acceptable to the Ionians and as sympathetic to the Greek cause since his wife was a Corfiote, whose first husband had apparently surprised them in the usual compromising circumstances.[52] They took a more active part in the life of the islands than the austere bachelor Maitland, including favouring the new university being organized by Lord Guilford, scorned by the self-educated Maitland, but which played an important part in the Greek linguistic and cultural revival. But experienced as Adam was, Bathurst had to remind him, when he referred to a private letter in a public despatch, that he must keep his official and private correspondence completely separate, since the latter was confidential to the Colonial Secretary, 'off the record', while the former might be produced in parliament.[53]

The British Empire in the Mediterranean was now too important and vulnerable to be combined under one individual, even if another Maitland could be found. Adam received only the Ionian islands and Malta was given to the sixty-nine-year-old Lord Hastings, the friend of George IV who, as Lord Moira, had been a candidate for Prime Minister in 1812. After ten years as Governor General of India he had returned in 1823 materially poor but rich in military and administrative experience and was grateful to receive the relatively lowly but nevertheless important appointment in a salubrious climate.

There was no shortage of other colonial issues in the early 1820s, but until 1823 none required as much of Bathurst's attention as the Ionian islands, literally within sight of the flashpoint of Greece which might ignite an international war at any moment. All around the world, however, the volume of colonial business was increasing beyond the capacity of the staff of the Colonial Office to handle it. The settlement colonies in North America, South Africa and even Australia were being transformed by postwar emigration, reflecting the agitation within Britain for parliamentary reform in their demands for more responsible and less authoritarian local government. There was also strong pressure to do something about the morally offensive institution of slavery. And all of this increased work and urgency occurred at a time when Lord Liverpool's government was threatened with collapse from within.

7

THE RESTRAINING AND LIBERATING HAND

Given the acrimony in the cabinet after the death of Castlereagh in 1822 as well as the increase in colonial business requiring his attention, it is hardly surprising that Bathurst withdrew more into his own department, and even away from the centre of conflict by spending more time in the country. He was no less concerned than before about foreign policy, but with Canning pursuing a course divergent from Castlereagh's he relied on Wellington to take the lead in opposition, while himself getting along well enough with the Foreign Secretary where their jurisdictions overlapped and on the colonial issues that required Canning's lead in the Commons.

After Liverpool's defection to Canning and his allies, Bathurst's relations with the Prime Minister became somewhat cooler and soon Wellington was the only leading minister to whom he was really close. The Duke in turn confided in Bathurst alone of his colleagues, which accounts for the jealous tone of some comments of his other confidante, Mrs Arbuthnot, good friend as Bathurst was to her husband. In 1822, for example, when, in a rare disagreement with her hero, Bathurst was sceptical of the Duke's proposal to reduce the cost of defending Canada by concentrating troops in a few places rather than spreading them along the frontier as well as his recommendation to improve the waterways, Mrs Arbuthnot, herself never in the van of reform except when it was advocated by Wellington, burst out that Bathurst was

a very bad minister for the present times, he likes everything to go on in the old way, likes a job for the sake of a job, not to get money in his own pocket, for there cannot be a more disinterested man, but he hates all innovation & wd have done perfectly & been considered a very upright minister in the time of Sir Robert Walpole.[1]

Her strong feelings surfaced again from time to time, but on this particular issue the ministers soon amicably patched up their differences and by 1826 work had begun on improving the Ottawa and Rideau Rivers at an eventual cost of over £6,000,000.

But even their close professional and personal relationship did not save Bathurst from occasional reprimand by the imperious Wellington, who had scarcely enough to do at the Ordnance and keeping a sharp eye on Canning to keep boredom at bay, whenever the Colonial Office or its agents were perceived as trespassing on his departmental authority. In the spring of 1824, complaining about a transgression of the Governor of the Leeward Islands, the Duke told Bathurst in uncompromising terms that he had no objection to surrendering all colonial concerns; but 'if the business is to be carried on by the Ordnance, the Governor and officers must be brought to their senses, or I must proceed in a manner which will certainly settle all these little questions, but which will be very disagreeable to me and to the officers on the spot'.[2] A few months later he was complaining about Bathurst himself issuing formal orders to the Ordnance for equipment and supplies for Sierra Leone without first discussing with him the need and the means of providing them. Again, it was no more than his duty to protest against 'a novel mode of conducting the business between the two departments, from which, in my opinion, the service has suffered very materially already, and will suffer more hereafter'.[3]

But, despite these occasional minor irritants, Wellington gave Bathurst another tangible mark of his high esteem in 1825 by sending an oil sketch of himself at Waterloo surrounded by his staff. This was the work of the Dutch artist Jan Willem Pieneman, the basis for the centrepiece of an enormous painting of the battle which had been exhibited in Hyde Park the year before. Bathurst replied that he would hang the picture in the new hall at Cirencester, where it remains today beneath Sir Thomas Lawrence's huge portrait of the Duke.[4]

Relations between Bathurst and Wellington may have been good and friction between the War and Colonial Office and the Ordnance the exception rather than the rule, but Wellington's annoyance was an indication that the Colonial Office had been increasing its control and trying to assert its supremacy in the colonies since the end of the war.[5] It was particularly concerned to impress its views on slavery, the leading humanitarian cause of the day, though this was by no means the only area in which it wanted to replace wartime neglect with central direction. Bathurst was much concerned that the colonies should be in harmony with the home government, but it was also his nature constantly to urge the governors that this conjunction would best be achieved by prudence and conciliation rather than heavy-handed imposition.

The increased work meant that Bathurst, who conducted the most important correspondence, his Under-Secretary Wilmot-Horton (who assumed the additional surname in accordance with his father-in-law's will in 1823), and even the clerks had to work harder for their reduced salaries by the early 1820s. As soon as he arrived at the end of 1821 Wilmot-Horton applied his ample though sometimes erratic energy to reorganizing, reforming and expanding the Office to deal with the additional business. In 1822 the empire was divided into four areas, each under a senior clerk who could develop specialized expertise: the West Indies; North America, including Newfoundland and Bermuda; the Mediterranean and Africa; and the eastern colonies of Mauritius, Ceylon and Australia. By 1824 the correspondence registers matched these geographical divisions. Many old and inefficient clerks were induced to retire on pensions and new ones were recruited and encouraged by establishing clerical grades and promising rapid promotion. This reform soon filled the senior ranks with relatively young men who blocked the advancement of others; but hardworking and promising clerks could be rewarded by what Bathurst defended a decade later as the 'economical and honourable way' of giving them colonial agencies in lieu of promotion and increased salary:

> He knows little of official life, or is little willing to give credit where credit is due if he can look with indifference on those who he sees toiling hourly under him, neither animated by the hopes of promotion, or the chance of being cheered in his labours by the gratifying voice of public approbation & applause.[6]

The most remarkable of the new individuals who joined the Colonial Office at this time was the barrister James Stephen, son of the prominent Evangelical Tory lawyer of the same name who had vigorously defended the Orders in Council, nephew of William Wilberforce, and son-in-law of the Evangelical rector of Clapham, John Venn. Stephen had been reviewing colonial acts at three guineas each since 1813, but they were now running at the rate of a hundred and fifty to two hundred and fifty a year and he was having trouble finding time for the rest of his practice. In 1823 he was granted an annual payment of £1000 in lieu of fees. Two years later, at the age of thirty-six, he became permanent counsel at the Colonial Office at a salary of £1500 a year (three-quarters that of the Under-Secretary), the extra £500 being provided by the Board of Trade for his services as its law clerk in succession of John Reeves, who retired after thirty-six years in the post. At this change the Colonial Office assumed the review of colonial acts from the Board of Trade. Stephen also poured his enormous energy into abolishing or at least improving the lot of colonial slaves. In 1836 he became Permanent Under-Secretary, leaving twelve years later to become Regius Professor of Modern History at Cambridge.

The other leading recruit was Henry Taylor, who had the unusual qualification of having actually served in the colonies. He had been in the navy at Quebec at the age of fourteen at the end of the war against the United States and had then become a clerk in the Storekeeper General's office for four years, including one at Barbados, until that department was abolished. With this useful experience he was appointed as a junior clerk in the Colonial Office in 1824. Bathurst was well pleased with his work and early in the following year Taylor was promoted to the position of senior clerk in charge of the West Indies; there he stayed for forty-seven years, at the end transacting business from Bournemouth where he lived for the sake of his health. He was also an essayist, poet and playwright, or more accurately melodramatist. In 1836 he published a satire on government and ambition, *The Statesman*, dedicated to Stephen, 'the man within the author's knowledge in whom the active and contemplative faculties most strongly meet'; but the parodies of cabinet ministers are based on Bathurst's successors rather than the one under whom Taylor began and for whom he retained the greatest admiration throughout his long years at the Colonial Office.[7]

In 1824 Major Thomas Moodie of the Royal Engineers was also appointed, ostensibly as home secretary to commissions investigating the colonies, but in fact as a senior adviser on the West Indies, colonial finance and emigration. He had served in the West Indies and studied the French and Dutch systems of colonial government as well as the theory of colonization. In the course of his research and observations, he had concluded that hot climates disposed blacks to laziness, a view from which Bathurst did not dissent. The Colonial Secretary also agreed with Moodie that slaves must be carefully prepared for freedom by a lengthy period of religious instruction, and that slave owners were entitled to compensation for loss of their property. The emancipationists, however, saw Moodie not as a gradualist but as an opponent of liberation and after Bathurst left the Colonial Office managed to have him removed in 1828.

Effective from 1 January, 1825, Archdeacon Anthony Hamilton, secretary of the Society for the Propagation of the Gospel in Foreign Parts, which supported colonial churches, missionaries and schools, was appointed Chaplain General for the Colonies, on the analogy of the Chaplain General of the Forces, at a salary of £500 a year and the services of a clerk; he was supervised by a board consisting of the Archbishops of Canterbury and York and the Bishop of London. His main job was to ensure a supply of qualified clergy, particularly for the West Indies where two new bishops and twenty clerics were sent to minister to the slaves under the programme of amelioration, but he also advised generally on religious matters and carried on most of the ecclesiastical correspondence.

One Church issue that was settled just before Hamilton's appointment was the retirement of the Bishop of Nova Scotia, Robert Stanser. The former rector of St Paul's in Halifax had been consecrated in 1816, but after a brief sojourn in his diocese returned to England in 1817 on grounds of ill-health and had never since felt well enough to return. In 1824 the Archbishop of Canterbury wrote to Bathurst strongly endorsing a letter from Stanser offering to resign and 'throw himself on the liberality of Government for such remuneration as his past services may be thought to deserve'. But the Archbishop also pointed out that this might well create a precedent since there was apparently no instance of a bishop retiring since the reign of Queen Elizabeth.[8] An appropriate form was eventually devised and Stanser was allowed to retire on a pension of £250 a year, over the objections of the residents of the adjacent colony of New Brunswick, who found themselves paying part of the allowance for a bishop who had never visited that part of his diocese.[9] The financial exaction, however, turned out to be brief since Stanser died three years later.

Perhaps encouraged by this agreeable arrangement, the novelist Maria Edgeworth wrote in 1825 to the Archbishop through Bathurst, asking the same relief for the Bishop of Quebec, the father of her near neighbour in Ireland.[10] Bishop Jacob Mountain, who had been agitating for translation to an English see, or even parish, for twenty years, was no great favourite with Bathurst for his intrigues against Governor Prevost, but the question of what, if anything, to do about him disappeared later in the year on his death at Quebec.

Within a couple of years between 1822 and 1824 the Colonial Office establishment had been restored to what it was at the end of the Napoleonic wars: from ten to fifteen clerks, one to two librarians, a practically full-time from a part-time counsel, two new registrars and a précis writer, and from one to three private secretaries. But even this more efficiently organized staff of two dozen under the Secretary of State and an Under-Secretary was scarcely adequate to administer a world-wide empire. Most of the detailed work of the enlargement and organizational improvements had fallen on Wilmot-Horton. But only Bathurst, by his high standing in the cabinet, could convince his colleagues that the budget of his department must be increased scarcely half a decade after it had been drastically reduced, though he was helped by the prosperity of the early 1820s and the general desire to strengthen the hand of the Colonial Office against the slave owners.

The keystone of the expanded Office also required all the Colonial Secretary's political credit. After persistent representations from Horton, Bathurst told the Prime Minister in October, 1824, that the work demanded a second Under-Secretary. His only hesitation was the attitude of the House of Commons, but he assured Liverpool that the Chancellor of the Exchequer had no objection to the expense, while Canning had told his friend Horton that he did not expect any political opposition. The Prime Minister did not object to the cost, but, despite Canning, feared that this was

> just the sort of question which might revive the ill humour of the House of Commons which is fortunately overcome, & will raise again the question so often agitated, as to the necessity of the Office of the Third Secretary of State, or the expediency (if it is necessary) of uniting it with the India Board, Board of Trade or some other Office.

He temporized by asking Bathurst and the others to consider some different appointment that would arouse 'less Observation & prejudice'.[11] But in the end Bathurst's colleagues supported him: his allies to show their confidence; the Prime Minister, Canning and his associates to mitigate Bathurst's reluctance to recognize the Spanish American states, on which Liverpool and Canning were then threatening to resign. The new post was easily approved by parliament, bent on improving the lot of the slaves, and an appointment was made on 6 July, 1825.

The new Under-Secretaryship was a permanent one, whose holder would continue from minister to minister and not sit in the House of Commons. To fill it Bathurst selected Robert W. Hay, a friend of Horton's from their days at Christ Church, Oxford, but a more reliable Tory. At the age of thirty-seven, Hay had much experience and had had plenty of time to demonstrate his political inclinations, having been private secretary for many years to the First Lord of the Admiralty, before serving in the Victualling Office. Although Horton assigned him the supervision of the Mediterranean, Africa, Asia and the Pacific colonies, keeping the Americas himself, Hay's principal task was to manage the Office while Horton represented it in the Commons. Hay lacked the relentless dedication of Stephen and Taylor, even Horton, and the first two were sharply critical of his casual style; but his gregariousness, wit, humour and easy manner pleased the similarly inclined Bathurst, who welcomed his refreshing presence among the more earnest and hard-working assistants.

However well they may have known each other before, Bathurst and Hay immediately established a far warmer relationship than ever existed between Horton or even Goulburn and their chief. Hay had scarcely arrived at the Colonial Office before Bathurst was inviting him to Cirencester in the bantering manner that characterized their correspondence: 'When are we to expect you? I will not say that there is a fatted calf ready for you, but there will be something akin to it; for there will be some fat despatches ready for your consumption.'[12] Three days later he wrote to the new Under-Secretary, stuck in the tedium of London in the middle of summer: 'I send you back a small Box much I imagine to your relief, as the dissipations of London must distract you with numerous engagements.'[13] Early in the next year Bathurst wrote from Brighton asking Hay for a gold or silver pen in place of the bad office ones. Hay promptly complied, but two days later Bathurst replied in a spidery hand illustrating his complaint: 'I am writing with the pen you sent me; I cannot make out the word by which you distinguish it; but until you send me a quire of glass, you need not send me a diamond pen.'[14] Later in the year he asked Hay to reply to an inquiry from Sir William Knighton, Keeper of the Privy Purse and the King's confidential adviser, about the equipment and passage for the son of a royal page who had been given an appointment in Ceylon:

> In saying this he puts in a parenthesis, that Mr. Whiting is now *always* on duty with the King as page. I consider therefore that I have made your fortune, by putting you in correspondence with this page. If you see his son, you may sit down in his presence, but of course you would not presume to do so, in the father's presence.[15]

Enjoying this pleasant and confidential relationship with Hay, and with the Colonial Office in good hands after a reorganization that would endure for twenty years, Bathurst could afford to spend more time away from London than he had since becoming President of the Board of Trade in 1807. Since the death of Castlereagh and the various retirements at the beginning of the decade, he was one of the most experienced ministers, having been in cabinet for eighteen years by 1825 and in various offices for twice as long.

He was highly favoured by the King and wise in the ways of government and the personalities of his colleagues. Having administered his present department for thirteen years, he had a firm grasp of the principles of the colonial direction, though he could not keep up with all the details of all the colonies, and his wide knowledge and natural caution often caused him to tone down the despatches of Wilmot-Horton, who did not spare himself in application but was more abrupt, impulsive and erratic.

Celebrating his sixty-third birthday in 1825, Bathurst was also by some margin the oldest senior minister, save only Lord Eldon who was seventy-four. Liverpool and Canning were both eight years younger; the Duke of Wellington was only a year older than they, and Peel was a mere thirty-seven. He was also beginning to show signs of his age. At the beginning of 1825 he assured Horton from the country that he was 'quite sound now; having had something like a return of the complaint I had last year'.[16] But this assurance was contradicted by the tone of the letters that followed. The next week he begged off an invitation to dine with Liverpool and Canning at Bath, at least in part because he was recovering from an attack of gravel: 'It would have been imprudent to have accepted the invitation, especially as travelling is not good for me at present, and it would have added to my journey to London, to which place I shall be setting off tomorrow'. And a year later he was complaining to Hay of 'something of the lumbago'.[17]

A touch of rheumatism, even painful crystals in the urinary tract, were nothing serious in an age when everyone expected to suffer chronic pain as a matter of course by middle age. Liverpool and Canning were racked by gout and even the Iron Duke, stoically as he bore his afflictions, was now permanently deaf in one ear and suffered periodic fevers and inflammations of the bowel in addition to arthritis and rheumatism. But Bathurst's aches and pains and advancing years did take the edge off the stimulation of political engagement, particularly in the present fractious state of the cabinet, while long experience justified the confidence that he could control all the important decisions in the Colonial Office as well as keep a sharp eye on policies and personalities within the cabinet as easily from the country as in the febrile atmosphere of London.

Even in the capital he had, like his colleagues, always done much of his work at home. When he did go to his office, it was now separate from the rest of the department. Since the new staff and rapidly accumulating correspondence were bulging out of the Colonial Office and there was no space available in the other government houses in Downing street, Bathurst gave up his own room, and chambers were rented for him in Whitehall. There he remained until the Office was able to take over the adjoining house after the change of government in 1827.[18] He probably welcomed this move, which gave him more privacy from the Canningite Horton, while still being only a stone's throw from the Under-Secretaries and the other busy workers in the hive.

Bathurst's frequent absences from the official seat of business seem on the face of it to explain such grumblings as that of the Governor General of Canada in the mind-numbing boredom of Christmas at Quebec in 1825 that the latest mail 'as usual brings me nothing official, but renews all my bitter complaints of the sad neglect in Lord Bathurst's department & officers'.[19] All governors (and most historians after them) naturally expected their particular concerns to be uppermost in the mind of the Colonial Secretary and senior officials, but even with the increased staff, there was still a press of business that had to be ordered into some hierarchy of importance and urgency. And however much Lord Dalhousie resented it, Canada did not at that time seem to present any great difficulties compared to other parts of the empire.

Spending more time outside London at his own or others' houses meant that Bathurst had to keep the Under-Secretaries informed of his movements for them to send him material. These migrations sometimes involved complicated logistical arrangements, as when he told Hay one Friday in the spring of 1826 from Dropdene that he was going to Mr Beauclerk's at St Leonard's Hill near Horsham and would then return to town on Monday:

> but as Lady Bathurst goes on to Brighton, and as Apsley took the post chaise up to London, in which I came to Brighton, I am *chaiseless*. I therefore wish you to order a messenger down to me on Sunday to Mr. Beauclerk's & to come down in the post chaise which will be ready for him. He may then go back by the stage.[20]

Such provisions were by no means unusual for ministers, particularly when parliament was not in session; and with an efficient postal system, or a messenger when necessary, the delay in sending or receiving letters from London was rarely more than a day each way in southern England, to which Bathurst largely confined himself.

There is also no reason to think that he paid any less attention to despatches in the country than when he was in London. Indeed the calmer atmosphere and pleasing distractions may have been more conducive to sustained work and thought than the press of small matters and social obligations in the capital. The notes accompanying official papers, generally addressed to Hay, show Bathurst's dedication to business, both in detail and broader issues. Writing from Lord Harrowby's house in the autumn of 1825, for example, he told Hay that he had not been able to consider the following documents in time for the next post: '1. The Malta Papers; 2. That on the State of the free people of Colour in Trinidad; 3. The Terms of the Company of Lower Canada; 4. Mr. Hopkin's Comments on the amended Charter for the W.I. Company.' But later the same day he returned the Malta materials along with a private letter to the Governor, then in England. In the interval before the Governor replied, he asked Hay to return the official despatch for his signature rather than including a blank signature for the fair copy: 'By this means I shall have again the opportunity of seeing the Instruction before it finally goes.'[21]

The fact that Bathurst engaged in the potentially risky practice of providing blank signatures is an indication of his confidence in them, to say nothing of the reliability and security of the post. But he was always careful about this, except for the most routine and unambiguous documents. Earlier in the same summer, sending a signature from Cirencester for a despatch to Barbados that he had amended and returned the previous day, he asked Hay to check the final copy carefully before sending it, 'as it will be well criticized by the Barbados Orators & if there be a doubt it may as well not go'.[22] His attention to the details and interests of his department from afar is also evident in a note a week earlier requesting Hay to ask Canning's private secretary if there had not recently been two vacancies among the foreign messengers, 'one of which should belong to me, as I have a great suspicion that his Master means to monopolize that Patronage'.[23]

Spending more time in the country also helped Bathurst to deal with time-consuming visits from colonial officials. A meeting with the Jove-like figure who had for so long influenced the destiny of their colony was always a highlight of any trip to England, a mark of the individual's standing with the home government, a reinforcement or enhancement of his place in local society and an opportunity for personal advancement. If Bathurst were away, they had to be content with an Under-Secretary, with whom in any event they would have more detailed discussions. But the honour of an invitation to visit Bathurst at his Gloucestershire seat was a far more glittering prize than a brief discussion in his office. It was something they could boast about for years, a reward that the Colonial Secretary knew how to bestow on particularly deserving individuals, further cementing their loyalty and co-operation.

In the summer of 1826 Bathurst told Wilmot-Horton that he consented to such an invitation for a day to W.B. Felton, a member of the Legislative Council of Lower Canada, in London to discuss emigration and land policy,

'as you assure me that he is a civilized Canadian, or rather that his long residence there has not savaged him: and that he does not eat his dinner with
his fingers, or has an uncontrolable passion to seize on a pig & eat him raw,
if he saw him running about'.[24] Despite this jesting tone Bathurst almost
certainly already knew Felton, a native of Gloucestershire and half-pay naval
officer to whom he had granted about 10,000 acres since his emigration in
1815. His confidence in this sound member of the colonial executive was
demonstrated during the visit when he read him the draft of a despatch to
the Governor General, discussing the necessity of an official allowance for
the Catholic Bishop of Quebec and what Dalhousie should do in his dispute
with the legislature over control of the revenue.[25] The invitation to
Cirencester may have helped to persuade Felton to abandon his proposal for
a private land company to promote settlement of the colony, in return for
which he was granted another 5000 acres and appointed commissioner of
crown lands in the following year. A similar invitation was extended that
summer to another reliable member of the same council, Chief Justice
Jonathan Sewell, who spent much of the latter part of that year advising
Wilmot-Horton.[26]

In writing, reviewing and altering the stream of despatches that followed
him around the country, Bathurst's main concern was to uphold the
authority of the crown, meaning the Colonial Office and its agents, against
what he considered the dangerously radical demands of local councils and
legislatures where they existed. Although he never asserted this in any
belligerent or provocative manner and was always willing to tolerate a wide
diversity of local customs and styles of governing, he nevertheless insisted
and firmly believed that central control was the only way to prevent the
empire from internal collapse.

This was well expressed in a letter to Hay, commenting on the issue
between General Sir Lowry Cole, Governor of Mauritius, and a member of
his council who was insisting on the Governor's full accountability to it.
Bathurst told Hay, who had been inclined to side with the councillor: 'No
distant Government can go on, if all its ordinary administration, all the
despatches, which I write, & all the answers which are given are to be
submitted to a Council.' Only the most formal and general documents
should be submitted and Cole's critic should be reproved for saying that the
Governor was answerable to the council for every act done without prior
communication, since that would make him subject to the council rather
than the home government. Bathurst even doubted that a councillor had the
right to enter a protest against the Governor for not consulting it: 'The duty
of a Councillor is to give his advice when summon'd. If he be not summoned

in common with the other Members, he has a right to protest; but if the Governor acts without their advice he is responsible to the King & not to the Council, for so acting'. Bathurst wanted Hay to draft a letter defending the authority of the Governor against such 'extravagant pretensions'; but it is significant that he did not propose cancelling the councillor's appointment as the Governor's secretary, or even publicly reprimand him, but merely proposed telling him privately that 'if he cannot act *under* and not in *common* with the Governor, he cannot be confirm'd Secretary'.[27]

Bathurst was always apprehensive that imperial authority would be destroyed and colonial government paralysed by rigid insistence on the power of the crown to the point of alienating the local élite who had a ready source of appeal in the parliamentary opposition in Britain. He never ceased trying to impart his own prudence and experience of administration to military veterans whose very different training led them to expect unquestioned obedience to orders from above. He understood well enough from his relations with Wellington and other commanders the impulse of hard-pressed governors to deal in a curt and confrontational manner with the ulcerous situations in which they often found themselves, but he warned them to use their powers with discretion and to be as conciliatory as compatible with upholding their position. In a memorandum written in 1825 or 1826 on the disputes in Australia over the decision to impose the British sterling standard on the various currencies circulating there, he advised:

When there are conflicting authorities, it is easy enough to preach temper, but it is perhaps difficult for those who are engaged in the contest to practise it. But in New South Wales, where the Governor's power is so manifestly paramount, he can afford to be forbearing – a readiness to accommodate, as far as is consistent with his duty, & a disposition to reconcile the quarrels which must be for ever recurring in such a society cannot be misunderstood.[28]

Bathurst may have been concerned to preserve the vast empire as it emerged from the Napoleonic wars but, as already seen in the case of Singapore, he was no enthusiast for acquiring new territories unless they offered some great economic or strategic benefit. To prevent promiscuous acquisition required keeping a close eye on local administrators, particularly in equatorial Africa, where the present possessions were a useful base for intercepting the transatlantic slave trade but otherwise seemed hardly worth the public expense for the guaranteed supply of gum, gold, spices and ivory. Bathurst shared the general desire of the government to reduce its costs and presence there,

166

though unlike some colleagues, he did not want to abandon it entirely.

Private British trading forts had been established on the coast of West Africa in the early seventeenth century. These were brought together in 1672 in the Royal Africa Company, from which Bathurst's great grandfather Sir Benjamin derived no small part of the family fortune. But despite its seemingly lucrative slave trade, the Company failed in the mid-eighteenth century, being succeeded by a loose coalition of the Company of Merchants trading into Africa organized by an act of parliament in 1750. This in turn faced collapse after the abolition of the British slave trade in 1807 and the advance against its forts of the aggressive Ashanti from the interior. At the same time Sierra Leone, a private settlement for freed slaves operated by British emancipationists since 1791, was taken over in 1808 as a crown colony when that noble experiment to demonstrate the superior efficiency of free labour over slavery proved economically disastrous. The number of freed Africans who were settled there increased rapidly after the Napoleonic wars, when the Royal Navy's African squadron could devote more effort to suppressing the slave trade. Between 1814 and 1824 about 16,000 freed slaves were landed, but the cost of administration also rose from about £24,000 in 1813 to £95,000 a decade later.[29]

In 1816 a select committee of the Commons recommended that Sierra Leone be kept, but that elsewhere the British presence be reduced to five forts. This drastic advice was not entirely adopted, but when the government felt compelled to take over the Company of Merchants in 1821 all of west Africa was combined under the Governor of Sierra Leone, Sir Charles Macarthy, who since 1816 had made his capital further north in the new post of Bathurst on the Gambia River. Macarthy was determined to bring British order to the Gold Coast by confronting the Ashanti with the grandiosely titled Royal African Colonial Corps, whose white troops were recruited from defaulters in the British army, in lieu of more immediate punishment. Disease and drunkenness were endemic in the humid tropical heat and it was difficult to find sufficient officers, even with the lure of promotion without purchase.[30]

Unfortunately for Macarthy, when his 5000-strong African Corps confronted the Ashanti on 21 January, 1824, the Ashanti were not only twice as numerous, twice as fit and twice as enthusiastic for battle, but were also well-equipped with arms and ammunition from the Dutch and the Danes. Macarthy's army was cut to pieces, he himself was killed and the skulls of the vanquished were used for years by the victors as ceremonial drinking cups.

When the news arrived in England, there were immediate demands for retribution. Bathurst did not share this anger and was satisfied with the repulse of the Ashanti from Cape Coast Castle in July of that year, but in the face of public opinion he and the government had little choice but to send a punitive expedition, the modest goal of which was low-cost punishment without further British involvement in that unpromising part of the world. Bathurst warned the new Governor, the Peninsular veteran Major General Charles Turner, on his appointment in June, 1824, not to enter into any new treaties with local rulers. Turner was even more pessimistic after he arrived, recommending withdrawing entirely from the Gold Coast, though, contrary to orders, he was soon trying to shore up the position by treaties.

Wellington and Huskisson agreed with Turner about abandonment, but Bathurst, unwilling to go that far, wanted to retain some toehold in the hope of trading opportunities with the interior of Africa. The compromise, he told Turner, was to preserve military forces at the strongholds of Cape Coast Castle and Accra but to abandon all other forts[31] since by this time a better centre for every British purpose had been found away from the heat, disease, vulnerability to attack and temptations of local disputes of the mainland. But finding efficient troops to garrison the two forts and deal with the Ashanti was no easy matter. The usual defaulters were rounded up in Britain, but when these proved insufficient by early 1826 it seemed inevitable that the Royal African Corps would become entirely native. Eleven Royal Artillerymen had been sent to Cape Coast Castle in 1824 to instruct the Corps in the use of guns and rockets, but with no conspicuous success.

To defend the two forts permanently Bathurst, in the summer of 1826, proposed raising an artillery corps from army pensioners, but for the present asked the Master General of the Ordnance to lend him a few of the regular artillery. Wellington was apoplectic at the suggestion, all the more because Bathurst had committed the grievous sin of sending an official request without discussing it beforehand. In a long, angry rocket, he wrote that the tropical African establishments were the most expensive and unhealthy of all the country's possessions, totally ineffective in stopping the growing slave trade by other countries, and it would be 'rather unjust to force the Royal Artillery upon an inglorious service on which death by sickness is certain, when other troops in his Majesty's service, excepting the volunteers in this local corps, or criminals, are exempt from it'. Of the eleven good artillerymen sent in 1824, only four had survived and two of those had had to be pensioned off as invalids. The Duke refused to commit any more without cabinet agreement to provide good fortifications, wholesome provisions, hospitals and convalescent ships, frequent relief and competent officers who would keep the troops in order and health. If the ministry insisted on continuing Britain's presence on the coast, despite 'the uselessness of these Posts and the experience of the past,' he helpfully recommended using seamen, since they received better provisions than the army and could more easily be evacuated 'if overtaken by those disorders to which man, even in a state of quiet, is liable in this most deleterious climate'.[32]

After receiving this letter, Bathurst went to Wellington's house in Hampshire, in part to reach some amicable agreement on the matter. The Duke essentially got his way, Bathurst telling Hay from Stratfield Saye to instruct Sir Neil Campbell, the new Governor succeeding Taylor, who had died of fever (as did Campbell), who was just leaving England, to withdraw the troops from Cape Coast Castle if it was safe and if he could make some friendly agreement with the Ashanti. The fort was to remain merely a trading post under the merchants. Campbell must make no commitment to provide troops for its defence, even in the event of an attack, though Bathurst added, 'he may engage generally that the Cape Coast will receive the protection of the Govt. in the same way as the other settlements are entitled to it'.[33] But less than a month after this arrangement the Royal African Corps inflicted a decisive though unauthorized defeat on the Ashanti on 7 August, 1826, at the battle of Dodowa (Katamansu). As a consequence, it took years to come to terms with the Ashanti and became practically impossible to remove the military force from the coast.

What persuaded Bathurst that the number of forts on the Gold Coast could be reduced and the troops evacuated, while maintaining British trading interests, was the Admiralty's proposal to occupy Fernando Po, a derelict island assumed to be owned by Portugal, 1000 miles east of Cape Coast and 2500 miles from Sierra Leone. This was not only supposed to be healthier than the mainland but was also closer to the cruising grounds of the anti-slavery squadron, enabling more freed slaves to be landed there than would survive the long voyage to Sierra Leone. In the spring of 1825 Bathurst circulated a minute to the cabinet recommending occupation, holding out the promise of being able to withdraw from Cape Coast Castle.[34] One of the Colonial Office clerks, however, discovered that the island had been sold by Portugal to Spain in 1778. Bathurst ruefully conceded to the Foreign Secretary: 'This makes an essential difference if correct, which I am inclined to doubt, as it is contrary to the general belief.'[35] The clerk, however, was right, and Canning insisted on caution, offering Spain cash or a West Indian island in exchange, until in 1827 Britain finally received provisional permission to use the island. But when it turned out to be no healthier than the coast, the government refused to pay Spain's £100,000 purchase price and in 1832 abandoned the establishment. The navy

169

continued using it for the next three years, but by 1835 there was more intense competition on the African coast and Spain wanted to use its own base. By then too, the British were being drawn back to the mainland by the lucrative exchange of manufactured goods for palm kernels and oil in the Niger, as well as timber and groundnuts (peanuts). Bathurst had tried to limit British involvement by disavowing the treaties of Turner, but if the lively prospect of profitable trade and resources had existed a decade earlier, he would undoubtedly have been more enthusiastic on maintaining at least the present position on the African coast.

The issue of tropical Africa was closely related to the campaign for the abolition of slavery, which became the major reform issue of the early 1820s. Far from objecting to the cost of the dangerous and unrewarding African coastal posts, many emancipationists thought that they should become bases for extending anti-slavery operations and sound moral and religious influences further into the continent. Cabinet ministers would not accept this, but they were grateful that emancipationists, the most vociferous of whom were among their parliamentary opponents, on this issue at least were prepared to regard government less as an expensive form of exaction, oppression and reward for the favoured few and more as an instrument for breaking the selfish interests of slave owners and imposing a righteous policy on them. But these new-found allies in turn expected effective action by the Colonial Office and were not slow to denounce what they regarded as reluctance to use the powers which they had helped to provide. The main area of contention was the West Indies, but the matter also extended to Mauritius in the Indian Ocean, where the illicit importation of slaves continued for almost a decade after its capture from the French in 1810, and the former Dutch colony at the Cape of Good Hope, where slavery had been established since the arrival of the Dutch in the middle of the seventeenth century.[36]

Abolition had been a recurring political issue since the beginning of Bathurst's political career in the 1780s when evangelical religion, the chief inspiration, was becoming widespread and respectable. In parliament the leader of the Saints was William Wilberforce, the friend of Pitt and old acquaintance of Bathurst. In 1807 they succeeded in getting the slave trade abolished within the British Empire and in 1808 the Portland government authorized the seizure and condemnation of slave vessels by prize commissions. But the right of violating foreign flags ended with the war and the Congress of Vienna's condemnation of the slave trade was little more than a pious declaration. The Foreign Office had some success in offering a variety of incentives to persuade other countries to accept treaties allowing the right of search to the anti-slavery squadron, but even these laudable and expensive efforts were not having marked success by the early 1820s.

Nor, despite the high hopes of 1807, had the lot of the slaves in British colonies improved since the trade was banned. With new supplies of vigorous young workers cut off, apart from smuggling, the owners simply worked the existing stock harder. The Saints concluded that the best way to stop this, and the illegal imports, was by slave registers in each colony, with copies in London. These were established by Orders in Council for the conquered colonies of Trinidad in 1812 and St Lucia in 1814, but when Wilberforce introduced a motion at the end of the war for general registration, Castlereagh persuaded him to give the colonial legislatures a chance to pass their own measures. This was echoed in the Lords by Bathurst, when Grenville raised the matter on 30 May, 1816. The Colonial Secretary told the House that it was better to let legislatures make their own laws than force measures on them, even though parliament had the undoubted right.

The West Indian assemblies bitterly resented what they saw as un-warranted interference in their internal affairs, seeing it as the first step towards emancipation.[37] They hotly denied that there was any illegal import-ation or mistreatment of slaves and adapted the argument of the American revolution in claiming that the slave registration fee was taxation without representation. But they finally accepted Bathurst's argument, presented through the governors, that it was better to concede in good time than rouse parliament to compel them, and by 1819 registers were operating in all the colonies.

During the registration contest Wilberforce took advantage of his connection to make direct appeals in person and long earnest letters to Bathurst and Goulburn, a pious Evangelical though also a slave-holder. After one of his more trying visits to the Colonial Office in 1819 pleading that the Governor of Sierra Leone be instructed to purchase a sufficient number of local women for the black regiments disbanded there, even the sympathetic Goulburn snapped to Bathurst after he left: 'I wish we could send some of our reforming countrywomen, but upon this I will defer saying more until I see you & only mention it to you because Wilberforce begged that not a day might be lost in calling your attention to it.'[38]

The registration struggle was a mere skirmish preparatory to the deter-mined campaign to improve the condition of the slaves that got underway in 1823. Since Wilberforce, Bathurst's senior by three years, felt too old and feeble to lead the revitalized cause, it fell to the devout thirty-seven-year-old MP Thomas Fowell Buxton, though the most powerful voice in the

Commons was that of Henry Brougham, the rising Whig lawyer who had defended Queen Caroline in 1820. The Anti-Slavery Society's ultimate aim was abolition, but the immediate task was improving the condition of the slaves in preparation for freedom. And since the new doctrines of political economy taught that free labour was more efficient than compulsion, the cause could claim the support of business principles as well as Christian morality.

In the spring of 1823 Buxton gave notice of a motion calling for the gradual abolition of slavery by an act of parliament declaring all slaves born after a certain date to be free. The government was caught in an awkward dilemma. Given the widespread support even among its own MPs, it could not oppose the motion and risk defeat, but emancipation by an imperial act would provoke resistance from the owners which in turn might produce slave revolts demanding the freedom granted by the parliament but denied by their masters. Before the debate in the Commons on 15 May a compromise was worked out with the representatives of the West Indian planters and merchants in Britain, a more moderate and amenable group than those resident in the colonies, providing for amelioration that would lead gradually to freedom, at which point the owners would receive compensation for their loss of property from the British government; the West Indian interest in return undertook to persuade colonial assemblies to pass their own legislation for this transformation. During the debate, in which Wilmot-Horton did not speak, Canning promised that the ministry would return to parliament for support if the assemblies did not co-operate. Wilberforce added his imprimatur and in the emotional atmosphere of the House and in view of public feeling, no one dared speak against these noble principles. Canning's resolutions passed without division, allowing Bathurst to tell the colonial governors, stretching the facts only a little, that the House had been unanimous in its support.

Ten days later Bathurst circulated a copy of the resolutions, which had been presented to the King by the ministers in the Commons, along with a copy of Canning's speech to the governors. Under threat of direct legislation, he advised the assemblies to adopt legislation forbidding the flogging of women, the carrying of whips by overseers in the field and also carefully to define and regulate the circumstances under which males might be beaten.[39]

A month later Bathurst issued two more circulars elaborating on the earlier despatch and adding further instructions. In one he pointed to the need for more clergy and teachers under clerical supervision, assuring those colonies that could not afford them that parliament would be well-disposed to help, provided that the assemblies substituted another market day for Sunday so that the Sabbath could be a day of rest and religious instruction. The additional clergy would enable slaves to contract regular religious and legal marriages, teach them the obligations of that honourable estate, and make it possible to give evidence in court. Indeed Bathurst requested immediate legislation admitting the testimony of any slave who could produce a certificate of religious instruction sufficient to understand the oath. Expanding on the restrictions to physical punishment, he called for laws forbidding it until the day following the offence, and then only in the presence of at least one free person other than the individual on whose authority it was inflicted. If more than three lashes were imposed, the details of the offence, the number of strokes and the names of the free persons in attendance were to be recorded in a book kept for the purpose that must be certified each quarter on oath before a magistrate.

To prepare for eventual emancipation, Bathurst called for the removal of obstacles to slaves purchasing their freedom. He also insisted on the laws on debt being altered so that, in cases of sale, domestic slaves would remain with the estate in the same way as those who worked in the field, and all families would be kept together. To encourage the habits and discipline of free labour, he directed that slaves be allowed to enjoy such property as they managed to accumulate. Legislatures were to establish savings banks like those in England, with provision for slave depositors to name beneficiaries in a declaration carrying the force of a will. He concluded with an exhortation to pass these improvements, 'not only with all possible dispatch but in a spirit of perfect and cordial co-operation with the efforts of His Majesty's Government'. But in case of serious opposition he ordered the governors to 'lose no time in transmitting to me the necessary communication in order that I may take the earliest opportunity of laying the matter before Parliament and submitting for their consideration such measures as it may be fit to adopt in consequence'.

The second circular was even more far-reaching, calling for the experiment of paying wages to slaves for some tasks to prepare both parties for a free labour market and proposing a modified version of Buxton's plan for emancipation. Colonial assemblies were to pass legislation freeing all female slaves born after a certain date in return for a period of apprenticeship work which would repay the cost of raising them. All children of these freed women, whether the fathers were free or slave, would also be free. Bathurst optimistically pointed out that the governors and planters would appreciate that this did not alter the present number of slaves but would extinguish the system 'progressively and almost imperceptibly at some definite and distant period'. By then the other measures he had proposed 'cannot fail to effect such a progressive change in the general character and habits of the slave population that when this distant period shall arrive the transition from slavery to freedom will be finally accomplished without revulsion or danger.'[40]

These generous interpretations of Canning's resolutions are a clear indication of the strength and sincerity of Bathurst's commitment to amelioration and eventual emancipation. But whatever the West India Committee had advised and expected, the reaction in the islands could not have been stronger if the despatches had been sent by the Anti-Slavery Society. The editor of a Jamaica newspaper wrote:

> When the inhabitants of this island bow the knee before that creature of a day, that tool and organ of the Saints, that fourth-rate fellow of a party, a Colonial Secretary of State, they will richly merit to be stript of their possessions, and to be scattered over the earth: unpitied victims of the unfledged oratory of a Buxton, and of the contemptible enmity of a Zachary Macauley.'[41]

The Jamaican assembly was no more restrained in unanimously rejecting the measures when they were recommended by the governor, insisting that the slave code was 'as complete in all its enactments as the nature of circumstances will admit, to render the slave population as happy and as comfortable in every respect as the labouring class of any part of the world'. They denied that they needed any 'Pharisaical dictator' to instruct them in their duty, insisting that they would, 'if left to their own guidance, steadily pursue the line of conduct which comports with the loyalty of their feelings, their regard to the safety, honour, and welfare of the island, and the peace and happiness of their fellow-subjects and dependants.'[42]

In Demerara 13,000 slaves reacted to what knowledge they had of Bathurst's proposals by a demonstration demanding the great improvement in their condition, which they believed was being withheld by the owners. Two whites were killed and the slaves were brutally suppressed. The planters, believing that they had been stirred up by a Dissenting missionary, had him tried by court martial; sentenced to death but recommended for mercy, he died in jail, perhaps of consumption from which he was already suffering. The only Anglican cleric in the colony was also expelled for his temerity in defending the missionary's innocence. This hardened convictions on both sides, the planters concluding that the demonstration was proof of the danger of interfering with the present system, the abolitionists pointing to the cruel treatment and death of the missionary as evidence that slave-owners would never voluntarily concede any improvement.

The first news of the trouble in Demerara, which reached England early in October, 1823, raised fears of other uprisings, prompting urgent consideration of troop reinforcements and the whole issue of the army for the country's domestic and imperial needs. Bathurst proposed sending at least two regiments to the West Indies and the Prime Minister agreed, not so much to deal with Demerara, where the situation would be resolved before they could arrive, but to prevent revolts elsewhere. The Duke of York, however, who had been waiting for such an opportunity ever since the postwar reductions, told Bathurst with grim satisfaction that it was impossible to furnish any reinforcement, 'however imperiously required, to any of our foreign possessions, without taking it from Ireland, where I am sure that there can be no difference of opinion that the force is already too small'. Wellington, after conferring with the Commander-in-Chief the next day, added his own great authority, telling Bathurst that the most that could be spared from Ireland was a single battalion. In the present mood of the slaves, excited by talk of emancipation, the Duke insisted that the West Indian garrisons must be permanently reinforced and a small reserve force provided to deal quickly with any insurrection.[43]

Despite the pressing claims of Ireland, Gibraltar and other British possessions, the need in the West Indies was so great that two battalions and two first-rate warships were immediately dispatched. But the strain that even this small force imposed on the army and the risks that it exposed called for deep thought by the cabinet. As Bathurst told Peel in summoning him to a cabinet for that purpose in mid-November: 'The present establishment is unfit for any thing but a state of absolute tranquillity'.[44] After much preliminary discussion by ministers scattered throughout the country, the cabinet decided to increase the army, with half-pay officers who had been yearning for employment since the end of the Napoleonic wars being appointed to the new units.[45] Three battalions of 800 each were raised at the end of 1823, six more in 1824, and in 1825 8,000 troops were added for service in Indian and other parts of the empire.[46] The era of postwar military reductions was over and, like the expansion of the Colonial Office, the main reason that the armed services could be increased, at least in the prosperity of the early 1820s, was that concern for slavery took precedence over the obsession with economy.

The reinforcements helped to maintain reasonable peace in the West Indies, but the necessity of sending them and the resistance of the planters to amelioration raised the question of what to do if the colonial assemblies persisted in refusing to pass the required legislation. As Liverpool put it to Bathurst and Canning early in 1824:

Are we prepared to enforce our new system and regulations by law and if necessary ultimately by force in those colonies to which we have granted constitutions? . . . I wish you would turn this part of the question most seriously in your thoughts, and when you have done so I shall be quite ready to talk to you and to give you my opinion.[47]

Whatever the Prime Minister had in mind, Bathurst had no intention of retreating from his demands, but neither did he intend to impose them by parliamentary legislation, which might require military support, until the process of persuasion was absolutely exhausted. Nor was he discouraged that the initial reaction was so unpromising. It had, after all, taken four years to get the colonies to accept slave registers and it was understandable that this greater step would take at least as long. But he never doubted that owners would eventually recognize the wisdom of voluntarily accepting improvement and eventual freedom in return for compensation and protection by the British government.

On 16 March, 1824, Bathurst took the opportunity of the presentation of petitions against slavery in the House of Lords to make a full public statement of his position. He produced the resolutions of the Commons and his three circulars to show the extent of the government's commitment and told the House that he felt 'in common with every man, the miseries and evils' of slavery. He was convinced that these could best be remedied by 'progressive measures of amelioration, by religious instruction, and a mitigation of the evils of slavery', and warned that such efforts would only be impeded by loud and angry discussions, 'as they but too generally tended to create in the mind of the owner an extravagance of fright, and in the slave an insubordination, both of which were in the end most pernicious to the security of the one, and to the improvement of the other'.

This firm and clear declaration further confirms Bathurst's dedication. His officials may have worked out the slavery details, but his was the presiding spirit which hovered over and encouraged them. Although he was not one of the reformers within the cabinet, this was the issue on which he parted from the doubts and reluctant assent of Wellington and other Ultra friends and found himself closer to Canning and the Liberal Tories. But the fact that he also enjoyed the Duke's confidence prevented the cabinet from splitting, as it did on so many other issues.

As an experiment to demonstrate the practicality of his slave programme,

Bathurst and his officials decided to impose it on the crown colonies (Trinidad, St Lucia, Demerara and Berbice) over which the Colonial Office had much clearer control than the chartered ones. A new slave code for Trinidad was drafted by the Governor and enforced by Order in Council in 1825. This went further than the 1823 proposals in providing for a Protector and Guardian of Slaves, who could not be an owner or mortgage-holder of a slave plantation on the island, and also in specifying that any owner convicted of cruelty a second time would be declared incompetent to own or supervise slaves.[48] This model code was adopted after some resistance by the nominated council of St Lucia in 1826. In Berbice the council flatly refused to accept the abolition of the whip and the flogging of women until 1826, when the Governor was instructed to replace the council with a more amenable one of his own appointees. In Demerara the code was denounced as a violation of the terms of capitulation of 1803, and in both Demerara and Berbice owners contested the legality of slaves being able to purchase their freedom. These issues were not resolved until 1829 when the Privy Council, with Bathurst as Lord President, pronounced against owners. In 1830, finally weary of this obstruction, the government of the Duke of Wellington, no less, imposed one uniform Order in Council on all the crown colonies.

The strength of Bathurst's commitment can also be seen in his correspondence with Wilmot-Horton, the Under-Secretary in charge of the West Indies. At the beginning of 1826 Horton, no Ultra-Tory sceptic of emancipation but a partisan of Canning, proposed to mollify the Demerara planters, and by implication those in other crown colonies, by altering to the advantage of the owners the terms on which slaves could purchase their freedom. Instead of the purchase price being the market value of the particular slave, it should be whatever any healthy slave might earn in a given number of years, with the owner being compensated from public funds for the difference between what the slave was required to pay for freedom and this standard price.

In what was for him an exceptionally long and rambling letter of thirteen sides, Bathurst flatly rejected the argument. He denied that owners had any claim to public compensation for a slave purchasing freedom and told Horton that he was not prepared to recommend such reimbursement to parliament. He also denied that the amelioration order injured slave owners. In what way, he asked, were they harmed by guaranteeing slave property, admitting slave evidence in courts, protecting them against arbitrary and excessive punishment, or encouraging them to marry? If there was anything in the new regulations that made the slaves idle and unfit for freedom, it should be removed by changing the provisions, not by compensating the owners. Unless Horton were prepared to admit that the interests of the slaves and owners were incompatible – 'and what an admission this would be to make' – the only justification for calling on the Commons to provide compensation for adopting the principle of amelioration would be to say that the House had been misled and had adopted the 1823 resolutions without sufficient inquiry. He also pointed out that Wilmot-Horton's scheme of a fixed price for all slaves would benefit those who treated their slaves badly and so reduced their value rather than those who were kindly and considerate: 'and would the House compensate an owner for the loss which he in fact sustain'd by reason of his past misconduct, or for the ill-will with which he may have executed the law[?]'

The only reimbursement that Bathurst was prepared to consider was for allowing slaves to go to market for part of a working day rather than Sunday, but since this was already allowed in all colonies, he did not think that the masters had any right to payment for losing what had not been enforced. He also revealed his own relaxed and by now rather old-fashioned religious views by saying that it would be better not to insist on prohibiting Sunday markets:

> Except where the distance is very great, the going to market is a pleasure not a fatigue & by closing the market before Church-time, it will not interfere with that service, and may even facilitate or encourage an attendance there. It is rather too puritanical to object to a poor Negro considering that day a day of cheerfulness as well as of devotion.

But although he was opposed to inflating the price of slave freedom, particularly at the expense of the British Treasury, Bathurst stood firmly by his conviction that 'the claim for compensation on the emancipation of the slave is irresistible. Emancipation cannot safely be accomplished by any act of an abstract kind. It must be through the instrumentality of the slave. It must be compulsory upon the master: it will not otherwise be accomplished.'[49] Later in the year he reiterated this in responding to the argument of the Rev Thomas Gisborne, a prominent emancipationist, that the public should compensate the slaves, not the owners, since they were stolen property. Bathurst thought the proposition 'Nonesense. If they are stolen goods, we must return them to those from whom we have stolen them,' dismissing Gisborne's case by saying: 'It is one thing to write essays, & another to make laws: and it must be as legislators, and not as essayists that we must act'.[50] But he continued to insist that the purchase price must be manifestly fair to the slaves: 'They ought not to be called upon to pay *now* more than the market price, on the plea that five or six years hence, the number in their class may be so diminished, & the demand for slaves to fill up the vacancies so increased, as to raise the price.'[51]

Once the slaves were free, Bathurst was also emphatic that they should be completely free labourers, without conditions. He rejected the idea of a transitional stage of apprenticeship to accustom them to their new condition as wage earners by pointing to the practical problems. Could individuals in this transitory condition be punished?: 'If so what progress are they making in civilization[?] If not, to what other employment can you assign them? I am afraid it would lead to no good'.[52] And he dismissed the presumption of the merchants in claiming compensation for the fall in sugar production since free blacks would not work as hard as slaves. If this happened, he argued, the investors could simply withdraw their capital and employ it elsewhere: 'I think the public must have become strangely cold on the slave question, if they will consent to secure this accumulated profit, of which the W.I merchants have not hitherto had the effrontery to state the amounts.'[53]

Bathurst's genuine solicitude for the slaves and surprising lack of partiality for the property and privilege of the planters and merchants was also reflected in the attention he devoted to the increased religious provision for the West Indies. After reading the new Bishop of Barbados's report on his parishes at the end of 1825, he wrote to express his pleasure at the evidence of the clergy's exertions. But he pointed out that the emphasis on the catechism over the bible for slave children was misguided since the catechism is 'the deductions which are drawn from the context of the Gospels and ought not to be substituted for it.' He was puzzled by the preference for the Old Testament over the New but approved the texts being accompanied by explanations of clergymen, 'whose professional pursuits have led them most seriously to consider it and whose experience must have shown them what is most fitting for those whom it is their duty to teach' since he did not accept the evangelical belief that 'the Gospel can be read as well or better without any comments'.

The importance of trained clergy brought Bathurst to the main point of his letter: the complaints of 'respectable Wesleyans' that the Church of England was trying to drive other denominations out of the islands. Bathurst had assured the Methodists that there was plenty of room for all and now told the Bishop that he had said this not 'with the plausible indifference of a man of the world to all sects, but from the persuasion that there is not so much of vital error in them as to make it desirable to endeavour their extirpation at the risk of overthrowing all religions'. He reminded the Bishop that if the Commons suspected that the extra funds being requested for the religious instruction of slaves were being used for 'supplanting those who have long laboured in the same calling without coming upon the public for remuneration, I am sure I need not tell you that there will be very great difficulty in procuring any pecuniary assistance from that Assembly'. He recommended instead acting in the spirit of Protestant comprehension rather than war 'with those who are in truth engaged in a common cause for the maintenance of what is essentially a common faith'.[54]

Another embarrassment of the state Church's privileged position that called for Bathurst's personal intervention was the new Bishop of Jamaica's intention of setting himself up in the style of a senior English ecclesiastic. When the Governor wrote to say that the Bishop desired an estate forty miles from the capital, Bathurst wrote directly to the Bishop pointing out that he would surely realize on reflection how objectionable this would be. In case he did not, Bathurst made it plain that he could not approve of living so far from the main business of his diocese; nor could he sanction the cost, even to that rich colony, of an estate of four or five hundred acres, particularly if any part were worked by slaves.[55]

In small matters as well as great, in symbol as well as substance, Bathurst did not spare himself in promoting the improvement of the lot of the slaves and the process of orderly emancipation. If he had not been so willing to engage his authority and prestige, as his successor from 1828 to 1830 was not, the prospect of success would have been even slimmer than it turned out to be after the high expectations of 1823. He concentrated his efforts on Jamaica since it was the largest and richest of the West Indian colonies and the one from which the others took their lead. The special position of this colony was acknowledged in 1826 when he and the Prime Minister were discussing a new Governor. Liverpool pointed out that the Jamaican appointment was of the very first rank, along with the embassies to Paris and St Petersburg, 'upon a different footing from the governments of Granada, St. Vincent etc., or the missions to Munich and Naples'.[56]

Such considerations had evidently not weighed so heavily with their predecessors, Castlereagh and Portland, who had appointed the Duke of Manchester in 1808 for no other obvious reasons than his grand title, aristocratic connections and firm attachment to the ministry. And yet Manchester had turned out to be a good Governor of Jamaica, gaining the goodwill of the planters, the free coloured population and even the slaves at times of unrest, while maintaining the confidence of the home government. In 1816 he had persuaded the assembly to accept a slave register, and the high regard in which he was held by the legislature moved it to vote 500 guineas to the surgeons who operated on him after he was thrown from his carriage and fractured his skull in 1820. His mental faculties were evidently not impaired and in 1823 Bathurst was confident that this seasoned Governor would again succeed in convincing the assembly to co-operate with the imperial parliament on amelioration. Unfortunately the task was beyond even Manchester. Bathurst could not conceal his disappointment that the Duke, like his counterparts elsewhere, was unable to secure a single one of the measures listed in his despatches. But in the hope of future success he praised Manchester for acting, 'not only in strict conformity with the Spirit of the Instructions, but in the manner in which the state of irritation in which the colony was placed, [was] most likely to be effective'.[57]

Despite this discouraging start, Bathurst and his officials continued to believe that exhortation and persuasion would eventually prevail. Every year until 1826 ministers were sincerely able to assure parliament of the strenuousness of the efforts. But still the colonial assemblies would not budge. When eight model bills based on the Trinidad Order in Council were circulated for their guidance in 1826, they received the same hostile reception as the 1823 despatches; but the legislatures cleverly managed to evade direct imposition from Britain by amending the existing slave codes in a mixture of old and new elements that prevented real change while making it difficult for the Colonial Office to disallow what they had enacted. This tactic succeeded until, on 2 February, 1830, after being distracted by more pressing domestic concerns for the last three years, the government issued an Order in Council overruling this ingenious tactic. Bathurst was then Lord President of the Council and took a leading part in devising the Order. In October, 1831, when the new Whig ministry was preparing to extend its provisions, no less an enthusiast for abolition than James Stephen paid a sincere tribute to the dedication of his Tory chief by saying:

> He conducted the correspondence respecting Slavery for the first five years of its continuance and was probably better qualified than any other man to take a comprehensive view of the subject. So much of the [1831] Order as rests on that [1830] foundation should be regarded as beyond the reach of present controversy. No objection was made by the West India Body on its promulgation.[58]

The Duke of Manchester, after a decade and a half in Jamaica before the amelioration pressure really got underway, grew weary of this additional burden and in 1826 submitted his claim for a post of high honour and light duties at home. He was eventually appointed Postmaster General, an undemanding office generally decorated by a deserving peer. But Bathurst asked him to remain for one more session of the assembly in the hope that he would finally persuade the slave owners to enact the draft bills and lead the West Indies in the cause of emancipation. 'I am sure it will be one of the happiest periods of your life,' he told Manchester with no exaggeration, 'if their Policy and wisdom shall enable you to lay at His Majesty's feet a Code of Laws with regard to the Slave Population, conformable to the Spirit of the Resolutions which met with the unanimous concurrence of the two Houses of Parliament'.[59] But the Duke had no more success than before, and nor did any other governor.

Nothing absorbed so much of Bathurst's time and effort in the years that he remained at the Colonial Office after 1823 as slavery, but it was by no means the only issue calling for his close attention, not even the sole one concerning the West Indies. In 1825 there was a complicated three-way dispute between the Treasury, the colonial legislatures and Colonial Office arising from Huskisson's crusade at the Board of Trade to remove financial barriers to commerce and the Treasury's continuing efforts to reduce colonial expenses. The conflict reveals the difficulties of the struggle to assert the supremacy of the Colonial Office as well as illuminating Bathurst's attitude and style of administration.[60]

The fees collected by customs officers appointed by the Treasury to the colonial ports had always been resented as an unnecessary addition to the cost of duties by merchants and shippers, to say nothing of those who purchased imported goods. The huge incomes of the officers (£2000 a year, equal to the salary of the Colonial Office Under-Secretaries, was by no means unusual in a large port) and the fact that this rich patronage was rarely bestowed on local residents were constant sources of grievance.

In 1825 parliament abolished the fees at the initiative of Huskisson, passively supported by Liverpool and the Chancellor of the Exchequer, without any consultation with the Colonial Office. No one seems to have considered the difficulties that would arise over paying the customs officers. Once the legislation had passed Huskisson was confident that the increase in colonial trade from lower costs would persuade the grateful assemblies to provide fixed salaries, lower than the fees in large ports but still very generous, without demanding in return any right of appointment or even a voice in setting the salaries. When Wilmot-Horton considered the matter in August, he realized that the colonial assemblies would never accept this without concession and cleverly proposed a Treasury order to the customs officers instructing them to withhold an amount equal to their salaries and expenses before remitting the duties to the colonial authorities.

Bathurst, who was in the country, immediately recognized that this would simply antagonize the colonial legislatures and wrote to defuse Horton's scheme. He doubted that the proposed order to the customs officers was even legal and pointed out that since no chartered colony had a financial surplus, they would have to raise taxes to make up for the reduced duties, in effect to pay the salaries, 'and I need hardly tell you that we can look only to a refusal from Legislative Assemblies'. Bathurst's solution was for parliament to provide a replacement in the next budget for the fees which it had abolished: 'It is the British Merchant who will be much more benefited than the poor planter by this arrangement, and it should be paid for by the British Treasury, not from the Colonies.' He added sharply in a postscript that he was 'most anxious not to be involv'd in a second battle with all the Colonies, in addition to the Slave Question. I see no reason why the Grace is to belong to one department, and the odium cast on another.'[61]

Bathurst was supported by James Stephen, who pronounced against both the legality and the expediency of Horton's intention, pointing out that any officer withholding revenue would be charged and tried by a colonial judge and jury, 'with what prejudices and prepossessions I need hardly mention'.[62] But for the political Under-Secretary, the House of Commons was a more present danger than any colonial assembly or court. Rather than risk being charged with increasing colonial costs to Britain under the guise of reducing them, which would incidentally benefit the slave owners in the West Indian colonies and give them further competitive advantage over the East Indies, Horton pressed on with his own plan. It is surprising that Bathurst did not forbid Horton from acting with the Treasury, get involved himself directly in the issue, even though technically it was outside his jurisdiction, or at least insist that this delicate matter be decided by the cabinet, all of which may indicate that he was preoccupied with slavery and other more pressing issues. But he did at least ensure that the circular on deducting salaries from customs duties went solely from the Treasury so that it alone would bear the colonial reaction.

The effect was exactly what Bathurst expected. Every legislature protested this new charge, imposed in a unilateral and high-handed manner by the home government. The most vituperative responses came from Jamaica, already inflamed over slavery, and from Lower Canada, where the assembly resented the Governor's considerable financial independence and where feelings still ran high over the 1822 proposal to unite the colony with Upper Canada. This last, apparently devised by Wilmot-Horton to settle the disputes between the two colonies over the division of import revenue, provide a more effective common defence against the United

States and reduce internal conflicts by increasing the power of the Governor, was opposed by both the French Canadians in Lower Canada and the English-speaking settlers in Upper Canada, each fearing that their interests would be subordinated to the other. When it was also criticized in the Commons by Whigs and Radicals, it was abandoned in 1823, to be revived in very different circumstances a decade and a half later, but in 1825 the memory helped fuel local bitterness and suspicion of the imperial government.

A further difficulty in the new scheme for paying customs officers was that the entire customs revenue in the smaller colonies was less than the salaries of those collecting it. When Bathurst himself finally intervened in this increasingly complex and contentious matter in 1826, the Treasury's response was to issue a general minute instructing all customs officers to remit only three-quarters of the duties they collected to the colonies, with any surplus after the salaries had been deducted from the remaining quarter being used to subsidize those colonies whose revenue was insufficient. But this equitable redistribution further angered the large and prosperous colonies, again principally Jamaica and Lower Canada.

Bathurst was so concerned about deteriorating relations between the legislatures and the home government that in August he wrote to Horton from Cirencester in terms that could have been used by a colonial politician, rebutting the familiar and apparently logical argument of Major Moodie that since colonial consumers would necessarily benefit from lower prices resultant upon abolishing the fees, they should be happy to pay the salaries. Bathurst argued that in fact the merchants would charge whatever the market would bear; in the long run the colonies might see some increased trade, but more immediately they would certainly have to raise taxes to make up for the loss of customs revenue. He also countered Horton's rationalism that colonies should not have the gross revenue without paying any of the costs by pointing out that 'unfortunately they have had up to this time that which you consider contrary to common sense. The charge of collection was not made on the gross revenue, but made out of fees, and we are now taxing the gross revenue which was heretofore at the disposal of the Colonies'. He added that, in this matter at least, he was more concerned about the North American colonies than the West Indies:

If they make a common cause, and a war with the United States should intervene, those colonies are gone. . . . I am more and more apprehensive that considering the many questions of difference between us and the United States, the time is not far distant, when we may be at war with them. It is the fear of this which perhaps makes me coward, & influences me strongly in all my proceedings with the N. American Colonial assemblies.

But if the Treasury insisted on persisting with its scheme, he wanted it clearly on the record that he was not responsible.[63]

By the time he wrote this protest Bathurst had only a little longer at the Colonial Office, though he had no intimation of it. A year later, when he was succeeded by the former Chancellor of the Exchequer, Lord Goderich (Frederick Robinson), and Canning was First Lord of the Treasury and Chancellor of the Exchequer, the liberal Tories recognized the error of their ways, saw the wisdom of Bathurst's anxiety and conceded the argument of the colonies. This time acting through the Colonial Office, the assemblies were granted the right to negotiate with the governors on the number and salaries of the customs officers in return for a permanent legislative provision of salaries. This was a considerable gain for local control, but although a repetition of the American revolt over unauthorized taxation was avoided, implementing the new system provided plenty of opportunity for tension for over a decade and in Lower Canada contributed to the rebellion of 1837. Bathurst had seen the danger of Huskisson's reform, but unfortunately not in time. Immersed in the many other problems of empire and at home in 1825, he had for once failed to impress his caution and experience on his enthusiastic Under-Secretary as well as on his cabinet colleagues.

8

BRAVE MEN IN TROUBLE

At the time of the well-intentioned but ill-considered abolition of customs fees in 1825, Bathurst was not only working hard to improve the lot of the slaves but was also deeply immersed in the sensitive difficulties of the Governors of New South Wales and the Cape Colony. Both places were being transformed by post-war emigrants who expected the freedoms, practices and institutions they had left behind, if not the reforms being demanded by radicals at home. The Governors, who had inherited authoritarian structures, appealed to the Colonial Secretary for support, while the grievances of the colonists and the conduct of the governors were always attractive to opposition politicians. Sensitive to parliamentary criticism as well as detached by time and space from the conflicts, Bathurst carefully considered the demands and struck a delicate balance in upholding the position of the governors and conceding adjustments to systems that had served well enough to the end of the Napoleonic wars.

Wilmot-Horton believed that a simple solution to many imperial and domestic problems lay in emigration to the colonies, and one of the great advantages for Horton in appointing Hay as second Under-Secretary in 1825 for Horton was that it gave him more time for this passionate crusade.[1] Removing the surplus population which had to be supported by poor relief from the British Isles - 'shovelling out paupers' as one of his critics caustically termed it - would in itself increase the nation's wealth, while transplanting them to Upper Canada, Australia or the Cape would provide them with opportunities to prosper and contribute to the development of the empire. The scheme had a pleasing symmetry which appealed to Horton's faith in rational political economy. But Bathurst, while by no means unsympathetic to emigration, was sceptical of this simple logic.

To divert the flow of settlers from the United States, the most common destination after 1815, Horton proposed public assistance to those who chose the British colonies. But in his enthusiasm he did not consider who would provide it: parliament, or the local parishes as an investment in lower poor rates; nor could he decide whether the money should be a loan or a grant. He also overlooked the difficulties that urban people in particular would face in opening and farming new land in climates very different from those at home. The result of these problems and Horton's boring monomania was that while the Commons investigated the subject at inordinate length it did not reach any conclusion in the 1820s. Only in the next decade, when Horton had gone to govern Ceylon, did a different government support the emigration of skilled, not destitute, workers primarily to assist the colonies rather than helping to solving Britain's own social difficulties.

In the years after 1815 Bathurst and Goulburn had provided incentives for war veterans to occupy Lower Canada between the St Lawrence River and the American border as a barrier to US expansion and a ready source of soldiers in the event of renewed war, which Bathurst was fearing in the mid–1820s. Even in the postwar obsession with retrenchment they had managed to find public money to settle emigrants on the vulnerable shore of the St Lawrence between Montreal and Kingston as well as giving some modest help to those who went to the Cape and Australia. But Bathurst had serious reservations about any large emigration scheme, questioning the wisdom of reducing the United Kingdom's population and being concerned that the most promising class of paupers would leave while the permanently indigent remained to be supported by the poor rates.

By paying closer attention than Horton to the actual experiences of those who went to the colonies, the cautious and pragmatic Bathurst was also not tempted to underestimate the difficulties they faced. On 2 December, 1826, when his personal friend the Whig Lord Lansdowne urged that emigration assistance be provided to destitute industrial workers, Bathurst told the Lords that he had great sympathy for the suffering that the poor had endured during the recent economic collapse but pointed out that it was already being relieved through public efforts, including the free importation of grain through the suspension of the corn laws. And he warned the peers not to consider emigration as an easy solution, since most of the colonies consisted of 'immense tracks of land, on which no house was erected, and which were covered with immense forests'. To send large numbers of people, particularly from the towns, to such conditions in the hope that they could support themselves was hazardous enough for the healthy but impossible for the aged, the sick and the infirm who would simply be exposed to calamity.

187

Peel, the Home Secretary, and most of the rest of the cabinet shared Bathurst's prudent but fundamentally humane attitude, and no extensive governmental programme was adopted in his time. Horton bitterly resented the lack of support for what he considered to be an economical and effective policy. But much of the blame, if blame there was, for doing little lay in his own failure to resolve the inconsistencies in his argument, to make it as appealing to the doubtful as to true believers, and his refusal to look plainly at how emigrants actually fared.

Apart from North America, particularly Upper Canada, the most attractive colonies for settlement were Australia and South Africa, but each of them presented greater challenges than eastern Canada, apart from longer and more arduous voyages. New South Wales, on the south-east coast of New Holland (the term Australia gained only gradual acceptance after 1815) had been founded as a convict colony in 1786 when the hulks and jails in Britain were bulging with prisoners after the American War of Independence closed that destination.[2] Botany Bay was an expensive seven months' voyage away, but once there escape was practically impossible. The First Fleet arrived at Sydney in January, 1788, but, despite the lash and the prospect of emancipation, the convicts were scarcely able to produce enough food to survive; only the supplies which arrived with the Second Fleet in June, 1790, saved the settlement from starvation.

The second expedition also brought news of the revolution in France, and after war began in 1793 New South Wales received only sporadic attention from Britain for twenty years. The number of transported convicts also fell as many were swept instead into the army. A new society emerged in this period, partly based on sporadic instructions from Downing Street, more on local necessity. The Governor was permitted to emancipate convicts for good behaviour and grant them land and supplies for a year; to others he could give tickets of leave, exempting them from compulsory work on public projects and allowing them to sell their labour. But since they could not return to Britain until the end of their term, and then only at their own expense, most of the emancipists remained, many prospering as traders and farmers and themselves employing convicts. The officers commanding the troops became the social élite, receiving large land grants, employing many convicts and selling the produce to the government as well as retailing goods purchased from visiting ships. At the bottom of the social hierarchy were the Irish Catholic convicts, the first of whom arrived in 1791, who were despised even by their self-consciously superior Protestant counterparts.

But while the colony became self-supporting, even throve, and a free society developed alongside the dwindling convict one, the powers of the Governor remained those of the military commander of a jail. When Captain William Bligh, of mutiny on the *Bounty* fame, exceeded even the customary standards of harshness and autocracy and was deposed by the army officers in January, 1808, Castlereagh, appointed Lt Colonel Lachlan Macquarie, who owed his selection to Sir Arthur Wellesley, the Irish Secretary, with whom he had served in India. Stern, dedicated and religious, the new Governor encouraged Evangelical churches and schools and worked to make New South Wales a model settlement for truly penitent and reformed convicts. Despite the resentment of the military officers and free settlers, he treated exemplary emancipists as the social and legal equals of free residents, appointing them as magistrates and even entertaining them in his home. Macquarie even wanted to ban further free settlers since they resisted association with former convicts. When the flood of convicts arrived from Britain in the troubled years after Waterloo, he put them to work on a vast programme of public works.

So successful was Macquarie in improving society that by the time Bathurst turned his mind to the colony in 1817 he feared that it was no longer fulfilling its original penal purpose. He told the Home Secretary that as long as it had consisted primarily of convicts and agriculture was not very developed, transportation had been 'the object of the greatest Apprehension to those who looked upon strict Discipline and Regular Labour as the most severe and least tolerable of Evils,' But New South Wales was now 'neither an object of Apprehension here nor the means of Reformation in the Settlement itself'. Wool and other products were making the colony a promising economic asset, and emancipists as well as free emigrants were claiming the same rights as British subjects elsewhere. To clarify his thoughts on reconciling a free and prosperous society in what was still in principle a convict colony, Bathurst proposed a commission to investigate and make recommendations.[3] Macquarie, who offered to resign at the end of the eight years for which he had been promised a pension by Castlereagh, was asked by Bathurst to remain until the investigation was complete.

In 1818 Bathurst appointed John Thomas Bigge as sole commissioner. A good Tory and Chief Justice of Trinidad for the past four years, who had pointed to useful improvements in the justice system inherited from Spain, he was in England at the time. Bigge arrived in New South Wales in September, 1819, and was soon at loggerheads with the Governor. Macquarie saw the commission as a criticism of his government while

189

Bigge, who did not appreciate Macquarie's achievement, all too readily accepted the complaints of his critics. After two years of collecting evidence in New South Wales and its dependency of Van Diemen's Land (Tasmania) Bigge returned to England and produced three stout reports, published by the House of Commons in 1822 and 1823. They contained much detailed criticism of government and the administration of justice, but the main charges were that Macquarie had been too lenient in his treatment of convicts and too extravagant in public works. Bigge recommended a clearer separation of convict and free society, stricter punishment and a distinct colony for hardened cases, restricting the privileges of ticket of leave holders and an end to granting land and office to emancipists. Convinced by the free settlers that the prosperity of New South Wales lay in sheep, he recommended that convicts be assigned to farmers as shepherds rather than used for public works. He also advised a separate government for Van Diemen's Land, which had a population of about 5,000, of whom half were convicts. In New South Wales only about 9,300 of its 24,000 Europeans had full convict status.[4] But Bigge rejected trial by jury, which he considered too risky for a society containing so many former lawbreakers.

Bigge's recommendations were generally accepted by Bathurst, who knew them long before they were made public. The ambiguity he had puzzled over in 1817 was resolved by recognizing New South Wales as being a free colony containing a prisoner community rather than primarily a penal settlement with some free inhabitants. Van Diemen's Land became a separate colony in 1825, and both received legislative councils of five to seven members specified by the crown, in effect the Colonial Secretary. But only the Governor might initiate legislation and could also proclaim laws without the council's assent so long as he gave written reasons. All acts were to be certified by the Chief Justice as not being contrary to British law, but could still be disallowed by the home government within three years. Trial by jury was denied, but all questions of fact in criminal cases were to be submitted to a jury of seven army or naval officers.

Even before the commission reports were published Bathurst appointed a new Governor to implement the changes. In 1820 he finally accepted the resignation of Macquarie who arrived in England in mid–1822, just as Bigge's volumes were beginning to appear and regarded them as a censure of all he had tried to do. Bathurst tried to assure him of the government's appreciation of his services and granted him a pension of £1000 a year (twice what he had expected), but Macquarie was beyond consolation and died a bitter man in 1824.

His suspicions were not unfounded. As new Governor Bathurst chose Sir Thomas Brisbane, who also owed his post to Wellington with whom he had served in Ireland in the 1790s, in the Peninsula and, after commanding troops against the United States, in the army of occupation in France. The Colonial Secretary kept a watchful eye on him from the beginning, to prevent him from falling into the same mistakes as Macquarie. Bathurst was not opposed to 'useful amelioration' of the convicts' lot, but even while the new Governor was still at sea privately asked Brisbane's comrade-in-arms, Sir George Murray to remind him of his main priority. 'The great error which his predecessor fell into,' he told Murray, 'was to consider the settlement as a colony, & not as a place of punishment and reform.' Bathurst accepted that New South Wales now deserved to be treated as a normal colony but this was secondary; Brisbane's first object should be

> to establish at some place far distant from the temptations and facilities of a town, a settlement composed exclusively of convicts, under constant control, severe discipline, and unremitting labour: the discipline and control in proportion to the character of the crimes for which they have been condemned, and their conduct since their arrival. Until the public here shall be convinced that this is the fate of those, who are sent there, more especially for crimes of the higher order, transportation cannot be considered as a punishment.[5]

The distinction between classes of convicts was quickly established. The worst kind, customarily those who had committed further offences after arrival, were segregated and, instead of Van Diemen's Land, were confined to various isolated penal settlements, the most fearsome being Norfolk Island, a speck in the ocean a thousand miles east of Sydney which was re-occupied in 1824 after being abandoned in 1806. The more promising convicts in New South Wales were dispersed and removed from the towns as well as the public charge by assigning them to farmers.

Brisbane strove to fulfil Bathurst's instructions, making the colony not only a harder place for convicts but also for emancipists, who were denied land and office, while making it a more flourishing one for free settlers, who received large land grants and a more generous supply of convict labour. He reduced the public building programme and employed government convicts in clearing land for sale, but retained the goodwill of the emancipists by commuting death penalties, reducing sentences and granting pardons. This humanitarianism and his involvement in factional quarrels, however, meant that Brisbane was no more successful than Macquarie in reconciling the élite to the emancipists or even new free settlers, and this failure also cost him his office.

Brisbane was particularly criticized for favouring Dr Henry Gratton Douglass, an emigrant who quickly became a magistrate and officer in several improving societies. Despite his useful medical and other talents, Douglass was resented as an interloper who enjoyed the confidence of the Governor. In letters to the Home Secretary he was accused of improper behaviour with a female convict who lived in his house, as well as cruelty and drunkenness. Brisbane, however, stood by him and early in 1824 sent him home on a mission.

While Douglass was in transit to England, Peel rerouted the list of allegations to the Colonial Secretary. Bathurst somehow got the impression that the letters had been authorized by Brisbane, and his disposition towards Douglass was not improved by discovering that the doctor had left England without authorization while on half-pay as a military officer and had refused to answer letters from his own War Department. He ordered Brisbane to dismiss Douglass as a magistrate[6] and had him summoned back to the army. But Douglas ignored the recall and forfeited his half-pay by returning to New South Wales. Brisbane then persuaded him to avoid the ignominy of dismissal by resigning from the bench.

Brisbane's partiality for Douglass and Bathurst's misunderstanding of their relationship certainly made this an embarrassment for the Colonial Secretary. Even more was the decision by Brisbane, himself a Scot, that Presbyterians, unlike Methodists and Roman Catholics, could afford to build their own church at Sydney without a government grant. Bathurst sharply told him that he should have handled this better. Although Presbyterians were not considered equal to Anglicans in the colonies, they were always favoured by the government. To make matters worse, Bathurst said that it was being put about in England that Brisbane and his wife had first subscribed to the building and then withdrawn on the advice of Major Frederick Goulburn, Secretary of the Colony and brother of the former Colonial Under-Secretary.

But the most serious charge to reach Bathurst was that Brisbane was abandoning government to Goulburn while devoting himself to astronomy and other personal interests. It was even reported that he was privately criticizing his own administration. Bathurst tactfully assured him that he was 'so fully aware of how easy it is to misrepresent good humoured expressions of regret addressed to persons who come to complain that I pay little attention to these representation,' but thought it only fair to warn Brisbane of 'the advantages which are taken of every expression which may escape from

192

you, which if they can be made to answer the object of the Reporters are sure to be circulated with exaggerations'. Anticipating criticism of both Brisbane and Goulburn when parliament next met, he advised Brisbane to prepare his defence: 'The honour of an absent Governor is in my custody, and when I see perpetual attempts made to impeach it, I am bound to apprise him of it, and enable him to put me in possession of his vindication.'[7]

Brisbane certainly gave Goulburn more scope than Macquarie had, but far from abandoning his official duties for research or idle dissipation, of which he was also accused, he was in fact being undermined by Goulburn who refused to carry out his instructions, withheld letters, answered them without consulting the Governor and even claimed that proclamations and orders were invalid unless issued through his office. Goulburn was no more liked by the local élite than Brisbane and their conflict practically paralysed the administration. In May, 1824, the Governor finally protested to Bathurst about Goulburn's conduct and pretensions. This was exceptionally awkward since Wellington took a close interest in Brisbane's career, while Henry Goulburn was the Irish Secretary. The only solution, which Bathurst aired to the Duke, was to recall both, since he could not tell which was more to blame: 'The fault of Sir Thomas is that he wished to throw everything upon others to have time to follow his own pursuits; the fault of the secretary is that he is a coxcomb without experience and little or no discretion.'[8] Much to Bathurst's relief Wellington did not leap to Brisbane's defence but philosophically wrote: 'He is a very good officer; with a great deal of science and very gallant in the field. I know nothing of him but in the field. But there are many brave men not fit to be governors of colonies!'[9]

When the news of his dismissal arrived like a bolt from the blue in September, 1825, Brisbane immediately wrote to defend himself to Bathurst and even more urgently to Wellington. He told the former that he had allowed himself to be misled by false reports and asked for a list of charges and persons making them when he returned, confident that he could defeat the accusations and restore his reputation.[10] To Wellington he wrote at greater length, explaining that New South Wales was a most difficult colony to govern since public officials were always in league against government and hostile to its measures. He enclosed an abstract of his rebuttal of the accusation of encouraging convict women to prostitution, which he thought was a major reason for his recall, and justified his decision to raise a troop of cavalry for use against aborigines and bushrangers (escaped convicts who lived on plunder) for which he had been censured by Bathurst on the grounds of cost and not demonstrating the necessity in advance.[11] He did not claim that his administration had been faultless, but he insisted that, as far as integrity and impartiality could be coupled with purity of intention and influenced by a loyalty, which has never yet been even suspected, I shall yield to none, and with confidence I assert that it will be discovered that my greatest aberration can only be imputed to errors in judgement.[12]

Brisbane's *cri de coeur* was similar to that of many another Governor caught in the factional disputes, resentments and ambitions of a small colonial society. He was treated well enough on his return, being appointed colonel of the 34th Regiment and being offered other colonial military, though not civil, commands. But he refused them all, retiring to his estate in Scotland where he perhaps derived some grim satisfaction from observing that his successors escaped no more lightly.

His immediate replacement, Sir Ralph Darling, seemed on the face of it particularly well prepared since he had served as an administrator at the Horse Guards from 1802 to 1818 and since 1819 had been Military Governor and occasionally Acting Civil Governor of Mauritius, where he had taken strong measures against the persistent illegal slave trade. But despite his considerable achievements in Australia – stabilizing the currency, reforming the banking system, increasing public revenue and including some non-official colonists in an expanded legislative council – his authoritarian, military manner soon led to familiar difficulties. Bathurst's successor but one at the Colonial Office, William Huskisson, told Horton in 1827 that he had known Darling at the Horse Guards, 'and although a very good plodding man of business in that department, I own that I should not have thought him well qualified to administer the Govt of such a country and such a society as New South Wales, and the people now settled there.' Not much better, however, could be expected until civilians were appointed instead of military officers. 'It may perhaps be difficult to find persons not of that profession of proper rank and qualification, to accept these places and submit to banishment,' Huskisson mused; 'but I trust some such may be found, and it is desirable to make the attempt.'[13] Civilian Governors, however, were not generally found, or even sought, until the 1830s when the senior veterans of the wars against France were getting long in the tooth. And of all the colonies New South Wales, with its large convict population, was the most risky place for such an innovation. The trials of the Governors were eased only after 1840 when transportation there was ended and a legislative assembly created which included elected as well as appointed members.

The problem of mixing convicts and free settlers in this increasingly conventional and valuable settlement colony by the mid–1820s also attracted the attention of the Home Secretary, who had charge of prisoners within the United Kingdom. In the summer of 1825 Peel told Bathurst that he had been considering how to reduce the number sent to New South Wales, but could see no easy solution. Since the population of the United Kingdom was increasing rapidly there was little hope of a decline in the number of criminals. The only alternatives to transportation were the already crowded jails and hulks; a few more might be crammed into penitentiaries if individuals showing promise of reformation could be found but the hulks were already bursting with 3378 inmates, from 2110 in 1815. Peel was willing to expand the number of hulks if nearby public works could be provided by the Treasury, the Ordnance, the Admiralty or Bathurst's own War Department.

Bathurst in reply thought that the real problem with transportation was not so much the actual numbers as the mixture of different classes of convicts. He was particularly concerned about those 'whose education & previous habits of life have placed them on a higher footing than the ordinary convicts . . . they are generally speaking those who are the most likely to be troublesome, more particularly when their time is out, or when they have received their pardon.' He wished that some place could be found for them other than New South Wales, where they might 'avail themselves of the number of convicts to make a formidable common cause against the government'. The only suitable location he could think of was one of the Seychelles Islands in the Indian Ocean, 'which are not unhealthy but are so thinly inhabited that they may be safely trusted with such an addition,' but perhaps Peel would prefer an island in Scotland: 'the expense of a long voyage would be saved & you would have the pleasure of keeping them under your immediate direction'.[14] Nothing came of either suggestion and early in the next year Bathurst himself rejected a new penal colony on Melville Island off the northern coast of Australia, since 'The best disposed would not much relish such a banishment, & the worst will require an additional force to protect the settlers.'[15] Not until the middle of the century was the issue of penal colonies settled by the general acceptance that transportation was a cruel and inhumane punishment and that the aim for all except those who were executed should be rehabilitation. Sentences by then were also shorter, but many new penitentiaries still had to be built. Only then could all the Australian colonies develop as entirely free communities.

The other settlement colony where the Governor's difficulties called for Bathurst's close personal attention was the Cape of Good Hope, misleadingly but effectively represented in travel accounts after Waterloo as a veritable Garden of Eden. Its first class governorship was the one most coveted by well-connected officers. But Bathurst would not remove the incumbent,

Lord Charles Somerset, whom he had appointed in the comparative dearth of candidates in 1813. Then forty-six Somerset had no impressive professional qualifications, having never been more than a district military commander in England (though he was nevertheless promoted to general in 1814); but he was a favourite of the royal family and brother of Bathurst's eminent neighbour in Gloucestershire, the Duke of Beaufort, as well as of Lord Fitzroy Somerset, the Duke of Wellington's Military Secretary since 1811. These attachments stood Lord Charles in good stead in the sea of troubles in which he found himself in the 1820s, but they also served to keep him in office too long for the benefit of the Cape and even his own reputation.[16]

When Somerset was appointed, it was by no means clear his term would be long since the British were mainly occupying the Cape, a Dutch possession since the seventeenth century, to prevent it from being used by France as a base for attacking India. The Governor like his Dutch predecessors was practically absolute, ruling by proclamation, and, apart from abolishing the slave trade as in all British possessions in 1807, the existing Dutch structure was scarcely altered. By the end of the Napoleonic Wars, however, the Cape had became an integral part of the British Empire, its wines being particularly favoured and protected as replacements for the French. In the peace negotiations the government placed a high priority on retaining it as a provisioning station and for the security of India, though with copper-bottomed ships it was no longer needed for the first purpose, as Pitt on the authority of Nelson, had pointed out at the time of the Treaty of Amiens.[17] Close relations between Britain and Holland persuaded the Dutch to cede the Cape in return for £6,000,000 to fortify the United Netherlands against France. And by the next year the Cape had a temporary importance in supplying the army and navy at St Helena so long as Napoleon lived.

Despite the transfer of sovereignty, Bathurst saw no pressing need to alter forms and practices that suited the 35,000 Dutch and French Huguenot cultivators, herdsmen and traders, or to replace the Governor who had been there for only a couple of years. The wisdom of his choice seemed confirmed when Somerset, in refreshing contrast to the West Indies, promptly imposed a slave register in 1816. But Bathurst was troubled by reports that Somerset had carried his courtier habits to the Cape, encouraging horse racing and tolerating gambling by military and civil officers in that Calvinist community. He not only wrote to Somerset himself but had his secretary Charles Greville, another devotee of the turf, ask Lord Edward Somerset to advise his brother to change his ways.

The Governor replied in injured tones, telling Bathurst that he had no idea where he got his misinformation and insisting that it was 'founded in the grossest misrepresentation and calumny'. He pointed out that racing had begun under the first British Governor twenty years before, had been supported by every one since in order to encourage horse breeding and was in fact popular with the Dutch. He admitted giving a plate at two annual meetings out of his private purse and offered to abandon this if Bathurst ordered. But he also observed that the races were not really suited to gambling since horses for that purpose were not bred at the Cape; even an expert gambler would not risk £5 on them. And he concluded with a fervent plea to the Colonial Secretary not to credit any other fabrications, or at least give him a chance to respond, since 'My mind is solely occupied by what can best promote the interests and welfare of the Colony – and my utmost ambition is that I may discharge my duty here as successfully as I feel I do – diligently – faithfully and conscientiously.'[18]

This was a trivial enough matter and Bathurst did not hesitate to accept Somerset's word. But it was an omen of the kind of charges that were hurled at Somerset after the arrival of British settlers in 1820. Somerset shared their desire to make the colony more British, but his Tory and aristocratic interpretation was at loggerheads with the conception of transplanted countrymen from a very different social class who soon denounced him as a despot worse than those at home. Like most of his kind, he was by nature authoritarian and was encouraged by his almost unlimited powers. But his anger and quarrels with everyone markedly increased after the death of his beloved wife in September, 1815.

Four of Somerset's six surviving children were with him at the Cape, two unmarried sons and two unmarried daughters, but in his bereavement the person who became his constant companion was Dr James Barry, Assistant Surgeon to the Forces, who arrived in August 1816. The young physician attracted immediate attention by his singular appearance: only five feet tall, he was slim, beardless and effeminate, wearing high heeled boots and, in military uniform, an exaggerated cocked hat and a huge sword. He was usually accompanied by a poodle and a large black servant with a parasol to shade his face from the sun. But no one doubted his professional skill and he quickly became a friend of the whole Somerset family. In 1817 he accompanied the Governor on a tour of the frontier and in December was appointed Somerset's official physician with a salary and a residence in the grounds of Government House.

The brusque Somerset's intimacy with the exotic doctor soon aroused malicious gossip, which might have been even greater if anyone had suspected that Barry was a woman (or possibly a male hermaphrodite with breasts and external female genitalia), which was only revealed at his death in 1865.[19] Somerset and Barry may have been lovers and may even have had a child, born in Mauritius while Somerset was on leave in England in 1820–21, but this is mere speculation. What is certain is that Barry nursed Somerset back to health after a severe illness in September, 1819. Relations then seemed to cool as the Governor prepared to sail home on leave with his daughters in January, but on his return in November, 1821, they became close again, even though Somerset brought with him a new wife by whom he subsequently had three children. A decade later, when Somerset was gravely ill in England, Barry rushed home from Mauritius without leave, protected against reprimand by Lord Fitzroy Somerset, Military Secretary to the Commander in Chief, to attend him until his death fourteen months later. This does not prove that they were lovers in any sense, but they were certainly extraordinarily devoted.

During Somerset's sojourn in England about 3500 British settlers arrived in the colony in the middle of 1820, aided by a parliamentary grant of £50,000 to take the edge off unrest in the year of Peterloo.[20] Most were sent to the eastern district of Albany where there was plenty of unclaimed land and where colonization would help to protect the frontier against increasing attacks from the Xhosa after the postwar economies had reduced the colony's military force from 4000 to 2400. Few of them had any experience of cultivation, though there had been some attempt to discourage those who were least suited, Goulburn having told the Duke of Newcastle that townspeople would be a burden to the colony and themselves: 'Their ignorance of agriculture is in itself a most serious obstacle and as far as my observation goes I should say they were less patient of inconvenience & therefore more easily disheartened.'[21]

But through no fault of their own all of those sent to the Eastern Cape became a burden. Despite the conviction in Britain that all of South Africa was more fertile than Canada, the soil in the Albany district was acidic, the streams unreliable and most of the water too bitter to drink, hence the Dutch term for the region Zuurveld, 'sour fields'. In time the settlers adapted to a land best suited to cattle grazing, but in the first few years they were afflicted by storms, drought, wheat blight and cattle raids by the Xhosa, and forced to depend on public and private charity just as the lucrative St Helena trade collapsed on Napoleon's death in 1821. Nor did they receive much sympathy from Somerset when he returned at the end of that year. Much as he welcomed the increase in British residents, now making up about 20% of the European population, he regarded this latest infusion as a collection of idle and dangerous whiners. He denied them permission to hold public assemblies to publicize their grievances, refused to meet them himself, and, whether they gathered at their new centre of Grahamstown, at Cape Town or elsewhere, he assumed that they were dangerous radicals as bent on destroying the settled order of the colony as the supporters of Queen Caroline he had recently seen in England.

In the face of Somerset's refusal to meet their requests, the settlers turned directly to Bathurst by sending him a petition bearing 171 signatures in March, 1823. They complained that it was their particular hardship to be situated in a remote corner of the British dominions, 'with their whole interests and prospects committed to the *unlimited control of one individual*, and possessing no security that their situation is thoroughly understood or properly represented' and that they were 'debarred by all means of expressing their collective sentiments upon matters of the utmost importance to their common interests'.[22]

Somerset himself had arrived back at the Cape in a foul mood even before he heard of these complaints. During his absence the acting governor had been Major General Sir Rufane Donkin, a veteran of the European wars who had been invalided to the Cape from India following the death of his young wife only three years after their marriage. Somerset had been annoyed enough to learn while in England that Donkin had departed from his own frontier policy, including halting work on the fortifications, and had taken advantage of his temporary position to make appointments. But this paled beside the insult which his eldest son, Captain Henry Somerset, Dr Barry, and the Assistant Quartermaster General came aboard to tell him about as soon as his ship anchored at Table Bay. Three months earlier Captain Somerset had criticized Donkin for removing some prize mules from the Governor's country residence of Newlands, contrary to his father's orders; when he insisted that they be returned, Donkin became so angry at the suggestion that he did not have full powers of government that he waved his carriage whip over the captain's head. This may not have been recounted in accurate detail, but Donkin had certainly placed Captain Somerset under open arrest and the offence to family honour was more than Lord Charles could bear. When Donkin sent word that a dinner in his honour was ready at Government House, Somerset replied that he would not disembark until the next day. Early that morning he entered the house by one door as Sir Rufane went out by another to greet him and the two did not meet in the three weeks before Donkin sailed for England.

Both Somerset and Donkin sent their version of this highly-publicized absurdity to Bathurst. After reading them, and before seeing Donkin who had just landed at Portsmouth, the Colonial Secretary reprimanded Somerset for his conduct, telling him curtly that if he had any reason to complain of Donkin's administration during his absence,

> anything was better than making it a matter of personal difference, & it would be paying you a very ill compliment to imagine that in the ordinary inter-course of Society you would not have had self consideration sufficient to keep up those public demonstrations of respect & attention to which it was the duty of each in your respective situations to observe towards each other, & which in the more elevated one in which in every way you enjoy, it was the more easy for you to exercise.

Bathurst agreed with Donkin that Somerset's refusal to land for dinner, the nature of his entry to Government House, and the abrupt, formal letter (of which he had enclosed a copy to Bathurst) saying that he would meet Donkin only by appointment if he had any official communication to make was 'a very rough way to turn him out of the house'. His advice was to 'oblit-erate the remembrance of this unfortunate affair' rather than causing dissent by repudiating all that Donkin had done: 'There is nothing which so weakens the authority of the State as the governor overturning the acts of his predecessor: nor is there anything so calculated to keep alive a party spirit in the Colony as such a system.'[23]

Far from following this wise counsel, however, Somerset was soon quarrelling with others, particularly Colonel Christopher Bird, the secretary of the colony since 1818. Having been at the Cape since 1797 with the exception of the years of Dutch reoccupation, Bird was one of the most experienced officials and had hitherto been highly regarded by Somerset. But he had supported Donkin during the Governor's absence, even taking Donkin's side in the dispute with Captain Somerset; and Bird compounded his sins by visiting Donkin frequently in the interval before he left. Both Bird and the Inspector of Lands and Woods, Charles D'Escury, also fuelled Donkin's vendetta in England by sending evidence of Somerset's arbitrary conduct. D'Escury, a Dutch refugee who had fled to England in 1795, was in financial straits as prices at the Cape were forced up by the demand from St Helena; since the Colonial Office would not increase his salary or Somerset appoint him to the Council of Justice, he hoped for better oppor-tunities under a new governor. In March 1823 he wrote to Bathurst accusing Somerset of receiving £750 in return for a land grant, disguised as payment for a horse that the Governor had personally imported.

Somerset told Bathurst that this accusation was part of Bird's campaign to get rid of him so that the Secretary could wield unbridled power. 'Colonel Bird's influence is so extensive in the Colony,' he wrote, 'that with the exception of the Chief Justice, the Auditor & three or four more, not a man *does* resist it. The Robespierrean terror in which he is held, excludes all representations of just grievances.' He added that he had accidentally opened a letter from Bird to Donkin which completely destroyed his confidence in the Secretary. And he complained bitterly of his staff writing directly to the Colonial Secretary: 'It is quite impossible that a Governor can advantageously administer his Govt. if the officers under him are permitted to correspond (except through him) with the Government at home. If a Governor refuses to send their representations they are at liberty to appeal to the Secretary of State.'[24]

Donkin meanwhile used the information from the Cape to blacken Somerset's reputation in England. When Bathurst refused to support Donkin's claim to a baronetcy for his acting governorship (he had already been promoted to lieutenant general in 1821), he became even angrier, turned to the receptive opposition and even tried to get into parliament himself. He did not succeed until 1832, by which time Somerset was dead, but his conduct hardened Bathurst's heart towards him and inclined him to give Lord Charles the benefit of the doubt. Donkin finally admitted his personal motives shortly after Bathurst left office, claiming that 'a very little consideration from [the Colonial Office] would have prevented those disclosures which I have been compelled publicly to make in my own satisfaction, and would have saved much uneasiness to a noble family for which I have always, with one exception, professed a high consideration'. He thought it astonishing that no one in the Colonial Office seems to have considered that an individual could combine 'profound Respect for official rank and station, with the most punctilious jealousy of his own honour as a soldier, united to the honest inflexible independence of an English gentlemen; my successful but rather arduous struggle in defence of both of which I look back on with pride and self-satisfaction.' Bathurst stiffly replied the next day that he was 'not conscious of having been wanting in that attention towards you which any General Officer returning from a temporary Command & Appointment in the Colonies is entitled to expect from the Colonial Minister'. He had never prevented Donkin from making 'disclosures which you might think requisite either for the King's service or your own vindication & I am bound to believe that you would not be inclined to make any to the prejudice of others, on any other ground whatever'.[25]

Somerset was supported in his quarrels not only by his powerful family but also of the conscience of the House of Commons, William Wilberforce, a great friend of the Evangelical Duchess of Beaufort and admirer of Somerset's imposition of a slave register. On 25 July, 1822, Wilberforce carried a vote in the Commons for an address to the King against extending slavery to the new Albany settlement, despite Horton's assurances that there was no slavery there and his warning that it was difficult to draw a territorial distinction in a colony where slavery had been long established. Later in the debate the Under-Secretary met this defeat by moving for a commission to report on the Cape, Mauritius and Ceylon, as well as the criminal justice system in the Leeward Islands. With the Under-Secretary's assurance that slavery at the Cape would be included in the instructions, which would also encompass the systems of government, ways to economize, currency, the legal systems and the administration of justice, Wilberforce also added his imprimatur.

Quick off the mark to improve his standing at home even before the commission began, Somerset, in March, 1823, issued a proclamation ameliorating the lot of the slaves: forbidding all but essential work on Sunday, legalizing slave marriages, admitting the oaths of Christian slaves in court; enforcing the baptism of Christian babies, requiring that slaves be educated in free schools, permitting them to own property, limiting the hours of work and providing payment for overtime, commanding that proper food and clothing be provided, restricting punishment, and protecting the slaves against maltreatment by their owners. This anticipated and even went beyond Bathurst's instructions to the colonial governors following the famous Commons debate two months later. When Somerset read the report of that, resting from his virtuous labours, he confidently awaited praise from the home government. But pleased as Wilberforce must have been, Lord Charles had exceeded his powers by issuing the proclamation without the Colonial Secretary's approval. Bathurst lauded Somerset for benevolent motives but had to rebuke him for taking matters into his own hand and insisted on a uniform ordnance based on the 1824 Order in Council for Trinidad. This was issued in 1826, but by then an advisory council had been established in the previous year, and great dispute arose as to whether or not he still had the authority to act unilaterally. This and opposition from the slave owners meant that the matter was not resolved until the home government issued its own general Order in Council in 1830. Somerset's well-intentioned but precipitate act had paradoxically delayed the improvement in slave conditions, but for a brief hour the autocrat was admired by reformers who suspected weaker governors of conniving in the owners' resistance.

To conduct the wide-ranging Commission of Eastern Enquiry called for by Horton's address, Bathurst appointed the veteran J.T. Bigge, just completing his publications on New South Wales, and Major William Colebrooke of the Royal Artillery, who was something of a local expert after fifteen years' service in India, Ceylon, Java and elsewhere in the east. But the colonies they were charged to investigate – the Cape, Mauritius and Ceylon – were so variegated and the terms of reference so sweeping that a third commissioner, William Blair, had to be added in 1825. Even then, they toiled for a decade before completing their task. Bigge's health did not survive the labour, but Colebrooke, only thirty-six when they began, later governed several colonies in the West Indies, as well as New Brunswick.

The first stop on the commissioners' tour was the Cape, where they arrived in July, 1823, and remained for three years. Somerset received them cordially, offering them Government House while he lived, as he preferred, at Newlands in the country. Opposition to Somerset was growing rapidly by this time and, in addition to their prescribed inquiries, Bigge and Colebrooke inevitably found themselves involved in the disputes, reporting to Bathurst on them and being instructed by him to investigate various issues as they arose.

The first accusation was D'Escury's, of improper horse trading and corrupt land granting. Somerset knew nothing of this until Bathurst's instructions reached the Cape in December, 1823, and was furious to learn of his own official's allegations in this manner. Bigge and Colebrooke spent three months examining the charge. Somerset insisted that the thirty-four horses he had imported from England entirely for the publicly-spirited purpose of improving the breed had cost him personally £5000. The commissioners also discovered that the horse supposedly sold as cover for a bribe had been bought by the farmer two years before the land grant, though the process of assigning the property had begun at the same time. In their report to Bathurst they concluded that Somerset was guilty of nothing worse than injudiciousness. Bathurst agreed, but Somerset was not best pleased by the censorious reminder that 'a Governor if he deals in horses will always be exposed to imputations if he happens to shew any thing which can be called a favour to any person to whom he is selling a horse'. The safe course Bathurst recommended was to refuse to sell horses to those applying for land grants.[26] D'Escury added to Somerset's discomfort by boasting that he had received very satisfactory letters directly from Bathurst, but his joy was short-lived: when Donkin published official documents supplied by D'Escury in a pamphlet at the beginning of 1827, D'Escury was dismissed for serious

203

breach of trust. He died on the way back to England, but, despite his conduct, the government granted his destitute widow a small pension.

Another matter that Bigge and Colebrooke could dispose of more promptly was the accusation that Somerset had improperly exchanged some prize slaves (captured by the anti-slavery squadron and apprenticed at the Cape for fourteen years in preparation for freedom) for a female slave to be employed, as they put it, for his 'personal and immoral gratification'. The story, probably inspired by Donkin, first appeared in *The Times* newspaper on 5 October, 1824. The commissioners concluded that there was no foundation for it, which was scarcely surprising since prize slaves fell under the Collector of Customs who jealously protected his rights. But they did establish that there had been a slave by the name of Carolina in Somerset's household whom he had freed before going on leave to England in 1820 and added that the relationship in which she was said to have lived with Somerset had entirely ceased since his return.[27] The second Lady Charles was no doubt similarly relieved, perhaps also Dr Barry, whose coolness on the eve of the Governor's leave may be thus explained.

Close friends again, Barry tried to reconcile Somerset and Bird while the commissioners were investigating the charges of D'Escury's, which were supported by Bird, and the Governor was embroiled in more disputes. An opportunity for this occurred in January, 1824, when Bird fell from a horse and broke his leg. Perhaps to avoid meeting the Governor, he used his convalescence to transact business at home, where he was attended almost daily by Barry. In October, as Bigge and Colebrooke were completing their report on D'Escury's allegations, Somerset told Bathurst that in May Barry had told him what no one else dared, 'that I was surrounded by unfaithful persons and that the only man that possessed the talent to assist me was Colonel Bird: and in the present dangerous state of Public Affairs, urged me to throw myself upon him.' Barry had also represented Bird as having the highest regard for Somerset, considering him to be the most scrupulous and conscientious person he had served under at the Cape. 'These words were so strongly and unequivocally expressed,' Somerset added with satisfaction, 'that I instantly made a minute of them. Of course I made no reply to the communication'.[28]

However much this endorsement might have served to raise Somerset in Bathurst's eyes on the eve of Bigge and Colebrooke's report on the sale of horses, it turned out to be yet another embarrassment. Six months earlier Bathurst had accepted Somerset's recommendation and discharged Bird for discreditable conduct towards the Governor. The order would have arrived at the Cape just after Barry's assurances of Bird's high esteem of Somerset.

When he was discharged Bird claimed that it was due to his Roman Catholicism, which had never previously been an impediment. The reason seemed plausible when he was granted a generous pension for his long service, but Lord Charles correctly claimed that it was due to his dissatisfaction with Bird's conduct.

Before Bathurst would take any account of Barry's surprising account of the now former Secretary's high regard for the Governor, he requested Somerset to have the doctor testify to its accuracy if memory still permitted. Somerset promptly returned a note signed by Barry that was a fairly close version of what he had earlier reported.[29] Three weeks later, however, this was undermined by Bird who, not knowing that it had been sent to London, told Bathurst that Barry had signed the paper without reading it; when he then asked to see it, Somerset refused; but Barry saw enough to realize that he had committed himself to a statement 'which was altogether false, it asserting among other things that I [Bird] had said it was impossible to call Lord Charles' probity into question'. Barry demanded the paper, Somerset again refused, 'the parties got warm, flat contradictions passed and it ended in Barry's protesting against any use being made of the certificate so surreptitiously obtained and in Lord C. forbidding Barry ever to enter his house again.' Barry appealed to the much put-upon Bigge and Colebrooke for assistance in recovering it, but they also failed. Bird rightly considered that Somerset had kept the document 'as a rebutter I suppose of my statement of his having purloined public money.'[30]

Early in 1826 Bigge and Colebrooke also told Bathurst that the dispute between Somerset and Barry, 'tho' partially accommodated, has become the subject of a more acute and serious breach of the very friendly & intimate relation that had long subsisted between them'.[31] Six thousand miles away Bathurst, though still disposed to believe Somerset, was sighing to his new Under-Secretary that Somerset had 'a happy knack of quarrelling with those whose support he wants – this quarrel with Dr. Barry is very inopportune'.[32] After reading the commissioners' account of how Barry had first deceived Somerset and then Somerset had deceived Barry, he concluded that the matter was 'nothing more than what I suspected, the contradictions & intrigues of a meddling physician [who first tried to bring his two patients together and afterwards tried to get himself out of the scrape]'. He told Bigge and Colebrooke that although Somerset's friends regretted 'the unfortunate influence which Dr Barry had at one time over him,' he was very able 'and it is well known that a skilful physician will gain by his habitual intercourse an ascendency over patients whose natural strength of mind would exempt them from such influence'.[33]

205

Barry's eagerness to reconcile Somerset and Bird was prompted by a new fight over freedom of the press that was shaking the colony to its foundations, and particularly alienating the new English arrivals. Whatever Bird's sins against the Governor in the past, Barry probably hoped that harmony would give Somerset the advantage of Bird's long experience in tackling his troubles. But even if Barry's too clever plan had succeeded before the order for Bird's dismissal arrived, there was not much chance that Bird or anyone else could have moderated Somerset's attitude towards the press and his tormentors.

There had never been a free press at the Cape and not much interest in it until the 1820 emigrants arrived when the issue was so contentious at home between Peterloo and Queen Caroline's trial. Somerset was instinctively hostile and his propensity was undoubtedly reinforced by the scurrilous publicity in favour of Caroline that he had seen in England. When two recently arrived printers applied for permission to publish periodicals in 1823, he immediately refused. The printers then appealed to Bathurst through Bigge and Colebrooke. The Colonial Secretary was no enthusiast for an uncensored press but, as he had at home, he recognized that denying it to British colonists would create greater controversy than allowing it. He gave a qualified assent, and on that authority two publications began in 1823 and 1824.

Somerset's ire was soon roused by the publishing of proceedings of two libel trials in which the defendant was one William Edwards, 'a soi-disant attorney' as Somerset accurately insisted, who later turned out to be Alexander Low Kay, a former law clerk escaped from New South Wales where he had been transported for theft. With little else by way of entertainment, large crowds flocked to the first trial to enjoy Edwards' unorthodox conduct and eloquent sarcasm. He was sentenced to a month in jail for contempt when he challenged the competence of the court, but was finally acquitted of the libel. This emboldened Edwards to write two letters to Somerset in which, as Bigge and Colebrooke delicately told Bathurst, 'after pretty plain allusion to occurrences, partly of a domestic and partly of a personal nature, His Lordship is charged with frequent violation of the laws, and in one instance, that had lately occurred, of a corrupt administration of it'. Somerset sent the letters to the legal officer to prosecute Edwards for libel against the authority and dignity of the Governor.

The second trial began in early May, 1824, and the court was once more attended by a host of spectators eager for another dramatic performance. On the first day, 'under pretence of making a technical objection to the charge,' Bigge and Colebrooke told Bathurst, 'he seized an opportunity, that ought not to have been allowed him, of making the most violent and indecent attacks upon the personal and domestic conduct of Lord Charles Somerset, as well as upon several persons, officers of the Government, who were known to be honour'd with his Lordship's friendship.' But Edwards was not allowed to call his huge list of witnesses, which included the Governor, and was prohibited from further personal attacks in presenting his defence. At the end of the trial he was found guilty and sentenced to seven years' transportation to New South Wales.

While in jail awaiting a ship, Edwards tried to apologize to Somerset, offering to withdraw his appeal to Britain against the irregularity of the trial if Lord Charles would forbear telling the Governor of New South Wales (where his identity was certain to be discovered) of his conduct at the Cape. Somerset rejected the bid with contempt. When the commissioners tried to discover his motives, Edwards told them that his resentment originated in the Governor's conduct towards his brother in England on some military issue. He also told them the even more improbable tale that he had a brother with a different name in the government of the Cape who provided him with information on the Governor's private life.[34]

The day before the second trial began, Somerset had instructed his legal officer to ensure that Edwards' outrageous court performance was not given wider publicity through the new journals, both of which had promised to avoid political and controversial topics. The officer called on one of the printers to obtain a financial guarantee of his promise, warned that trials should not be reported until they were completed, and insisted on seeing page proofs. The printer reacted by inserting a notice that his periodical would cease publication until freed from censorship, and drew even more attention to the matter by issuing handbills. Somerset then ordered the press sealed and the printer to leave the colony within a month. Although the Governor relented on the banishment order, the printer resolved to take the matter to England. The other publication gave offence at the same time by blaming the difficulties of the Albany settlers on incapacity and abuses within the colonial government. When the editors were warned by the legal officer to avoid such topics, they also decided to suspend publication, producing a violent outburst by Somerset against one of the editors.

This was bad enough, but early on the morning of 1 June, the day after Somerset confirmed Edwards' sentence, a placard appeared in Cape Town accusing the Governor of 'an unnatural crime' with Dr Barry.[35] This was seen by only two people before it mysteriously disappeared, one a naval captain in dressing gown and slippers out to see if there were any ships arriving, but it was immediately the talk of the town. Somerset, Barry and others offered a total reward of £1575 for information. Somerset was convinced that Edwards was to blame, even though he was in jail, but when the huge sum produced no response, it was impossible to charge him with libel and slander.

The early months of 1824 had severely tested Somerset's precarious equanimity. But by the middle of the year the level of acrimony had fallen to the customary level in such a society with such a Governor and Lord Charles could take comfort in the thought that by firm action he had rid himself and the colony of the most dangerous and disruptive individuals. But the attacks had merely shifted to London where his opponents were now gathering. And even Bathurst was shaken by the news of Somerset's high-handed conduct towards the publishers.

At the end of October he wrote a long letter from Cirencester telling Somerset that the case of Edwards and the sealing of the press were not satis-factorily explained and that he needed more information in order to defend the Governor. Until he had a report of the trial Bathurst would not confirm Edwards' sentence of transportation, since it sounded 'very harsh to English ears; and you yourself seem to be aware of it, for you add that the severity of the punishment arose from his conduct at the trial'. In sealing the press and banishing the printer Somerset had also 'unfortunately stirr'd two most delicate questions to which every English feeling is most likely to be alive. The one, the freedom of the press: the second, the power of expulsion without trial, by the exercise of your own individual authority.' The former would certainly be raised in parliament, where some even thought that publication should be unfettered in India, 'although every reflecting man must see that a free press in that country is incompatible with those principles of government by the maintenance of which we can alone hope to retain that Empire'. Bathurst was relieved that the Chief Justice at the Cape had given his authority to seizing the press, but he still required docu-mentary evidence that could be produced in parliament. He also pointed out that while Somerset had the right of expulsion under his instructions, not everyone agreed that the Crown had the right to assign such power. It should in any event be reserved for 'the suppression of some extreme Case of danger where the ordinary administration of the law will not admit of timely assist-ance'. Imprudent use would undermine it, and Bathurst could not see that the presence of the printer in the colony constituted a danger to trade or anything else.

Reflecting on Somerset's conduct and the criticisms of other governors for authoritarianism, he wrote that, although he was inclined to wait for the commissioners' report, if it were delayed he intended to protect Somerset like the Governor of New South Wales by establishing an advisory council, which he did a few months later in February 1825. In the meantime he reminded Lord Charles that 'command of temper is the most serviceable of all qualities in men vested with authority'. The great advantage of a council was that it gave governors time to reflect when provoked by their opponents; another was that it made parliament more willing to entrust authority to colonial governors. But council or no, Bathurst told Somerset that he should not have allowed himself to be so easily aroused. And he warned that even though Somerset thought criticism of him outrageous, it did not appear so in England where libellous matter was published daily and where the Governor's response would be condemned as harsh and arbitrary.[36]

Everything transpired exactly as Bathurst gloomily expected. The attack in the Commons in 1826 was led by Henry Brougham, amply briefed by Somerset's opponents. Lord Charles angrily told Bathurst that accusations of arbitrary conduct were as unfounded as the charges of homosexuality which had appeared on the placard, and that he was as incapable of the one as the other. He entreated Bathurst to defend him,

> [not] in Yr. Lordship's station in the state; nor as the Head of the Department under which I have the honour to serve the King – nor as the much-valued & highly respected friend of my family; nor as an individual to whom I am & have long been largely indebted – but I appeal to Your Lordship on this occasion, as my fellow man.[37]

Even before receiving this plea, however, Bathurst had written to tell Somerset that he could not support his handling of the press, to reproach him for refusing to transmit the publisher's appeal to the Privy Council and suggesting that he come home on leave.[38]

Somerset was getting the same advice from his family, and early in March, 1826, he sailed for England. There were two dinners in his honour before he left, and the staunchly Tory Dudley Perceval, son of the assassinated Prime Minister who had been given a minor post at the Cape by Bathurst the previous year, told the Colonial Secretary that there had never been 'a more unsolicited, a more unequivocal proof of respect and attachment,' claiming that this amounted to a satisfactory answer to nine-tenths of the charges against Somerset, though Bigge and Colebrooke seemed not to appreciate it.[39] The weary commissioners themselves finally completed their much interrupted investigations after Somerset sailed and left for the relative calm of Mauritius, where they were followed by Dr Barry.

The attacks on Somerset in the Commons continued while he was at sea,

Horton successfully beating off the critics by demanding specific charges that could be properly investigated rather than general condemnations. By the time Somerset arrived in the middle of May, political attention was diverted by the general election the following month. But even before that, allegations about the Governor at the Cape had to compete for attention with the more pressing matters of Catholic emancipation, the economic collapse and bad harvest of 1825, the suspension of the corn laws and argument over their permanent alteration. Bathurst was also too immersed in these issues as well as the threats to international peace to spend much time on Somerset's troubles. But he continued to be circumspectly well-disposed to him and his powerful family, early in 1827 appointing Herbert Cornwall, who had married the youngest daughter of Somerset's first marriage at the Cape in 1822, to the new office of Surveyor of the Customs in Lower Canada. This was bitterly resented by the Governor General, both on grounds of cost and the individual, who was so profligate that his father, the Bishop of Worcester would not permit him to return to England; though Dalhousie had to concede that Cornwall's advantageous marriage entitled him to the Colonial Secretary's notice.[40] The appointment did not, however, mean that Bathurst would defend Somerset's conduct to the point of calling his own administration into question or exposing the government to risk.

After dragging into 1827, the Somerset issue was settled in an unexpected way by Lord Liverpool's collapse. Calculating that he had little to hope for from a government headed by Canning that even included Whigs, Somerset resigned his office. Canning's precarious ministry did not want to add to its troubles with the Ultra Tories by provoking him, and in relieved tones Bathurst's successor assured Lord Charles that his accusers' failure to bring their charges to the parliamentary test entitled him to consider himself 'absolved from all imputations touching your personal honour and character, and no one can with justice represent your Lordship's resignation of your appointment as proceeding from an unwillingness to meet any accusation which it might have been intended to make against you'.[41] Although no friend of Canning's government, Bathurst must have been relieved by this happy issue out of an affliction that had plagued the Colonial Office during his last five years.

9

A FRIEND OF THE DUKE OF WELLINGTON, 1826–28

In addition to the distant problems of his own department Bathurst had many other concerns at home and in Europe to occupy him in 1826. There had been riots against the corn laws in the industrial towns in the winter following the economic collapse and the wet spring raised the prospect of a bad harvest. In May, before dissolving parliament for the general election in June, the government prudently obtained authority to release wheat in bonded warehouses at a fixed low duty and the right to admit further imports by Order in Council before the new parliament assembled, when, Liverpool warned the Lords, there would have to be some permanent adjustment of the corn laws.

The election was no more exciting than usual, despite the issue of agricultural protection. The other major question postponed to the new parliament was Catholic emancipation, on which both sides were eager to increase their number of MPs. There was a particularly bitter contest at Cambridge University where two Protestant ministers, Sir John Copley, the Attorney General, and Goulburn, the Irish Secretary, declared their candidacies as early as December, 1825, against the ministerial incumbents, the pro-Catholic Lord Palmerston, Secretary at War, and the Protestant but embarrassing Henry Bankes, who had recently eloped with Lady Buckinghamshire. For departmental as well as political reasons, the Duke of York was especially keen to be rid of Palmerston, and many strong

Protestants agreed. Bathurst was no admirer of Palmerston, but despite his Protestant views he did not engage in the campaign against the Secretary at War, though he did support Goulburn. Palmerston complained about Bathurst's refusal to help him, remarking that it was certainly unusual that 'an official man should find himself endangered in a seat which he has held for fourteen years, by the undisguised competition of two of his colleagues in office'. And he was not mollified by Bathurst's explanation that his desire to use what little influence he had there for Goulburn did not imply hostility to any other candidate.[1] The four fought it out to the bitter end, with Palmerston being returned second to Copley (Goulburn was at the bottom of the poll), in an even more peevish mood than before. The overall result throughout the United Kingdom was about the same proportion of pro- and anti-Catholic MPs as before.

Of far greater concern to Bathurst early in the year than the impending election was the consequence of the death of the Russian Emperor on 13 December, 1825. He feared that the new Tsar would find it necessary to strengthen himself by going to war for the Greeks against the Turks which would not only expand the Greek conflict and threaten the Ottoman empire but even, as he told Canning, increase the banking crisis by encouraging currency speculation and hoarding.[2] There was uncertainty over the Russian succession and a revolt of army officers until it was confirmed that the rightful heir was the younger of Alexander's two brothers. Nicholas I turned out to be a more determined autocrat and opponent of liberalism than Alexander had become by the time of his death, but to sound him out and keep him on the right track about Greece, the British government sent the Duke of Wellington with official condolences to the funeral, which was deferred until April. Bathurst told him that it was 'a very handsome thing of you to consent to so long a journey, and at such an inclement season',[3] particularly since he was recovering from an illness and would have to travel long days for a month over the thawing roads of northern Europe to St Petersburg. Canning more tartly observed that 'the selection of *another* person would have done his health more prejudice than all the frosts and thaws of the hyperborean regions can do it'.[4]

The war in Greece, now in its sixth year, was at a critical stage. Early in 1824, having failed to make much headway against the Greeks, the Sultan had practically handed over the Peloponnesus to Mehemet Ali, the ruler of Egypt and his nominal vassal, who despatched his son Ibraham with a huge fleet and an army. The Greeks, with the aid of foreign recruits, managed to hold their own at sea, but when the Egyptians carried all before them on land in 1825, Greeks and philhellenes clamoured for British protection.

Despite Greek piracy and their atrocities against the Turks at every opportunity, the British public still generally saw only Turkish outrages. Writing to wish Wellington well on his travels at the beginning of February, Bathurst reminded him, if he needed any reminding, of the true situation in Greece.[5] But even Bathurst was incensed by news that the Egyptians intended to expel the Greeks and repopulate the Peloponnesus with people from North Africa. On the same day that he wrote to the Duke, he issued orders to the Admiralty for an officer to obtain a written undertaking from Ibraham Pasha renouncing any such intention under threat of British naval intervention.[6]

By this time Bathurst had a personal as well as official interest in the eastern Mediterranean. On 16 March, 1825, in the fashionable St George's, Hanover Square, his second daughter Emily, then twenty-seven, had married the forty-two year old Colonel Frederick Ponsonby, a veteran of the Peninsula and Waterloo, where he had suffered terrible wounds and been left on the field for dead all night. By virtue of his imminent connection with the Secretary of State for War and the Colonies, Ponsonby had been appointed inspecting field officer of the Ionian islands in January and two months after the marriage he was promoted major general. Lady Emily's father also bestowed £4000 of his £20,000 marriage settlement for the younger children on her.[7] As the couple prepared to leave for Corfu at the beginning of July, Bathurst told Canning that he was going into the country with his wife for a couple of days to spare her the agony of parting.[8] Six months later, however, there was great rejoicing when news arrived of the birth of the first of the Ponsonbys' six children. Bathurst told Hay, who forwarded the letter to Brighton: 'We are all in delight; altho' the Grandfather and Grand Mother feel that we have become much older bodies by it'.[9]

As Wellington, briefed by the Ionian intercepts, pondered the issue he was going to discuss during his journey to St Petersburg, he told Bathurst in a long letter from Berlin that although the conflict between the Greeks and Turks was in itself trifling, if it led to Russian intervention and a general European war, 'sooner or later we shall be forced to enter as principals, if our essential interests or honour do not oblige us to commence it'. With his great military authority, he pronounced that since the Greeks were superior at sea, neither side could really win and the best solution would be some compromise short of Greek independence which he hoped to arrange directly with the Russians since he did not believe that it could be settled by another great power conference where British proposals were not well received.[10]

The Duke found that the agreeable new Tsar, unlike his predecessor, had a low regard for the rebellious Greeks, though no less interest in Russian expansion against the Ottoman Empire. He told Bathurst that he had deterred Nicholas from fighting the Turks by reminding him that although he could determine the time of the first shot, 'he might as well talk of stopping the course of the Neva as of fixing the limits of his operations if once he goes to war'.[11] A month later Wellington signed a protocol by which the two countries offered mediation between the Greeks and Turks in order to achieve local autonomy for the Peloponnesus within the Ottoman Empire. France and Austria added their influence and the Sultan seemed to assent, though fighting still continued.

Within a few months Bathurst and the Duke were complaining that Canning was twisting the protocol into a requirement that Britain force the Turks to concede Greek autonomy. When asked to review the instructions for Stratford Canning, the Foreign Secretary's cousin and ambassador to the Porte, Wellington expostulated to Bathurst that Canning was 'certainly a most extraordinary man':

> Either his mind does not seize a case accurately, or he forgets the impression which ought to be received from what he reads or is stated to him; or knowing and remembering the accurate state of the case, he distorts and misrepresents facts in his instructions to his [diplomatic] ministers with a view to entrap the consent of the cabinet to some principle on which he would found some new-fangled system.[12]

But Bathurst and the Duke were sure that their vigilance would preserve the careful compromise worked out at St Petersburg to maintain the Ottoman Empire and the peace of Europe.

Apart from the Mediterranean and the looming danger in Portugal, where the death of John VI in March revived the threat to the constitutional system and the prospect of a Spanish invasion, Bathurst and the other ministers were increasingly worried by September about the prospective food shortage, particularly in Ireland where a severe drought had apparently ruined the oats and the potatoes. They issued an Order in Council admitting oats and oatmeal, rye, beans and peas at duties to be specified later, but since only wheat had been specified in the enabling legislation in the spring, parliament had to be recalled in November to set the amounts and to indemnify the ministers for their decision. By the time it was recalled, however, the Order turned out to have been unnecessary since the potato crop was sufficient and the rise in the price of oats would have allowed imports under the existing corn laws.

Ministers would not be criticized for their prudence and concern for the poor, but they had to prepare for a potentially damaging discussion on changing the corn laws, on which they were profoundly divided. When Robinson, Chancellor of the Exchequer suggested a large reduction, Bathurst warned the sympathetic Horton of the danger from the government's own landed MPs: 'He may depend upon it that if he means to make bread cheap to become popular, the country gentlemen will in return make themselves popular by voting cheap estimates.' A week later he cautioned his Under-Secretary not to be taken in by private promises of support for reducing the tariff from agriculturalists: 'My own opinion is that the admitting of foreign wheat in at 15 shillings [a quarter duty] when the market price is as low as 5s, would bring on a great agricultural distress.'[13] A few weeks later Horton concluded that cheap grain was a less effective answer to distress than his customary one of emigration, telling Bathurst: 'It would have only the effect of giving the Master Manufacturers higher profits, as they would then be *enabled* to lower the wages, which now they are obliged to give to sustain the life of the workman, and that is all that they now give.'[14]

Despite the disagreement on the corn laws, Bathurst from Cirencester expressed the hope to the Prime Minister at the end of October that it would not be necessary for the cabinet to meet every day of the week before parliament opened since only the indemnity bill must be dealt with before Christmas. Liverpool irritably replied that it was essential to agree on the changes promised for 1827 lest ministers be led into expressing their individual views in the November session, 'and I need not add (for past experience proves it) what inconvenience might result from the occurring in the present state of opinion upon this question.' He also added that 'Cabinets are *very much wanted* on many points in no ways connected with the early meeting of Parliament.'[15]

The only solution to the never-ending corn question was a sliding scale of duties that would admit wheat at a lower initial price than the 80 shillings (£4) a quarter set in 1815, but provide increasing protection as the domestic price fell. After two weeks' discussion, on 22 November the cabinet agreed to allowing imports at a duty of one shilling when wheat was at seventy a quarter, rising to twenty when the price fell to sixty, but refused to be goaded into revealing the scale in parliament before the Christmas recess. By the time the Lords debated the indemnity bill on 11 December, Liverpool had collapsed of exhaustion and Bathurst had to defend the Order in Council. But having already delivered its main attack on the corn laws, the opposition gave him an easy ride, merely charging that the Order

215

had made imports of oats more difficult and expensive than under the existing laws.

The next day Bathurst was on his feet again in place of the Prime Minister to explain the more controversial decision to send 5000 troops to Portugal in response to that government's appeal to the treaty between the two countries. The absolutists who had fled to Spain after the death of King John were now returning with the assistance of Spanish irregulars, none too covertly encouraged by Ferdinand VII. After failing to persuade Spain to desist by diplomatic means for months, Canning convinced his colleagues that only prompt military assistance would embolden the Portuguese government to defeat the challenge and repel the Spanish incursion. He told the Commons: 'We go to plant the standard of England on the well-known heights of Lisbon. Where that standard is planted, foreign domination shall not come.' Referring to the French army which was supporting Ferdinand VII in Spain, he linked the Portuguese cause to his wisdom in insisting on recognition of its former colonies: 'I resolved that if France had Spain, it should not be Spain "with the Indies". I called the New World into exist-ence to redress the balance of the Old.'

There was no such dramatic performance in the Lords, but also no collapse such as Canning suffered after his histrionic triumph. Apart from their differences in style, temperament and the fact that Bathurst was no great orator, he also had less objection to absolutism than Canning and more scepticism about the consequences of this new involvement in the Peninsula. Instead of a ringing call to fly to the aid of Portuguese freedom, he subjected the peers to a long, dry narrative of recent events leading to the necessity of fulfilling the country's obligation to defend the Portuguese government. His true feelings on the subject were revealed in the private observation to Wellington, as the British troops approached Lisbon, that their effect would be to support the revolutionary party in power against the wishes of the Portuguese people.[16]

The Duke, who had supported Bathurst in the Lords by expressing the hope that the British expedition would bring the Spanish King to 'that sense of what was due to himself and his own dignity, which would pre-vent him from allowing any aggression on the territories of his neighbour, our near ally,' was even cooler in his private estimate of the intervention, telling Bathurst: 'Our business is to drive out the enemy. Nothing else'. But it was not even clear to the War Minister who the enemy really was. He thought it more likely to be the Portuguese deserters combined with the local population than the Spanish or French troops. He did not doubt that the insurgents could be beaten, but considered this to be none of the proper business of the British army, which was solely to uphold the constitutional government by putting down insurrections at Lisbon and encouraging a reconciliation of all factions. He was even prepared to leave British troops for a time to ensure lasting peace through a general amnesty, but Wellington argued for his more restricted interpretation that the force should simply drive any invaders over the Spanish border. If the Portuguese insurgents were dispersed within the country and could be dealt with by the government, this would amount to the same thing. A British proposal of a general pardon would entail too great a commitment to Portuguese affairs.[17]

Even as Bathurst and the Duke were discussing the limits on British intervention, the commander of the expedition, Sir William Clinton, MP, recently appointed as Wellington's assistant at the Ordnance, was telling the Secretary of State that his troops had not been hailed with delight when they arrived at Lisbon on Christmas Day, save by the government and a few respectable individuals. This indifference, even hostility, surprised those officers who had served there during the Peninsular War (which Clinton had not), but Bathurst assured him that this was due entirely to resentment of Britain. 'Even the Government who owe their existence to your arrival,' he wrote, 'are obliged to consult their feelings of jealousy by refusing to admit British officers to discipline their army, which by all accounts is in a very disorganized state'. But this was none of Clinton's concern; following the exchange with Wellington, Bathurst warned Clinton not to become implicated in any clashes apart from those directed to overthrowing the government, but to concentrate on driving out the invaders. Bad as the condition of the Portuguese army might be, Bathurst was sure that 'the insurgents must be still worse: & I have no idea that they would stand the appearance of the Corps of one of your Grenadiers'.[18]

Canning's expectation of the British intervention seemed justified in the short run as the Portuguese government struck out against its opponents. Even more gratifying was the retreat of the Spanish monarch in face of the British action. At the beginning of February the Foreign Secretary gleefully countered Bathurst's scepticism by sending him a despatch from Frederick Lamb, the ambassador at Madrid, reporting that the reaction there was 'MORE *satisfactory* than that which Lamb would have been authorized to take as *satisfactory*.'[19] Perhaps this happy state of affairs might have endured, but when Wellington became Prime Minister and withdrew British troops a year later Portugal was plunged into six years of civil war which ended only when new governments in Britain and France rallied to the cause of constitutional government in both peninsular countries.

In addition to Bathurst, Wellington and Canning, the other person occupied with the expedition to Portugal was the Commander in Chief of the Army, the Duke of York, who had been prone to dropsy since the summer of 1826. He was operated on in September, but continued to deteriorate. Bathurst nevertheless assured the King early in December that making the troop arrangements for the Peninsula had 'much enliven'd His Royal Highness, instead of depressing him & had serv'd to awaken him from that state which his great suffering was gradually beginning to reduce him'.[20] A few days later, however, Bathurst had cause to regret that York's interest remained so keen.

On the evening of 14 December, learning of the death of the Marquess of Hastings, Governor of Malta, Bathurst immediately recommended to the King that the island be reduced to a second class government and given to his son-in-law, General Ponsonby, who would continue as commander of the troops and second-in-command to the High Commissioner of the Ionian islands. Apart from Ponsonby's military claims and 'the interests of a dear daughter', Bathurst added that 'such an appointment will come so much within the range of personal intercourse that Lady Bathurst & myself may feel that his professional pursuits will not altogether estrange our daughter from us, and that even with Lady Bathurst's health she may be able occasionally to visit them'.[21] George IV had no objection to accommodating his highly favoured minister, but York protested that he should at least have been consulted. He was feeling particularly sensitive about neglect and, although not disapproving of Ponsonby personally, did not think that he should be promoted to Lieutenant Governor of Malta on the basis of family connection. But his Military Secretary, in conveying his complaint to Wellington, assured him that York would treat the matter as a royal command and say nothing to Bathurst, asking Wellington to do the same.[22] Ponsonby was of course overjoyed at this unexpected and munificent appointment, though anxiously inquiring if the salary would start from the date of appointment or from his actual arrival at Malta.[23]

This expression of annoyance was practically the Duke of York's last pronouncement. On Christmas Eve Bathurst wrote from Brighton to ask Hay if a Secretary of State was required to carry on official business in the event of the Commander in Chief's death.[24] The military secretary replied directly from the Horse Guards on 30 December saying that the Duke was not expected to live more than forty-eight hours but informing Bathurst, who after four decades in office still did not understand all the complicated divisions of power, that the Secretary at War (Palmerston) was the person designated to perform the duties when there was no Commander.[25]

When the Duke of York died on 5, January, 1827, it was obvious to practically everyone that the only person to succeed him was Wellington, though George IV had some bizarre thought of commanding the army himself, or at least giving it to another brother, the Duke of Cambridge. Wellington, always more sensitive than he appeared, even interpreted Bathurst's silence when they discussed the succession as an indication that he was not going to be appointed. Mortified at the misunderstanding, Bathurst immediately told the Prime Minister that he had not given the Duke any assurance only because he thought that Wellington realized that none was necessary.[26] Liverpool agreed and lost no time in recommending Wellington to the King, who accepted without a murmur. But since the Prime Minister had no intention of depriving his government of this national icon, the Duke also continued in cabinet as Master General of the Ordnance.

Even before arriving at the Horse Guards, Wellington showed himself a worthy defender of the army by grumbling to Bathurst that the Duke of York's funeral at Windsor on 20 January could not be a military one 'because we have not men enough to bury a Field Marshal!'[27] It could nevertheless not have been mistaken for anything else. Wellington was naturally a pall-bearer and Bathurst was an assistant to the chief mourner, the Duke of Clarence, the new heir presumptive. The cold was so intense in St George's chapel during the inexplicable two-hour wait for the coffin that it seemed that others would follow it into the grave. The Bishop of Winchester, Pitt's friend and biographer Pretyman Tomline, died from the effects, and many others, including Wellington and Canning, were ill for some time. Bathurst, given his age, was lucky to escape unscathed. Lady Bathurst was remembered by a lock of York's hair to mark a friendship going back to his refusal to fire at her brother, the future Duke of Richmond, when challenged to a duel in 1789.[28]

A month after the funeral Lord Liverpool suffered a stroke at his breakfast table on 17 February, his nervous temperament strained to the breaking point by the divisions within the cabinet during the past five years. But, in contrast to the Duke of York, there was no obvious person to replace him in keeping together Liberal Tories and Ultras, Protestants and Catholics. Bad as his condition was, it suited everyone's convenience to postpone the difficult decision by hoping that he would recover. As the King told Bathurst in the course of a rambling two-hour monologue a week later, it would be highly indelicate to presume that Liverpool's illness was hopeless, particularly when the Prime Minister recovered his senses sufficiently to realize what had happened.[29] When Liverpool did rally, six weeks later, it was only sufficiently to respond to his wife's assurances that he would soon be well enough to resume his duties by saying, 'No, no, not I - too weak, too weak'.[30]

The Ultra Tories naturally looked to Wellington as the next Prime Minister and now regretted that he had taken the command of the army. But since he insisted that his proper place was at the Horse Guards he and others pinned their hopes on Bathurst, who as the senior minister was by default acting Leader of the Lords. The Duke of Buckingham, despite being pro-Catholic, saw the way the wind was blowing and promptly wrote to Bathurst offering his services as Governor General of India, being so financially hard pressed that he was forced to close his great house at Stowe. He claimed that he had been assured the year before, presumably by his nephew Charles Williams Wynn, President of the Board of Control, that if the sub-continent were at peace he would have no rival. None too subtly, Buckingham told Bathurst that if he wanted the support of Buckingham's MPs he would be 'so good as to permit Lord Chandos [his son] to converse with you upon the subject, and it will gratify me much on private as well as on public grounds if the result shall prove satisfactory to us both'.[31] As other candidates for Prime Minister were proposed Buckingham hawked his offer to them in similar terms.

His first overture, however, was based on a misassumption, since Bathurst had no interest in the premiership nor any intention of being pushed into it. Not only was he eight years older than Liverpool and a poor speaker, he also disagreed with the revision of the corn laws, the major issue to which the ministry was committed. At the cabinet hastily assembled two days after Liverpool's stroke at the house of William Huskisson, who was too ill to go out, it was resolved that ministers would assure the Commons that Canning, who was also ill, would proceed with the bill as scheduled but that the proposed simultaneous discussion in the Lords would be postponed until the bill actually arrived there since, as Huskisson told Canning, it was clear that 'Bathurst will not undertake it'.[32]

But the desire to be Prime Minister burned as strongly as ever in Canning. When he was well enough to return to parliament on 1 March he demonstrated his fitness by dividing the opponents of the corn bill and getting it passed by early April. The Lords, of course, was another matter. When the peers staked out the grounds for their opposition on 8 March Bathurst rejected the suggestion that revision had been forced on Liverpool when he was ill and pointed out that the sliding scale would moderate the erratic 'open and shut' system which permitted a sudden flood of imports, but his heart was clearly not in it and he raised no objection to a select committee.

By the time Lady Liverpool conveyed her husband's acquiescence in resignation at the end of March opinion among the ministers and their supporters had hardened for and against Canning. The King's hope that the government could continue as it was under Bathurst or Lord Bexley (the former Nicholas Vansittart) was not acceptable to Canning, who was well aware of his worth and the fear of his opposition. If not nominally Prime Minister, he insisted on determining policy on such leading questions as the corn laws, Catholic relief and foreign policy. After sending Peel on the hopeless mission to inquire if Canning and his associates would serve under Wellington, George IV faced the inevitable by commissioning Canning to form a government on the same basis as Liverpool's, though leaving the way open to some compromise Prime Minister by not actually naming him to the office. Canning informed his colleagues and asked to see Bathurst among others at his convenience. The Colonial Secretary replied the next morning saying that he would be at his office between one and two, remaining until five, and would be ready to talk to Canning 'either during that interval, or any hour you choose to send for me on this day'.[33] After they had met Bathurst sent Canning another note asking if he had understood him correctly to say that if the Catholic question could be put aside Peel would serve under him, since Bathurst had seen letters from Peel to Eldon saying the opposite: 'Altho' I do not mean that such an information, if made, would make any essential difference in the decision I may make, any more than his retreat, absolute and entire of itself would be conclusive, I should be glad to know if I misunderstood you'.[34]

Caught by his own deviousness Canning hurried to Bathurst's office to defend his interpretation of Peel's refusal, only to find that he had left. The Foreign Secretary scribbled a line saying that it would take 'more time that I can possibly find to answer your note in writing,' and asking Bathurst to call at the Foreign Office for five minutes on his way to dinner with most of their colleagues at the President of the Board of Control's house.[35] If Bathurst saw Canning that evening, there is no record of it.

Conspicuous among those absent from the dinner were Peel and Wellington. When the Duke received Canning's circular, he asked, as Canning had when Liverpool was trying to form a government in 1812, who was to be Prime Minister. Canning used this letter to get the King to state that he intended him to be Premier, then haughtily informing Wellington that this was so generally understood that he had not troubled to mention that the usual form would be followed on this occasion. This was not the tact which others were careful to use with the Great Man, but even if Canning had handled the matter more gracefully Wellington would

221

have left, having determined years ago that he would not serve under Canning. Perhaps hoping to stop him in his tracks, the Duke wrote to the King the next day resigning not only the Ordnance but also, more surprisingly, the command of the army. This settled the matter for Bathurst and many others. The following day the Colonial Secretary told Canning that he must also leave, excusing himself for not giving reasons since it was better 'to avoid any thing which would lead to discussion, as it is too apt on these occasions to widen the breach, which separation must in some measure effect'. But he did sharply add that, after talking to Peel, he had discovered that the King had completely misunderstood the Home Secretary's attitude about continuing under Canning.[36]

A total of over twenty members left the administration. The only Protestant who remained was Lord Bexley, Chancellor of the Duchy of Lancaster, for whom Canning had not hitherto demonstrated any conspicuously high regard. Bathurst's friend Lord Harrowby, a pro-Catholic though a person of almost legendary moderation who had served in every ministry save the Talents since Pitt's day, added his prestige by continuing as Lord President of the Council. But it seemed that the mass of Tory resignations would frustrate Canning. 'No man ever took office under more humiliating circumstances or was placed in a more difficult and uncertain situation,' wrote Charles Greville, who was informed of the negotiations by Lady Bathurst and her daughter Georgina: 'indeed a greater anomaly cannot be imagined. Canning, disliked by the King, opposed by the aristocracy and the nation, and unsupported by the Parliament is appointed Prime Minister.'[37] But Canning managed to lure in the Protestant Copley, with whom he had been quarrelling in the Commons over Catholic emancipation only a month before, by making him Lord Chancellor as Lord Lyndhurst, and inducing another Protestant, Lord Anglesey, to succeed Wellington at the Ordnance.

Thus encouraged, Canning turned again to Bathurst, the most moderate of Wellington's associates, offering him the Home Office in place of War and the Colonies, which was too close to his own interests and was given to Frederick Robinson, who went to the Lords as Viscount Goderich. The chances of acceptance must have seemed high to Canning. He and Bathurst had always got along well enough in their overlapping departments; Bathurst was a reliable and efficient minister, unlike the embarrassing Eldon; he showed less strain of office than many younger colleagues and, since he was not rich by aristocratic standards, the £6000 salary made a greater difference to him than to such ministers as Wellington and Westmorland. The Home Office was also senior to the War and Colonies, though technically all three

222

Secretaries of State were equal, so the exchange could be represented as a promotion. Citing the examples of Bexley and Copley and alluding to Anglesey, not yet confirmed, Canning optimistically claimed to find in Bathurst's letter of resignation 'no reason alleged by you against accepting (or retaining) office, except the want of countenance from other individuals holding the same opinions on the questions which divide us, as yourself'. But Bathurst was not tempted to abandon Wellington by this or any other blandishment. Pointing to the wave of resignations, he politely but firmly declined an offer which 'would not be creditable to me and could not therefore be serviceable to his Majesty,' though he agreed to Canning's request to say nothing about refusing the Home Office, which might 'embarrass you in your negotiations and would tend to lessen the value of the obligation to the individual on whom it may be ultimately conferred'.[38]

Canning then applied to the opposition and most Whigs decided to support him as a lesser evil than the Ultra Tories. On this basis he put together a government that he could comfort himself was no more shaky or unimpressive than the one constructed by his hero Pitt at the end of 1783.

The seals of departing ministers were transferred on 31 April, the day before parliament reassembled after the Easter recess. But Bathurst prepared to leave as soon as Goderich was named. In order to protect Hay's position he wrote a memorandum on 20 April setting out Lord Liverpool's agreement to the appointment of a Permanent Under-Secretary similar to the one at the Treasury, adding that the choice of Hay had been approved by the Prime Minister and that the expectations of him had been amply justified during the past two years. Hay was delighted, but Bathurst assured him: 'You are very good in considering an act of justice towards you, as proof of friendship,' adding that it would 'add much to my regret at quitting office if I thought it was to separate us in personal life'.[39] Their friendship did endure, as they continued exchanging information and advice, though necessarily less often than when they had worked together.

Bathurst also wrote to express his appreciation to James Stephen and to Adam Gordon, the chief clerk (beavering away ever since the establishment of the War Department in 1794), asking him to convey his thanks to the senior clerks. And finally he wrote to Wilmot-Horton, since 'It would look as if I were insensible of what I feel towards you, were I to omit addressing a letter to you'. Despite their different political outlooks, Bathurst assured him, 'I have never had any reason to think that your official as well as your personal attachment to me was not every thing I would wish: and I have always found you my zealous defender in the H. of Commons, & a most efficient assistant in my Office,'asking him to accept 'my most sincere thanks for all your able exertions and kind attention'. Horton was also pleased with his letter, telling Bathurst that there was no document to which he attached so much value, 'especially as I feel that you have not exaggerated my official and personal attachment to yourself – which, I believe, was well known to all persons, whatever their shades of political opinion might be'. He was well aware that those acting together in public life should ideally be in complete harmony and it was therefore 'with *peculiar* satisfaction that I reflect on our five long years of official connection, & the commentary upon them which you have this day sent me, *notwithstanding* the absence of that condition'. He trusted that the sincerest respect for his departing chief would 'stand the test of *any time* that may be *at hand*'.[40]

At the resumption of parliament, the first item was the new governmental arrangements and the explanations of those who had resigned. In the Lords, which met on 2 May, former ministers sat on the cross benches, indicating that they were neither supporters of the administration nor truly in opposition to it. The main attention was naturally directed to Wellington, who declared that he could not remain at the Horse Guards after the rebuke from Canning in response to his inquiry as to who was to be Prime Minister, asserted that he had never wanted that position himself and denied that there was any concerted action to stop Canning. This last theme was reiterated by others, including Bathurst, who in his own brief statement told the House that he had followed those in whom he had confidence, contending that it was impossible for him to sit in a cabinet in which only three of twelve ministers were anti-Catholic, unlike Liverpool's in which there had been an equal division. When these opening salvoes made it clear that there would be no reconciliation between Canning and his former colleagues, three more Whigs were admitted to the cabinet, further increasing the hostility of the Tories who defeated the corn bill on a wrecking amendment from the Duke. This led the overwrought Canning to tell the Commons on 18 June – Waterloo Day no less – that Wellington, whom he was trying to win back to the command of the army, was 'a tool in the hands of more crafty intriguers'.

After the failure of his one major piece of legislation, Canning turned to the pressing issue of the war in Greece. Unable to persuade Austria and Prussia to accept a joint demand to the Ottoman Empire that Greece become a self-governing province, he took advantage of French agreement to raise the protocol to a treaty, signed in London by representatives of the three powers on 6 July. A new secret clause was added providing for a joint force, in practice a naval squadron, to end the fighting if the Turks and the Greeks did not accept their mediation. This was obviously well known in political circles, and Bathurst, appalled at the escalation of diplomatic pressure, told Arbuthnot on the eve of the signing, 'It appears to me that what is going on is a system of unusual injustice & improvidence'. Apart from interference in the internal affairs of the Ottoman Empire, Britain was demanding for the vanquished Greeks the terms of victors. Having threatened the Turks (more accurately the Egyptians) when they had indicated that they would expel all the Greeks from the Peloponnesus, the country was now requiring the ejection of the Turks at the end of the war, 'practising towards our Allies in time of peace the same measure, which we declared to be too bad for the Turks to commit against their antagonists in time of war'. He also warned that joint naval action would invite a Russian fleet into the Mediterranean, which Britain had always tried to prevent and which was unnecessary since the Royal Navy, with or without the French, could easily handle the situation.[41] If Bathurst had remained in the cabinet and known that the Russians were prepared to act alone, he might have accepted the necessity of joint naval as well as diplomatic action, but he would have tried to avoid it and would at least have argued for a Russian agreement to withdraw after the action.

Just a month after concluding this treaty Canning died in excruciating agony on the morning of 8 August. The day before, Hay sent an account of his condition to Cirencester. Much as he had objected to Canning's policies and manner, Bathurst magnanimously replied, 'He never enjoy'd what had been the whole object of his life to attain; & I believe latterly was more annoy'd by his old friends than by his new ones.'[42] Wellington, made of sterner stuff, assured Bathurst on the authority of one Dr Farr that 'it was Canning's temper that killed him'.[43] George IV, despite disliking the Whigs, decided to continue the ministry under Lord Goderich rather than embark on the strenuous course of trying to reunite the Tories. But he insisted that the cabinet not touch Catholic relief or parliamentary reform, that no more Whigs be admitted and that the sound Tory J. C. Herries, Financial Secretary to the Treasury and one of the commissioners for the restoration of Windsor Castle, be appointed Chancellor of the Exchequer. The day before this was confirmed, Bathurst presciently told Wellington that, although Goderich was 'as amiable and as honourable a man as the King could have selected. . . I doubt whether he will be equal to the task imposed upon him'. He also alerted the Duke, who was just leaving for Dorset and would stop at Cirencester on the way back, that it would be difficult to refuse the command of the army now that Canning was dead.[44]

Bathurst also warned Hay not to jeopardize his position by going on a foreign holiday during the ministerial shuffle that brought Huskisson to the

Colonial Office and raised the prospect of Wilmot-Horton being promoted. He reminded him that since the advantage of a Permanent Under-Secretary was that 'there is always some one in the Office who can be safely consulted by the in-comers,'his absence would provide the new minister with a good reason to replace him: 'It would be consider'd either that you had neglected your duty, when it was most required, or that you did not consider yourself a permanent Under-Secretary & that your services as such might be not unfairly dispensed with.' Hay was duly grateful for this good counsel.[45]

As Bathurst predicted, Lord Anglesey, the Master of the Ordnance, followed Wellington with letters from the King and Prime Minister inviting the Duke back to the Horse Guards. On his way back to London, Wellington paused overnight at Cirencester to discuss his situation with Bathurst. He had already begun the task of justifying his ways to the Ultras, most of whom accepted the necessity of his decision, but Mrs Arbuthnot was so angry that only a fierce quarrel which threatened to end their friendship reconciled her to his inability to refuse. The more moderate Bathurst merely warned that the Duke's position would be awkward since any independent political action would be seen as opposition to the government which gave him his official authority. Since Canning had already gratified the heir presumptive by taking the Admiralty out of commission and appointing the Duke of Clarence Lord High Admiral, Bathurst was also concerned about making the heads of both fighting services professional rather than political appointments. Separation from government was praised by liberals, but he considered that the advantages, 'whatever they may be', were outweighed by the 'irresponsibility of those whose councils ought to influence the government in the administration of public affairs'. He thought it unlikely in particular that a First Lord of the Admiralty in cabinet would have agreed to the Treaty of London, surrendering British supremacy in the Mediterranean. But he recognized that even the Duke could do nothing about the situation unless he had insisted on a seat in the cabinet, and Wellington had no intention of being any closer to the ministry than absolutely necessary.

The Duke assured Bathurst that, although his position would be difficult, cabinet ministers at least had no reason to complain since they would not have to contend with his opposition to 'all their Portuguese and Greek follies'. He stoutly insisted that he would not abandon his views on foreign policy, the corn laws or appeasement of Catholics in the next parliamentary session. And since he had made his independence clear, ministers 'must blame themselves if they should represent that they have been deceived, as nobody else is'.[46] This was never put to the test, and certainly the determined opposition of the Commander-in-Chief to the government in parliament would have been carrying division of powers to ludicrous lengths.

A week after the Duke stopped at Cirencester Lord Grey arrived with his wife and two daughters. Even though Bathurst told Wellington that they were there by invitation of Lady Bathurst the year before, the visit could not avoid having political overtones.[47] The arrogant and difficult Grey was even more opposed to Canning and Goderich than he had been to Liverpool and strongly critical of those Whigs who accepted office. Like all of his persuasion he wanted Greek independence, but he was as disparaging of the Treaty of London as Bathurst and Wellington, also fearing that it would open the way to French and Russian expansion into the eastern Mediterranean. More concerned to preserve the Ottoman Empire than most of his colleagues, he thought that the Sultan would be perfectly justified in rejecting the three-power demand for local Greek autonomy. Such congenial discussions were bound to make it seem that Bathurst was acting on Wellington's behalf to form a combination against the government before parliament met in 1828.

This impression was strengthened by Bathurst's travels in the autumn. The Mediterranean was too dangerous for the promised visit to the Ponsonbys at Malta after the Sultan's rejection of the joint demand for an armistice on 16 August, but in October and November Bathurst, his wife and their daughter Georgina ventured into the equally unfamiliar north, as far as the highlands of Scotland. The weather was poor but Bathurst told Wellington that his wife bore the strain of travel reasonably well.[48] To the suspicious, however, this uncharacteristic journey seemed a pretext for further negotiations with Grey at his rural fastness in Northumberland.

Bathurst was at Grey's house on his way home when he learned from Hay that the combined British, French and Russian squadrons had destroyed the Egyptian fleet at Navarino on 20 October. Although Canning had expected that the ultimatum from Britain, France and Russia alone would be sufficient to get the Turks to accept Greek autonomy, Stratford Canning interpreted the demand for an armistice to mean the use of force if necessary, and his instruction was readily accepted by the three sympathetic admirals. The inevitable battle ensued when the Egyptian commander at Navarino Bay refused to accept their humiliating restriction that his ships could sail only for Constantinople or Alexandria.

Navarino was hailed as a victory for Greek liberty by philhellenes all over Europe, and in Britain also as a triumph for the Royal Navy. As Bathurst told Hay, the pretext 'matters little to John Bull, as he is always pleas'd with fighting and glory; & there has been enough of each: for no one can deny the gallantry of the achievement.'[49] But he and Wellington

227

feared for the consequences for Britain's position in the Mediterranean, its relations with Russia and France and the future of the Ottoman Empire after a battle undermining the announced British intention of a diplomatic settlement for Greece. Bathurst told the Duke that Grey had also been thrown into great irritation for the same reason.[50] When the King anxiously asked Wellington if Navarino meant war, the latter told Bathurst that he had responded, 'Why, Sir, there is war!' The Duke urged immediate reinforcement of the Mediterranean fleet before the French and Russians secured bases in the Greek islands and told Bathurst with satisfaction, 'I believe I there hit the right nail'.[51]

After reading the official account of the battle, Wellington told Bathurst that 'as a military feat it is a mere humbug! The Allies had eleven sail of the line against three, and on the whole more large ships than the Turks'.[52] Bathurst agreed that this superiority was too great to make it a real triumph, but pointed out that it would only create jealousy if army people disparaged the navy. Both men were critical of the British admiral, Sir Edward Codrington, and Bathurst recollected warning the First Lord of the Admiralty when Codrington was appointed to the Mediterranean station at the end of 1826 that he was 'hasty, though a gallant and excellent officer'.[53] They could not prevent him from being loaded with honours by all three allies, including a Knighthood of the Bath, but when they got back into government they ensured that he was recalled, with no stated reason, in the summer of 1828.

By the time Bathurst reached the Midlands on his way home, he learned, as expected, that Goderich had decided to promote Wilmot-Horton. But when Horton was offered the Board of Trade he sought the advice of his former chief, saying that he was inclined to refuse unless he could either be re-elected for Newcastle-under-Lyme without much expense or the government provided a seat, which it showed no sign of doing. Bathurst agreed that the ministry had a duty to provide a seat if it could, but warned that it 'very rarely happens that vacancies are obtained Scot-free', that Horton must expect some outlay in return for a higher office and that declining for that reason would put him in the wrong and provide a ready excuse for offering him nothing further.[54] In the end Horton decided to stay at the Colonial Office, but just over a month later he was turned out by the fourth government within a year.

By December the cabinet was being shaken to its foundation by quarrels and the Prime Minister was trying in vain to persuade the King to admit more Whigs. Finally, on 8 January, 1828, he told the monarch that the government could not continue. Goderich was then allowed to slope off, later reappearing in both Whig and Conservative governments between 1830 and 1846, a resurrection accompanied by the promotion and change of title to Earl of Ripon in 1833. By not meeting parliament, the only Prime Minister who never did, he avoided the ignominy of having to defend Navarino. George IV turned to Lord Chancellor Lyndhurst, who recommended Wellington, and with an eye to his own interests undertook to bring him to Windsor the next day.

As soon as the Duke returned to London from this interview he summoned Peel, the indispensable Leader of the House of Commons, and Bathurst, his most intimate colleague. The latter had remained in the country during the final days of the Goderich ministry, mainly because his sister-in-law, Lady Mary Lennox, had suffered a stroke. But as soon as he received Wellington's letter at 10 pm, he immediately responded to the challenge by saying that he would set off in the morning, hoping to be at Apsley House by three.[55]

10

RELUCTANT REFORMER, 1828–30

The difficulties of restoring the good old order after the Canning-Goderich interlude were glaringly revealed when Wellington, Bathurst and Peel began discussing the composition of the ministry on 11 January, 1828. Bathurst wanted to bring back all those who had left with the Duke the previous April, even unto the seventy-six-year-old Lord Eldon who was keen for nominal office if he could not have the woolsack again, while Peel was principally concerned to be supported by good speakers which meant keeping many of the Canningites. Compromises were eventually devised which pleased no one but resulted in a reasonable facsimile of Liverpool's government. The Canningites retained most of their good offices and even a few Whigs remained, leaving little for the returning Wellington loyalists. Bathurst could have had almost any post he wanted, though it would have been difficult to move Huskisson from the Colonial Office, where the Canningite Wilmot-Horton was now pushed out to make way for Lord Francis Leveson-Gower, son-in-law of the Duke's old love, Lady Charlotte Greville. Bathurst was in fact perfectly content to be Lord President of the Council where the duties were light, his chief function being to serve as the Duke's chief adviser and confidant.

The Privy Council met about once a week in its chamber in Whitehall. Its business was organized by the Clerk, the familiar Charles Greville. Bathurst was generally present, as was the Master of the Rolls; otherwise few other Privy Councillors troubled to attend, unless there was some matter that concerned them. And as usual in such departments, the Clerk alone simply read routine orders into the minutes. The main occupation of 'a Committee of the Lords of His Majesty's Most Honourable Privy Council' was to consider petitions and act as the final court of appeal for the colonies, India, the Channel Islands and the Isle of Man. Hitherto it had also formally approved or disallowed acts of colonial legislatures, but Bathurst, having been concerned about the slow process as Colonial Secretary, soon secured authority for acts to be transmitted directly (without an Order in Council) to the Board of Trade which in turn had for the past five years referred them to the Colonial Office, a modification of the system of reviewing colonial legislation which continued until 1856.[1] The Council also approved new churches and schools and dealt with charters to municipalities, corporations and companies, university statutes and even cattle diseases.[2] On one occasion the Duke of Wellington attended when the Council dealt with the Cinque Ports of which he became Lord Warden after Lord Liverpool died at the end of 1828, but its business generally attracted little attention from other cabinet ministers.

It was as well that the Privy Council left Bathurst plenty of time to assist the Duke in a general way since the two factions of the cabinet treated each other with the courtesy of men who had just fought a duel.[3] Many staunch Tories were reconciled to the necessity of accommodation with the Canningites by the Prime Minister's renunciation of the army, but this sacrifice did nothing to improve the disposition of the Canningites who remained, to say nothing of those who were ejected, who bitterly criticized their former colleagues for coming to terms with their opponents. The reference in the Speech from the Throne to Navarino as 'an untoward event' seemed an indication of what the Canningites had had to swallow to stay in office, while Ultra Tories' suspicions were roused by Huskisson blurting out at the by-election required on his transfer to the Colonial Office that he had insisted on guarantees that the ministry would continue the same policy as Canning's, a claim angrily denied by the Duke in the Lords on 11 February.

Tensions over the implications of Navarino were glaringly obvious when Lord Dudley, who remained as Foreign Secretary, wanted to extend the naval blockade of the Ottoman forces in order to secure a larger autonomous Greek province than had been agreed to by Wellington at St Petersburg and Canning in the Treaty of London. Bathurst told the Duke, who was unable to attend the cabinet on the subject, that 'Lord Dudley, Lord Palmerston, and Mr. Huskisson contended that the larger operation might be necessary for the more limited object, but the more limited operation would be decisive against the larger boundary'. Bathurst himself feared that this might lead to the allied admirals assisting the Greeks with ammunition and

231

provisions in the event of an attack on Athens. Dudley agreed to modify the British admiral's instructions,[4] but the dispute dragged on until the Greek situation was transformed by the Russian declaration of war against the Ottoman Empire at the end of April, news of which arrived just as the cabinet was splitting on the corn laws.

As every government since 1826 had been committed in principle to changing agricultural protection, it could not be abandoned by Wellington and Bathurst, much as they would have liked. But the Canningites threatened to leave if they did not get every particular of the bill that Wellington had destroyed in the Lords the year before; the Duke, Bathurst and others demanded a higher level of protection, and Peel made it clear that he would resign as Leader of the Commons if the Canningites went into opposition. When the protectionists made concessions, which were rejected by those demanding freer trade, Bathurst expostulated to Lord Aberdeen that they were in effect claiming the right to dictate the measure; in twenty years in cabinet he had never seen 'such a party spirit exist, acting so avowedly without any public principle, but on a broad avowal of a private league & covenant'. And he refused to accept Peel's fatalistic view that the ministry could not continue without the four Canningites, much less that 'we hold our seats dependent on their good will and pleasure'.[5]

Ultimately the cabinet agreed to a sliding scale of twenty shillings duty when the price of wheat was sixty-six a quarter, falling to a nominal one shilling when the price rose to seventy-three. Bathurst assured the great northern magnate Lord Lonsdale that this scale, along with increasing the number of towns at which the average price was taken and including the price of Irish wheat, which always sold for less than British, would increase agricultural protection by lowering the official domestic price as well as making it more difficult for speculators to manipulate the price in the towns on which the average was based.[6] In fact, though no one seems to have thought of it at the time, speculators could now reduce the duty considerably by forcing up the price only slightly. But the corn laws were such a contentious issue that no party cared to touch them again for over a decade.

The opposition tried to exploit the obvious divisions within the government by introducing a motion for the repeal of the Test and Corporations acts, which in principle, though not in practice, prevented non-Anglicans from holding public office. Dissenters had hitherto accepted the acts on the ground that removing them would open the way to Catholic emancipation, but after the 1826 election, in which they strongly supported the Protestant cause, they claimed an end to their second class status. The motion was a matter of considerable embarrassment to the Protestant ministers. But when they discovered that even the Bishops and the universities favoured concession to relieve the Church of the embarrassment of occasional conformity as well as to build a wider defence against Catholic demands, they prudently decided that it was better to manage the inevitable change than have it humiliatingly forced on them. The measure nevertheless encountered strong resistance from the King and was denounced in parliament by Lord Eldon and the Duke of Cumberland, who hurried back to England after a decade in Germany. But the cabinet remained intact.

The Whigs had better luck with parliamentary reform. The boroughs of Penryn in Cornwall and East Retford in Nottinghamshire had been found guilty of such flagrant corruption at the 1826 general election that in 1827 the House of Commons moved to extend the boundaries of Penryn to embrace its hundred (the next largest county unit) and to transfer East Retford's seats to Birmingham. When the new parliamentary session began in 1828 the Whigs improved on this by introducing bills to give Penryn's MPs to Manchester in addition to East Retford's to Birmingham. This was too much for Wellington and Bathurst who were opposed to enfranchising turbulent new towns. They wanted to throw both boroughs into their hundreds, but the Canningites finally managed to get the transfer of Penryn's to Manchester and the Tories the hundred for East Retford. When the former bill went to the Lords, the latter remained in the Commons as a hostage. But the arrangement fell apart when the peers were so impressed by the solemn testimony of the Penryn voters that even the Whig in charge of the measure moved to throw it into the hundred.

Ministers in the Commons now felt released from the compromise. But before the confusion could be resolved Peel voted to extend East Retford's boundaries to its hundred while Huskisson voted with the opposition to transfer the franchise to Birmingham. Rather than waiting for the cool light of day to see how this might be healed, Huskisson wrote to Wellington offering as a matter of honour to resign before he went to bed. When the Duke read the letter in the morning he went to Bathurst who advised taking Huskisson at his word. Bathurst had already protested at the time of the corn bill about the Canningites acting too much as a group in cabinet, constantly threatening resignations which they thought the Prime Minister dared not accept. But Huskisson and his friends were stunned when Wellington briskly accepted the offer. After five days of entreaties and threats, during which the Duke insisted that unless Huskisson formally withdrew his resignation he would effectively be Prime Minister, on 25 May, Palmerston, Grant, Dudley and William Lamb, the Irish Secretary, followed Huskisson out of office.

Great was the rejoicing of the Ultras. And the reorganization of the ministry along more Tory lines cleared the air on two important issues about which Wellington and Bathurst felt strongly: there would be no armed intervention in the war between Russia and the Ottoman Empire nor in the civil war between absolutists and constitutionalists in Portugal. The British force had already been withdrawn in April and the cabinet now regarded the conflict as an entirely internal one. It also seemed axiomatic that nothing would now be done about Catholic emancipation.

When this question was aired in the Lords on 9 June on the eve of the arrival of an emancipation bill from the Commons, Bathurst joined a list of other Protestants in offering his views on the subject. In an uncharacteristically long speech he maintained that the exclusive and authoritarian nature of the Catholic Church made it incompatible with other denominations. If there were to be any alteration in the restrictions on Catholics there must be securities for the Protestant state. And although he insisted that he would be happy to see the matter finally settled if such assurances could be obtained, he certainly gave the impression that he was a staunch defender of the present system. The next day, when the relief bill was formally debated and defeated, Wellington spoke more ambiguously to the same effect, saying that if only the agitation in Ireland and emotional discussion would cease, something constructive might be done. This was generally interpreted as a firm refusal of emancipation, though some were willing to bet that it meant that there would be Catholics in parliament in 1829.[7] The reason that the Bathurst and Duke spoke in such equivocal terms was that they were preparing the ground for the removal of some Catholic disabilities. Peel, the indispensable Leader of the Commons, had thrown the cabinet into disarray by insisting that concession could not be delayed much longer; but apart from insisting that his own Protestant reputation made it impossible for him to manage a settlement, though he promised to support one from the back benches, he had no practical advice on how to proceed.[8] The best that Wellington and Bathurst could do in the Lords until the cabinet settled the crisis, so similar to that of 1825, was to temporize. The day after his speech the Duke told his colleagues at dinner at Apsley House that no one wanted to settle the issue more than he but he could not 'see daylight'.[9]

Two weeks later the sun rose in the west. In Ireland as elsewhere Wellington's speech was construed both ways. Among those who concluded that it meant that there would be no change was Daniel O'Connell, founder of the Catholic Association to press for full political rights in 1823, who now decided to stand in the by-election in County Clare occasioned by Vesey Fitzgerald becoming President of the Board of Trade. Although no Catholic could take the oath to sit in parliament, O'Connell cleverly saw that there was no bar to Catholics being elected. Four days after he issued his election address, an Irish correspondent told Bathurst in great alarm that O'Connell's real object was revolution or a foreign war that would embarrass England. He claimed that the Association could be stopped by the resentment of the Catholic clergy and the Bishops' desire to cast off the great liberator and urged the government to negotiate a settlement with the moderate Bishop of Kildare and Leighton, Dr James Doyle, who had fought with the Spanish and aided the British during the Peninsular war.[10] But this presupposed that the cabinet was determined on Catholic relief.

Whatever the various ministers were considering, the Clare election strengthened the case for concession. When O'Connell piled up a two to one lead during the first five days of polling Fitzgerald abandoned the contest and Wellington concluded that solving the Catholic question was essential to prevent the breakdown of order, if not rebellion, in Ireland. An escalation of this issue was postponed only by O'Connell deciding not to claim his seat until the 1829 session. The Duke thought that the best solution was to allow Catholics to sit in parliament under a special oath, with the government licensing and paying the clergy and the forty shilling franchise in Ireland being restricted by requiring the payment of some specified amount of the county rate in order to have the vote.[11] But the King refused to allow the Prime Minister to do any more than study the matter with the reliably Protestant Peel and Lyndhurst, though in fact Wellington also confided in Bathurst, who now accepted the necessity of concession, as he had in 1801, to avoid something far worse.

The problem was to devise a form of emancipation that would also keep Peel. The sticking point, Bathurst told Arbuthnot who also knew what was afoot, was not so much the Home Secretary's strong Protestantism, since he had 'long been strangely ashamed of the question, and of the eager Protestants,' as his fear of inconsistency, as well as the advantage of being the head of the Church of England party, if relief did not produce tranquillity in Ireland. Bathurst thought it far more important to have some offer to meet parliament in 1829 than to keep Peel, however great his influence in the Commons and however much his departure would distress the Duke: Wellington must now 'go on and die game'.[12]

Three days later Bathurst had a long conversation with the Duke at Cheltenham, taking him back to Cirencester for dinner. As well as Catholic relief and events abroad, they discussed what to do about the Duke of Clarence, Lord High Admiral for the past year, who was not only quarrelling with his council but had recently gone to sea for ten days without anyone knowing where he was.[13] He was dismissed and the Admiralty returned to a board under Lord Melville, the First Lord throughout Liverpool's ministry. 'H.R.H. is certainly somewhat mad,' Bathurst told Lord Aberdeen; 'if however there be not method, there is certainly judgement and spirit in his madness.' But despite Clarence's anger at being ejected, he philosophically saw some public benefit by it: 'Well after all the Duke of Wellington is the man who ought to be Minister of this Country, for no other man would dare to act by the Heir to the Throne in the way he has done'.[14] But Bathurst nevertheless counselled Wellington to refute what Huskisson was representing him as saying about the departure of the heir presumptive: 'There is no mistake, and there shall be no mistake'.[15]

As he remained at Cirencester throughout the autumn, Bathurst also kept in touch with Robert Hay, who sent Colonial Office papers for his consideration, probably with the approval of the inexperienced and harassed Colonial Secretary, Sir George Murray. In October Hay also sought Bathurst's advice on a political career. Clearly anticipating the political situation after the Catholic issue had been resolved, Bathurst firmly discouraged him from leaving the 'honorable civil situation out of the vortex'. Recent events had dissolved all the attachments that had kept Liverpool's powerful party together and at each ministerial reconstruction, which Bathurst evidently considered would be frequent, Hay would have to consider whether or not to remain, and 'where the political changes which take place have more of personal jealousies or animosities than public differences, the staying in, or going out always gives rise to squabbles, & estrangements in private life; much more than on graver occasions'. By remaining where he was Hay would gain in authority year by year, 'and there is no Colonial Secretary who will not be too happy to look to your assistance.' At the end of this long letter Bathurst added a light note which he knew would appeal to Hay: 'When you said that the King had "sunk three feet in girth" did you mean that his belly had sunk lower down so much, or only that he was less around in girth by three feet [?]'[16] Hay took Bathurst's advice, but the advantages of a permanent Tory Under-Secretary were not so obvious to Colonial Secretaries after 1830, nor to more earnest senior Colonial Office officials. In 1836 he was pushed out and succeeded by the Evangelical workaholic James Stephen with the acquiescence of the Whig Colonial Secretary Lord Glenelg, the former Canningite Tory Charles Grant.

A poignant reminder of the political stability that Bathurst lamented forever appeared at Cirencester in December when the cortège escorting the body of Lord Liverpool to burial at the family home of Hawkesbury near Bristol paused for refreshment. Events had moved so quickly during the past two years that the former Prime Minister was almost forgotten, The hearse was accompanied by very few carriages, though they included the Duke of Clarence's. Bathurst did not go to see it but was told that the procession 'made a sad appearance, which is the case generally with these last journies, until they approach the place of interment'. He offered the escort of his own carriage for the first mile out of town but the undertaker declined since the attendants were not formally dressed and the carriages were covered with mud.[17]

A notionally happier event at the same time was the invitation to Bathurst's son-in-law, General Frederick Ponsonby to add the lustre of his office as Lieutenant Governor of Malta to the Order of St Michael and St George. Ponsonby was reluctant to accept this uncertain honour, but Bathurst, who had helped to invent it and understood its local purpose, agreed to pay the fees and urged Ponsonby to use the title 'Sir' rather than disdaining the provincial knighthood as inferior to his rank as the younger son of an earl. 'His not taking the Title now would appear very extraordinary, & be invidiously interpreted,' Bathurst told Hay.[18] But Ponsonby's chagrin lasted only until 1831 when, still at Malta, he became a Knight Commander of the less ambiguously Honourable Order of the Bath.

The inconclusive musings meanwhile on the Catholic question through the summer and autumn were not made easier by the Irish Viceroy's conversion to the necessity of concession following O'Connell's election. Lord Anglesey, who had been appointed at the end of the Goderich ministry and confirmed by Wellington, assumed that the cabinet was still determined to resist emancipation. On his own he tried to reduce the tension by not arresting agitators, receiving O'Connell and even warning him of an impending proclamation against assemblies so that he could issue his own address and take credit for tranquillity. But whatever the cabinet decided to do, it would not condone the slightest approval of the Catholic Association or allow the impression that it was influencing their decisions. At the end of September Bathurst, undoubtedly acting for Wellington, reproved the Lord Lieutenant for his dangerous conduct, telling him that his essential task was 'to preserve the Peace, & to ensure the loyalty & good-will of all H. M.'s subjects by protecting the lives & property of all.' He reminded Anglesey that the Catholic question could not be settled without the agreement of the King, who could not hear or even think about it without distress, and warned the Viceroy that he was rousing his suspicions and Protestant ones in all three kingdoms.[19]

Anglesey did not understand this hint or alter his method. Two months later the Prime Minister expostulated to Bathurst: 'Lord Anglesey is gone mad. He is bit by a mad Papist; or instigated by the love of popularity.' If only he would take a firm stand with the Catholic Association, Wellington thought 'we should have the whole game in our hands. But he is looking after a low popularity!'[20] Finally on Christmas Eve the exasperated Duke summoned the cabinet ministers he could find in London, who unanimously agreed to the Viceroy's recall. Bathurst, at Cirencester, thought this risky considering Anglesey's popularity but agreed that it was probably the least difficult course.[21]

The next step was to find a good successor at this delicate moment. The King's mind turned immediately to the good and faithful Protestant Bathurst, of whose changed attitude he had no inkling. But Wellington had no intention of losing his valuable adviser, and Bathurst had no intention of going. 'Nothing would induce me to go there as Lord-Lieutenant,' he told Wellington.[22] The Prime Minister instead sent the Duke of Northumberland, hitherto a strong Protestant, who had come to the pleasing conclusion that the time had arrived for Catholic relief under Wellington's careful management.

On 12 January, 1829, just three weeks before parliament opened, Peel finally accepted that a satisfactory settlement of the Catholic issue depended on his remaining. But even then Bathurst suspected from two or three words in Peel's memorandum which Wellington sent to Cirencester that he 'reserved to himself the right of deciding whether consistent with his past conduct he would belong to such a cabinet'.[23] The ambiguity was cleared up in the next few days, but at the cost of the Duke and Bathurst surrendering all the controls on the Catholic church that had been considered. With Peel secure, Wellington turned his attention to the King, who gave separate interviews to the Protestant ministers, including Bathurst, and was shaken to discover that they were all agreed on the necessity for emancipation. With not a single ally to appeal to, George IV allowed the entire cabinet to discuss the matter, though ominously warning that he was not committed to accepting their conclusions.

With the monarch in this unhelpful mood, and knowing that many of its customary supporters in parliament would be just as hostile, the cabinet decided to proceed first with measures for peace and order in Ireland and Protestant securities before removing the Catholic disabilities. The Catholic Association was to be suppressed, the voting qualification in Ireland raised and the Crown would receive the right to ban unacceptable priests, prevent the use of the same territorial titles as the established Church, the wearing of religious dress in public and the founding of new religious houses. It would also gain some authority over St Patrick's College, Maynooth, which had been training priests with government support since 1795. Once all this was enacted, Catholics would be permitted to sit in both Houses of Parliament and to hold all offices save those of Prime Minister, Lord Chancellor of Britain and Ireland, Secretary of State, and all posts in Oxford, Cambridge and royal schools requiring the holders to be members of the Established Church. But Wellington had his work cut out simply persuading the King to accept the principles in the Speech from the Throne.

When parliament was opened on 5 February by a commission which included Bathurst, the announcement of Catholic emancipation produced a sensation. The rejoicings of the Whigs and the Canningites were tempered only by bitterness that it was being sponsored by those who had opposed it for thirty years; the anger came from the Ultra Tories, whose fears on repealing the restrictions against Dissenters were now fulfilled. Lord Eldon, in great wrath, accused his former colleagues at length of surrendering their principles. Of all the ministers in the Lords, Bathurst, who had been a close fellow Protestant of the former Lord Chancellor for twenty years, most felt the sting of this attack. But he was also well prepared. Rising immediately after Eldon, he insisted, to the surprise of many of his listeners who had forgotten or not known his attitude in 1801, that he had never been 'one of those who had declared a determination never to consent to any further concessions to the Roman Catholics'. Circumstances had changed recently and he had not hesitated to change when necessary for the good of the country, despite his previous votes and charges of inconsistency. Catholic emancipation officially recommended by the King was a very different proposition from when it was proposed by those without the responsibility of office. This, he maintained, was the correct way to bring the matter forward, the way intended by Pitt, and when Pitt had been unable to get the agreement of the monarch and ministers he had resigned. But now it was not only imperative but finally safe to settle the Catholic issue.

This was a plausible explanation of Bathurst's changed attitude, but to many outside the cabinet it seemed like unprincipled expediency. Charles Greville was delighted that Catholics were receiving political rights, but thought that 'even those idiots' the extreme Protestants had behaved respectably compared to Bathurst and other previously strong defenders of the Church who had abruptly reversed themselves. Whatever the virtue and necessity of the step, he predicted that 'a blow will have been given to the reputation of publick men in general which will, I suspect, have an important though not immediate effect upon the aristocratic influence in this country, and tend remotely to increase the democratic spirit which exists'.[24] One of the peers who had given his proxy to Bathurst was so taken back by the revelation of what was intended that he wrote emphatically to revoke it except for the purpose of suppressing the Catholic Association until he was 'more enlightened *by what is to come*, and *that I am fully convinced of the* (more than) *safety of the Protestant establishment* of these kingdoms'.[25]

The clash of arms and high feelings on the first day of the parliamentary session was a portent of the 'battle like Waterloo', as Wellington called it, that raged for the next two months. After six weeks Lady Georgina Bathurst told a friend, 'Nobody thinks or dreams of any thing but the [Catholic] Question'. The King and the Ultras, including Bathurst's nephew and Wellington's former aide, the Duke of Richmond, contested the surrender every inch of the way and the Prime Minister was goaded into a duel, of which in principle he disapproved, with pistols by young Earl of Winchilsea. The Duke of Cumberland raced back from Germany, emotionally rejecting the pleas of Lady Georgina Bathurst and others not to denounce the bill in the Lords and stiffen the King's wavering resistance. But Lady Georgina was confident that Wellington was 'more *powerful*. Our Gracious [sovereign] is in a terrible way between them'. And indeed with the support of the Whigs and Canningites the eventual passage of the measure was practically assured.

When the strife was over, the battle won, the ailing Lord Grenville wrote to tell Bathurst how glad he was to have been spared to see the granting of the concession which had first divided them so long ago.[26] The following year the archdeacon son of Bishop Bathurst, his father's long support of the measure finally vindicated, applied to the Prime Minister for promotion on that ground.[27] Nothing was forthcoming for him or his eighty-six-year-old father, though two years later Bishop Bathurst declined as too little, too late the Primacy of Ireland from his Whig friends.

In the aftermath of this wrenching conflict Wellington's government tried to attract more parliamentary support. But the Ultras kept their anger warm, seeking issues on which to bring down the apostates and even flirting with the hitherto radical idea of parliamentary reform in order to reduce the influence of the ministry and make the Commons more reflective of the Protestant majority in Britain. The Canningites, despite supporting relief, were no less irate over their ejection the year before and would return only on their own terms. Lord Grey, who was close to Wellington and Bathurst on foreign policy, was still not acceptable to the King, but a couple of similarly-minded Whigs were appointed. Bathurst of all people, perhaps on the strength of his recently founded friendship with Grey, urged taking in even more, but Wellington was determined to trust to his policies and the passage of time to reconcile his natural Tory friends to the wisdom of his decision on the Catholic question.[28]

In the fragile and bitter political situation of 1829 the ministry was at least fortunate that its opponents were divided. It could also rest fairly easy about the international situation. The Russo-Turkish war ended without Russia obtaining any territory in Europe or the Mediterranean, but with the way open for a much larger and truly independent Greece the Duke gloomily concluded that the Ottoman Empire was destroyed. Bathurst was less dismayed, perhaps relieved that the consequences of Navarino and the Russian declaration of war had not been far worse. He spent the autumn at Cirencester but was in London for a cabinet on the Mediterranean when his third surviving son, Seymour, now thirty-four, married Julia, three years his junior, the only daughter of the widowed Mrs John Hankey on 6 October in St George's, Hanover Square.[29] Wellington wrote to Bathurst from Stratfield Saye the day before to apologize that he could not be in town for the wedding of his former aide, though he would have arranged it if he had known sooner, but he hoped that his colleague would remain for the cabinet the next day and have dinner with him.[30]

The couple soon left for Malta, where the bridegroom was Treasurer, but the marriage lasted only four and a half years. Two daughters, born in 1830 and 1831, died soon after birth; in 1832 they had a son, Allen Alexander and in 1834 a daughter, Mary Selina, both of whom lived a normal span. But Seymour himself died in the spring of 1834, just a few months before his father. His widow lived another forty-three years, dying the year before her son succeeded his two unmarried uncles as sixth Earl Bathurst in 1878.

Wellington's government was even sooner doomed. Despite what some, though not Bathurst, expected of emancipation, a poor harvest fuelled a high level of violence in Ireland in the autumn. The Catholic Association was revived, there were demands for the restoration of the forty shilling franchise and the old cry for repeal of the union was raised again. In Britain the high price of food was exacerbated by an industrial depression. When the Speech from the Throne on 4 February, 1830, blandly assured parliament that the situation was due to the weather and other causes beyond political control, amendments were moved in both Houses for the first time since the end of the wars against France. The Ultras, with Richmond prominent in the van, stood forth as champions of hapless agricultural workers and the ministry was saved only by the Canningites and Whigs, who had no interest in assisting a faction that they considered far worse than the present administration.

So long as its opponents remained separate, Wellington's ministry could continue, hoping that passions would abate and its friends return. But the situation became more uncertain with the King's declining health. If he died there would have to be a general election, otherwise not necessary until 1833. On edge about this latest addition to his troubles, when the cabinet in April wanted to counter newspaper speculation by issuing more medical bulletins, which George IV still had the strength to oppose, the Duke uncharacteristically burst out to his closest colleague, 'Well, Lord Bathurst, you are the President of the Council. Will you have the goodness to go down to Windsor & say to the King all you are saying here? Perhaps you will prevail upon him, but I have done all I can & can't succeed.'[31] By the end of May the monarch had to accept that he was too weak to sign documents, and on 26 June his much abused frame finally succumbed to its various ailments. Bathurst was one of the ministers who accompanied the Prime Minister and the Lord Chancellor to inform the Duke of Clarence of his brother's death and his own succession. Despite his dismissal two years earlier, the new William IV affirmed his strong confidence in Wellington and all the present ministers.

The old sailor, who had lived to sixty-five in relative poverty and obscurity save for his brief moment as Lord High Admiral, was beside himself with excitement, showing himself to his subjects so frequently and informally as to raise questions about his sanity. During these appearances he demonstrated that the Bathursts stood as high as ever in royal favour. After reviewing troops in Hyde Park he went for breakfast afterwards once to Wellington but three times to the Bathursts, then living in Great Cumberland Street north of the park. On one day there was a kind of royal drawing room, with Lady Bathurst presenting the ministers' wives to Queen Adelaide.[32]

Since an election had to be held within six months, the government decided to strike before its opponents found common cause. As usual only about a quarter of the seats were contested. But what the ministry gained in those boroughs it controlled, hitherto held by Canningites, it lost in other boroughs, while in the counties there was a general revolt against all authority, Whig and Tory, with many MPs being returned in favour of some kind of reform. The final stages of the election coincided with the revolution in Paris, which deposed Charles X and established a more limited constitutional government under Louis Philippe, and was followed by the revolt of the Belgians against the union with Holland, both of which raised the familiar spectres of real revolution and war on the continent.

At the moment of the Belgian uprising the Bathursts' youngest son, the Rev Charles, married Lady Emily Bertie, youngest daughter of the Earl of

242

Abingdon, at the end of August.[33] A few months before, undoubtedly prompted by the Lord President of the Council, Wellington had given the bridegroom an early wedding present in the form of the living of Southam in Wiltshire (in addition to Siddington just outside Cirencester). The new rector gratefully hoped that the Prime Minister and his father, even the inhabitants of the parish, would not regret the choice.[34] Bathurst himself settled £4000 on his son a month before the marriage.[35] But Charles lived only one year longer than his brother Seymour, dying in 1842 at the age of forty. His widow, like Seymour's, lived for another forty years. This third wedding turned out to be the last for the Bathurst children since the three oldest, Lord Apsley, William and Georgina, never married. Georgina, who died at the age of eighty-two in 1874, continued at the edge of the court circle until 1857 as lady in waiting to the Duchess of Gloucester, widow of George III's nephew.

A couple of weeks after this marriage Wellington tried to take the opportunity of another happy social occasion to win back the Canningites. This was the opening of the first long-distance railway, the thirty-mile Liverpool-Manchester line, attended by William Huskisson as MP for Liverpool. When the train carrying them from Liverpool to Manchester stopped to take on water the passengers strolled around the tracks, but as George Stephenson's 'Rocket' came hurtling down the second track Huskisson failed to scramble back into the carriage. His leg was crushed by the train and he died in the nearest town, the first passenger line claiming its first victim on the first day. Probably nothing would have come of the overture and Palmerston, the new leader, insisted on a reconstruction of the government that would amount to control by the Canningites.

Thus rebuffed, the Duke tried to reassure the Ultras that he would defend the present order against any further challenge, at home or abroad. But the opening of parliament on 2 November did just the opposite. The Speech from the Throne, read by William IV himself, blandly assured the legislators that, amidst the upheavals of Europe, they lived in the most peaceful, prosperous and free of all countries, expressed concern over the revolt of the Belgians, announced the intention of recognizing the absolutist Miguel as King of Portugal (as he had practically been since 1828) and promised to suppress the agricultural riots and punish the leaders. More astonishing, given the support for various reforms at all levels of society, it contained not a word about changing parliament or anything else. The tumult in the Lords began as soon as the King left, with Winchilsea and Richmond leaping again to the defence of honest, hard-pressed agricultural labourers. But the main attack came from Lord Grey. Now that the proscription on his appointment to office had been lifted with the death of George, he made a bid for disaffected Tories of all stripes by demanding a reduction in taxes; he also rejected the characterization of the Belgians as 'revolted subjects' and insisted that there was no reason for British interference except as mediator, opposed recognizing Miguel and warned that if the ministry did not reform parliament it would be challenged as it had been on Catholic emancipation. Knowing that even some Ultras were sympathetic to MPs being more independent of government influence than they had been on Catholic emancipation, Grey astutely reminded the Lords that never throughout his long career had he supported universal suffrage, but he did believe that some extension of the franchise was imperative to secure the constitution against the storm of change that was raging over Europe.

The Duke responded with a ringing declaration that the present legislature was better than any individual could devise, that he had no intention of reforming it and that he would oppose any proposal for change. But even those Ultras who shared these sterling sentiments remembered similar assurances on the eve of Catholic relief. Despite the disposition of some ministers to introduce a small measure of parliamentary reform, the cabinet decided to stand by Wellington's refusal when the subject was debated in the Commons on 16 November. Lady Bathurst told Charles Greville that her husband was encouraging the Prime Minister to stand or fall on the issue, though he feared that the Duke would be tempted to make some concession.[36] But when the cabinet cancelled the Lord Mayor of London's annual banquet, fearing that demonstrations for reform would get out of hand, it was Bathurst who realized after Wellington and Peel had gone to inform the King that this capitulation to popular pressure would 'put an end to the Government, and carry Reform'.[37] The former humiliation was avoided only by the unexpected defeat in the Commons on William IV's civil list on 15 November. The Duke resigned on this minor point and Grey quickly formed a coalition ministry with the Canningites that even included the Duke of Richmond.

This anticlimactic end of Wellington's government was no personal disappointment for Bathurst. He was now sixty-eight, only two years older than Grey, but in contrast to the new Prime Minister had been in government almost continuously for close to half a century. He was ready to retire and had already offered to surrender his office if it would help Wellington's recruitment of others. But in one way the timing was extremely awkward. Just the day before the vote in the Commons the Joint Clerk of the Privy Council, James Buller, died after a minor operation, being eulogized by his colleague Greville as 'a very honourable, obliging and stupid man, and a great loss to me'. When Greville told Bathurst the next day that the appointment was in the gift of the crown, he hurried to the King to propose his own son William, then thirty-nine, a lawyer and a clerk in the Victualling Office. William IV, who himself had nine illegitimate children to provide for, assured his favoured servant, 'I can never object to a Father's doing what he can for his own children'. But it seemed too late. When Wellington announced his resignation to the Lords the following day, 16 November, Lord Grosvenor prolonged the sitting long enough to ask Bathurst if the Clerkship had been filled, anticipating the expected answer by saying that it was unbecoming to fill so lucrative an office so quickly. But Bathurst answered what was perfectly true, that no appointment had been made.

When the ministers went to submit their resignations, the King told Bathurst that he was still anxious to secure his son's appointment and asked if there was anything he could sign to ensure it. Bathurst thanked him but said that it was too late. In fact, as Greville pointed out, it could still be rushed through, but since the salary depended on an annual vote of the Commons the new government could in effect rescind it. A month later, however, the new Lord President of the Council, Bathurst's friend Lord Lansdowne, appointed William Bathurst at the reduced salary of £1200 a year and there he remained for thirty years. Lansdowne had consulted the King, who confirmed what he had told Bathurst,[38] but Grey's goodwill towards the man whose colleague he might easily have become during the last three years and whose views he had so recently shared was undoubtedly also an important factor. Gratifying a moderate and influential figure might well temper the opposition of Wellington and more determined adversaries in the battles that loomed ahead on a variety of reforms.

11

CROSSING THE BAR,
1830–1834

Immediately after resigning as Lord President of the Council Bathurst returned to Cirencester. He told Wellington early in December, sending him half of one of his highly praised does, that the county was quiet following agricultural riots but he thought that the magistrates had made a mistake in making too many promises in return for peace and in committing 200 of those awaiting trial to the prison at Gloucester which was too small to accommodate them. The city was tense and lancers had been requested to guard the jail and other places where prisoners were being held.[1] Wellington, who was directing operations against the rioters in Hampshire as well as keeping a close eye on the new ministers in London, told Bathurst the next day that what Gloucestershire needed was a special commission to deal with capital cases and make strong examples of serious infringements of the law.[2] The new Home Secretary, Lord Melbourne, meted out swift and exemplary punishment and by the time rioting ended in 1831, nineteen people had been executed and many sentences commuted; about 450 people were transported to Australia and several hundred were in jail in England.

These challenges to the social and political order were serious enough, though no worse than those during the wars against France and the early years of peace, and were soon overshadowed by the government's astonishing proposal for parliamentary reform. Grey and his colleagues decided that only an extensive measure would conciliate the country, bring potential leaders of revolt into the pale of the constitution and solve an issue that had been a lively recurring matter of dispute since the middle of the eighteenth century. A quarter of the seats would be transferred from small boroughs to heavily populated towns and counties and the bewildering variety of urban franchises would be replaced by a uniform qualification giving the vote to prosperous male heads of households owning or renting residences worth £10 a year; in the counties a similar extension would add substantial long-term leaseholders to the traditional 40s. freeholders.[3]

When Lord John Russell introduced this sweeping bill in the Commons on 1 March, 1831, Tories such as Bathurst and Wellington were astounded at the intention of destroying the excellent aristocratic and monarchical order that had served the country so well since the Glorious Revolution. By tipping the balance fatally to democracy it would inevitably lead to the demolition of the House of Lords, the Church of England, the monarchy and all forms of hereditary privilege. Most of the Ultras, though not Richmond, flocked back in alarm to the Duke, who after the unpleasantness of the past two years kept his distance from these repentant allies.

After a mere two days' debate, the bill squeaked through its second reading in the Commons on 22 March by 302 votes to 301, accompanied by a denunciation from Wellington in the Lords. Bathurst tried to restrain him by advising the Duke not to speak on it again as MPs prepared to debate it clause by clause since the bill might well arrive in their House in a very different form.[4] Blood up, however, Wellington could not resist repeating his condemnation at even greater length on 28 March. Bathurst, for his part, gloomily told Charles Greville's father that of the 301 votes against the bill, 'I do not hear of fifty who are not nominal reformers, and there are about a hundred of them, who have each their own pet plan, which each intends to press upon the Committee'. Instead of these propositions being beaten in turn, Bathurst hoped for some comprehensive motion that would unite the various opponents and those who had voted for the bill but were looking for an opportunity to oppose it, conceding that this would not be easy to accomplish.[5] What achieved it was the proposed reduction of the number of English MPs and their proportion of representation in the Commons. The amendment preserving the total number of English seats was carried against the government early in the morning of 20 April by 299 votes to 291. Later in the day William IV gave in to a cabinet ultimatum and agreed to dissolve parliament.

A combination of traditional government influence and fervour for change produced a ministerial majority of at least 130 by the time the general election ended in early June. Tory anger at the result was reflected in Lady Bathurst's sister, Lady Mary Lennox, telling Seymour Bathurst that she had settled on him Wood End, the family home near Chichester which she had inherited from her mother the previous Christmas Day, with instructions never to '*lett* it, *lend* it, *give* it, *sell* it, or *leave* it' to any '*Patriotic radical Whig families*'.[6]

A second, slightly modified bill began its slow progress through the Commons in July, the main point of the opposition being to buy time until the reaction in the country became strong enough to justify rejection by the Lords. Bathurst meanwhile was furious that the international danger from Belgium was being neglected while 'six of the Cabinet Ministers, including the Foreign Secretary & first Lord of the Admiralty have nothing better to do, than sit debating in the H of Commons whether North Shield & South Shield should belong to Schedule D.' It was bad enough that Grey's ministry had accepted Belgian independence rather than some form of local autonomy within the United Netherlands, thereby destroying the barrier to French expansion so carefully constructed at the end of the Napoleonic wars; far worse was its response to the appeal from the new King of the Belgians, Leopold of Saxe-Coburg (who would now have been the British royal consort if Princess Charlotte had lived to succeed George IV), when his country was attacked by the Dutch. Britain promptly despatched a naval squadron, while France sent an army. Bathurst agreed that the Dutch had acted improperly in using armed force against the Belgians, but so had Leopold by sending individual requests rather than appealing collectively to the five powers which had ordered an armistice just before the Duke's government went out of office. He told Lord Aberdeen that this was giving France its long-sought opportunity to control Belgium, while Britain was in the awkward position of having to join France in attacking Holland, a reversal of its policy ever since the reign of Charles II.[7]

By the time the reform bill reached the Lords on 22 September, however, the Belgian crisis had abated and peers could also turn their full attention to the matter. The day before, Bathurst and fifteen or sixteen other peers dined with Wellington to discuss their opposition. They agreed to allow the first reading but thereafter to make every effort at defeat. The evening before the real debate on the second reading, Monday, 3 October, there was a similar dinner at Apsley House, but this time no happy agreement. Some thought that the only prudent course was to concede the principle of reform but propose more restricted change. Lord Wharncliffe, who had urged moderation from the very beginning, suggested an address to the King stating that, although the House of Lords rejected '*this Bill*, we were ready to consider the state of the representation & to make such changes as might be consistent with the practice of the Constitution'. But Bathurst objected that this would be 'a declaration of the incompetence of the Parliament as it was,

& leave it to go on without proposing any plan of change.' The sense of the meeting was against Wharncliffe, but Lord Ellenborough feared that 'the want of union amongst us as to what should be done will give great advantage to our antagonists in debate'.[8]

The debate raged for five nights and was a great event for the House of Lords. Instead of the customary handful of peers around the table, galleries were erected as they had been during Queen Caroline's trial. Bathurst was present but did not speak. On the last night Lord Chancellor Brougham declaimed for over three hours, refreshed by three tumblers of mulled port which Bathurst told his daughter the Tories had considerately provided. At one point Brougham put the tumbler on the bench next to Bathurst, who had the reputation of being a good drinker, but, 'thinking it in danger, he stopped in the middle of a sentence and removed it to the table in front of him, amidst some laughter'. Brougham carried on in good form to the end, despite the 85F heat, but a more effective speech on undecided votes was that by Bathurst's moderate and relatively unpartisan colleague of many decades, Lord Harrowby. A fine though more restrained orator than Brougham, he urged defeat by saying that the ministry should have brought in a more limited reform. When the vote was taken at about 5 a.m. on the morning of 8 October the bill was decisively rejected by 199 to 158.

As soon as Bathurst returned to his house he went to his daughter Georgina's bedroom to tell her what had happened. She in turn relayed the news to her friend Ralph Sneyd. Reflecting her father's views, she thought it unlikely that the government could persuade the King to create enough peers – it would take about sixty – to ensure passage. As for riots, 'In London unless they are got up by the Govt we shall have none; there has been no mob about the H. of Lds.' It was probably no comfort to Sneyd, whose home was in Staffordshire, that she complaisantly added, 'There may be breezes in the North; as the Reformers will take care to excite the people in every possible way.'[9] But contrary to Lady Georgina's expectations there were soon huge protests in London as well as Birmingham, Nottingham, Exeter and Bristol and smaller ones elsewhere. Parliament was prorogued while the government considered what to do and the self-appointed peacemakers, Lords Wharncliffe and Harrowby, tried to use the size of the majority against the bill to persuade the cabinet to make substantial reductions in their reforms. But these waverers did not speak for the more determined opponents, while the ministry refused to concede more than small modifications before beginning the legislative process again.

Four days before parliament reassembled after the two-month recess to consider the third version of the bill, Bathurst advised Wellington not to commit himself to proposing any specific measure of reform, though he might go so far as to say that he was willing to consider whatever bill actually arrived in the Lords. Bathurst also warned him not to be carried beyond what he intended in the strain and excitement of debate by being careful of his words and ensuring that they were accurately reported, presumably by giving a text to Hansard's reporters.[10] This time Wellington followed Bathurst's recommendation and resisted the temptation to speak on the measure while it was in the Commons.

The new reform bill, introduced in the Commons on 12 December, contained enough concessions to justify acceptance by those who were alarmed by the recent violence or finally weary of the tiresome process. After five nights it passed the second reading by 324 votes to 162, but the real question was whether or not the concessions and the majority would persuade enough peers to accept it. To increase the chances, the cabinet in January added the threat of the King's promise to create sufficient peers if necessary. Harrowby and Wharncliffe canvassed support for the bill in order to avoid a dilution of the peerage and when it arrived in the Lords on 26 March they announced that they would vote for the second reading in expectation that the opposition would be allowed to make extensive amendments in committee.

Bathurst deplored this division among the Conservatives, as opponents of parliamentary reform were being called, wanting them to remain solidly united under Wellington who on the same day told the Lords that he would fight the bill all the way. Bathurst considered that the waverers were being deceived by the ministers, who would insist on new peers if defeated on a major clause. Lady Georgina's daughter told Ralph Sneyd that her father thought that the Duke could not reverse himself without discredit, as he had on Catholic emancipation, and sponsor a reform bill, but his resistance allowed him to accept a more limited measure sponsored by some less adamant opponent. But since the Conservatives could not agree or rely on each other, Bathurst's best hope was that 'something as the time draws near will happen that may avert such a misfortune as the carrying of such a Bill'.[11]

Bathurst finally spoke publicly on the subject for the first time on 3 April when presenting a petition from Oxford University in place of its Chancellor, Lord Grenville, who was too ill to attend. Although he confined himself to summarizing the university's case against the bill, this was obviously no uncongenial task. He told the House that the scholars judged the reorganization of the Commons to be hazardous, violent and unsafe. Many boroughs were being disenfranchised for no obvious reason and others given representation on no principle; the changes went far beyond what even reformers had expected and the measure would produce hostility towards the Church and even greater public excitement and confusion than had been suffered since its introduction. Lord Grey, now heartily sick of the whole matter, wearily responded that he would reserve his comments until second reading the following week.

On the first day of that debate, 9 April, Bathurst rose again to insist that the measure would not reform but rather destroy the constituency of the country. He admitted that in the rapturous early dawn of Pitt's government he had also supported change, but that was on the careful basis of maintaining the total number of MPs and disenfranchising no borough without proof of corruption. His main fear of the present, more radical change was that the £10 franchise was so low as to give permanent control of elections to the radical urban political unions formed to agitate for parliamentary reform.

There was no novelty in this conventional objection, and the general reprise of familiar arguments made debate flatter than the first round. The real excitement was over the vote, and once again the galleries had to be erected. Lady Georgina wrote that the waverers who would vote for the second reading and then press for amendments were deluding themselves: 'the Lords are not *youths*, and they will soon get tired of fighting night after night & the other [Whig] party with their new Peers will make a point of regular attendance from their friends & the alterations will end in nothing being done'. Some reform was now inevitable, but as her father had said, the best hope was to defeat the present measure and have an independent peer present a more moderate one in the next session.[12] But when the House divided at 6.30 am on Saturday, 14 April about two dozen opponents supported second reading, allowing it to pass by 184 to 175.

During the three-week Easter recess there was much consultation between waverers and ministers and waverers and Tories about what would happen in committee. Bathurst told the Duke that he agreed with Lyndhurst that the most promising course was to 'strike at three or four great blots in the bill, and not attempt at re-modelling it'. In particular he recommended restricting the franchise by an additional requirement that qualified house-holders must have lived in the same house and paid the poor rate for half a year before the annual revision of the voters' register. He also recommended preserving the present proportion of county to urban members by giving many of the new towns one MP instead of two, which would 'diminish the number of those who will be disappointed at having no representative, while it keeps down the amount of the town representation'. And he thought that it would be a great improvement for the landed interest if radicals were

251

confined to urban areas by insisting that the new boundaries (a separate bill already in parliament) be passed at the same time as the main reform bill.

Wellington, however, was still poised for a decisive blow and refused to concede that minor improvements were the most that could be achieved. He told Bathurst that he was still 'very averse to the whole measure. I don't see how it is possible to govern the country under such a system, amend it as we may'. But since an entirely new bill would undoubtedly fail, the best aim was to try to form something as close as possible to the present system out of the measure, and if the Tories were determined and united, they could outvote the government and waverers combined. He hoped to isolate radicalism within forty-five new urban seats by excluding from the county vote those who owned property in towns and raising the urban franchise requirement, even to £25. Although this might not be practical it was highly desirable since the people, although well inclined, had been corrupted by the newspapers: 'Plunder is everywhere the object; and the lower we go, the stronger we find the desire for plunder.' With the Duke in this eupeptic mood, Bathurst did not try to deflect him from his heroic course but confined himself to pointing out that there were probably not more than half a dozen towns where the franchise could be raised to the level he suggested, and even that would not keep them out of the hands of the radicals, but it would raise the demand for a lower qualification elsewhere, throwing even more places into radical hands.[13]

The only thing that the waverers and Conservatives had agreed on by the time parliament resumed on 7 May was to postpone consideration of the first clause, completely disenfranchising fifty-six small boroughs, until they saw what changes they could achieve. When Grey declared this a matter of confidence, the opposition regarded it as an empty threat and deferral was carried by 151 to 116. While the vote was being taken, Bathurst joined a hasty conference with Wellington, Lyndhurst, Aberdeen, Wharncliffe and Harrowby at which they decided to undermine the government's case for new peers by putting up Ellenborough to sketch out their proposed amendments. When he told the House that the Conservatives would in due course accept abolition of all the boroughs in the first clause, the Ultras were more thunderstruck than the ministers. The next morning the entire cabinet, save the Duke of Richmond who was having second thoughts, formally advised the King to create enough peers to pass the bill. But William IV refused to go beyond twenty. The following day, 9 May, the government resigned and the King summoned Lyndhurst to advise on a ministry that would carry a large measure of reform without additional peers.

Lyndhurst went straight to Wellington, who did not think the commission hopeless but would not himself propose a reform bill and insisted that the Prime Minister should be in the Commons. The obvious candidate was Peel, who would not compromise his reputation and who now believed that there was no alternative to accepting the present bill. Harrowby and various other candidates were also canvassed without success, until finally the Duke declared that he at least would not be found wanting in his duty to King and country. He was not deterred by the Common Council of London entreating the Commons not to pass the budget until the reform bill became law, by monster petitions organized in towns which saw the prospect of representation in jeopardy or by plans for a national tax strike and an immediate financial crisis by withdrawing cash from the Bank of England. Placards appeared in London urging the population 'To Stop the Duke, Go for Gold'.

Most of Wellington's friends wished him well, but from a safe distance. Only Generals Hardinge and Murray, who had learned their duty to the Duke in a hard school, accepted office. Even Bathurst, devoted as he was to the Duke and the existing parliamentary system, had no heart to participate in this desperate enterprise. On 10 May he wrote to forestall an invitation by saying that he would not alter his determination when he left office in 1830 never to return. But he encouraged Wellington to form a ministry to pass a reform act, saying that Grey had put his resignation on such grounds that if there were any loyalty in the country at all, he could no longer expect support. No one had ever been so intoxicated with power, to the point of engaging in a 'personal contest with his Sovereign, by undisguisedly requiring the uncontrolled exercise of the highest prerogative of the Crown – that of creating hereditary Peers of Parliament; and this for the avowed purpose of insuring to himself an undisputed ascendency in that House'.[14]

Abandoned by his friends and unable to find ministers who could make a dent in the hostility of the Commons, where he was even attacked by some Ultras for lack of principle, the Duke was forced to tell the King on 15 May that it was impossible to form a government. William IV in turn had no choice but to recall Grey, whom he tried to persuade to alter the bill to make it acceptable to the Conservatives. But Grey had no need to make any concessions and insisted on a written pledge to create sufficient peers when Wellington, after privately promising to stay away from future debates on the subject, denounced the bill on 17 May at the end of his explanation to the Lords of the attempt to devise a ministry. The King's guarantee finally decided the matter. The ministry accepted a few small amendments from the few remaining die-hards who did not follow Wellington in staying away until the measure was passed. On 7 June, with the opposition benches conspicuously empty, a royal commission quietly gave assent to the bill.

It gave a nice symmetry to Bathurst's half-century career that it should end with the same issue as it began. Now that a more extensive measure than had ever been dreamed of by Pitt before industry and urbanization greatly shifted the distribution of wealth and population had been enacted, he was as fearful of the future as his Tory friends. When the first general election was being held under the new arrangements in December, 1832, Lady Georgina gloomily told her brother, safely sheltered from the storm in the Privy Council Office: 'All the agricultural interest must be overpowered by the towns – & as to the Radicals the Govt may say what they please, but there are quantities of them.'[15] In fact, although there were 50 or 60 Radicals, 39 Irish Repealers and only about 150 Conservatives among the 658 MPs, the social composition of the new House was not much different from the old, with aristocracy remaining the dominant element. This continuity was reflected in the unopposed return of Apsley and Joseph Cripps for Cirencester which, with a population of 5400 and a total electorate of 604, still had two MPs as it had since the Middle Ages. One of the seats was eliminated by the second reform bill of 1867 but not until the third reform bill of 1884 did the ancient town cease to have its own separate representation in the Commons.

Even the Duke of Wellington recovered from a far darker despair than Bathurst's and was soon enjoying gratifying success in using the massive Conservative majority in the Lords as a bastion of traditional arrangements. Bathurst himself was practically detached from diurnal politics, but the habits of a lifetime did not allow him to abandon his interest in such international issues as the Belgian question, which lingered on to 1839, and he was greatly heartened by the Duke's domestic campaign. When a stalking horse for other privileged institutions appeared in 1833 in the form of a bill to reform the vulnerable Church of Ireland, he told Apsley that he agreed with Wellington's decision to amend the measure in the House of Lords, despite Lord John Russell's announcement that he would not accept any changes beyond those already conceded to Peel, since he was sure that not all the cabinet were so unyielding.[16] Not only did this turn out to be the case, but by 1834 the Whig cabinet was fundamentally split on further Church reform.

By now, however, his time was primarily devoted to Cirencester, to his family and his friends. He was particularly distressed about Lord Grenville, 'the oldest & most valued friend I have,' who had been in poor health since a stroke a decade earlier. He suffered another in November, 1833, and at first seemed to be recovering, but it was soon obvious that he was failing. Bathurst was well prepared for the news of his death when it arrived in January, telling Thomas Grenville that his brother's consciousness of losing his speech and his total helplessness must have made the release a mercy to him as well as those around him. But the irrevocable parting from the companion of his youth and age and 'one of the best men our time has produced'[17] was a severe blow, a forceful intimation of mortality and one of the last milestones towards the end of his own course.

While Grenville was hovering at the door of death, the attention of the political world turned to the Chancellorship of Oxford as it had when the Duke of Portland was moribund a quarter of a century before. Conservatives in the university were determined to have a powerful defender of the Church in the House of Lords which had fought to save the Irish Church. When a delegation approached the Duke of Wellington, he told Bathurst that he had responded that 'it would occur to every body that I was an example of success in life without academical education and an example to be avoided, rather than an example for the university to hold forth to the youth of the country' and recommended that they consider Bathurst among others.[18] Bathurst ignored this flattery and was delighted at the prospect of the Conservative hero becoming Chancellor. But, remembering 1809, he warned the Duke that it could become a bitter party question, adding the next day that losing the election would be 'a great blow to the cause, and there is no exertion which the Government could not make which would not be made against you'. Wellington should not allow himself to become a candidate until he was assured that some of the leading colleges would support him as a body.[19]

The Duke was characteristically confident that the Conservatives could beat any Whig: 'I don't believe that there is a gentleman of property or education who would vote for any of them who is not one of their majority in one or other of the Houses of Parliament.' But it was beneath his dignity to campaign for the honour: 'It must be imposed upon me by the university; and I certainly cannot allow myself to be put forward as a candidate if any other fit person should be willing to come forward.'[20] When various other individuals declined, including Peel who was mortified by his university's choice and Wellington's obliviousness to his own yearning for the distinction, Wellington received the post by acclamation a week after Grenville's death.

The installation in June was a huge Tory celebration that lasted for a week. Bathurst presumably attended as an honorary doctor as well as the Duke's great friend and colleague for a quarter of a century, though just two months earlier he had suffered another severe loss with the unexpected death of his son Seymour, only thirty-eight, in London on 10 April, 1834. His correspondence came to an abrupt end, and the grief may have hastened his own sudden decline. Still he probably went as usual to Wellington's Waterloo dinner at Apsley House on 18 June, as the former War Minister the only civilian customarily invited to mark the day with the senior officers. That year's dinner was particularly joyful, in the midst of the Duke's parliamentary victories and immediately following the triumphal reception at Oxford.

About a month later, after seventy-two years of good health, Bathurst fell suddenly ill in London, probably of a heart attack, since the symptoms of a stroke were well known. Early on Friday morning, 25 July Apsley wrote to reassure Wellington about his father's condition[21] but then took alarm when summoned to his bedside at 9 a.m. Bathurst had asked for his son at five, but when told the hour had asked the servants to wait. When Apsley arrived, his father said in a firm but deep voice, 'I can not bear the idea of dying without having a Clergyman by my bedside to pray for me, I wish you to think of some one.' Seeing his son's anguish he comforted him by saying, 'Tomorrow or the next day will do – this is a distressing interview.' Lady Bathurst and Lady Georgina meanwhile read prayers to him whenever he felt equal to it. When Lady Georgina could not think of a parish clergyman in London with whom their father was intimate, Apsley consulted the Archbishop of Canterbury, William Howley, Bathurst's friend and contemporary, who offered to come himself. When he reported this his father responded that he had done the right thing and that he would see the Archbishop the next day. Although he did not feel strong enough for a religious examination, he did wish 'to be put in the way of a few short prayers'. Bathurst's medical attendant, Mr More, nevertheless thought that there was no cause for alarm, while Sir Henry Halford, the fashionable physician to the aristocracy, assured Lady Georgina that her father's symptoms were so favourable that he felt free to go into the country, perhaps to attend Mrs Arbuthnot who was stricken by the cholera epidemic.

Bathurst may have had a better sense of his condition than the doctors, or perhaps, his life's work done and a son recently dead, he had lost the will to live and was ready to give up the ghost. He told Apsley that no one was to speak to him about anything that was going on in the world or bring him any newspapers, though in fact none had been brought to him lately. But he had been told their astonishing contents: the Whig government, so seemingly unassailable on the morrow of the reform act two years earlier, was crumbling as its members divided on further changes to the Church; several

256

ministers resigned over secular appropriation of Irish Church revenues, including the Duke of Richmond, and Lord Grey himself retired in disgust on a related Irish issue a few days later. The King instructed the new Prime Minister, Lord Melbourne, the least radical of those who remained, to seek a coalition with Wellington and Peel, but, with brighter prospects than anyone could have imagined even a year before, they refused.

However exciting these events were to the living, they were of no significance to the dying. In the midst of this astonishing drama on the national stage where he had been a leading player for so long Bathurst, lately a backstage spectator in the wings, slipped silently away. He died with his age, not in the very midst of it like Pitt or long after it like the Duke of Wellington, but in his last active days he had the comfort of expecting that the essential social and political order he had defended all his life would endure despite the great adjustments of the past half decade.

When the Archbishop came on the Saturday afternoon, Bathurst at first felt too weak to receive him, telling Apsley that he might return in a day or two, but then changed his mind, invited Howley into his room and requested that he pray for him. These were almost his last words. After the Archbishop left, he asked to be left alone, and scarcely spoke again. At midnight, hearing Apsley's voice, he called to him but then said nothing. At seven the next morning he again heard Apsley's voice and beckoned but did not try to speak. At half past two that Sunday afternoon, 27 July, he ceased breathing without a struggle.[22]

Like the death of Lord Liverpool at the end of 1828, in the eventful summer of 1834 the death of a retired cabinet minister, however important he might have been in his day, did not attract much attention. Even the Duke of Wellington was preoccupied with parliamentary battles and within a week was devastated by the unexpected death of his beloved Mrs Arbuthnot on 2 August. But at Cirencester Bathurst remained a great figure and his passing was a major event. He had specified that the funeral be private but it was a miniature counterpart of the national commemoration of the Duke of Wellington eighteen years later, a small local state ceremony.

The hearse drawn by six horses which took him home arrived the following Saturday, when all the shops in the town closed for the day. Seymour's body was disinterred from the new Kensal Green cemetery in London and also brought for reburial with his father. The two coffins lay in state in the hall, with Bathurst's coronet on a velvet cushion on top of the oak coffin draped in ornamented black velvet. The walls were hung with black cloth painted with his various orders, the windows were covered and the room was lit by candles on pedestals. On Monday, the day before the funeral, the hall was open to the public for six hours and thousands came from the town and the surrounding countryside to pay their respects.

At six o'clock on 5 August the bells of the Abbey church began to toll. The shops were again closed for the day and by nine o'clock three hundred tenants and gentlemen in deep mourning had gathered in the courtyard. Most of the population of the town lined the route of the procession from the house to the church. Seymour's coffin was carried in front of his father's and behind followed the chief mourners: the new Lord Bathurst, William and the Rev Charles Bathurst. At the end of the service the coffins were lowered into the family vault to join their forbears back to the first Earl.[23]

On the day of the funeral Charles Greville, returning to London from the Duke of Richmond's Goodwood races full of self-reproach for his idleness and dissipation, wrote a peevish assessment of this old family friend, his former chief at the War and Colonies Office and the Privy Council and father of his fellow Joint Clerk, William Bathurst. In his surly mood he blamed Bathurst for reinforcing his lack of ambition and his lack of achievement by not working him harder and involving him more in business twenty years earlier. Even though he had known Bathurst all his life, the usually penetrating diarist confessed that he had never managed to pierce the defences of formality and wit. 'He was nervous and reserved, with a good deal of humour, and habitually a jester,' Greville rightly wrote, though greatly exaggerating when he added that 'His conversation was generally a series of jokes, and he rarely discussed any subject but in ludicrous vein'. From what he had learned from others, he was inclined to rate Bathurst's political and administrative abilities higher than most people did, but still judged him, rightly enough, to be 'the friend and devoted admirer of Pitt, and a regular Tory of the old school, who felt that evil days had come upon him in his old age'. His final summary was that Bathurst was 'a very amiable man and with a good understanding, though his talents were far from brilliant, a High Churchman and a High Tory but a Cool Politician, a bad speaker, a good writer, greatly averse to changes, but unwillingly acquiescing in many'.[24] This was perceptive enough as far as it went, if harsh, and certainly more thoughtful than the curt dismissal of Mrs Arbuthnot in a couple of sentences the same day.

A rather different appraisal some thirty years later was contained in the autobiography of Sir Henry Taylor, who by 1865 had acquired almost legendary status after four decades as a senior clerk in the Colonial Office. Taylor was no aristocrat and never had Greville's opportunity of knowing the minister and his family socially, but in the three years that they worked

together Bathurst made a lasting impression on him. In old age he was mortified at the recollection of his awkwardness when he entered the Colonial
Office at the age of twenty-four: 'In my utter ignorance of society and of
relative social positions, I was afraid of seeming to defer too much to rank
and station, and affected not to recognize them at all.' He now realized that
there had been many reasons for him to treat Bathurst with respect: 'office,
rank, age, manners, and talents; and I had a very genuine admiration and
respect for him, and would have expressed it by a duly deferential manner
if I had known how.' Throughout Taylor's career Bathurst's manner
remained the ideal standard. 'I could not have fallen in with any man in
whose official style there was more of the dignity of good-nature,' he
appreciatively wrote: 'He could be severe when necessary; but in his severity
there was generally a parental tone; and to the severest of his rebukes he
could contrive to give a colouring of consideration for the culprit.' As an
example Taylor recalled a Scottish cleric returning from British Guiana and
abusing the Governor: 'Lord Bathurst answered that he would have wished
to send the letter to the Governor for his explanation of the facts alleged,
but that he felt a difficulty in doing so, not only out of respect for the
Governor, but from an unwillingness "to expose a Minister of the Gospel".'[25]

Taylor's view is certainly closer than Greville's to the esteem in which
Bathurst was held during his lifetime by monarchs, prime ministers and
cabinet colleagues, those who worked for him in various offices and his many
friends including political adversaries. The Whig Lord Holland, who had
never let being Lady Bathurst's second cousin temper his criticism of government or of Bathurst himself, described him shortly after his death as 'the most
amiable and nearly the most sensible of our tory opponents'.[26]

Holland, if pressed, might even have conceded that, apart from the
confinement of Napoleon at St Helena, Bathurst had served the state well
for half a century and directed the empire in no despotic fashion for a
momentous decade and a half of war and peace. But by the relative peace
and security of the mid-Victorian years, Bathurst's reputation fell along
with that of his colleagues. They were conventionally seen as reactionary,
repressive mediocrities who had no idea how best to prosecute the Great
War against France or even govern the country in peacetime, and in the
fervour for empire later in the century they were further accused of indifference and neglect of the colonies. In the very last year of the nineteenth
century, the Liberal imperialist Lord Rosebery, who had managed to be
Prime Minister for a year and leader of his party for two, expressed the
standard view in trenchant terms in the course of denouncing the treatment
of Napoleon, his hero, after Waterloo. 'Who was Bathurst?' he demanded,

and, answering, said, 'One of those strange children of our political system who fill the most dazzling offices with the most complete obscurity.' Speaking more generally he pronounced in lapidary terms, 'Liverpool, Eldon, Bathurst, Castlereagh, and Sidmouth were men whose names can scarcely be said to glow in history. . . . They were honest men acting up to their lights: we can only regret that the men were dull and the lights were dim.'[27]

A hundred years later little remains of this view. Apart from the availability of archives and a flood of well-researched books on the late eighteenth and early nineteenth century, the events of the twentieth century have been a hard education in the kind of problems that Bathurst and his contemporaries faced in their day. Wars that have dwarfed the Napoleonic ones, the difficulties of transition from war to peace, the reordering of the political geography of Europe, social protest, revolutions and coups d'état, decolonization, the disappearance of freedom in constitutional countries and threat of it elsewhere: all encourage a more sympathetic understanding of those who governed Britain and the Empire in the age of the French Revolution. Castlereagh and Liverpool in particular have risen far above their Victorian characterization and it can now be seen that their close associate and confidant was, like them, efficient and humanitarian, striving to preserve as much as possible of the aristocratic order which seemed to be the best guarantee of true freedom against despotism on the one hand and anarchic democracy on the other. Even Bathurst's instinctive mistrust of the consequences of most proposals for reform caused moderate proponents at least to reconsider their first impulses, thereby contributing to the compromise between innovation and stagnation that characterized Britain in his day and afterwards and which helped to safeguard it from the upheavals that ravaged so many other countries.

NOTES

ABBREVIATIONS

BP: Bathurst Papers (British Library)
CHBE: *Cambridge History of the British Empire*
CP: Cirencester Papers (Earl Bathurst)
HMCB: Historical Manuscripts Commission, Report on the Manuscripts of Earl Bathurst
WD: Wellington Despatches
WSD: Wellington Supplementary Despatches
WND: Wellington Despatches, Correspondence and Memoranda
WP: Wellington Papers (University of Southampton)

Introduction (PAGES 1–3)

1   Maria Edgeworth to Sophy Ruxton, 19 September 1819. Edgeworth, *Letters from England 1813–1844*, p. 232.
2   'Those two fat volumes, with which it is our custom to commemorate the dead – who does not know them, with their ill-digested masses of material, their slipshod style, their tone of tedious panegyric, their lamentable lack of selection, of detachment, of design?' *Eminent Victorians*, preface.
3   C. M. Woolgar, 'Wellington's *Dispatches* and their editor, Colonel Gurwood,' Woolgar, *Wellington Studies*, I, p. 199. The letter books are WP 10 in the Wellington Papers.
4   N. D. McLachlan, 'Bathurst at the Colonial Office, 1812–1827: A Reconnaissance,' which is practically confined to the last five years. The relevant papers, however, are also well used in Rory Muir, *Britain and the Defeat of Napoleon, 1807–1815*.

Chapter 1 (PAGES 3–26)

1 Lord Apsley to Rev Dr [Henry] Bathurst, 13 March 1781. BP, vol. 2.

2 Walpole to Rev William Mason, 21 December 1775. Lewis, *Walpole Correspondence*, vol. 28, p. 239.

3 Colley, *In Defiance of Oligarchy*, pp. 239–41.

4 *Ibid.*, p. 289.

5 Lord North to Lord Chancellor Apsley, [August 1772]. HMCB, pp. 12–13.

6 Lees-Milne, *Earls of Creation*, chapter 1; Hussey, *English Gardens and Landscapes 1700–1750*, chapter 9; and Martin, *Pursuing Innocent Pleasures*, chapter 3. The first two contain a good deal of information about the first Lord Bathurst; indeed Lees-Milne's chapter is his only real biography. See also Hussey, 'Cirencester House', *Country Life*, 16 & 23 June 1950; and *Country Life*, 8 August 1908.

7 Chambers, 'The Legacy of Evelyn's *Sylva* in the Eighteenth Century.'

8 The only full, but hostile, account of the second Earl is in Campbell, *Lives of the Lord Chancellors*, vol.6.

9 [Mrs Mary Dodd to Lady Apsley], 20 January; Dr William Dodd to [Lord Chancellor], 30 January 1774. *HMCB*,pp.13–15.

10 Dodd [i.e. Johnson] to [Earl Bathurst], 8 June 1777. *HMCB*, pp. 15–16. Barker, 'Samuel Johnson and the Campaign to Save William Dodd'.

11 Valentine, *Lord North*,vol. I, pp. 313–14 & 321.

12 Bathurst to [Lord North], 9 December 1777. *HMCB*,pp. 16–17.

13 Valentine, *Lord North*, vol. II, pp. 3–15.

14 *Ibid.*,p. 155.

15 Lady Bathurst to [Mr Porter, estate agent], 11 June 1780. BP, vol. 76.

16 Hardy, 'The Building and Decoration of Apsley House'.

17 The King to Bathurst, 26 February 1783. *HMCB*,p. 19.

18 The King to Lord Sydney, 10 July 1786. Aspinall, *The Later Correspondence of George III*,vol. I, p. 220.

19 Pitt to the King & the King to Pitt, 10 July 1786. *Ibid.*, vol. I, pp. 237–38.

20 BP, vols. 75 & 76.

21 Walpole to Lady Ossery, 1 February 1775. Lewis, *Walpole Correspondence*, vol. 32, p. 236.

22 Thistlethwaite, *Memoirs and Correspondence of Dr. Henry Bathurst, Lord Bishop of Norwich*, pp. 11–12.

23 Portland to the King, 20 June 1808. Aspinall, *Later Correspondence of George III*, vol 5, p. 86.

24 Butler, *The Eldest Brother: The Marquess Wellesley, 1760–1842*, p. 33.

25 Edward Copleston q.in Bill, *Education at Christ Church Oxford 1660–1800*, from which this description of the college in Apsley's time is drawn.

26 Apsley to Dr Bathurst, 13 March 1781. BP, vol. 2.

27 Prince Frederick to Prince of Wales, 29 March 1782. Aspinall, *The Correspondence of George, Prince of Wales 1770–1812*, vol. I, p. 85.

28 Apsley to Sir R. M. Keith, 7 March & 11 April [1783]. Add. MSS. 35,525 (Hardwicke Papers).

29 Jennings, 'The Cirencester Contest and its Aftermath'; Porritt, *The Unreformed House of Commons*, vol. I, p. 198.

30 Bathurst to Mr Porter, 5 April [1784]. BP, vol. 76.

31 Q. in Rodger, *The Admiralty*, p. 95.

32 *Ibid.*, pp. 61–7.

33 Thistlethwaite, *Memoirs and Correspondence of Dr. Henry Bathurst,* p.34.

34 Lady S Lennox to Lady Susan O'Brien, 5 March 1780. Ilchester and Stavordale, *The Life and Letters of Lady Sarah Lennox 1745–1826*, vol. I, pp. 306–7. For Lady Sarah and her sisters see also Tillyard, *The Aristocrats.*

35 Lady Sarah Lennox to Lady Susan O'Brien, 29 May 1789. Illchester & Stavordale, *Life and Letters of Lady Sarah Lennox*, vol. II, p. 72.

36 Pitt to the King, 29 June 1789. Aspinall, *Later Correspondence of George III*, vol. I, p. 436.

37 Q. in Rodger, *The Admiralty*, p. 95.

38 Treasury Minute Books (T 29). PRO.

39 Pitt to the King, 9 June 1791. Aspinall, *Later Correspondence of George III*, vol. I, p. 542.

40 Board of Control Minutes and Secret Board of Control Minutes. India Office Library.

41 Bathurst to Camden, 27 November 1795. U840 C226/2 (Camden Papers); Camden to Bathurst, 3 December 1796. BP vol. 2.

42 Grenville to the King, the King to Grenville, 6 October 1796. Aspinall, *Later Correspondence of George III*, vol. II, pp. 507–8 & n. 1; Mornington to Camden, 24 November 1796. U840 C121/3 (Camden Papers).

43 Mornington to Bathurst, 5 July. *The Wellesley Papers*, vol. I, p. 32; Dundas to Bathurst, 5 July. BP, vol. 2; Bathurst to Mornington , 5 July. Add. MSS. 37,308 (Wellesley Papers); Mornington to Bathurst, 25 July 1797. *Wellesley Papers*, vol. I, pp. 37–8.

44 Camden to Bathurst, 18 February 1798. *HMCB*, pp. 22–23.

45 Fortescue, *The County Lieutenancies and the Army 1803–1814,*p. 5. Fortescue points out that almost nothing is known about the provisional cavalry beyond this comment.

46 Bathurst to Mornington, 29 April 1798. Add. MSS. 37,308 (Wellesley Papers); Bathurst to Dundas, 16 April 1798. Melville Papers (Clements Library).

47 Bickley, *Glenbervie Journals*, vol. I, pp. 400–1 & n.

48 Lady Berkeley to Admiral Berkeley, 1 April 1799. BP, vol. 2.

49 Johnson, *The Gloucestershire Gentry*, p. 165 & entry for Pitt in Thorne, *The House of Commons 1790–1820*.

50 Pitt to Bathurst, 16 April; Admiral Berkeley to Bathurst, [April] & 24 April 1799. BP, vol. 2.

51 Pitt to Bathurst, 19 May & 18 June 1799. *Ibid*.

52 Entry for Berkeley in Cockayne, *The Complete Peerage*.

53 Pitt to Bathurst, 23 October 1811. BP, vol. 4.

54 Bathurst received copies of the correspondence between Pitt and the King, as no doubt did other members of the administration. BP, vol. 2.

55 Bathurst to Mornington (*sic*), 28 May 1800. Add. MSS. 37,308 (Wellesley Papers).

56 Harcourt, *The Diaries and Correspondence of the Right Hon. George Rose*, vol II, p. 243 (diary, 2 February 1806).

57 Pitt to Bathurst, 2 October 1801. *HMCB*, p. 25.

58 Bickley, *Glenbervie Journal*, vol. I, p. 272 (diary, 25 October 1801); Malmesbury, *Diaries and Correspondence of James Harris, First Earl of Malmesbury*, vol. IV, pp. 62–3 (diary, 1 October 1801).

59 Bathurst to Pitt, 16 October 1801. PRO 30/8, vol. 112 (Chatham Papers).

60 Pitt to Bathurst, 18 October 1801. *HMCB*, p. 26.

61 Camden to Bathurst, 24 October 1802. *Ibid*., pp. 29–30.

62 Harcourt, *Diaries and Correspondence of George Rose*, vol. I, p. 497 (diary, 23 November 1802).

63 Malmesbury, *Diaries and Correspondence of Malmesbury*, vol. IV, p. 155 (diary, 18–20 December 1802) & p. 335 n.

64 Pitt to Bathurst, 12 May 1804. *HMCB*., pp. 41–2; Bathurst to Pitt, 14 May 1804. PRO 30/8 (Chatham Papers).

65 Samuel Lysons to Bathurst, 5 April 1805. BP, vol. 85; Craig, *The Mint*, pp. 257–71.

66 Pitt to Bathurst, *Ibid*., pp. 49–50.

67 Same to same, 1 January 1806. *Ibid*., pp. 50–1.

68 Col Herbert Taylor to Bathurst, 9 January 1806. BP, vol. 2.

69 Bathurst to Wellesley, 9 January 1806. Add. MSS. 37,309 (Wellesley Papers).

70 Butler, *Eldest Brother*, p. 371.

71 Wellesley to Bathurst, 22 January 1806. *The Wellesley Papers*, vol. I, p. 190.

72 Bishop Tomline to his wife, 24 January 1806. HA 119/T99/27 (Pretyman Tomline Papers).

73 Bathurst to Grenville, 28 January. *HMCB*, p. 51; Grenville to Bathurst, 29 January 1806. BP, vol. 2.

74 Bathurst to Camden, 3 July & 26 & 28 September 1806. U840 C226/10, C226/14 & C226/11 (Camden Papers).

75 Bathurst to Grenville, [11 March ?]; Grenville to Bathurst, 11 March 1807. *HMCB.*, pp. 54–5.

76 Grenville to Bathurst, 18 March 1807. *Ibid.*, pp. 55–6; Jupp, *Lord Grenville*, pp. 388–412.

Chapter 2 (PAGES 27–50)

1 Portland to the King, 25 March 1807. Aspinall, *Later Correspondence of George III*, vol. IV, p. 542.

2 Chester, *The English Administrative System 1780–1870*, pp. 271–2; Sainty, *Officials of the Boards of Trade 1660–1870*.

3 Privy Council Minutes (P.C. 4), P.R.O.

4 Harrowby to Bathurst, 27 March 1807. *HMCB*, p. 57.

5 Wellesley to Bathurst, 22 March 1807. *Ibid.*, p. 56.

6 Bathurst to Wellesley, [October 1807]. Add. MSS. 37,309 (Wellesley Papers).

7 *Victoria History of the County of Surrey*, vol. IV, p. 81; Bathurst's successive London addresses were: Curzon Street to 1812; Portman Square, 1812–13; Mansfield Street, 1813–20; Stanhope Street, 1821–28; Mansfield Street, 1829; Great Cumberland Street, 1829–30; Arlington Street, 1831–34. I am grateful to Judy Collingwood for providing this information from various directories.

8 Bathurst to Grenville, n.d.; Grenville to Bathurst, 25 March 1807. BP, vol. 3.

9 Berkeley to [Bathurst?], 13 & 17 August 1807. *HMCB*, pp. 63–5; Perkins, *Prologue to War*, p. 140 ff.

10 Lord Mulgrave to Bathurst, 24 November 1808. BP, vol. 3.

11 Wellesley to Wellesley-Pole, 26 January 1810. Webster, *Some Letters of the Duke of Wellington to his brother William Wellesley-Pole*, pp. 30–1.

12 Memorandum on Drafts of Orders in Council of 11 November 1807. Q. in Gray, *Spencer Perceval*, p. 170.

13 Printed instructions on Orders in Council to naval commanders, Admiralty Office, 3 February 1808. BP, vol. 20.

14 *Parliamentary Debates*, 1st. series, vol. 10, cols. 469–73 (15 February 1808). The best work on the Orders in Council is Crouzet, *L'economie britannique et le blocus continental, 1806–1813*.

15 Board of Trade Minutes, 3 December 1808. B.T., vol. 18.

16 Bathurst to Canning, 13 September 1808. Canning Papers.

17 Canning to Bathurst, 16 September 1808. *HMC*, pp. 75–6.

18 Canning to Bathurst, 9 January 1809. *Ibid.*, pp. 83–4.

19 Grenville to Bathurst, 7 & 23 September & 8 October. BP, vol. 3; Canning to Bathurst, 30 October 1808. Canning Papers.

20 Bathurst to Richmond, 1 March 1809. Aspinall, *Later Correspondence of George III*, vol. V, p. 214n.

21 Bathurst to Wellesley, 10 August [1809]. Add. MSS. 37,309 (Wellesley Papers).

22 Wellesley to Bathurst, 19 September 1809. BP, vol. 4.

23 Bathurst to Rose, 23 August [1809]. Add. MSS. 42,773 (Rose Papers).

24 Bond, *The Grand Expedition*, p. 159. There is also a fine thesis by Carl A. Christie, 'The Walcheren Expedition, 1809' (University of Dundee Ph.D., 1975).

25 Negotiations of 1809 [September 1809], *Ibid.*, pp. 112–19, preceded by numerous letters, pp. 90–112.

26 Portland to Bathurst, 4 May 1809. *Ibid.*, p. 92.

27 Camden to Bathurst, [8 September 1809]. *Ibid.*, pp. 101–2.

28 Harcourt, *Diaries and Correspondence of George Rose*, vol. II, pp. 377 & 380. (diary, 18 & 19 September 1809)

29 Bathurst to Malmesbury, 8 October 1809. Malmesbury ed., *A Series of Letters of the First Earl of Malmesbury*, vol. II, p. 149.

30 Wellesley to Bathurst, 30 October 1809. BP, vol. 4. (p.pr. in *HMCB*, p. 130).

31 Bathurst to Richmond, 6 November; Richmond to Bathurst, 4 December 1809. Aspinall, *Later Correspondence of George III*,vol. V, pp. 464–5.

32 Perceval to Bathurst, 28 April 1810. *HMCB*, pp. 140–1.

33 Thomas Grenville to Lord Grenville, 30 November 1809. *HMC Report Fortescue*, vol. IX, pp. 391–2; Jupp, *Lord Grenville*, pp. 416–17; Sack, *The Grenvillites*, pp. 117–19.

34 Wellesley to Marquis of Buckingham, 16 December 1809. Buckingham and Chandos, *Memoirs of the Courts and Cabinets of George the Third*, vol. IV, pp. 407–8.

35 Bathurst, Answer to the Tyrolese; Bathurst to King, 10 November; W. R. Hamilton to Bathurst, 5 November; King to Bathurst, 11 November; Charles Stuart to W. R. Hamilton, 15 November 1809. *HMCB*, pp. 130–6.

36 Bathurst to Prince Starhemberg, 13 November 1809. BP, vol. 4.

37 Canning to Bathurst, 12 October; Gentz to [Canning], 29 September; the King to Bathurst, 27 October 1809. *HMCB*, pp. 119–126 & 130.

38 Journal of Mrs Benjamin [Phillida] Bathurst's four months travels on the Continent to discover the mysterious fate of her husband. BP, vol. 79.

39 Apsley to Bathurst, 5 January 1815. BP, vol. 9.

40 George Galway Mills entry in Thorne, *The House of Commons 1790–1820*; Hall, *Four Famous Mysteries*.

41 Bathurst to Sir Thomas Brisbane, 5 January 1824. *Historical Records of Australia*, 1st. series. Vol. XI, p 192; Sir Ralph Darling to Bathurst, 15 February 1828. *Ibid.*, Vol. XIII, pp. 784–5.

42 The King to Bathurst, 24 November; Malmesbury to Bathurst, 12 October 1809. *HMBC*, pp. 136 & 128.

43 Richard Ryder, Home Secretary, to Lord Harrowby, 20 September 1810. Aspinall, *Later Correspondence of George III*, vol. V, p. 635.

44 Berkeley to Bathurst, 10 & 14 October 1810. *HMCB*, pp. 150–1.

45 Berkeley to Bathurst, 30 September 1810. *Ibid.*, pp. 148–9.

46 Bathurst to Richmond, 11 November 1810. Aspinall, *The Correspondence of George, Prince of Wales, 1770–1812*, vol. VII, pp. 72–3.

47 Matthew Baillie to Bathurst, 15 December 1810. *HMCB*, p. 152.

48 [Bathurst] to Col John McMahon, 1 December; Charles Arbuthnot to McMahon, 10 December 1811. Aspinall, *Correspondence of Prince of Wales*, vol. VIII, pp. 235–6 & 245.

49 Earl Temple to C. W. Williams Wynne, 15 September 1811. Q. in Harvey, *Britain in the Early Nineteenth Century*, p. 280.

50 Bathurst, Notes of a Conversation with Lord Wellesley, 17 January 1812. *HMCB*, pp. 160–1.

51 Bathurst, Notes concerning Lord Wellesley's Resignation, 17 February 1812. *Ibid.*, pp. 164–6.

52 Bathurst, Memorandum respecting the Assassination of Spencer Perceval, 11 May 1812. *Ibid.*, pp. 172–3.

53 Bathurst to Rose, 24 May 1812. Harcourt, *Diaries and Correspondence of George Rose*, vol. II, p. 510.

54 Bathurst to Prince Regent, 29 May 1812. *HMCB*, p. 176.

55 Richmond to Bathurst, 12 June 1812. *Ibid.*, pp. 179–80.

56 Bartlett, *Castlereagh*, p. 111.

Chapter 3 (PAGES 51–74)

1 The standard work on the Colonial Office in this period is Young, *The Colonial Office in the Early Nineteenth Century*. There is a shorter, more wide-ranging and recent discussion in Buckner, 'The Colonial Office and British North America, 1801–50,' *Dictionary of Canadian Biography*, Vol. VIII. There is no comparable work on the War Office for this period.

2 The various officials and their responsibilities are described in detail in Clode, *The Military Forces of the Crown*.

3 Bunbury, *Memoir. . . of Lieutenant-General Sir Henry Edward Bunbury*, p. 61.

4 Goulburn, draft memoirs (Goulburn Papers, 304, Box 68). The standard biography is Brian Jenkins, *Henry Goulburn 1784–1856: A Political Biography*.

5 Bentinck to Bathurst, 1 September 1812. *HMCB*, p. 210.

6   Strachey & Fulford, *Greville Memoirs*, vol. III, p. 66 (5 August 1834).

7   The best book on government policy and the Peninsular War and other campaigns is Muir, *Britain and the Defeat of Napoleon 1807–1815*; briefer and more generally, Muir and C. J. Esdaile, 'Strategic Planning in a time of Small Government: the Wars against Revolutionary and Napoleonic France, 1793–1815' in Woolgar, *Wellington Studies*, I.

8   Liverpool to Wellington, 10 June 1812. Yonge, *The Life of. . . Liverpool*, vol. I, pp. 399–400.

9   Gordon to Bathurst, 7 July [1812]. *HMCB*, pp. 184–5.

10   Wellington to Bathurst, 4 July & 3 August 1812. *WD*, vol IX, pp. 269–70 & vol. V, p. 329.

11   Bathurst to Wellington, 22 September 1812. WP/1/350 (WP); Clapham, *The Bank of England*, vol. II, p. 35.

12   Herries, *Memoir of. . . Herries*, vol. I, pp. 68–76. Herries was Commissary in Chief from 1811 until 1816, when the office was abolished.

13   Bathurst to Wellington, 23 July 1812. BP, vol. 60.

14   Wellington to Bathurst, 24 July 1812. *WD*, vol. IX, pp. 308–9.

15   Bathurst to Wellington, 6 August 1812. *WSD*, vol. VII, pp. 374–5.

16   Same to same, 16 August 1812. *Ibid.*, pp. 383–4.

17   Wellesley to Bathurst, 16 August 1812. Add. MSS. 37,314 (Wellesley Papers).

18   Liverpool to Bathurst, 16 August; *HMCB*, pp. 195–6; Bathurst to Wellington, 20 & 22 August; Liverpool to Wellington, 22 August. *WSD*, vol. VII, pp. 404–8; Wellington to Bathurst, 24 August 1812. *WD*, vol. IX, p. 378.

19   Mulgrave to Bathurst, 24 August 1812. *HMCB*, pp. 201–2.

20   Bathurst to Prince Regent, 21 August 1812. *Ibid.*, pp. 201–2.

21   Wellington to Bathurst, 9 September 1812. *WD*, vol. IX, pp. 352–5.

22   Bathurst to Wellington, 9 September 1812. *WSD*, vol. VII, p. 417.

23   Wellington to Bathurst, 18 August 1812. *WD*, vol. X, pp. 368–71.

24   Bathurst to Wellington, 31 August 1812. *WSD*, vol. VII, pp. 412–13.

25   Bathurst to Wellington, 22 September 1812. WP/1/350 (WP). Since specie was always sent at its intrinsic value while Wellington acknowledged it at the nominal value, there was much disagreement and confusion about the actual amount.

26   Harrowby to Bathurst, 17 September 1812. *HMCB*, pp. 213–14.

27   Bathurst to Wellington, 6 March 1813. BP, vol. 61.

28   *Ibid.*, 20 April 1813. WP/1/368 (WP).

29   Mulgrave to Bathurst, 24 August 1812. *HMCB*, pp. 202–4.

30   Wellington to Bathurst, 14 April 1812. *WD*, vol. X, pp. 295–7.

31   Bathurst to Wellington, 25 May 1813. WP/1/369 (WP).

32   Bathurst to Liverpool, 3 October 1812. Add. MSS. 38,250 (Liverpool Papers).

33 Wellington to Bathurst, 11 May 1813. *WD*, vol. X, pp. 371–3.

34 Bathurst to A'Court, 27 March 1813. Add. MSS. 41,512 (Heytesbury Papers).

35 Stagg, 'James Madison and the Coercion of Great Britain'.

36 Brock to Liverpool, 25 May 1812. *HMCB*, pp. 174–5.

37 O'Toole, *Honorable Treachery*, pp. 89–91.

38 Bunbury to Bathurst, 7 October 1812. *HMCB*, pp. 216–17.

39 Bathurst to Wellington, 6 October 1812. *WSD*, vol. VII, p. 442.

40 Wellington to Bathurst, 25 July 1812. *WD*, vol. IX, pp. 312–13.

41 Bathurst to Wellington, 8 October 1812. *WSD*. Vol. VII, p. 446.

42 *Ibid.*, 12 November 1812. BP, vol. 60.

43 Wellington to Liverpool, 23 November 1812. *WD*, vol. IX, pp. 570–4.

44 Wellington to Bathurst, 19 November 1812. WP/1/351 (WP).

45 Bathurst to Wellington, 17 March 1813. *WSD*, vol. VII, p. 588.

46 Wellington to Bathurst, 11 & 25 May 1813. *WD*, vol. X, pp.371–3 & 400.

47 Bathurst to Wellington, 25 August. *WSD*, Vol. VIII, p. 209; Wellington to Bathurst, 3 September 1813. *WD*, vol. XI, p. 76.

48 Bathurst to Wellington, 3 July 1813. *WSD*, vol. VIII, p. 49.

49 Parliamentary Debates, 1st. series, vol. 26, cols. 1123–25 (7 July 1813).

50 Bathurst to Lord Melville, 24 July. BP, vol. 107; Melville to Bathurst, 28 July 1813. *WSD*, vol. VIII, pp. 144–47.

51 Bathurst to Wellington, 22 July. *WSD*, vol. VIII, p. 109; Wellington to Bathurst, 18 August 1813. *WD*, vol. XI, pp. 11–12.

52 Bathurst to Wellington, 9 October 1813. WP/1/378 (WP).

53 Wellington to Bathurst, 10 July. *WD*, vol. X, pp. 522–23; & 19 August 1813. *Ibid.*, vol. XI, pp. 17–19.

54 Melville to Wellington, 28 July & 3 September 1813. *WSD*, vol. VIII, pp. 144–7 & 223–6.

55 Bathurst to Wellington, 5 November 1813. *Ibid.*, vol. VIII, p. 337.

56 *Ibid.*, 20 October 1813. *Ibid.*, pp. 318–19.

57 Wellington to Bathurst, 21 November 1813. *WD*, vol. XI, pp. 303–7.

58 Goulburn, draft memoirs (Goulburn Papers).

59 Bathurst to Wellington, 24 November 1813. *WSD*, vol. VIII, p. 390.

60 Wellington to Bathurst, 21 December 1813. *WD*, vol. XI, p. 384–7.

61 Bathurst to Wellington, 31 December 1813. *WSD*, vol. VIII, pp. 450–2.

62 *Ibid.*, 7 January 1814; [Col Bunbury], 'Memorandum on the Present State of Affairs and the Military Operations which might be Pursued,' 31 December 1813. *WSD*, vol. VIII, pp. 491 & 457–62.

63 Bathurst to Wellington, 12 January 1814. BP, vol. 63.

64 Wellington, Memorandum for Colonel Bunbury, 1 February 1814. *WD*, vol. XI, pp. 492–3.

65 Bathurst to Wellington, 10 February. *WSD*, vol. VIII, p. 683; William Manning, Gov. of Bank of England, to Bathurst, 8 February 1814. *HMCB*, p. 265; Herries, *Memoir*, vol. I, pp. 85–7.

66 Wellington to Bathurst, 22 February 1814. *WD*, vol. XI, pp. 525–6.

67 Prince of Orange to Bathurst, 21 December 1813. *HMCB*, p. 250.

68 Bathurst to wife, 13 December 1813. CP.

69 Strachey & Fulford, *Greville Memoirs*, vol. I, pp. 3–4 (11 February 1814).

70 Stewart to Bathurst, 2 April 1814. *HMCB*, p. 273.

71 Bathurst to Wellington, 23 March 1814. *WSD*, vol. VIII, p. 676.

72 Bunbury to Bathurst, 16 April 1814. BP, vol. 57.

73 Bathurst to Wellington, 29 March 1814. *WSD*, vol. VIII, pp. 702–3.

74 *Annual Register*, 1815, Chronicle, pp. 32–7.

75 Bathurst to Wellington, 23 & 28 April 1814. *WSD*, vol. IX, pp. 29–30 & 53.

Chapter 4 (PAGES 75–83)

1 Apsley to Lady Bathurst, 25 April [1814]. CP.

2 Seymour Bathurst to Lady Bathurst, 28 May 1814. BP, vol. 7.

3 Prince of Orange to Bathurst, 24 April 1814. HMCB, p. 273.

4 Bathurst to Prince of Orange, [April 1814]. *Ibid.*, p. 275.

5 *Ibid.*, 11 May 1814. *Ibid.*, pp. 277–8.

6 Princess Charlotte to Lady Bathurst, [June 1814]. CP.

7 Bathurst to Wellington, 28 January 1814. WSD, vol. VIII, p. 547.

8 Wellington to Bathurst, 22 February 1814. WD, vol. XI, pp. 525–6.

9 Bathurst to Wellington, 14 April 1814. WP/1/409 (WP).

10 Wellington to Castlereagh, 4 October 1814. WSD, vol. IX, pp. 314–16.

11 Bathurst to Goulburn, 21 October 1814. Goulburn Papers, vol 2. (Clements Library).

12 HMCB, pp. 285–6 & 290–4.

13 Bathurst to Peel, 19 August 1814. Add. MSS. 40,238 (Peel Papers).

14 Bathurst to Wellington, 25 October 1814. WP/1/431 (WP).

15 Wellington to Bathurst, 30 October 1814. HMCB, pp. 302–3.

16 *Ibid.*, 4 November 1814. *Ibid.*, p. 303.

17 Wellington to Liverpool, 9 November 1814. WSD, vol.IX, pp. 424–6.

18 Memorandum from Murray to Bathurst, 21 September. BP, vol. 22; Bathurst to Murray, 13 December 1814. Murray Papers, vol. 120.

19 Bunbury, *Memoir*, vol. I, pp. 64–72.

20 Liverpool to Bathurst, 11 September 1814. WSD, vol. IX, p. 240.

21 Bathurst to Goulburn, 12 September 1814. Goulburn Papers, vol. 2 (Clements Library).

22 Apsley to Bathurst, 2 & 5 January 1815. HMCB, pp. 319–20.

23 Castlereagh to Bathurst, 27 April 1814. *Ibid.*, p. 274.

24 Augustus Foster to Bathurst, 14 July 1814. *Ibid.*, pp. 280–1.

25 Bathurst, Note of a conversation with Mr. Anker, 9 November 1814. *Ibid.*, p. 308.

26 Countess of Pembroke to Bathurst, 15 September 1815. *Ibid.*, pp. 289–90.

27 Castlereagh to Bathurst, Apsley to Bathurst, 4 October 1814. *Ibid.*, pp. 295–6.

28 Apsley to Bathurst, 9 November 1814. *Ibid.*, pp. 304–5.

29 Pembroke to Bathurst, 2 December 1814. *Ibid.*, pp. 310–11.

30 Castlereagh to Bathurst, 18 December. *Ibid.*, pp. 316–17; Bathurst to Wellington, 23 December 1814. WP/1/437 (WP).

31 Apsley to Bathurst, 22 January 1815. HMCB, pp. 327–8.

32 Bathurst, Foreign Policy, 12 December 1814. *Ibid.*, pp. 314–15.

33 Liverpool to Bathurst, 21 January 1815. *Ibid.*, pp. 326–7.

34 Harrowby to Bathurst, 17 January 1815. *Ibid.*, p. 325.

35 Apsley to Bathurst, 22 January 1815. *Ibid.*, pp. 327–8.

36 Liverpool to Bathurst, 17 January 1815. WSD, vol. IX, pp. 540–1.

37 Apsley to Bathurst, 30 January 1815. HMCB, p. 336.

38 Wellington to Castlereagh, 12 March 1815 (two letters). WD, vol. XII, pp. 267–8.

39 Prince of Orange to Bathurst, 13 March. BP, vol. 9; Bathurst to Prince of Orange, 21 March 1815. HMCB, p. 342.

40 Bathurst to Wellington, 14 March 1815. WP/1/452 (WP).

41 Prince of Orange to Bathurst, 17 March. BP, vol. 9; Bathurst to Wellington, 20 March 1815. WP/1/10/2 (WP; pr. along with Duke's commission as dated 28 March in WSD, vol. X, p. 5).

42 Bathurst to Murray, 20 March 1815. Murray Papers, vol. 120.

43 Wellington to Bathurst, 17 April 1815. WP/1/458 (WP).

44 Herries, *Memoir*, vol. I, pp. 98–101.

45 Wellington to Bathurst, 6 April 1815. WD, vol. XII, pp. 291–2.

46 Sir Henry Torrens to Bathurst, 7 April 1815. WSD, vol. X, pp. 40–1.

47 Apsley to Bathurst, 22 April 1815. BP, vol. 9.

48 Richmond to Bathurst, 10 April 1815. HMCB, pp. 344–5.

49 Harrowby to Castlereagh, 7 April & Liverpool's memorandum, 1 April 1815. WSD, vol. X, pp. 31–7.

50 Wellington to Lord Stewart, 8 May 1815. WD, vol. XII, p. 358.

51 Bathurst to Wellington, 13 April 1815. WP/1/454 (WP).

52 Bathurst to Wellington, 16 May & 2 June. WSD, vol. X, pp. 305–6 & 411–13; Liverpool to Wellington, 14 April 1815. HMCB, pp. 345–6.

53   Bathurst to Wellington, 11 April 1815. WSD, vol. X, pp. 218–19.

54   Mulgrave to Bathurst, 9 April 1815. HMCB, p. 344.

55   Wellington to Bathurst, 21 April 1815. WD, vol. XII, pp. 319–20.

56   Bathurst to Wellington, 13 & 16 June 1815. WP/10/1/2 & 1/468 (WP).

57   Bathurst to Wellington, 18 May 1815. WP/1/462 (*Ibid*).

58   Bathurst to Murray, 30 March. Murray Papers, vol. 120; Murray to Bathurst, 30 May 1815. BP, vol. 9.

59   Wellington to Bathurst, 4 May 1815. WSD, vol. X, pp. 218–19.

60   Swinton, *A Sketch of the Life of Georgina, Lady De Ros*, pp. 124–3. In 1815 Lady De Ros was Lady Georgina Lennox.

61   Lady Georgina Lennox to Lady Georgina Bathurst, 16 June 1815. CP (typescript).

62   Lady Georgina Lennox to Lady Georgina Bathurst, 17 June 1815. *Ibid*.(typescript).

63   Richmond to Bathurst, 18 June 1815. BP, vol. 9 (p.pr. in HMCB, p. 356).

64   Gore, *Creevey*, pp. 141–2; Lady Sarah Lennox to Lady Georgina Bathurst, 19 June 1815. CP. (typescript).

65   Goulbourn, draft memoirs (Goulburn Papers, 304/Box 68).

66   Colby, *The Waterloo Despatch*.

67   Bathurst to Wellington, 23 June 1815. WSD, vol. X, p. 563.

68   Wellesley to Bathurst, 23 June 1815. WSD, vol. X, p. 563.

69   Apsley to Bathurst, 19 June. HMCB, p. 357; Seymour Bathurst to Lady Bathurst, 19 June 1815. CP.

70   Lady Georgina Lennox to Lady Georgina Bathurst, 22 June 1815. CP (typescript).

71   Seymour Bathurst to Bathurst, 22 June 1815. *Ibid*.

72   Wellington to Bathurst, 25 June 1815. WD, vol. XII, pp. 507–9.

73   Bathurst to Wellington, 26 June 1815. WSD, vol. X, p. 593.

74   Wellington to Bathurst, 25 June 1815. WD, vol. XII, p. 509.

75   Apsley to Bathurst, 25 June 1815. BP, vol. 9.

76   Bathurst to Wellington, 24 June 1815 (2 letters). WSD, vol. X, pp. 571–2 & WP/1/468 (WP).

77   Seymour Bathurst to Lady Bathurst, 2 July 1815. CP.

78   Wellington to Bathurst, 2 July 1815. WD, vol. XII, pp. 532–8.

79   Seymour Bathurst to Lady Bathurst, [July 1815]. CP.

80   Seymour Bathurst to Lady Bathurst, 22 July 1815. *Ibid*.

81   Liverpool to Castlereagh, 15 July 1815. Yonge, *Life of Liverpool*, vol. II, p. 196.

82   *Ibid*., 21 July 1815. WSD, vol. XI, p. 47.

83   Bathurst to Wellington, 24 July 1815. *Ibid*., vol. XI, pp. 55–6.

84   Goulburn, draft memoirs (Goulburn Papers, 304/Box 68).

85 Bunbury to Bathurst, 31 July. HMCB, p. 365; Notes [on Napoleon], 31 July 1815. Bunbury, *Memoir*, pp. 297–307.

86 William Lennox Bathurst to Bathurst, 31 July 1815. HMCB, p. 364.

87 Eldon to Bathurst, 1 September & n.d., 1815. *Ibid.*, pp. 375–80.

88 Bathurst to Lowe, 15 April 1816 (2 letters). Forsyth, *History of the Captivity of Napoleon at St. Helena*, vol. I, pp. 167–8.

89 The debate is printed in *Ibid.*, vol. II, pp. 371–89.

90 Stanhope, *Notes of Conversations with the Duke of Wellington 1831–1851*, pp. 104–4 & 325–7 (16 October 1837 & 21 December 1848).

Chapter 5 (PAGES 106–134)

1 Seymour Bathurst to Lady Bathurst, 22 July 1815. CP.

2 Apsley to Bathurst, 14 September 1815. *Ibid.*

3 Bathurst to Wellington, 15 July 1815. WP/10/1/2 (WP); same to same (2 letters), 10 July 1815. WSD, vol. XI, pp. 23–4.

4 Liverpool to Bathurst, 12 October 1815. HMCB, pp. 388–9.

5 Bathurst to Liverpool, 19 October 1815. *Ibid.* pp. 390–1.

6 Bathurst to Cumberland, 4 September; Liverpool to Prince Regent, 6 September 1815. Aspinall, *The Letters of George IV 1812–1830*, vol. II, pp. 102–4 & 106; Bathurst to Prince Regent, 4 September & Regent to Bathurst, 5 September 1815. HMCB, pp. 382–4.

7 A good study of the army after 1815 is Padgett, 'The Making of Military Policy in Early Victorian England, 1815–1827'(Ph.D. thesis, Stanford University, 1979).

8 Bathurst to Wellington, 20 October 1815. WSD, vol. XI, pp. 204–5.

9 Wellington to Bathurst, 23 October & to Sir Henry Torrens, 4 November 1815. WD, vol. XII, pp. 668–9 & 680–2.

10 Bathurst to Wellington, 9 April & Wellington to Bathurst, 15 April 1816. WSD, vol. XI, pp. 354 & 365–6.

11 Wellington to Castlereagh, 9 February & circular to rulers of lesser powers, 11 February 1817. *Ibid.*, pp. 626–7.

12 Goulburn, draft memoirs (Goulburn Papers, 304/Box 68).

13 Bunbury to Bathurst, 16 May 1815. *HMCB*, p. 349; Bunbury, *Memoirs*, pp. 78–85.

14 Young, *The Colonial Office*, pp. 78–85.

15 Goulburn to his wife, 31 January 1816. Goulburn Papers.

16 Bathurst to the Ladies Bathurst, [June 1817]. CP.

17 Eldon to Bathurst, [June 1817], Wellington to Bathurst, 18 June 1817. *Ibid.*

18 Prince Regent to Northumberland, 23 January 1818. Aspinall, *Correspondence of Prince of Wales*, vol. VIII, p. 427.

19 Memorandum for Lord Bathurst; Knight Commander [invoice], n.d. CP.

20 Bathurst to wife, [July 1817]. *Ibid.*

21 Garter King of Arms to Bathurst, 13 August 1817. BP, vol. 22.

22 Wellington, *A Selection from the Private Correspondence of the First Duke of Wellington*, p. 158.

23 Prince Hardenberg to Bathurst, 20 June 1818. HMCB, p. 450.

24 Bathurst to wife, 4 November 1817. CP.

25 Bathurst to Prince Regent, 5 November 1817. Aspinall, *Letters of George IV*, vol. II, p. 211.

26 M. Baillie to Bathurst, 2.10 & 2.30 a.m., 6 November 1817. BP, vol. 11.

27 Bathurst to Liverpool, 8:30 a.m., 6 November 1817. Add. MSS. 38,269 (Liverpool Papers).

28 Bloomfield to Bathurst, 8 November 1817. BP, vol 11.

29 Liverpool to Bathurst, 6 November 1817. *Ibid.*

30 Arbuthnot to Bathurst, 14 April 1818. HMCB, pp. 447–8.

31 *Gentleman's Magazine*, 1819, p. 479.

32 Captain Charles Jones (A.D.C.) to Bathurst [May 1818]. BP, vol. 12.

33 Young, *The Colonial Office*, pp. 26–7.

34 Goulburn to wife, 30 January 1816. (Goulburn Papers, 304/Box 62B).

35 Tunstall, 'Imperial Defence, 1815–1870,' CHBE, vol. II; Manning, *British Colonial Government After the American Revolution*, p.495ff.

36 Bathurst to Macquarie, 24 July 1816. *Historical Records of Australia*. Series I, vol. V, pp. 150–1.

37 Brownrigg to Bathurst, 29 April 1817. Add MSS 38,741 (Huskisson Papers).

38 Lady Sarah Lennox to Lady Georgina Bathurst, 4 August 1815. CP (typescript).

39 Richmond to Bathurst, 16 May 1817. BP, vol. 11.

40 Wellington to Combermere, 3 December 1817. WSD, vol. XII, p. 154.

41 Bathurst to Newcastle, 2 October 1819. NeC5, 152 (Newcastle Papers).

42 *Ibid.*, 9 October 1819. NeC5, 153 (*Ibid.*).

43 Bathurst to Lonsdale, 3 November 1815. D/Lons/L44 (Lonsdale Papers).

44 Richmond to Bathurst, 28 February 1818. BP, vol. 12.

45 *Ibid.*, 27 March 1818. *Ibid.*

46 *Ibid.*, 13 April 1818. *Ibid.*

47 Whitelaw, *The Dalhousie Journals*, vol. I, pp. 78–80 (1, 17 & 24 May 1818).

48 Richmond to Bathurst, 11 August 1818. HMCB, pp. 450–1.

49 *Ibid.*, 21 August 1818. *Ibid.*, p. 454.

50 [Transcript of the Duke of Richmond's last remarks], 27 August [1819]. BP, vol. 12; Wellington to Bathurst, Memorandum on the Defence of Canada, 1

March 1819. WND, vol. I, pp. 36–44. The map illustrating the plan is in the possession of the Duke of Wellington.

51 Maitland to Bathurst, 2[shd. be 5] September 1819. BP, vol. 12.

52 *Ibid.*, 13 September 1819. *Ibid.*

53 Whitelaw, *The Dalhousie Journals*, vol. I, pp. 160–1 & 172–3 (11 & 15 September & 21 November); Dalhousie to Bathurst, 15 September 1819. BP, vol. 12.

54 Bathurst to Wellington, 10 October 1819. WP1/632/4 (WP).

55 Bathurst to Wellington, 2 October. WP1/632/4. *Ibid.*; & 5 October 1819. HMCB, p. 478.

56 Bathurst to Liverpool, 6 October 1819. Add. MSS. 38,280. (Liverpool Papers).

57 Kempt to Wellington, 3 October. WP1/632/6; Wellington to Bathurst, 5 October. HMCB, p. 478; Bathurst to Wellington, 10 October 1819. WP1/632/15. (WP).

58 Bathurst to Castlereagh, 20 October 1818. Londonderry, *Memoirs and Correspondence of Castlereagh*, vol. XII, pp. 55–8.

59 P. J. Marshall, 'British Assessments of the Dutch in Asia in the Age of Raffles' and Robert Van Niel 'Dutch Views and Uses of British Policy in India around 1800' in P. J. Marshall *et al.* eds., *India and Indonesia during the Ancien Regime*.

60 Hastings to Bathurst, 23 March 1819. HMCB, pp. 468–71. H. H. Dodwell, 'The Straits Settlements, 1815–1863,' CHBE, vol. II.

61 Marks, *The First Contest for Singapore, 1819–1824* contains a detailed account of the negotiations.

62 Liverpool to Bathurst, 27 September 1818. HMCB, p. 456.

63 Bathurst to Liverpool, 8 October 1818. Add. MSS. 38,273 (Liverpool Papers).

64 W. H. Fremantle to Marquess of Buckingham, 18 November 1819. Buckingham, *Memoirs of the Court of England During the Regency 1811–1820*, vol. II, pp. 373–4.

65 The best work on the subject is still Tumelty, *The Ionian Islands under British Administration, 1815–1864*. Pratt, *Britain's Greek Empire*, based on Tumelty, is more accessible. Dixon, *The Colonial Administration of Sir Thomas Maitland* is also useful.

66 Bathurst to Wellington, 13 January 1815. WSD, vol. IX, pp. 534–5.

67 Castlereagh to Bathurst, 14 August 1815. HMCB, p. 372.

68 Exmouth to Bathurst, 5 May 1816. *Ibid.*, pp. 412–13.

69 Exmouth to Bathurst, 30 August 1816. *Ibid.*, vol. 11.

70 Bunbury to Bathurst, 25 October 1815. *Ibid.* pp. 392–3.

71 Extract of Bathurst's instruction to Governor Sir T. Maitland, 28 July 1813. BP, vol. 89.

72 Maitland to Bunbury, 18 February 1816. *Ibid.*, vol. 24.

73 Eldon to Bathurst [June 1817]. CP.

74 Maitland to Goulburn 3 November 1819. BP, vol. 28.

75 Bathurst to Lord Melville, 13 August 1819. *Ibid.*, vol. 107.

76 Wellington to Bathurst, 26 August 1819. WP1/629/8 (WP).

77 Bathurst to Wellington, 27 August 1819. WP1/630/11 (*Ibid.*)

78 Castlereagh to Bathurst, 28 & 30 August 1819. HMCB, pp. 473–6.

79 Bathurst to Wellington, 29 August. WP1/630/14; Wellington to Bathurst, 30 August 1819. WP1/629/11 (WP).

80 Lady Georgina Bathurst to Ralph Sneyd, 26 August 1819. Sneyd Papers.

81 Capodistria, from Warsaw, to Wellington, 18 October 1819. WP1/632/25 (WP).

82 Bathurst to Wellington, 3 September. WP1/631/4; Count Lieven to Wellington, 13 September 1819. WP1/631/13 (*Ibid.*)

83 Maitland to Bathurst, 10 December 1819 & 22 July 1820. BP, vols. 28 & 29.

84 Goulburn to Bathurst, 7 September 1819. *Ibid.*, vol. 12.

85 Bathurst to Wellington, 27 August 1820. WP1/653/8 (WP).

Chapter 6 (PAGES 135–154)

1 Bathurst to Liverpool, 26 June 1820. Add. MSS. 38, 285 (Liverpool Papers).

2 Bathurst to Liverpool, 8 August 1820. Add. MSS. 38,286 (*Ibid.*)

3 Liverpool to Arbuthnot, 13 November 1820. Aspinall, *The Correspondence of Charles Arbuthnot*, p. 21.

4 Arbuthnot to Bathurst, 29 November 1820. HMCB, pp. 489–90.

5 Liverpool to Bathurst, 7 January 1821. *Ibid.*, pp. 493–4.

6 Bunbury to Bathurst, 27 June; Sir Thomas Maitland to Goulburn, 24 July 1821. BP, vol. 40; Young, *The Colonial Office*, pp. 41 & 263.

7 Goulburn to Bathurst, 13 August 1821. HMCB, p. 508.

8 Bathurst, Instructions for Preserving Order at the Queen's Funeral, [13/14 August 1821]. *Ibid.*, p. 509.

9 Bathurst to Eldon, 30 August 1821. BP, vol. 13.

10 Liverpool to Bathurst, 3 September 1821. HMCB, p. 514.

11 Wellington to Liverpool, 4 September. WP1/680/4 (WP); Wellington to Bathurst; York to Bathurst, 5 September 1821. HMCB, pp. 514–15.

12 Liverpool to Bathurst, 6 September; Melville to Bathurst, 10 September 1821. HMCB, pp. 515–16.

13 Liverpool to Bathurst, 16 September 1821. *Ibid.*, p. 517.

14 Lady Holland to Bathurst, 16 July 1821. BP, vol. 13.

15 A lengthy selection was published a decade after Lowe's death in Forsyth, *History of the Captivity of Napoleon at St. Helena*.

16 Bathurst to Lowe, 28 November 1823. *Ibid.*, vol. I, pp. 191–2.

17 Benjamin Bloomfield to Bathurst, 21 November 1821. BP, vol. 82.

18 Harrowby to Bathurst, 24 November 1821. HMCB, pp. 522–3.

19 Jenkins, *Henry Goulburn*, pp. 131–2.

20 Goulburn to Bathurst, n.d., 28 & 29 November 1821. *HMCB.*, pp. 523–4.

21 Wynne to Duke of Buckingham, 17 January 1822. Buckingham, *Memoirs of the Court of George IV*, vol. I, p. 274.

22 Bathurst to Wellesley, 30 November 1821. Add. MSS. 37,310 (Wellesley Papers).

23 Goulburn to Bathurst, 29 November 1821. BP, vol. 13 (p.pr. in HMCB, p. 524).

24 *Ibid.*, 3 December 1821. BP, vol. 13.

25 Hyde, *The Strange Death of Lord Castlereagh.*

26 Londonderry to Bathurst, 26 August 1822. WP1/749/1 (WP).

27 Strachey & Fulford, *The Greville Memoirs*, vol. I, p. 130 (22 September 1822); Wellington to King, 7 September 1822. WND, vol. I, pp. 274–6.

28 Bathurst to Penn, 13 February 1832. Add. MS. 40,880 (Ripon Papers).

29 Bamford & Wellington, *Journal of Mrs. Arbuthnot*, vol. I, p. 211 (3 February 1823).

30 Bathurst to Wellington, 25 February 1823. WND, Vol. II, p. 46; Bamford & Wellington, *Journal of Mrs. Arbuthnot*, Vol. I, pp. 211 & 219 (3 & 25 February 1823).

31 *Ibid.*, pp. 210–11 (3 February 1823).

32 *Ibid.*, p. 220. (27 February 1823).

33 Countess Lieven to Mettternich, 28 March 1828. Quennell, *The Private Letters of Princess Lieven to Prince Metternich, 1820–1826*, pp. 199–202.

34 Arbuthnot to Bathurst, 24 March 1824. HMCB, p. 565.

35 Bathurst to Canning, 29 March 1824. (Canning Papers).

36 Dawson, *The First Latin American Debt Crisis* (p. 100 for reference to Wellington).

37 Bathurst to Liverpool, Liverpool to Bathurst, 4 May 1825. *HMCB*, pp. 579–81.

38 Bathurst to Peel, 16 May 1825. Add. MSS. 40,378 (Peel Papers).

39 Liverpool to Bathurst, 18 May 1825. HMCB, p. 583.

40 *Ibid.* 22 May 1825. *Ibid.*, pp. 583–4.

41 Bathurst to Liverpool, 23 May 1825. *Ibid.*, pp. 584–5.

42 The best even-handed account of the Greek war for independence is St. Clair, *That Greece Might Still Be Free.*

43 St. Clair, *That Greece Might Still Be Free*, ch. 15; Dakin, *British Intelligence in Greece 1824–1827,* containing some of the transcripts; for British intercepts generally see Ellis, *The Post Office in the Eighteenth Century*, ch. 6.

44 Bathurst to Aberdeen, 25 & 27 December 1821. Add. MSS. 43,231 (Aberdeen Papers); Chamberlain, *Lord Aberdeen*, pp. 199–200.

45 Londonderry to Lord Strangford, 14 July 1821. WP1/674/4 (WP).

46 Maitland to Wilmot, 25 July 1822. BP, vol. 35.

47 Maitland to Bathurst, 29 September 1822. *Ibid.*

48 Bamford & Wellington, *Journal of Mrs. Arbuthnot*, Vol. I, p. 230 (29 April 1823).

49 Bathurst to Melville, 26 August; Melville to Bathurst, 29 August 1823. BP, vol. 107; Davis, 'Greek Slaves at Tunis in 1823'.

50 Maitland to Bathurst, 15 January 1824. BP, Vol. 54.

51 Adam to Wellington, 27 January; WP1/782/13; Beresford to Wellington, 19 February 1824. WP1/785/6 (WP).

52 Pratt, *Britain's Greek Empire*, pp. 171–2.

53 Bathurst to Adam, 16 July 1824. BP, Vol. 67.

Chapter 7 (PAGES 155–185)

1 Bamford and Wellington, *The Journal of Mrs. Arbuthnot*, vol. I, pp. 158–9.

2 Wellington to Bathurst, 6 May 1824. WND, Vol. II, p. 263.

3 *Ibid.*, 30 August 1824. *Ibid.*, pp. 304–6.

4 Wellington to Bathurst, 4 September; Bathurst to Wellington, 9 December 1825. WP1/828/1 & WP1/833/3 (WP). The painting of the battle, purchased by the King of the Netherlands, is now in the Rijksmuseum, Amsterdam; the individual sketches of Wellington's commanders are in Apsley House (Wellington Museum).

5 Young, *The Colonial Office*, chapter 2; Sainty, *Colonial Office Officials*; Chester, *The English Administrative System*, esp. pp. 239–41; Snelling & Baron, 'The Colonial Office and its permanent officials 1801–1914'; Murray, *The West Indies and the Development of Colonial Government 1801–1834*, chapter 7.

6 Bathurst to Richard Penn, 13 February 1832. Add. MS. 40,880 (Ripon Papers).

7 Taylor, *Autobiography*, vol. I, pp. 68–72.

8 Canterbury (Charles Manners-Sutton) to Bathurst, 18 August 1824. BP, vol. 56.

9 Lt-Gov Sir Howard Douglas to Bathurst, 28 October 1824. *Ibid.*

10 Maria Edgeworth to Archbishop of Canterbury [1825]. *Ibid.*, vol. 23.

11 Bathurst to Liverpool, 3 October; Liverpool to Bathurst, 5 October 1824. Add. MSS. 38,299 (Liverpool Papers).

12 Bathurst to Hay, 12 August 1825. BP, vol. 57.

13 *Ibid.* 15 August 1825. *Ibid.*

14 *Ibid.*, 13 & 15 January 1826. *Ibid.*, vol. 58.

15 *Ibid.*, 28 June 1826. *Ibid.*

16 Bathurst to Wilmot-Horton, 2 January 1825. Wilmot-Horton Papers (Mitchell Library).

17 Bathurst to Liverpool, 10 January 1825. Add. MSS. 38,299 (Liverpool Papers); Bathurst to Hay, 18 January 1826. BP, Vol. 58.

18 Young, *The Colonial Office*,pp. 124–8.

19 Whitelaw, *The Dalhousie Journals*, Vol. II, p. 41 (25 December 1825).

20 Bathurst to Hay, 3 March 1826. BP, vol. 58.

21 *Ibid.*, 12 October 1825 (2 letters). *Ibid.*, Vol. 57.

22 *Ibid.*, 23 August 1825. *Ibid.*

23 *Ibid.*, 14 August 1825. *Ibid.*

24 Bathurst to Wilmot-Horton, 3 August 1826. Wilmot-Horton Papers (Mitchell Library).

25 *Ibid.*, 22 August 1826. *Ibid.*

26 *Ibid.*, 7 August 1826. *Ibid.*

27 Bathurst to Hay, 22 June 1826. BP, Vol. 58.

28 Bathurst,memorandum on New South Wales [1825–26]. C.O. 324/75, f. 11.

29 Metcalfe, *Maclean of the Gold Coast*, pp. 13–14; A. P. Newton, 'British Enterprise in Tropical Africa, 1783–1870', C.H.B.E., Vol. II.

30 Metcalfe, *Maclean of the Gold Coast*, pp. 10 & 14–15.

31 Bathurst to Turner, 5 July 1825. Harlow & Madden, *British Colonial Developments, 1774–1834*, pp. 495–6.

32 Wellington to Bathurst, 30 June & 4 July 1826. WND, Vol. III, pp. 344–9.

33 Bathurst to Hay, 13 July 1826. BP, Vol. 58.

34 Bathurst, Colonial Minute to cabinet on the Island of Fernando Po, 25 March 1825. *Ibid.*, Vol. 89.

35 Canning to Bathurst, 12 August; Bathurst to Canning [August] 1825. HMCB, pp. 585–7.

36 Of the vast literature on abolition and amelioration, the most useful for this study were Walvin, *England,Slaves and Freedom, 1766–1838*, esp. ch. 6; Murray, *The West Indies and the Development of Colonial Government 1801–1834*, esp. ch. 4; Ward, *Colonial Self-Government*; Klingberg, *The Anti-Slavery Movement*; Hurwitz, *Politics and the Public Conscience*; and Craton, Walvin & Wright, *Slavery, Abolition and Emancipation*.

37 The West Indies colonies with legislatures were Antigua, Bahamas, Barbados, Dominica, Grenada, Jamaica, St Kitt's, St Vincent and Tobago.

38 Goulburn to Bathurst, 17 August 1819. BP, Vol. 12.

39 .Bathurst to Governor John Murray & Lt Governor Henry Beard (Demerara & Berbice respectively), 28 May 1823. Harlow & Madden, *British Colonial Developments, 1774–1834*, pp. 560–1. (The same despatch was sent to all West Indies governors.)

40 Two Circular despatches from Lord Bathurst to Certain West India Governors, 9 July 1823. *Ibid.*, pp. 562–5.

41 *Jamaica Journal*, 11 October 1823. Q. in Mellor, *British Imperial Trusteeship 1783–1850*, p. 91.

42 Jamaica: Address and Resolutions of the Assembly, 11 December 1823. Harlow & Madden, *British Colonial Developments, 1774–1834,*pp. 565–6.

43 Liverpool & York to Bathurst, 13 October. HMCB, pp. 545–6; Wellington to Bathurst, 14 October 1823. WND, Vol. II, pp. 147–8.

44 Bathurst to Peel, 21 October 1823. Add. MSS. 40,358 (Peel Papers).

45 HMCB, pp. 546–52.

46 Fortescue, *A History of the British Army*, vol. XI, pp. 86–7.

47 Liverpool to Bathurst, 12 January, enclosing Liverpool to Canning, 9 January 1824. HMCB, pp. 559–61.

48 Harlow & Madden, *British Colonial Developments, 1774–1834*, pp. 567–73.

49 Bathurst to Wilmot-Horton, 11 January 1826. Wilmot–Horton Papers (Mitchell Library).

50 *Ibid.*, 1 April 1826. *Ibid.*

51 *Ibid.*, 6 November 1826. *Ibid.*

52 *Ibid.*, 11 January 1826. *Ibid.*

53 *Ibid.*, 6 November 1826. *Ibid.*

54 Bathurst to Bishop of Barbados, 3 November 1825. C.O. 324/74.

55 Bathurst to Bishop of Jamaica, 7 December 1826. *Ibid.*

56 Liverpool to Bathurst, 16 July 1826. HMCB, pp. 605–6.

57 Bathurst to Manchester, 14 February 1824. BP, Vol. 8.

58 Stephen, 'Answer to Objections to the Proposed Order in Council respecting Slavery' [October 1831], Bell and Morrell, *Select Documents on British Colonial Policy 1830–1860*, pp. 377–8.

59 Bathurst to Manchester, 29 July 1826. C.O. 324/74.

60 The issue is masterfully dissected by Young, *The Colonial Office*, chapter 7.

61 Bathurst to Wilmot-Horton, 2 September 1825. Q. in *Ibid.* pp. 215–16.

62 Stephen to Wilmot-Horton, 15 September 1825. *Ibid.*, pp. 216–18.

63 Bathurst to Wilmot-Horton, 16 August 1826. Wilmot Horton Papers.

Chapter 8 (PAGES 186–210)

1 The standard work is Johnston, *British Emigration Policy 1815–1830*.

2 The best general work on this period is the first two volumes of Clark, *A History of Australia*. There is a very graphic account of the convicts in Hughes, *The Fatal Shore*; but powerful as the description is, it does not relate the dreadful lot of

the convicts to the hard life of agricultural labourers, miners, soldiers, sailors and other manual workers at the time.

3   Bathurst to Sidmouth, 23 April 1817. Clark, *Select Documents in Australian History 1788–1850*, pp. 315–17.

4   Clark, *A History of Australia*, Vol. I, appendices I & II.

5   Bathurst to Murray, 11 November 1822. BP, Vol. 64.

6   Bathurst to Brisbane, 18 July 1824. NLA MS 4036 (NK6787) (Brisbane Papers).

7   Bathurst to Brisbane, 23 August 1824. BP, Vol. 64.

8   Bathurst to Wellington, 13 November 1824. WP1/804/10 (WP).

9   Wellington to Bathurst, 20 November 1824. HMCB, p. 576.

10 Brisbane to Bathurst, 10 September 1825. WP1/827/22 (WP).

11 Bathurst to Brisbane, 22 December 1824. NLA MS. 4036 (NK6787) (Brisbane Papers).

12 Brisbane to Wellington, 19 September 1825. WP1/827/21 (WP).

13 Huskisson to Wilmot-Horton, 18 September 1827. Catton Papers, D3155 2818.

14 Peel to Bathurst, 13 July; Bathurst to Peel, [July 1825]. Add. MSS. 40,380 (Peel Papers).

15 Bathurst to Hay, 29 March 1826. BP, Vol. 58.

16 Millar, *Plantagenet in South Africa* is a very favourable biography.

17 Graham, *Great Britain in the Indian Ocean*, pp. 27–40.

18 Somerset to Bathurst, 14 March 1815. BP, Vol. 87.

19 The two biographies, neither very satisfactory, are Rae, *The Strange Story of Dr James Barry* and Rose, *The Perfect Gentleman*. The latter contains more on Barry and Somerset. The best discussion, summarizing the medical literature on Barry's sex, is the entry in the *Canadian Dictionary of Biography*, vol IX by Charles G. Roland, M.D. Contrary to the *Dictionary of National Biography*, Barry is referred to here as 'he' which was the contemporary usage.

20 See Johnston, *British Emigration Policy 1815–1830*, chapter 3.

21 Goulburn to Newcastle, 5 September 1819. Newcastle Papers NeC 5, 155.

22 Harlow & Madden, *British Colonial Developments, 1774–1834*, pp. 475–6.

23 Bathurst to Somerset, 19 February 1822. BP, Vol. 65.

24 Somerset to Bathurst, 2 December 1824. *Ibid.*, Vol. 87.

25 Donkin to Bathurst, 25 June; Bathurst to Donkin, 26 June 1826. *Ibid.*, Vol. 18.

26 Bathurst to Somerset, 19 February 1825. *Ibid.*, Vol. 65.

27 Bigge & Colebrooke to Bathurst, 14 February 1825. *Ibid.*, Vol. 87.

28 Extract of letter from Somerset to Bathurst, 16 October 1824. *Ibid.*

29 Bathurst to Somerset, 14 February; Somerset to Bathurst, 7 May 1825. *Ibid.*

30 Bird to Bathurst, 25 May 1825. *Ibid.*

31 Bigge & Colebrooke to Bathurst, 9 February 1826. *Ibid.*, Vol. 88.

32 Bathurst to Hay, 20 January 1826. *Ibid.*, Vol, 58.

33 Bathurst to Commissioners at the Cape, 29 April 1826. *Ibid.*, Vol. 65. The passage in square brackets is crossed out.

34 Bigge & Colebrooke to Bathurst, 14 July 1824. *Ibid.*, Vol. 87.

35 Somerset to Bathurst, 12 October 1825. *Ibid.*, Vol. 88.

36 Bathurst to Somerset, 29 October 1824. *Ibid.*, Vol. 65.

37 Somerset to Bathurst, 12 October 1825. *Ibid.*, Vol. 88.

38 Bathurst to Somerset, 10 November 1825. *Ibid.*, Vol. 65.

39 Perceval to Bathurst, 4 March 1826. *Ibid.*, Vol. 23.

40 Whitelaw, *Dalhousie Journals*, Vol. III, p. 53. (7 May 1826).

41 Lord Goderich to Somerset, 21 June 1827. Q. in Millar, *Plantagenet in South Africa*, p. 250.

Chapter 9 (PAGES 211–229)

1 Palmerston to Bathurst, 12 January; Bathurst to Palmerston, 15 January 1826. HMCB, pp. 598–9.

2 Bathurst to Canning, 19 December 1825. Canning Papers.

3 Bathurst to Wellington, 20 January 1826. WP1/847/7 (WP).

4 Hinde, *George Canning*, p. 405.

5 Bathurst to Wellington, 8 February 1826. WP1/849/3 (WP).

6 Bathurst to Lords Commissioners of the Admiralty, 8 February 1826. WND, Vol. III, pp. 82–3.

7 *Gentleman's Magazine*, 1825, pp. 272 & 364; Bathurst Papers D2525 F (Gloucestershire Record Office).

8 Bathurst to Canning, 1 July 1825. Canning Papers.

9 Bathurst to Hay, 6 January 1826. BP, Vol. 58.

10 Wellington to Bathurst, 17 February. WND, Vol. III, pp. 113–16; Bathurst to Wellington, 20 January 1826. WP1/847/7 (WP).

11 Wellington to Bathurst, 7 March 1826. *WND*. Vol. III, pp. 159–60.

12 Wellington to Bathurst, 7 September 1826. WP1/861/30 (WP) (part of letter not printed in WND, Vol. III, pp. 402–3.

13 Bathurst to Wilmot-Horton, 11 & 17 September 1826. Wilmot-Horton Papers (Mitchell Library).

14 Wilmot-Horton to Bathurst, 21 October 1826. BP, Vol. 17.

15 Bathurst to Liverpool, 23 October. Add. MSS. 38,302; Liverpool to Bathurst, 25 October 1826. Add. MSS. 38,303 (Liverpool Papers).

16 Bathurst to Wellington, 24 December 1826. WP1/867/40 (WP).

17 Wellington to Bathurst, 27 December; Bathurst to Wellington, 28 December;

Wellington to Bathurst, 30 December 1826. WND, Vol. III, pp. 505–6 & 509–10.

18 Clinton to Bathurst, 1 January; Bathurst to Clinton, 25 January 1827. BP, Vol. 90.

19 Canning to Bathurst, 1 February 1827. HMCB, p. 629.

20 Bathurst to King, 11 December 1826. RA 23685 (Royal Archives).

21 Bathurst to King, 14 December 1826. Aspinall, *The Letters of King George IV*, Vol. III, pp. 186–7.

22 Sir Herbert Taylor to Wellington, 15 December 1826. WP1/867/25 (WP).

23 Ponsonby to Bathurst, 15 January 1826 [shd. be 1827]. BP, Vol. 18.

24 Bathurst to Hay, 24 December 1826. *Ibid.*, Vol. 58.

25 Sir Herbert Taylor to Bathurst, 30 December 1826. Taylor, *The Taylor Papers*, pp. 191–2.

26 Bathurst to Liverpool, 6 January 1827. HMCB, pp. 619–21.

27 Wellington to Bathurst, 9 January 1827. *Ibid.*, pp. 626–7.

28 *Gentleman's Magazine*, 1827, p. 170.

29 Bathurst to Peel, 23 February 1827. BP, Vol. 17.

30 Brock, *Lord Liverpool and Liberal Toryism*, p. 283.

31 Buckingham to Bathurst, 26 February 1827. Aspinall, *The Formation of Canning's Ministry*, p. 27.

32 Huskisson to Canning, 19 February 1827. *Ibid.*, pp. 4–5.

33 Bathurst to Canning, 11 April 1827. CP.

34 *Ibid.*, 11 April 1827. *Ibid.*

35 Canning to Bathurst, 11 April 1827. Aspinall, *Formation of Canning's Ministry*, p. 61.

36 Bathurst to Canning, 12 April 1827. BP, Vol. 18.

37 Strachey & Fulford, *Greville Memoirs*, Vol. I, p. 172. (13 April 1827).

38 Canning to Bathurst, Bathurst to Canning, 15 April 1827. HMCB, pp. 632–3.

39 Bathurst, Memorandum on the Circumstances of Appointing Mr. Hay Under-Secretary of State, 20 April. BP, Vol. 18; Bathurst to Hay, 21 April 1827. *Ibid.*, Vol. 59.

40 Bathurst to Wilmot-Horton, 26 April. Wilmot-Horton Papers; Wilmot-Horton to Bathurst, 26 April 1827. Catton Papers, D3155/WH 2749.

41 Bathurst to Arbuthnot, 4 July 1827. Aspinall, *Correspondence of Charles Arbuthnot*, pp. 87–8.

42 Bathurst to Hay, 9 August 1827. BP, Vol. 59.

43 Wellington to Bathurst, 10 August 1827. WND, Vol. IV, p. 76.

44 Bathurst to Wellington, 12 August 1827. *Ibid.* p. 81.

45 Bathurst to Hay, 14 August. BP, Vol. 59; Hay to Bathurst, 15 August 1827. *Ibid.*, Vol. 18.

46 Bathurst to Wellington, 22 August; Wellington to Bathurst, 25 August 1827. WND, Vol. IV, pp. 104–6.

47 Bathurst to Wellington, 28 August 1827. WP1/895/49 (WP).

48 Bathurst to Wellington, 27 October 1827. WND, Vol. IV, p. 140.

49 Bathurst to Hay, 12 November 1827. BP, Vol. 59.

50 *Ibid.*, 15 November 1827. W.N.D., Vol. IV, pp. 158–9.

51 Wellington to Bathurst, 12 November 1827. HMCB, pp. 647–8.

52 *Ibid.*, 13 November 1827. *Ibid.*, p. 648.

53 Bathurst to Wellington, 16 November 1827. WND, Vol. IV, pp. 159–60.

54 Bathurst to Wilmot-Horton, 27 November 1827. Catton Papers WH 2748.

55 Wellington to Bathurst, 10 January (2 letters). HMCB, p. 652; Bathurst to Wellington, 10 January 1827. WND, Vol. IV, p. 185.

Chapter 10 (PAGES 230–245)

1 P.C. 4, Vol. 17 (PRO) (28 May 1828). The Order in Council was issued on 30 May 1828; Swinfen, *Imperial Control of Colonial Legislation 1813–1865*, pp. 16–20.

2 Chester, *The English Administrative System*, pp. 273–4.

3 Ellenborough, *A Political Diary*, Vol. I, p. 3 (22 January 1828).

4 Bathurst to Wellington, 5 March 1827. WND, Vol. IV, p. 299.

5 Bathurst to Aberdeen, 15 March 1828. Add. MSS. 43,231 (Aberdeen Papers).

6 Bathurst to Lonsdale, 31 March 1828. D/Lons/L44 (Lonsdale Papers).

7 Strachey & Fulford, *Greville Memoirs*, I, p. 212. (18 June 1828).

8 Peel, *Memoirs*, I, pp. 127–8.

9 *Ellenborough Diary*, I, p. 143 (11 June 1828).

10 George Villiers to Bathurst, 28 June 1828. BP, vol. 18.

11 Bamford and Wellington, *Journal of Mrs. Arbuthnot*, vol. II, pp. 198–200 (29 July 1828).

12 Bathurst to Arbuthnot, 15 August 1828. Aspinall, *Correspondence of Charles Arbuthnot*, pp. 105–6.

13 *Ibid.*, 19 August 1828. *Ibid.*, p. 106.

14 Bathurst to Aberdeen, 21 August 1828. Add. MSS. 43,232 (Aberdeen Papers).

15 Bathurst to Wellington, 19 August 1828. WND, vol. IV, p. 637.

16 Bathurst to Hay, 23 October 1828. BP, vol. 59.

17 Bathurst to Arbuthnot, 19 December 1828. Aspinall, *Correspondence of Charles Arbuthnot*, pp. 112–13.

18 Bathurst to Hay, 27 & 30 November 1828. BP, vol. 59.

19 Bathurst to Anglesey, 28 September 1828. *Ibid.*, vol. 18.

20 Wellington to Bathurst, 24 November 1828. WND, vol. V, p. 281.

21 Bathurst to Wellington, 29 December 1828. WP1/973/12 (WP).

22 *Ibid.*, 29 December 1829. WND, vol. V, p. 376.

23 Bathurst to Wellington, 13 January 1829. WP1/989/2 (WP).

24 Strachey & Fulford, *Greville Memoirs*, I, pp. 248–9 (6 February 1829).

25 Lord Bagot to Bathurst, 13 February 1829. WND, V, pp. 502–3.

26 Grenville to Bathurst, 10 May 1829. HMCB, p. 659; Lady Georgina Bathurst to Ralph Sneyd (22 March 1829) Sneyd Papers.

27 Archdeacon Henry Bathurst to Wellington, 13 September 1830. WP1/1141/4 (WP).

28 Bamford and Wellington, *Journal of Mrs. Arbuthnot*, II, p. 293 (3 July 1829).

29 *Gentleman's Magazine*, 1829, p. 364.

30 Wellington to Bathurst, 5 October 1829. WND, VI, p. 198.

31 *Journal of Mrs. Arbuthnot*, II, pp. 352–2 (22 April 1830).

32 Strachey & Fulford, *Greville Memoirs*, II, p. 7 (20 July 1830); *Journal of Mrs. Arbuthnot,*II, p. 373 (21 July 1830).

33 *Gentleman's Magazine* 1830, p. 176.

50 .Rev C. Bathurst to Wellington, 23 May 1830. WP1/1115/11 (WP).

35 Glos R O D2525 F (Bathurst Papers), 26 July 1830.

36 Strachey & Fulford, *Greville Memoirs*, II, pp. 60–1 (16 November 1830).

37 Ellenborough, *Diary*, II, p. 420 (7 November 1830).

38 *Greville Memoirs*, II, pp. 58–62 & 83–4 (15–17 November & 12 December 1830); Bathurst to Wellington, 10 December 1830. WP1/1156/3 (WP).

Chapter 11 (PAGES 246–260)

1 Bathurst to Wellington, 6 December 1830. WP1/1158/9 (WP).

2 Wellington to Bathurst, 7 December 1830. HMCB, pp. 622–3.

3 The best work on the subject is Brock, *The Great Reform Act*.

4 Bathurst to Wellington, [27 March 1831]. WP1/1179/9 (WP).

5 Bathurst to Charles Greville Snr., 2 April 1831. CP.

6 Lady Mary Lennox to Seymour Bathurst, 20 July 1831. CP; *Gentleman's Magazine*, 1830 (notice of Lady Lennox's death).

7 Bathurst to Aberdeen, 7 August 1831. Add. MS. 43,236 (Aberdeen Papers).

8 Aspinall, *Three Diaries*, pp. 138–40 (Ellenborough, 1 October 1831).

9 G Bathurst to Sneyd [8 October 1831]. Sneyd Papers; Aspinall, *Three Diaries*, p. 147 (Littleton, 8 October 1831).

10 Bathurst to Wellington, 2 December 1831. WP1/1204/5 (WP).

11 Lady Georgina Bathurst to Sneyd, 'Wednesday' [28 March 1831]. Sneyd Papers.

12 *Ibid.*, 'Thursday' [12 April 1832]. *Ibid.*

13 Bathurst to Wellington, 24 April; Wellington to Bathurst, 27 April; Bathurst to Wellington, 29 April 1832. WND, VIII, pp. 281–2; 285–8; 290–1.

14 Bathurst to Wellington, 10 May 1832. *Ibid.*, VIII, pp. 304–5.

15 Lady G Bathurst to William Bathurst [18 December 1832]. CP.

16 Bathurst to Apsley, 16 July 1833. BP, vol. 18.

17 Bathurst to Thomas Grenville, 5 November 1833 & 15 January 1834. CP.

18 Wellington to Bathurst, 28 November 1833. Brooke & Gandy, *Wellington: Political Correspondence*, vol. I, pp. 361–3.

19 Bathurst to Wellington, 30 November & 1 December 1833. *Ibid.*, pp. 364–8.

20 Wellington to Bathurst, 3 December 1833. HMCB, pp. 664–5.

21 Wellington to Apsley, 25 July 1834. BP, vol. 18.

22 Lord Apsley's account of his Father's last hours. CP.

23 *Times* newspaper, 7 August 1834.

24 Strachey & Fulford, *The Greville Memoirs*, Vol. III, pp. 65–6 (5 August 1834).

25 Taylor, *Autobiography*, Vol. I, pp. 68–72.

26 Kriegal, *The Holland House Diaries 1831–1840*, p. 265 (October 1834).

27 Rosebery, *Napoleon: The Last Phase*, pp. 117–18.

BIBLIOGRAPHY

MANUSCRIPT SOURCES

Bathurst Papers (British Library, Loan 57)
Cirencester Papers (The Earl Bathurst)
Bathurst Papers (Gloucestershire Record Office)
Royal Archives (Windsor Castle)
Wellington Papers (University of Southampton)
British Library:
    Aberdeen Papers
    Hardwicke Papers
    Huskisson Papers
    Liverpool Papers
    Peel Papers
    George Rose Papers
    Wellesley Papers
Brisbane Papers (National Library of Australia)
Camden Papers (Kent Archives Office)
Canning Papers (West Yorkshire Archives Service)
Catton [Wilmot-Horton] Papers (Derbyshire Record Office)
Goulbourn Papers (Surrey History Centre and Clements Library, University of Michigan)
Lonsdale Papers (Cumbria Record Office)
Melville Papers (Clements Library, University of Michigan)
Murray Papers (National Library of Scotland)
Napier Papers (Bodleian Library, Oxford University)
Newcastle Papers (Nottingham University)
Portland Papers (Nottingham University)
Sneyd Papers (University of Keele)
Tomline Papers (Suffolk Record Office)
Wilmot-Horton Papers (Mitchell Library, Sydney)

Public Record Office:
Chatham Papers
Admiralty Board Minutes
Treasury Minute Books
Board of Trade Minutes
Colonial Office Papers (C.O. 74 & 75)
Privy Council Minutes
Board of Control Minutes & Secret Board of Control Minutes (India Office Library)

PUBLISHED SOURCES

Andersson, Ingvar, *A History of Sweden*, 2nd. ed. trans. Carolyn Hannay and Alan Blair, London, Weidenfeld & Nicolson [1965], 1970.

Annual Register.

Aspinall, A., ed., *The Correspondence of Charles Arbuthnot*, London, Royal Historical Society, 1941 (Camden Society, Third Series, vol. LXV).

Aspinall, A., ed., *The Correspondence of George, Prince of Wales 1770–1812*, 8 vols., London: Cassell, 1963.

Aspinall, A., ed., *The Later Correspondence of George III*, 5 vols., Cambridge, Cambridge University Press, 1962.

Aspinall, A., ed., *The Diary of Henry Hobhouse (1820–1827)*, London, Home & Van Thal, 1947.

Aspinall, A., ed., *The Formation of Canning's Ministry, February to August 1827: Edited from Contemporary Sources*, London, Royal Historical Society, 1937 (Camden Society, Third Series, vol. LIX).

Aspinall, A., ed., *The Letters of King George IV 1812–1830*, 3 vols., Cambridge, Cambridge University Press, 1938.

Aspinall, A., ed., *Letters of the Princess Charlotte 1811–1817*, London, Home & Van Thal, 1949.

Aspinall, A., ed., *Three Early Nineteenth Century Diaries* [Sir Denis LeMarchant, Edward John Littleton and Lord Ellenborough, November 1830–June 1834], London, Williams & Norgate, 1952.

Australian Dictionary of Biography.

Baddeley, Welbore St. Clair, *A History of Cirencester*, Cirencester, Cirencester Newspaper Company, 1924.

Bamford, Francis and the Duke of Wellington eds., *The Journal of Mrs. Arbuthnot 1820–1832*, 2 vols., London, Macmillan, 1950.

Barker, A. D., 'Samuel Johnson and the Campaign to Save William Dodd,' *Harvard Library Bulletin*, vol. 31 (Spring 1983), pp. 147–80.

Bartlett, C.J., *Castlereagh*, London, Macmillan, 1966.

Barman, Roderick J., *Brazil: The Forging of a Nation, 1798–1852*, Stanford, Stanford University Press, 1988.

Bate, Walter Jackson, *Samuel Johnson*, New York, Harcourt Brace Jovanovich, 1975.

Bathurst, A. B., *History of the Apsley and Bathurst Families*, Cirencester, G. H. Harmer, 1903.

Bayly, C. A., *Imperial Meridian: The British Experience and the World 1780–1830*, London, Longman, 1989.

Bell, Kenneth N. and W. P. Morrell, eds., *Select Documents on British Colonial Policy 1830–1860*, Oxford, Clarendon Press, 1928.

Bickley, Francis, ed., *The Diaries of Sylvester Douglas (Lord Glenbervie)*, 2 vols., London, Constable, 1928.

Bill, E. G. W., *Education at Christ Church Oxford 1660–1800*, Oxford, Clarendon Press, 1988.

Bond, Gordon C., *The Great Expedition: The British Invasion of Holland in 1809*, Athens, University of Georgia Press, 1979.

Bourne, Kenneth, *Britain and the Balance of Power in North America 1815–1908*, Berkeley, University of California Press, 1967.

Bourne, Kenneth, *Palmerston: The Early Years 1784–1841*, New York, Macmillan, 1982.

Brock, Michael, *The Great Reform Act*, London, Hutchinson University Library, 1973.

Brock, W. R., *Lord Liverpool and Liberal Toryism 1820–1827*, Cambridge, Cambridge University Press, 1941.

Brooke, John, *King George III*, New York, McGraw-Hill, 1972.

Brooke, John and Julia Gandy, *Wellington: Political Correspondence*, vol. I: 1833–November 1834, London, HMSO, 1975.

Buckingham and Chandos, Duke of, *Memoirs of the Courts and Cabinets of George the Third*, 4 vols, London, Hurst and Blackett, 1853–55.

Buckingham and Chandos, Duke of, *Memoirs of the Court of England During the Regency, 1811–1820*, 2 vols, London, Hurst and Blackett, 1856.

Buckingham and Chandos, Duke of, *Memoirs of the Court of George IV, 1820–1830*, 2 vols, London, Hurst and Blackett, 1859.

Buckner, Phillip, 'The Colonial Office and British North America, 1801–50', *Dictionary of Canadian Biography*, vol. VIII.

Bucker, Phillip A., *The Transition to Responsible Government in British North America: British Policy in North America, 1815–1850*, Westport, Connecticut, Greenwood Press, 1985.

Bunbury, Sir Charles J. F., ed., *Memoir and Literary Remains of Lieutenant-General Sir Henry Edward Bunbury, Bart*, London, Spottiswoode & Co., 1868.

Burt, Alfred LeRoy, *The British Empire and Commonwealth from the American Revolution*, Boston, D.C. Heath, 1956.

Butler, Iris, *The Eldest Brother: The Marquess Wellesley, 1760–1842*, London, Hodder & Stoughton, 1973.

Byrne, Patrick, *Lord Edward Fitzgerald*, London, Staples Press, 1955.

Cambridge History of the British Empire, The, vol. II: *The Growth of the New Empire*

1783–1870, eds. J. Holland Rose, A. P. Newton and E. A. Benians, Cambridge, Cambridge University Press, [1940] 1968.

Cambridge History of British Foreign Policy 1783–1919, vol. I, eds. Sir A. W. Ward and G. P. Gooch, Cambridge, Cambridge University Press, 1922.

Campbell, John *Lives of the Lord Chancellors and Keepers of the Great Seal of England, From the Earliest Times Till the Reign of Queen Victoria*, new ed., ed. John Allen Mallory, 10 vols, Toronto, Carswell, 1876.

Cell, John W., *British Colonial Administration in the Mid-Nineteenth Century: The Policy-Making Process*, New Haven, Yale University Press, 1970.

Chamberlain, Muriel *Lord Aberdeen: A Political Biography*, London, Longman, 1983.

Chamberlain, Muriel E., *'Pax Britannica'?: British Foreign Policy 1789–1914*, London, Longman, 1988.

Chambers, Douglas, 'The Legacy of Evelyn's *Sylva* in the Eighteenth Century,' *Eighteenth Century Life*, vol. 12, n.s. (February 1988), pp. 29–41.

Chester, Sir Norman, *The English Administrative System 1780–1870*, Oxford, Clarendon Press, 1981.

Christie, Carl A., *The Walcheren Expedition, 1809* (Ph.D. thesis, University of Dundee, 1975).

Christie, Ian, *Stress and Stability in Late Eighteenth Century Britain: Reflections on the British Avoidance of Revolution*, Oxford, Clarendon Press, 1984.

Christie, Ian R., *Wars and Revolutions: Britain 1760–1815*, London, Edward Arnold, 1982.

Clapham, Sir John, *The Bank of England: A History*, vol. II, Cambridge, Cambridge University Press, 1945.

Clark, J. C. D., *English Society 1688–1832*, Cambridge, Cambridge University Press, 1985.

Clark, C. M[anning]. A., ed., *Select Documents in Australian History 1788–1850*, Sydney, Angus & Robertson, 1950.

Clark, Manning, *A History of Australia*, vols. I & II, Melbourne, Melbourne University Press, 1962 & 1968.

Clode, Charles M., *The Military Forces of the Crown; Their Adminstration and Government*, 2 vols., London, John Murray, 1869.

Cockayne, G. E., *The Complete Peerage*, rev. ed., 6 vols, Gloucester, Alan Sutton [1910–59], 1982.

Colby, Reginald, *The Waterloo Despatch*, London, HMSO, 1965.

Cochester, Lord ed., *The Diary and Correspondence of Charles Abbot, Lord Cochester*, 3 vols., London, John Murray, 1861.

Colley, Linda, *In Defiance of Oligarchy: The Tory Party 1714–60*, Cambridge, Cambridge University Press, 1982.

J. E. Cookson, 'Political Arithmetic and War in Britain, 1793–1815,' *War and Society*, vol. I (September 1983), pp. 37–60.

Cory, G. E., *The Rise of South Africa: A History of the Origins of South African Colonization and of its Development towards the East from the Earliest Times to 1857*, vols. I & II, Cape Town, Struik [1910 & 1913], 1965.

Craig, Gerald, *Upper Canada: The Formative Years 1784–1841*, Toronto, McClelland and Stewart, 1963.

Craig, Sir John, *The Mint: A History of the London Mint from A.D. 287 to 1948*, Cambridge, Cambridge University Press, 1953.

Craton, Michael, James Walvin and David Wright, *Slavery, Abolition, and Emancipation: Black Slaves and the British Empire: A Thematic Documentary*, London, Longman, 1976.

Crouzet, Francois, *L'économie britannique et le blocus continental 1806–1813*, 2 vols., Paris, Presses universitaires de France, 1958.

Cunningham, Audrey, *British Credit in the Last Napoleonic War*, Cambridge, Cambridge University Press, 1910.

Dakin, Douglas, ed., *British Intelligence in Greece, 1824–1827: A Documentary Collection*, Athens, Extracted from the Bulletin of the Historical and Ethnographical Society of Greece, vol. XIII, 1959.

Davenport, T. R. H., *South Africa: A Modern History*, 4th. ed., London, Macmillan [1977], 1991.

Davies, K. G., *The Royal African Company*, London, Longmans, Green, 1957.

Davis, G., 'Greek Slaves at Tunis in 1823,' *English Historical Review*, vol. 34 (1919), pp. 84–9.

Dawson, Frank Griffith, *The First Latin American Debt Crisis: The City of London and the 1822–25 Loan Bubble*, New Haven, Yale University Press, 1990.

Dickinson, H. T., ed., *Britain and the French Revolution, 1789–1815*, London, Macmillan, 1989.

Dictionary of Canadian Biography.

Dictionary of National Biography.

Dixon, C. Willis, *The Colonial Administration of Sir Thomas Maitland*, London, Frank Cass [1939], 1968.

Duhamel, Jean, *The Fifty Days: Napoleon in England*, trans. R. A. Hall, London, Rupert Hart–Davis, 1969.

Edgeworth, Maria, *Letters from England 1813–1844*, ed. Christina Colvin, Oxford, Oxford University Press, 1971.

Ehrman, John, *The Younger Pitt*, 3 vols., London, Constable, 1969, 1983 & 1996.

Eldridge, Herbert G., 'The Paper War Between England and America: The *Inchiquin* Episode, 1810–1815,' *Journal of American Studies*, vol. 16 (April 1982), pp. 49–68.

Ellenborough, Lord, *A Political Diary 1828–1830*, ed. Lord Colchester, 2 vols., London, Richard Bentley & Son, 1881.

Ellis, Geoffrey, *Napoleon's Continental Blockade: The Case of Alsace*, Oxford, Clarendon Press, 1981.

Ellis, Kenneth, *The Post Office in the Eighteenth Century*, London, Oxford University Press, 1958.

Emsley, Clive, *British Society and the French wars 1793–1815*, London, Macmillan, 1979.

Fabel, Robin F. A., 'The Laws of War in the 1812 Conflict,' *Journal of American Studies*, vol. 14 (August 1980), pp. 199–218.

Feiling, Keith Graham, *The Second Tory Party 1714–1832*, London, Macmillan, [1938], 1951.

Forsyth, William, *History of the Captivity of Napoleon at St. Helena; From the Letters and Journals of the Late Lieut.-Gen. Sir Hudson Lowe, and Official Documents Not Before Made Public*, 2 vols., New York, Harper & Brothers, [1853], 1855.

Fortescue, J. W., *The County Lieutenancies and the Army 1803–1814*, London, Macmillan, 1909.

Fortescue, J. W., *A History of the British Army*, 13 vols., London, Macmillan, 1899–1930.

Foss, Arthur, *The Ionian Islands: Zakynthos to Corfu*, London, Faber & Faber, 1969.

Francis, Mark, *Governors and Settlers: Images of Authority in the British Colonies, 1820–60*, London, Macmillan, 1992.

Frankel, Jeffrey A., 'The 1807–1809 Embargo Against Great Britain,' *Journal of Economic History*, vol. XLII (June 1982), pp. 291–307.

Fritz, Paul S., *The English Ministers and Jacobitism Between the Rebellions of 1715 and 1745*, Toronto, University of Toronto Press, 1975.

Fryman, Mildren L., *Charles Stuart and the 'Common Cause': The Anglo-Portuguese Alliance, 1810–1814* (Ph.D. thesis, Florida State University, 1974).

Galpin, W. Freeman, *The Grain Supply of England During the Napoleonic Period*, New York, Macmillan, 1925.

Gash, Norman, *Aristocracy and People: Britain 1815–1865*, London, Edward Arnold, 1979.

Gash, Norman, *Lord Liverpool: The Life and Political Career of Robert Banks Jenkinson Second Earl of Liverpool 1770–1828*, London. Weidenfeld & Nicolson, 1984.

Gash, Norman, *Mr. Secretary Peel: The Life of Sir Robert Peel to 1830*, London, Longmans, 1961.

Gash, Norman, *Sir Robert Peel: The Life of Sir Robert Peel after 1830*, Longmans, 1972.

Norman Gash. ed., *Wellington: Studies in the Military and Political Career of the First Duke of Wellington*, Manchester, Manchester University Press, 1990.

Gates, David, *The Spanish Ulcer: A History of the Peninsular War*, London, George Allen & Unwin, 1986.

Gentleman's Magazine.

Glover, Michael, *'A Very Slippery Fellow': The Life of Sir Robert Wilson 1777–1849*, Oxford, Oxford University Press, 1977.

Glover, Michael, *Britannia Sickens: Sir Arthur Wellesley and the Convention of Cintra*, London, Leo Cooper, 1970.

Glover, Michael, *The Peninsular War 1807–1814: A Concise Military History*, Newton Abbot, David & Charles, 1974.

Glover, Richard, 'Arms and the British Diplomat in the French Revolutionary Era,' *Journal of Modern History*, vol. 29 (September 1957), pp. 199–212.

Glover, Richard, *Peninsular Preparations: The Reform of the British Army 1795–1809*, Cambridge, Cambridge University Press, 1963.

Goldenberg, 'The Royal Navy's Blockade in New England Waters, 1812–1815,' *The International History Review*, vol. VI (August 1984), pp. 424–39.

Gordon, Hampden, *The War Office*, London, Putnam, 1935.

Gore, John, ed., *Creevey*, rev. ed., London, John Murray, 1948.

Graham, Gerald S., *Great Britain in the Indian Ocean: A Study of Maritime Enterprise 1810–1850*, Oxford, Clarendon Press, 1967.

Gray, Denis, *Spencer Perceval: The Evangelical Prime Minister 1762–1812*, Manchester, Manchester University Press, 1963.

Gregg, Edward, *Queen Anne*, London, Routledge & Kegan Paul, 1980.

Hall, Henry L., *The Colonial Office: A History*, London, Longmans Green, 1937.

Hall, Sir John, *Four Famous Mysteries*, London, Nisbet & Co., 1922.

Harcourt, Leveson Vernon, ed., *The Diaries and Correspondence of the Right Hon. George Rose*, 2 vols., London, Richard Bentley, 1860.

John Hardy, 'The Building and Decoration of Apsley House,' *Apollo*, September 1973, pp. 170–79.

Harlow, Vincent and Frederick Madden, eds., *British Colonial Developments, 1774–1834: Select Documents*, Oxford, Clarendon Press, 1953.

Harvey, A. D., *Britain in the Early Nineteenth Century*, London, Batsford, 1978.

Henning, Basil Duke, *The House of Commons 1660–1690*, 3 vols., London, Secker & Warburg, 1983.

Herries, Edward, *Memoirs of the Public Life of the Right Hon. John Charles Herries*, 2 vols., London, John Murray, 1880.

Hibbert, Christopher, *George IV: Regent and King*, New York, Harper & Row, 1973.

Hill, B. W., *British Parliamentary Parties 1742–1832: From the Fall of Walpole to the First Reform Act*, London, George Allen & Unwin, 1985.

Hilton. Boyd, *Corn, Cash, Commerce: The Economic Policies of the Tory Governments 1815–1830*, Oxford, Oxford University Press, 1977.

Hinde, Wendy, *Castlereagh*, London, Collins, 1981.

Hinde, Wendy, *George Canning* London, Collins, 1973.

Historical Records of Australia, Series I: Governors' Despatches to and from England, 26 vols., Sydney, Library Committee of the Commonwealth Parliament, 1914–25.

Horsman, Reginald, *The Causes of the War of 1812*, New York, Octagon Books, [1962], 1972.

Horward, Donald, 'British Seapower and its Influence Upon the Peninsular War (1808–1814)', *Naval War College Review*, vol. 31 (1978), pp. 55–71.

Howson, Gerald, *The Macaroni Parson: A Life of the Unfortunate Dr. Dodd*, London, Hutchinson, 1973.

Hughes, Robert, *The Fatal Shore: A History of the Transportation Convicts to Australia, 1787–1868*, London, Collins Harvill, 1987.

Hurwitz, Edith, *Politics and the Public Conscience: Slave Emancipation and the Abolitionist Movement in Britain*, London, Allen & Unwin, 1973.

Hussey, Christopher, *English Gardens and Landscapes 1700–1750*, London, Country Life, 1967.

Hyde, H. Montgomery, *The Strange Death of Lord Castlereagh*, London, Heinemann, 1959.

Ilchester, Countess of and Lord Stavordale, eds., *The Life and Letters of Lady Sarah Lennox 1745–1826*, 2 vols., London, John Murray, 1901.

Jarrett, Derek, *Pitt the Younger*, London, Weidenfeld & Nicolson, 1974.

Jenkins, Brian, *Henry Goulburn 1784–1856: A Political Biography*, Montreal: McGill-Queen's University Press, 1996.

Jennings, R. W., 'The Cirencester Contest and its Aftermath,' *Transactions of the Bristol and Gloucestershire Archeological Society*, vol. 92 (1973), pp. 157–68.

Johnson, Joan, *The Gloucestershire Gentry*, Gloucester, Alan Sutton, 1989.

Johnston, H. J. M., *British Emigration Policy 1815–1830: 'Shovelling Out Paupers'*, Oxford, Clarendon Press, 1972.

Jones, J. R., *Britain and the World 1649–1815*, London, Fontana, 1980.

Jupp, Peter, *Lord Grenville 1759–1834*, Oxford, Clarendon Press, 1985.

Klingberg, Frank J., *The Anti-Slavery Movement in England: A Study in English Humanitarianism*, New Haven, Yale University Press, 1976.

Knaplund, Paul, *James Stephen and the British Colonial System 1813–1847*, Madison, University of Wisconsin Press, 1953.

Knox, Bruce, 'British Policy and the Ionian Islands, 1847–1864: Nationalism and Imperial Administration,' *English Historical Review*, vol. 99 (July 1984), pp. 503–29.

Kreigel, Abraham D., ed., *The Holland House Diaries 1831–1840: The diary of Henry Richard Vassall Fox, third Lord Holland with extracts from the diary of Dr John Allen*, London, Routledge & Kegan Paul, 1977.

Langford, Paul, *A Polite and Commercial People: England 1727–1783*, Oxford, Clarendon Press, 1989.

Langford, Paul, *The Eighteenth Century 1688–1815*, London, Adam & Charles Black, 1976.

Lees-Milne, James, *Earls of Creation: Five Great Patrons of Eighteenth Century Art*, London, Hamish Hamilton, 1962.

Lewis, W.S. et. al., ed., *The Yale Edition of Horace Walpole's Correspondence*, 48 vols., New Haven, Yale University Press, 1937–1983.

Londonderrry, Marquess of, ed., *Correspondence, Despatches, and other Papers of Viscount Castlereagh*, 12 vols., London, John Murray, 1848–53.

Lucas, Colin, 'Great Britain and the Union of Norway and Sweden,' *Scandinavian Journal of History*, vol. 15 (1990), pp. 269–78.

Mackesey, Piers, 'Problems of an Amphibious Power: Britain against France, 1793–1815,' *Naval War College Review*, vol. 30 (Spring 1978), pp. 16–25.

McLachlan, N. D., 'Bathurst at the Colonial Office, 1812–27: A Reconnaissance,' *Historical Studies; Australia and New Zealand*, vol. 13 (1967–69), pp. 477–502.

Mack, Maynard, *Alexander Pope: A Life*, New Haven, Yale University Press, 1985.

Malmesbury, Third Earl of, ed., *Diaries and Correspondence of James Harris, First Earl of Malmesbury*, 2nd. ed., 4 vols., New York, AMS Press [1845], 1970.

Malmesbury, Earl of, ed., *A Series of Letters of the First Earl of Malmesbury, His Family and Friends from 1745 to 1820*, 2 vols., London, Richard Bentley, 1870.

Manning, Helen Taft, *British Colonial Government After the American Revolution*, Hampden, Connecticut, Archon Books, [1933] 1966.

Manning, Helen Taft, *The Revolt of French Canada 1800–1835: A Chapter in the History of the British Commonwealth*, Toronto, Macmillan, 1962.

Manning, Helen Taft, 'Who Ran the British Empire – 1830–1850?', *Journal of British Studies*, vol. 5 (1965), pp. 88–121.

Marcus, G. J., *The Age of Nelson*, London, George Allen & Unwin, 1971.

Marks, Harry J., *The First Contest for Singapore 1819–1824*, 'S Gravenhage, Marinus Nijhoff, 1959.

Marshall, P. J., *Problems of Empire: Britain and India 1757–1813*, London, George Allen & Unwin, 1968.

Marshall, P. J. et al., *India and Indonesia During the Ancien Regime*, Leiden, E. J. Brill, 1989.

Martin, Peter, *Pursuing Innocent Pleasures: The Gardening World of Alexander Pope*, Hampden, Connecicut, Archon Books, 1984.

Mellor, George R., *British Imperial Trusteeship 1783–1850*, London, Faber & Faber, 1951.

Melville, Lewis, ed., *The Huskisson Papers*, London, Constable, 1931.

Melvin, F. E., *Napoleon's Navigation System*, New York, AMS Press, [1919] 1970.

Metcalfe, G. E., *Maclean of the Gold Coast: The Life and Times of George Maclean, 1801–1847*, London, Oxford University Press, 1962.

Middleton, Charles R., *The Administration of British Foreign Policy 1782–1846*, Durham, Duke University Press, 1977.

Millar, Anthony Kenal, *Plantagenet in South Africa: Lord Charles Somerset*, Cape Town, Oxford University Press, 1965.

Moore, Thomas, *The Life and Death of Lord Edward Fitzgerald*, 2 vols., New York, J. & J. Hope, 1831.

Muir, Rory, *Britain and the Defeat of Napoleon 1807–1815*, New Haven, Yale University Press, 1996.

Murray, D. J., *The West Indies and the Development of Colonial Government 1801–1834*, Oxford, Clarendon Press, 1965.

Namier, Sir Lewis and John Brooke, *The House of Commons 1754–1790*, 3 vols., London, HMSO, 1964.

Newbury, C. W., *British Policy Towards West Africa: Select Documents 1786–1874*, Oxford, Clarendon Press, 1965.

O'Toole, G. J. A., *Honorable Treachery: A History of U.S. Intelligence, Espionage, and Covert Action from the American Revolution to the CIA*, New York, Atlantic Monthly Press, 1991.

Ouellet, Ferdnand, *Lower Canada 1791–1841*, trans. and adapted by Patricia Claxton, Toronto, McClelland & Stewart, 1980.

Padgett, Nancy Jo, *The Making of Military Policy in Early Victorian England, 1815–1827* (Ph.D. thesis, Stanford University, 1979).

Parker, Charles Stuart, ed., *Sir Robert Peel from his Private Papers*, 3 vols., New York, Kraus Reprint, [1891] 1970.

Peel, Sir Robert, *Memoirs*, 2 vols., New York, Krause Reprint, [1856–7], 1969.

Perkins, Bradford, *Castlereagh and Adams: England and the United States, 1812–1823*, Berkeley, University of California Press, 1964.

Perkins, Bradford, *Prologue to War: England and the United States 1805–1812*, Berkeley, University of California Press, [1961] 1974.

Phillips, C. H., *The East India Company 1784–1834*, Manchester, Manchester University Press [1940], 1961.

Porritt, Edward, *The Unreformed House of Commons: Parliamentary Representation before 1832*, vol. I: England and Wales, Cambridge, Cambridge University Press, 1903.

Pratt, Michael, *Britain's Greek Empire: Reflections on the history of the Ionian Islands from the fall of Byzantium*, London, Rex Collings, 1978.

Pugh, R. B., 'The Colonial Office,' *The Cambrige History of the British Empire*, vol. III, eds. E. A. Benians, Sir James Butler and C. E. Carrington, Cambridge, Cambridge University Press, 1959.

Quennell, Peter, ed., *The Private Letters of Princess Lieven to Prince Metternich 1820 to 1826*, London, John Murray, 1948.

Rae, Isobel, *The Strange Story of Dr James Barry: Army Surgeon, Inspector-General of Hospitals, Discovered on Death to be a Woman*, London, Longmans, Green, 1958.

Reese, M. M., *Goodwood's Oaks: The Life and Times of the Third Duke of Richmond, Lennox and Aubigny*, London, Threshold Books, 1987.

Reilly, Robin, *Pitt the Younger*, London, Cassell, 1978.

Report on the Manuscripts of B. Fortescue, Esq., Preserved at Dropmore, vol. IX, London, Historical Manuscripts Commission, 1912.

Report on the Manuscripts of Earl Bathurst, Preserved at Cirencester Park, London, Historical Manuscripts Commission, 1923.

Rodger, N. A. M., *The Admiralty*, Lavenham, Suffolk, Treence Dalton, 1979.

Rose, June, *The Perfect Gentleman: The remarkable life of Dr James Miranda Barry, the woman who served as an officer in the British Army from 1813 to 1859*, London, Hutchinson, 1977.

Rosebery, Lord, *Napoleon: The Last Phase*, London, Hodder & Stoughton [1900], 1922.

Roseveare, Henry, *The Treasury 1660–1870: The Foundations of Control*, London, George Allen & Unwin, 1973.

Ryan, A. N., 'Trade with the Enemy in the Scandinavian and Baltic Ports During the Napoleonic War: For and Against,' *Transactions of the Royal Historical Society*, 5th. series, vol. 12 (1962), pp. 123–40.

St Clair, William, *That Greece Might Still Be Free: The Philhellenes in the War of Independence*, London, Oxford University Press, 1972.

Sack, James J., *The Grenvillites: Party Politics and Factionalism in the Age of Pitt and Liverpool*, Urbana, Illinois, University of Illinois Press, 1979.

Sainty, J.C., *Admiralty Officials 1660–1870*, University of London, Insitute of Historical Research, 1975.

Sainty, J. C., *Colonial Office Officials 1794–1870*, University of London, Institute of Historical Research, 1976.

Sainty, J. C., *Officials of the Boards of Trade 1660–1870*, University of London, Institute of Historical Research, 1974.

Sainty, J. C., *Treasury Officials 1660–1870*, University of London, Institute of Historical Research, 1972.

Schroeder, Paul W., *The Transformation of European Politics 1763–1848*, Oxford, Clarendon Press, 1994.

Seaton, R. C., *Napoleon's Captivity in Relation to Sir Hudson Lowe*, London, George Bell & Sons, 1903.

Sedgwick, Romney, *The House of Commmons 1715–1754*, 2 vols., New York, Oxford University Press, 1970.

Semmel, Bernard, *Liberalism and Naval Strategy: Ideology, Interest, and Sea Power During the Pax Britannica*, London, Allen & Unwin, 1986.

Severn, John Kenneth, *A Wellesley Affair: Richard Marquess Wellesley and the Conduct of Anglo-Spanish Diplomacy, 1809–1812*, Tallahassee: University Presses of Florida, 1981.

Sherwig, John M., *Guineas and Gunpowder: British Foreign Aid in the Wars with France 1793–1815*, Cambridge, Harvard University Press, 1969.

Sichel, Walter, ed., *The Glenbervie Journals*, London, Constable, 1910.

Snelling, R. C. and T. J. Barron, 'The Colonial Office and its permanent officials 1801–1914,' Gillian Sutherland ed., *Studies in the Growth of Nineteenth Century Government*, London, Routledge & Kegan Paul, 1972.

Stagg, J. C. A., 'James Madison and the Coercion of Great Britain: Canada, the West Indies, and the War of 1812,' *William and Mary Quarterly*, 3rd. series, vol. 38 (1981), pp. 3–34.

Stanhope, Philip Henry, 5th. Earl, *Notes of Conversations with the Duke of Wellington 1831–1851*, 3rd. ed., London, John Murray, 1889.

Strachey, Lytton and Roger Fulford, eds., *The Greville Memoirs 1814–1860*, 8 vols., London, Macmillan, 1938.

Sutherland, L. S. and L. G. Mitchell, eds., *The History of the University of Oxford*, vol. V: *The Eighteenth Century*, Oxford, Clarendon Press, 1987.

Swinfen, D. B., *Imperial Control of Colonial Legislation 1813–1865*, Oxford, Clarendon Press, 1970.

Swinton, Mrs. R. J., *A Sketch of the Life of Georgina, Lady DeRos*, London, John Murray, 1893.

Tangeraas, Lars, 'Castlereagh, Bernadotte and Norway,' *Scandinavian Journal of History*, vol. 8 (1983), pp. 193–223.

Taylor, Ernest, ed., *The Taylor Papers: Being A Record of Certain Reminiscences, Letters and Journals in the Life of Lieut.-Gen. Sir Herbert Taylor*, London, Longmans, Green, 1913.

Taylor, Sir Henry, *Autobiography 1800–1875*, 2 vols., London, Longmans, Green, 1885.

Thistlethwaite, Mrs. [Tryphena], *Memoirs and Correspondence of Dr Henry Bathurst, Lord Bishop of Norwich*, London, Richard Bentley, 1853.

Thompson, Neville, *Wellington After Waterloo*, London, Routledge & Kegan Paul, 1986.

Thorne, R. G. ed., *The House of Commons 1790–1820*, 5 vols., London, Secker & Warburg, 1986.

Thornton, Michael John, *Napoleon After Waterloo: England and the St. Helena Decision*, Stanford, Stanford University Press, 1968.

Tillyard, Stella, *Aristocrats: Caroline, Emily, Louisa and Sarah Lennox 1740–1832*, London, Chatto & Windus, 1994.

Trulson, Sven G., *British and Swedish Policies and Strategies in the Baltic after the Peace of Tilsit in 1807*, Lund, CWK Gleerup, 1976.

Tumelty, J. J., *The Ionian Islands under British Administration, 1815–1864* (Ph.D. thesis, Cambridge University, 1953).

Turberville, A. S., *The House of Lords in the Age of Reform, 1784–1837*, London, Faber & Faber, 1958.

Twiss, Horace, *The Public and Private Life of Lord Chancellor Eldon With Selections From His Correspondence*, 2nd. ed., 3 vols., London, John Murray, 1844.

Valentine, Alan, *Lord North*, 2 vols., Norman, University of Oklahoma Press, 1967.

Victoria County History of Surrey, 4 vols., London, University of London, 1902–1912.

Walvin, James, *England, Slaves and Freedom, 1776–1838*, London, Macmillan, 1986.

Ward, John Manning, *Colonial Self-Goverment: The British Experience 1759–1856*, Toronto, University of Toronto Press, 1976.

Webster, C. K., *Britain and the Independence of Latin America, 1812–1830: Selected Documents from the Foreign Office Archives*, 2 vols., London, Oxford University Press, 1938.

Webster, Sir Charles, *The Foreign Policy of Castlereagh 1812–1815: Britain and the Reconstruction of Europe*, London, G. Bell & Sons, 1950.

Webster, Sir Charles, *Some Letters of the Duke of Wellington to his brother William Wellesley-Pole*, London, Camden Miscellany, vol. XVIII (Camden Society Third Series, vol. LXXIX), 1948.

Walpole, Sir Spencer, *A History of England from the Conclusion of the Great War in 1815*, rev. ed., 6 vols., London, Longmans, Green, 1913.

Wellesley Papers, The, by the editor of the Windham Papers, 2 vols., London, Herbert Jenkins, 1914.

Whitelaw, Marjory, *The Dalhousie Journals*, 3 vols., Toronto, Oberon Press, 1978–82.

Wellington, Duke of, *The Dispatches of Field Marshal the Duke of Wellington, 1799–1815*, ed. Col. John Gurwood, 12 vols, London, John Murray, 1835–38.

Wellington, 2nd. Duke of,ed., *Despatches, Correspondence,and Memoranda of Field Marshal Arthur, Duke of Wellington, K.G.*, 8 vols., London, John Murray, 1867–80.

Wellington, 2nd. Duke of, ed., *Supplementary Desptaches, Correspondence, and Memoranda of Field Marshal Arthur, Duke of Wellington, K.G.*, 15 vols., London, John Murray, 1858–72.

Willis, G. M., *Ernest Augustus, Duke of Cumberland and King of Hanover*, London, Arthur Barker, 1954.

Wilson, Monica and Leonard Thompson, eds., *The Oxford History of South Africa*, vol. I: *South Africa to 1870*, Oxford, Clarendon Press, 1969.

Woodhouse, C. M., *The Battle of Navarino*, London, Hodder & Stoughton, 1965.

Woodhouse, C. M., *Capodistria: The Founder of Greek Independence*, London, Oxford University Press, 1973.

Watson, J. Steven, *The Reign of George III 1760–1815*, Oxford, Clarendon Press, 1960.

Woodward, Sir Llewellyn, *The Age of Reform 1815–1870*, 2nd. ed., Oxford, Clarendon Press, [1938] 1962.

Woolgar, C. M. ed., *Wellington Studies*, I, University of Southampton: Hartley Institute, 1996.

Yonge, C. D., *The Life and Administration of Robert Banks, Second Earl of Liverpool, K.G.*, 3 vols., London, Macmillan, 1868.

Young, D. M., *The Colonial Office in the Early Nineteenth Century*, London, Longmans, 1961.

INDEX

B = Bathurst **Bn = Baron** **V = Viscount**
E = Earl **M = Marquess** **D = Duke**

Aberdeen, 4th E of, 150–1, 236, 248, 252.
Adam, Sir Frederick, High Commissioner, Ionian Islands, 153–4.
Addington, Henry, see Sidmouth.
Adelaide, Queen, 242.
Admiralty, B a civil lord, 1783–9, 12–14.
Africa, W equitorial, 166–70.
Algiers, 61, 129–4, 153.
Anglesey, 1st Marquess of (E of Uxbridge to 1815), Waterloo, 93–4, 98; 99; in Canning's ministry, 222–3, 226; dismissed as Ld Lt of Ireland, 237–8.
Anne, Queen, friend of Bathurst and Apsley families, 2; Cirencester statue, 5.
Apsley, Lord, see 2nd, 3rd, 4th E Bathurst.
Apsley House, 1, 7–8, 30.
Arbuthnot, Charles, 97, 114, 136, 144, 146, 225, 235.
Arbuthnot, Harriet, 143, 145, 152; estimation of B, 155–6; 226; death, 257–8.
Australia, vii, 116, 154, 157, 166, 186, 188–95, 207, 208–9, 246.
Austria, 1809 revolt, 36, 40; 67;

Bank of England, specie exports, 59–60.
Bankes, Henry, 211.
Barbados, 117, 119–20, 164; Bp of, 179–80.
Barry, Dr James, and Lord Charles Somerset, 197–8, 199, 204–6, 207, 209.
Bathurst, Allen, 1st E, Tory career, Cirencester house & park 2–5, 9.
Bathurst, Apsley, B's brother, 20, 111.
Bathurst, Benjamin, envoy to Austria, 1809, 36; mysterious death, 41–2.
Bathurst, Rev Charles, B's son, marriage & preferment, 242–3; 258.
Bathurst, Emily, B's daughter, marries F. Ponsonby, 213.

Bathurst, Georgina, Countess, marries B, 1789, 14–15; delicate health, 23; 78, 108, 112, 213, 218–19, 222, 227, 242, 256.
Bathurst, Lady Georgina, B's daughter, 133, 222; on Catholic emancipation, 240; 243; parliamentary reform, 249, 251, 254; 256.
Bathurst, Henry, 2nd E, character, 3, 8–9; burns father's papers, 3; early career, 5; Judge & marriages, 1754–71, 5–6; Ld Chancellor (Apsley to 1775), 1770–8, 6–7; Ld President 1779–82, 7–8; builds Apsley House, 7–8; and George III, 8; wants B to join Fox–North ministry, 11; supports Pitt, 12; death, 16.
Bathurst, Henry, 3rd E (Ld Apsley, 1775–94), epitome, vii–x; characterizations and opinions of: Maria Edgeworth, ix; Goulburn, 53–4; George IV, 139–40; C Greville, 54, 258; H Taylor, Ld Holland & Ld Rosebery, 258–60; birth and ancestry, 1–2; childhood, Eton and Oxford, 9–10; completes Cirencester house, 4; Teller of Treasury, 1790, 8, 15, 111; friend of Wellesley and Grenville, 9; visits France and Germany, 10–11; on Fox–North ministry, 11; MP for Cirencester, 1782–94, 11; Civil Ld of Admiralty, 1782–89, 12–14; betrothal to Miss Copley and her death, 14; marriage to Georgina Lennox, 1789, 14–15; jr Ld of Treasury, 1789–91, 15–16; member of Board of Control, 1793–1801, 16; succeeds as 3rd E, 1794, 16; death of infant son Peter, 16–17; maiden speech in Lords, 1796, 17; declines Madras, 17; corresponds with Wellesley in India & Camden in Ireland, 18; commander of Glos provisional

Bathurst, Henry, 3rd E (Ld Apsley, 1775–94)
(*continued*)
cavalry, 1798, 18–19; investigates E of
Berkeley's marriage, 19; resigns with Pitt,
1801, 20; Clerk of Crown in Chancery,
1800, 20; lends money to Pitt, 20;
disagrees with Pitt over Treaty of Amiens,
21; and Addington ministry, 21–2; tries to
reconcile Grenville and Pitt, 22; Master of
Mint, 1804–6, 22–3; Pitt's failing health
and death, 23–45; refuses office under
Grenville, 24–5; and Ministry of All
Talents, 25–6; President of Board of Trade
& Master of Mint, 1807–12, 27–9; sells
Apsley House to Wellesley, 30; Orders in
Council, 31–2; and Heligoland pilots, 33;
on Convention of Cintra, 34; breach with
Grenville, 30, 35; on D of York's
resignation as Commander in Chief, 35;
Benjamin Bathurst's mission to Austria &
death, 36, 41–2; Canning's scheme to
replace Castlereagh with Wellesley, 36–8;
Wellesley's embassy to Spain, 36–7;
Walcheren campaign, 37; Foreign
Secretary, 1809, 38–41, 43; explains
Wellesley's KG to Richmond, 39; supports
Grenville for Chancellor of Oxford, 38–9;
Wellesley as Foreign Secretary, 42; on
George III's insanity, 44–5; helps Regent
with imports, 45; defends government
loans to merchants, 1811, 45; Wellesley
attempts to become Prime Minister end of
friendship, 46, 48; defends Orders in
Council, 1812, 47; Sec of State for War
and Colonies, 49–50, 51–4; relationship
with Wellington, 55–6; provides specie to
Wellington, 56–7, 59–60; Salamanca,
57–8; horses and food for Peninsula, 60–1;
food from US & Barbary states, 60–1; war
with U S and defence of Canada, 62–3,
67–8, 78–81; treaty of Ghent, 82–4;
Napoleon's invasion of Russia, 63–4;
Wellington's retreat to Portugal, 1812,
64–5; defends Peninsular policy against
Wellesley, 65; Vitoria, 67; missing
battering train, 68; Wellington's
complaints of navy, 68; sack of San
Sebastian, 68–9; praises Wellington's
advance into France, 69; sends Bunbury to
soothe Wellington, 69–70; Pr of Orange's
betrothal to Pss Charlotte, 70–1, 77–1;
acting Foreign Secretary, 1814–15, 72, 76,
81, 107; peace terms with Napoleon,
1814, 72–3; Bourbon restoration, 73–4;
congratulates Wellington on end of war,
74; DCL, Oxford, 77; transfer of Norway
to Sweden, 1814, 84–5; Lord Herbert's
Sicilian marriage, 85–6; secret alliance with
France and Austria, 87–8; Waterloo
campaign, 89–99; Napoleon's capture and
exile to St Helena, 99–105; D of
Cumberland's marriage, 108; army & Col
Office reductions, 109–111, 126; KG,
1817, 112; receives Lawrence portrait from
Wellington & porcelain from K of Prussia,
113; death of Pss Charlotte, 113–14;
administration of Col Office, 114–20; D of
Richmond as Gov Gen of Canada, 120–4;
acting Foreign Sec & Congress of
Aix–la–Chapelle, 1818, 124–5; overture to
Grenville, 127; 1816 expedition vs Barbary
pirates, 129; acquisition & administration
of Ionian Islands, 128–9, 129–34; Q
Caroline's trial & funeral, 135–8; death of
Napoleon and Lowe's grievances, 138–9;
reconciliation with Grenville, 140;
Wellesley as Ld Lt of Ireland, 140–1; 1821
Col Office salary cuts, 141; Castlereagh's
suicide, 1822, 142; conflict with Canning's
as Foreign Secretary, 142–7 Catholic
question, 1825, 148–9; Greek revolt &
Ionian Islands, 150–4; 1823 expedition vs
Barbary slavery, 153; close relations with
Wellington after 1822, 155–6; Bps Stanser
& Mountain, 159; Col Office expansion,
1822–5, 160; relations with Hay, 160–1;
administrative style & habits, 1820s, 161–6;
and equitorial Africa, 166–70; slavery
amelioration, 170–82; dispute over
customs fees, 182–5; emigration, 186–8;
Australia, 188–95; Cape Colony, 195–210;
1826 Cambridge election, 212; state of
Greek revolt, 1825–6, 212–14; opposes
lowering corn duties, 1826–8, 215, 220;
troops to Portugal, 1826, 216–18; appoints
Ponsonby Lt Gov of Malta, 218; death of
D of York, Wellington Commander in
Chief, 1827, 218–19; Liverpool's stroke, B
possible successor, 219–21; Canning tries
to keep, resigns, 221–3; farewell to Col
Off, 223–4; defends resignation, 224;
appalled at Treaty of London, 225; on
Canning's death & Goderich as Prime
Minister, 225; on Wellington's return as
Commander in Chief, 225–6; advises Hay,
225–6; concerns about D of Clarence as
Ld High Admiral, 226; visits Scotland &
Ld Grey, 227–8; Navarino, 227–8, 241;

advises Wilmot–Horton on political career, 228; Ld Pres in Wellington's ministry, 1828–30, 229–31; disputes with Canningites over Greece & corn laws, 231–3; Catholic emancipation, 234–5, 237–40; dimissal of D of Clarence, 235–6; Ponsonby's knighthood, 237; dimissal of Anglesey, 237–8; refuses Ld Lieutenancy of Ireland, 238; marriage of Seymour B, 241; death of George IV, accession & favour of William IV, 242; marriage & preferment of Rev Charles B, 242–3; end of Wellington's ministry, William B Joint Clerk of Privy Council, 244–5; agricultural unrest in Glouestershire, 1830, 246; opposes parliamentary reform, 1831–2, 247–54; Belgian revolt, 248; approves Wellington's opposition to reforms, 254; death of Grenville, 254–5; supports Wellington as Chancellor of Oxford, 255; death, 256–7; funeral, 257–8.

Bathurst, Rev Henry, Bp of Norwich, tutor & friend of B to 1805, 9–10; 14; 36; hopes for promotion, 1829, 240.

Bathurst, Henry George, 4th E, ix; Paris, 1814, 75–6; Congress of Vienna, 42, 84, 86–8; Waterloo, 91, 94, 98; Paris, 1815, 106–7; 243, 254; father's death & funeral, 256–8.

Bathurst, Peter George, B's son, death at age 3, 16–17.

Bathurst, Seymour, B's son, ix; visits Wellington, 1814, 70; Bordeaux, 1814, 76; Waterloo, 91, 94, 98–9, 118; Paris, 1815, 100, 106; agent for Malta, 137; marriage, 241; 247; death, 241, 256; funeral with father, 257–8.

Bathurst, William Lennox, 5th E, to Spain with Wellesley, 36–7; sees Napoleon at Plymouth, 101–3; father's deputy at Exchequer & lawyer 111; 243; Joint Clerk of Privy Council, 244–5, 254; 258.

Bayham, V, see Camden.

Beaufort, 3rd D of, 4; 6th D, 39–40; 196.

Belgium, annexed by Holland, 76–7; 1830 revolt, 242–3, 248.

Berbice, 177.

Berkeley, 5th E of, disputed marriage, 19–20.

Berkeley, Admiral Sir George, and E of Berkeley's supposed marriage, 19–20; Chesapeake affair, 30–1; Lisbon, 31, 37, 44; 94.

Bermuda, 157.

Bexley, Bn, see Vansisttart.

Bigge, J T, Australian inquiry, 189–90; Cape inquiry, 203–7, 209.

Bird, Christopher, 200–1, 204–6.

Birmingham, 233.

Board of Control for India, B a member, 1793–1801, 16, 18; 125–6.

Board of Trade, composition and function, 27–8.

Brisbane, Sir Thomas, Gov of N S Wales, 191–4.

Brock, Sir Isaac, and war of 1812, 62.

Brougham, Henry (1st Bn, 1830), 209, 249.

Brownrigg, Sir Robert, Gov of Ceylon, 117–18; 120.

Buckingham, 1st D, 142, 220.

Bunbury, Col (Sir, 1815) Henry, Military Under–Secretary, 1809–16, 53, 55; on fall of Detroit, 62–3; mission to Wellington, 1814, 70, 73; opposes New Orleans expedition, 81, 92; 101; interview with Napoleon, 1815, 101–2; 105; post abolished, 1816, 111; 128; 130; punished for supporting Q Caroline, 136–7.

Buxton, Thomas Fowell, and slavery abolition, 171–2, 174.

Camden, 1st M (V Bayham 1786–94, E Camden, 1794–1812), friend of B, 15, 17; Ld Lt of Ireland, 18; critical of Pitt, 21–2; 25; Ld Pres of Council, 29, 38; 52; 112; 120.

Campbell, Sir Neil, 115; Gov of W Africa, 169.

Canada, vii; war of 1812, 61–3, 67–8, 78–81; 107, 116, 119, 120–3; defence, 155–6; 157–8, 163–5; customs officers, 183–5; 186–8, 210.

Canning, George, viii–x, 15; Foreign Secretary 1807–9, 29, 33–5, 36–7, 41; 46–7; Pres, Bd of Control, 1817–21, 124, 135; 140–1; Foreign Secretary, 1822–7, & cabinet division, 142–6; independence of Spanish & Portuguese colonies, 146; Catholic emancipation, 147–9; Greek revolt, 152; 160, 162, 164, 169, 214, 224–5; slavery, 172, 174, 176; 185, 216, 219; Prime Minister, 1827, 210, 220–4; tries to keep B, 221–3; Treaty of London, 224–5; death, 225; 227.

Canning, Stratford, 227.

Cape Coast Castle, 168–9.

Cape Colony (Cape of Good Hope), 21, 116, 119–20, 139, 154, 170, 186, 195–210.

Capodistria, Count John, and Ionian Islands, 127–8, 132–3, 153.
Caroline, Queen , 70, 77; divorce trial and death, 135–7, 199, 206; 249.
Castlereagh, V (M of Londonderry, 1821), ix–x; in Portland ministry, 29, 32, 34 36, 37–38; 46; Foreign Secretary, 1812–22, 46, 49; 52; at allied headquarters, 1814, 71–3; peace conferences, 1814–15, 75–6, 81–3, 85–8, 97, 107; 109–10, 112, 116, 124–5, 128, 132–3, 137; suicide, 141–2; 143, 146–7, 152, 171, 180; 189, 260.
Catholic Emancipation, 1827–8, viii, 234–5, 237–40, 244.
Ceylon, 116–20, 130, 157, 187, 202–3.
Chamberlain, Joseph, vii.
Charlotte, Princess, and Pr of Orange, 70–1, 77–8; death, 113–14; 248.
Chatham, 2nd. E of, 13–14, 24, 37.
Chesapeake affair, 1807, 30–1.
Cintra, Convention of, 34.
Cirencester, Bathurst family settled there, 2; house and park 4–5; elections, 11; 19; loses 1 seat in 1832, 254; B's funeral, 257–8.
Clarence, D of, see William IV.
Clinton, Sir William, 217.
Codrington, Admiral Sir Edward, Navarino & recall, 228.
Colebrooke, William, Cape inquiry, 203–7, 209.
Cole, Sir Lowry, Gov of Mauritius, 155.
Colonial Office, see War and Colonies.
Combermere, Lord, 99; Gov of Barbados, 119–20;
Continental System, 31–3, 45, 128.
Copley, Sir John, see Lyndhurst.
Convicts, transportation to Australia, 188–9, 194–5.
Corn Laws, suspended, 1826, 214; amendment of, 1827–8, 215, 224, 232.
Cornwallis, 2nd E, 17–18.
Cumberland, D of, marriage, 108–9; 112, 114, 233; opposes Catholic emancipation, 240.
Dalhousie, 9th E of, Lt Gov of Nova Scotia, 121; Gov Gen of Canada, 123–4, 163, 165, 210.
Darling, Sir Ralph, Gov of N S Wales, 194.
Demerara, 117, 174–5, 177.
Denmark, 33, 83.
D'Escury, Charles, 200, 203–4.
Dodd, Rev William, 6.
Donkin: Sir Rufane, dispute with Ld C Somerset, 199–201, 203.

Douglass, Dr H G, 192.
Dudley, 1st E of, 231, 233.
Dundas, Henry (1st V Melville, 1802), Pres, Bd of Control, 16, 18; Sec of State for War, 19, 52; 24.

East India Company, 11, 16, 18, 125–6.
East Retford, 233.
Edgeworth, Maria, novelist, 159; characterization of B, ix.
Edwards, William (Kay), 206–8.
Eldon, 1st Earl of, Lord Chancellor, 1801–6, 1807–27, 29, 39–40, 72; custody of Napoleon, 103; 112, 114; Ionian constitution, 131; 138, 162, 222, 233; denounces Catholic emancipation, 239; 260.
Ellenborough, 2nd Bn, 249, 252.
Emigration, 186–8, 198–9.
Exmouth, Admiral, 5th V, 129, 153.

Fernando Po, 169–70.
Felton, W. B., 164–5.
Fitzgerald, Ld Edward, 14–15.
Fitzgerald, Vesey, 234–5.
Fox, Charles James, 8, 11, 15, 22–3, 24–5.
Frederick, Prince of Wales (d. 1751), 3, 5.

George, Prince of Wales and Pr Regent, see George IV.
George I, 2.
George II, 3.
George III, friend of Bathursts, viii, 3, 17, 8; 11–12, 17, 14; Pitt's resignation, 1801, 20; Pitt second ministry, 1804–6, 22–4; Ministry of All Talents, 24–5; Portland ministry, 1807–9, 27, 38, 40–1; thanks B for serving as Foreign Secretary, 43; mental incapacity & regency, 44–5; death, 127.
George IV, 11; assumes Regency, 44–6; and Ld Wellesley, 46–8; 53, 57–8, 67; Pss Charlotte's betrothal to Pr of Orange, 70–1, & her death, 113–14; 73–4, 77, 97; D of Cumberland's marriage, 108; B's Garter, 112; becomes K, 127; 131; Q Caroline's trial & funeral, 135–8, opinion of Liverpool ministry and B, 138–9, 145–6; Canning as Foreign Secretary, 142, 147; 218; Liverpool's stroke, 219; Canning Prime Minister, 221–2; Goderich Prime Minister, 225, 226, 228; Navarino, 228; Wellington Prime Minister, 229; Catholic emancipation, 235, 238, 240; 236; death, 242; 244.
Goderich, 1st V, see Robinson.

Gordon, Adam, Chief Clerk, War & Cols, 223.

Gordon, Lord George, 1780 riots, 7.

Goulburn, Frederick, 192–3.

Goulburn, Henry, Col Under–Secretary, 1812–21, estimation of Bathurst, 53–4; 69; Ghent treaty negotiations, 79, 82–3; 97, 101; post–war reductions, 110–11; administration of Office, 114–16, 122; Ionian Islands, 134; 137; Irish Sec, 140–1; slavery, 171; 192, 198; Cambridge election, 1826, 211–12.

Greece, revolt, 1821–30, 150–3, 212–14, 224–5; Navarino, 227–8, 231–2, 241.

Grenville, William, 1st Bn, 1790, friend of B, viii, x, 9, 14, 12, 17; critical of Pitt, 21; allies with Fox, 22–4; Prime Minister, 1806–7, 24–6; 29; breach with B, 35; 38, Chancellor of Oxford, 39–40; 48, 51; supports Liverpool govt, 127; 136; reconciliation with B, 140; 171, 250; death & B's tribute, 254–5.

Greville, Charles, B's private secretary, 1812–21, estimation of B, 53–4, 258; 111, 196; on Canning ministry, 222; Clerk of Privy Council, 230; Catholic emancipation, 239; William B as colleague, 244–5.

Grey, 2nd E, 38, 48, 94; and B, 1827, 227–8; 240; attacks Wellington's govt, 243–4; Prime Minister, 1830–4, 244–5; parliamentary reform, 246–53; retires, 257.

Grosvenor, 2nd E, 245.

Halford, Sir Henry, 256.

Hamilton, Achdeacon Anthony, Chaplain General for Colonies, 159.

Hardinge, General Henry, 253.

Harrowby, 1st E, 29, 53, 59, 72, 88, 91, 97, 140; 164; in Canning's ministry, 222; moderate on parliamentary reform, 249–50, 252.

Hastings, 1st M of (E of Moira to 1817), 46; Gov Gen of India, 125; Gov of Malta, 154, 164; death, 218.

Hay, Robert W: Colonial Under–Secretary, 1825–36, relations with B, 160–1; 164–5, 169, 186, 213, 218; B protects appointment, 223; advice from B, 225; 227, 236; dismissed, 236.

Heligoland, 33, 44, 115.

Herbert, Lord, Sicilian marriage, 85–6.

Holland, 69; proposed dynastic link, 70–1, 77–8; annexes Belgium, 76–7; Singapore, 125–6; Cape Colony, 196; revolt of Belgium, 242.

Holland, 3rd Bn, Napoleon's captivity, 103–4; opinion of B, 259.

Holland, Lady, and Napoleon, 138–9.

Howley, William, Archbishop of Canterbury, 256–7.

Huskisson, William, Pres of Board of Trade, 1823–7, 142–5; customs officers' fees, 182, 185; on col govs, 194; 220; Col Sec, 1827–8, 225–6, 230–1; resigns, 233; 236; killed by train, 243.

Ionian Islands, British protectorate, 127–4; and Greek revolt, 150–4; 213.

Ireland, 1798 rebellion, 15, 18; union with Britain, 20; 120, 140, 147–8; 1826 drought, 214; 232; Catholic emancipation, 1828–9, 234–5, 237–41.

Jamaica, 117, 174, 180–3.

Jenner, Dr Edward, 16–17.

Kempt, Sir James, Lt Gov of Nova Scotia, 124.

Lamb, Frederick, 217.

Lamb, William, see Melbourne.

Lansdowne, 3rd M, 187, 245.

Lawrence, Sir Thomas, artist, Wellington commissions equestrian portrait for B, 1818, 112–13; George IV commissions portrait of B for Windsor Castle, 139–40.

Lennox, Ld George, Lady B's father, 14.

Lennox, Georgina, see Bathurst, Countess.

Lennox, Georgina, daughter of D of Richmond, Waterloo letters, 95, 98; 123.

Lennox, Lady Mary, sister of Countess B, 247–8.

Lennox, Lady Sarah, aunt of Lady B, 14, 53.

Leopold, Prince, marriage to Pss Charlotte, 78, 114; K of Belgians, 1831, 248.

Liverpool, 2nd E, (Robert Banks Jenkinson, Ld Hawkesbury, 1796–1808), viii, x, 16, 29, 32; Prime Minister, 1812–27, 48–9; 52, 55, 58, 69; Treaty of Ghent, 82–3; transfer of Norway, 84; Congress of Vienna, 87–8; 91, 107, 109, 112, 114, 124, 126; Q Caroline's trial and funeral, 135–8; 140; Canning as Foreign Secretary, 142–7; Catholic question, 1825, 147–9; Col Office expansion, 160; 162; slavery, 175–6; 180, 182, 215; Wellington as Commander in Chief, 219; stroke & resignation, 219–20; 227; death, 231, 236–7; 257, 260.

Londonderry, 3rd E (Sir Charles Stewart to 1822), 73; Congress of Vienna, 87; 142.
Lonsdale, 1st E, 120, 232.
Louis XVIII, King of France, 73–4, 89–90, 99–100, 107, 128, 144.
Lowe, Sir Hudson, Gov of St Helena, 101, 103–4; grievances, 139.
Lyndhurst, 1st Bn (Sir John Copley to 1827), 211–12; Ld. Chancellor in Canning ministry, 222–3, 229; in Wellington's, 235; first reform bill, 251–2.

Macarthy, Sir Charles, Gov of W Africa, 167.
Macquarie, Lachlan, Gov of N S Wales, 117, 189–91, 193.
Maitland, Sir Peregine, Lt Gov of Upper Canada, 118–19, 121–3.
Maitland, Sir Thomas, Gov of Malta, High Commissioner, Ionian Islands, 129–34, 151–4.
Malmesbury, 1st E, admires B, 22, 43.
Malta: 116, Maitland's administration, 129–30; 154, 164, 218.
Manchester, 5th D, Gov of Jamaica, 180–2.
Mauritius, 157, 165–6, 170, 198, 202–3, 208.
Melbourne, 2nd V (William Lamb to 1828) 233, 246; Prime Minister, 257.
Melville, 2nd V: First Ld of Admiralty, 53, 72, 124, 138, 142, 152, 236.
Mills, George, 43.
Moira, 2nd E of, see Hastings, M.
Moodie, Major Thomas, home sec to commissions of enquiry, Col Off, 158, 184.
Moore, Sir John, death at Corunna, 34–5.
Morocco, 61, 129.
Mountain, Jacob, Bishop of Quebec, 159.
Mulgrave, 1st E, Master General of Ordnance, 53, 60, 92, 126.
Murray, Sir George, in Canada, 1814–15, 80–1, 89–90, 93, 191; Col. Sec., 1828–30, 236; 253.

Napier, Lady Sarah, see Lennox.
Napoleon (Bonaparte) I, Emperor, x; Continental System, 31–2, 44, 45; Tilsit, 33; Portugal & Spain, 33–4; Austrian revolt, 1809, 37, 40; and Benjamin Bathurst, 41–2; 47; invasion of Russia, 63–4; Leipzig, 67; 1814 abdication, 72–3; on Wellington, 76; returns, 89–90; Waterloo, 93–6; 1815 abdication & St. Helena, 99–105, 106–7, 111; 128; 130; death, 138–9; 259.
Navarino, 1827, 227–9, 231–2.

New Brunswick, 159, 203.
Newcastle, 4th D of, 119–20, 198.
Newfoundland, 28, 76, 157.
New South Wales, see Australia.
North, Lord, Prime Minister, 6, 8, 11.
Northumberland, 3rd D of, 238.
Norway, transferred from Denmark to Sweden, 84–5.
Nova Scotia, 30, 119, 121, 123–4, 159.

O'Connell, Daniel, 234–5.
Orange, William, Hereditary Prince, 69–70; betrothal to Pss Charlotte, 70–1, 77–8; 89.
Orders in Council, regulating shipping to Napoleonic Europe, 1807–12, 29, 32–33, 47, 49.
Ottoman Empire, Greek revolt against, 150–3, 212–14, 224–5; Navarino, 227–8, 231–2; 234, 241.
Oxford University, 2, 5, 9–10, 36; Grenville Chancellor, 39–40, 77; Wellington Chancellor, 255–6.

Palmerston, 3rd V, 13; 1826 Cambridge election, 211–12; 218, 231; reigns, 233; rejects Wellington's overture, 243.
Parliamentary reform, 233, 240, 243–4; reform bill, 1831–2, 246–54.
Peel (Sir 1830) Robert, 53; Home Secretary, 1821–7, 140, 142; opposes Catholic emancipation, 1825, 148–9; 162, 175, 188, 192; convict transportation, 194–5; 221–2, 229; Home Secretary, 1828–30, 232; Catholic emancipation, 235, 238; 253–5, 257.
Pembroke, 11th Earl of, son's Sicilian marriage, 84–5.
Penryn, 233.
Perceval, Dudley, 209.
Perceval, Spencer, Chancellor of Exchequer, 1807–9, 29, 32; Prime Minister, 1809–12, 38–9, 45–6; assassination, 47; 53, 209.
Percy, Major Henry, 95–6.
Peterloo, 126–7, 198, 206.
Pieneman, Jan Wilhelm, painting of Waterloo, sketch given to B by Wellington, 156.
Pitt, Joseph, investigates Berkeley marriage, 19–20.
Pitt, William, Prime Minister, 1783–1801, viii, ix–x, 12–13, 15–16, 18; resigns, 20; and Addington, 21–2; Prime Minister, 1804–6, 22–3; death, 24; 38–9, 51, 145, 196, 239, 254, 257.
Plumptre, Rev John, 9.
Ponsonby, Frederick (Sir), 98; marries Emily

B, posted to Ionian islands, 213; Lt Gov of Malta, 218; knighthoods, 237.

Pope, Alexander, 3–4.

Portland, 3rd D of, 11, 25; Prime Minister, 1807–9, 27, 38; death, 39; 52, 53–4, 180, 255.

Portugal, 30, 1808 revolt, 33; 44, 59, 64–6, 93, 144, 214; independence of colonies, viii, 146–7; 169; British troops to defend, 1826–8, 216–18, 234; 244.

Prevost, Sir George, Gov Gen of Canada, war of 1812 and recall, 79–81, 123; 159.

Privy Council, duties of, 28–9; & B Ld Pres of, 230–1; 54.

Raffles, Sir Stamford, 125.

Reeves, John, 28.

Richmond, 4th D of, Ld Lt of Ireland, 1807–13, 30, 39, 44, 48; 77, 80; Waterloo, 91, 94–6; 118–19; Gov Gen of Canada, 1818–19, & death, 120–3; 219.

Richmond, 5th. D of, opposes Catholic emancipation & Wellington's govt, 240–1, 243; in Grey's ministry, 244, 247, 252; resigns, 257.

Robinson, Frederick (1st. V Goderich, 1827), viii, Chancellor of Exchequer, 1823–7, 143, 144–5; 160; and customs officers, 182; 185, 215; Col Sec, 1827, 210, 222–3; Prime Minister, 1827, 225–7; reigns, 228–9.

Rose, George, 15; Vice–Pres., Bd of Trade, 1807–12, 28, 37–9, 48.

Rosebery, 5th. E of, low opinion of B, 259–60.

Rothschild, Nathan, 70, 97.

Russell, Lord John, 247, 254.

St Lucia, 171, 177.

Sewell, Jonathan, 165.

Sherbrooke, Sir John, Gov Gen of Canada, 1816–1818, 121.

Sidmouth, 1st. V (Henry Addington to 1804), viii; Prime Minister, 1801–4, 20–2; 23, 25, 47; 52; Home Sec, 1812–21, 107–8, 114, 116, 124, 137, 140, 189, 260.

Sierra Leone, 156, 167, 169, 171.

Singapore, British acquisition, 125–6; 166.

Slavery, 26, 76; Barbary States, 129, 153; 156–7, 160; 167–8; amelioration, viii, 170–82; Cape Colony, 196, 202, 204.

Smirke, Sir Robert, 4, 23.

Sneyd, Ralph, friend of Georgina B, 249.

Somerset, Henry, son of Ld Charles, 199.

Somerset, Lord Charles, Gov of Cape Colony, 1813–27, 120, 195–210.

Somerset, Lord Fitzroy, 98, 120, 144, 196, 198.

Spain, 1808 revolt, 33; Moore's retreat, 34–5; Talavera, 36; Ld Wellesley's embassy, 36–7; Ciudad Rodrigo, 47: Badajoz, 49; Salamanca, 49, 57; Madrid, 58–9, 64; Wellington army commander, 59; Vitoria, 66–7; San Sebastian, 68–9; Pamplona, 69; 144; independence of colonies, viii, 146–7; Fernando Po, 169–70; 216–17.

Stanser, Robert, Bishop of Nova Scotia, 159.

Stephen, James, 116; Colonial Office counsel, 157–8; 161; praises B's slavery efforts, 181; and customs officers, 183; B's appreciation, 1827, 223; 236.

Stewart, Sir Charles (Lord), see Londonderry.

Sweden, 32; acquires Norway from Denmark, 66, 84–5.

Taylor, Henry, Snr Clerk for West Indies, 158; 161; high regard for B, 258–9.

Test & Corporations acts, repeal, 1828, 232–3.

Trafalgar, 23.

Treasury, 15–16; and customs fees, 182–5.

Trinidad, 164, 171, 177, 181, 189, 202.

Tripoli, 61, 129.

Tunis, 61, 129, 152.

Turner, Charles, Gov of W Africa, 168.

United States, revolution, 6–7, 12; Chesapeake affair, 30–1; and Orders in Council, 33, 45, 47, 49; war of 1812, 49, 61–3, 67–8; 78–81; Peninsula food supplies, 60–1; Treaty of Ghent, 79, 82–3; 184, 187.

Uxbridge, E of, see Anglesey.

Vansittart, Nicholas (1st Bn Bexley, 1823), 107, 124, 221, 222–3.

Victoria, Queen, birth, 114.

Vienna, Congress of, 77, 86–8, 128.

Walcheren expedition, 1809, 37–8.

Walpole, Horace, on 2nd E B, 3, 8–9.

Walpole, Sir Robert, 3, 5, 156.

War and Colonies Office, structure & B's administration, vii, x, 52–4; 'sink of papers', 67; post–war reduction & patronage, 110–20; 1822 salary cuts, 141; increases authority, 156–7; reoganization & expansion, 1822–25, 157–60; customs dispute with Treasury, 182–5; 231.

Wellesley, (Sir) Arthur, see Wellington.

Wellesley, Henry, 29, 76.

Wellesley, Richard, 1st. M (2nd E of Mornington, 1781–99), friend of B, x, 9, 14; at Treasury, 15–16; Bd of Control, 16; Gov–Gen of India, 17–18; returns, 24;

Wellesley, Richard, 1st. M (2nd E of Mornington, 1781–99) (*continued*) declines Foreign Office, 1807, 29; buys Apsley House, sells to Wellington, 1817, 30; ambassador to Spain, 36–7; Foreign Secretary, 1809–12, 38–40, 43, 45–6; tries to become Prime Minister, forced to resign & break with B, 46, 48; 51; 55; 57–8; denounces government on Peninsula, 65; 67, 91; Waterloo campaign, 94, 97; 125; Ld Lt of Ireland, 140–1.

Wellesley–Pole, William, 29; refuses War Department and joins opposition, 1812, 49, 53, 55; Master of Mint, 1814–23, 91, 98, 107–8.

Wellington, 1st D of, viii–x; Apsley House, 7–8; 18, 30; Irish Secretary, 29–30; expedition to Portugal & Convention of Cintra, 1808, 33–4; returns to Portugal, 1809, 36; on Ad Berkeley, 31; Talavera, 36; lines of Torres Vedras, 44; Ciudad Rodrigo, 47; Badajoz, 49; Salamanca & Madrid, 49, 57–8; relations with B, 55–6; shortage of specie, 56–7, and horses, 59–60; commander of Spanish army, 59; Napoleon's invasion of Russia, 63; on state of army 1812, 64–5; Vitoria, 66–7; complaints of missing battering train & navy, 68; sack of San Sebastian, 68–9; Pamplona, 69; complains of troops for Holland, 69–70; Bunbury reassures, sufficient specie, 70; Bordeaux, 73; Toulouse, B's congratulations, promoted to D, 74; mission to Spain, 76; 1814 celebrations, 77; war of 1812, 78–80; 86; Congress of Vienna & Napoleon's return, 88–90; Waterloo campaign and Napoleon's 1815 abdication, 89–101; on Sir H Lowe, 104–5; occupation of France, 1815–18, 106–7, 109–10; on B's KG, 112; gives equestrian portrait to B, 112–13; 114; colonial patronage, 118–19, 123–4; 124; Master Gen of Ordnance, 1819–27, 126; Ionian Islands, 132–3; 138; disputes Canning's foreign policy, 142–7, 214; Catholic question, 1825, 148–9; Greek revolt, 152; relations between Ordnance & Col. Office, 155–6; 162; opposes troops for W Africa, 168–9; expansion of army, 175; 176–7; 189; and Sir T Brisbane, 191, 193–4, 196; West Indies, 116, 156–9; slavery, 170–82; 184, 202; Greece & 1826 mission to Russia, 212–14; on troops to Portugal, 1826, 216–17; 218; Commander in Chief, 1827, 219–20; resigns on Canning becoming Prime Minister, 220–4; on Canning's death, 225; returns as Commander in Chief, 1827, 225–7; on Navarino, 227–8; Prime Minister, 1828–30, 229–31; disputes & resignation of Canningites, 231–3; Catholic emancipation, 234–5, 237–40; dismisses D of Clarence, 235–6; and Anglesey, 237–8; threats to government, 241–2; gives living to Rev Charles B, 243; death of Huskisson, overture to Palmerston rejected, 243; fall of ministry, 244–5; 1830 agricultural unrest, 246; opposes parliamentary reform, 1831–2, 247–53; tries to form a ministry, 1832, 253–4; opposes reforms in House of Lords, 254; 257.

Westmorland, 10th E of, 120, 222.

Wharncliffe, 1st Bn, parliamentary reform moderate, 248–50, 252.

Wilberforce, William, 111, 170–1, 201.

William IV (D of Clarence), viii, 138; Ld. High Admiral, 226; dismissed, 235–6; 237; accession, favours Bathurst, 242; 243; Wellington's resignation, favours William B as Joint Clerk of Privy Council, 245; 247; parliamentary reform, 247, 250, 252–3.

Williams–Wynne, Charles Watkin: Pres, Bd of Control, 1822–8, 140, 220, 221.

Williams–Wynne, Henry, 35, 140.

Wilmot (–Horton, 1823), Robert, Col Undersecretary, 1821–8, 141; supports Canning, 144; reorganization of Col. Office, 157, 160–3; 164–5; slave amelioration, 177–8; and customs officers, 182–5; and emigration, 186–8; 194, 215; B's appreciation of, 1827, 223–4; 226; B advises on proposed promotion, 228; dismissed, 230.

Wilson, Sir Robert, 138.

Winchilsea, 10th Earl of, 240, 243.

Windham, William, 18.

York, Prince Frederick, D of, 11; resigns as Commander in Chief, 1809, 35–6; re-appointed, 1811, 45; 93; post–war army reductions, 109, 126; 112, 138; expansion of army, 175; and Palmerston, 211; death, 218–19.